Modern Studies in Philosophy

SPINOZA

MODERN STUDIES IN PHILOSOPHY is a series of anthologies presenting contemporary interpretations and evaluations of the works of major philosophers. The editors have selected articles designed to show the systematic structure of the thought of these philosophers, and to reveal the relevance of their views to the problems of current interest. These volumes are intended to be contributions to contemporary debates as well as to the history of philosophy; they not only trace the origins of many problems important to modern philosophy, but also introduce major philosophers as interlocutors in current discussions.

MODERN STUDIES IN PHILOSOPHY is prepared under the general editorship of Amelie Oksenberg Rorty, Kings College, Cambridge University.

MARJORIE GRENE is Professor of Philosophy at the University of California at Davis. She is the author of *Sartre, Approaches to Philosophical Biology, Introduction to Existentialism, Martin Heidegger, Portrait of Aristotle,* and *Knower and the Known.*

Modern Studies in Philosophy

Amelie Oksenberg Rorty
General Editor

SPINOZA

A Collection
of Critical Essays

EDITED BY MARJORIE GRENE

1973
Anchor Books
Anchor Press/Doubleday
Garden City, New York

This anthology has been especially prepared for Anchor Books and has never before appeared in book form.

Anchor Books edition: 1973

ISBN: 0-385-01216-0
Library of Congress Catalog Card Number 72–96276
Copyright © 1973 by Marjorie Grene

"Behind the Geometrical Method," from *The Philosophy of Spinoza*, by H. A. Wolfson, Cambridge, Massachusetts, Harvard University Press, 1934, Vol. 1, Chapter 1, pp. 3–31. Reprinted by permission of the author and of Harvard University Press.

"Spinoza and Language" by David Savan, from *The Philosophical Review* 67 (1958), pp. 212–225. Reprinted by permission of the author and of *The Philosophical Review*.

"Language and Knowledge in Spinoza" by G. H. R. Parkinson, from *Inquiry* 12 (1969), pp. 15–40. Reprinted by permission of the author and of *Inquiry*.

"Spinoza's Theory of Knowledge in the Ethics" by Guttorm Fløistad, from *Inquiry* 12 (1969), pp. 41–65. Reprinted by permission of the author and of *Inquiry*.

"Spinoza and the Theory of Organism" by Hans Jonas, from *Journal of the History of Philosophy*, Vol. 3 (1965), pp. 43–58. Copyright by the Regents of The University of California. Reprinted from the *Journal of the History of Philosophy*, Vol. 3, No. 1, pp. 43–58, by permission of the Regents.

"The Two Eyes of Spinoza," translated by Mr. Oscar Swan from Leszek Kolakowski, "Dwoke Oczu Spinozy," *Antynome Wolnosci*, Wilna, 1966, pp. 219–229, by permission of the author and his agent.

"Spinoza and the Idea of Freedom" by Stuart Hampshire, from the *Proceedings of the British Academy* 46 (1960). Reprinted by permission of the author and of The British Academy.

"Substance and Its Modes," from *Benedict de Spinoza* by H. F. Hallett, London, The Athlone Press, 1957, Chapters I–III, pp. 9–43. Reprinted by permission of The Athlone Press.

"Spinoza's Letter on the Infinite," translated by Kathleen McLaughlin from Martial Gueroult, *Spinoza*, Vol. I, Paris: Aubier-Montaigne, 1968, Appendix IX, pp. 500–528. By permission of the author and the publisher.

"The Ontological Argument in Spinoza" by William A. Earle, from *Philosophy and Phenomenological Research* 2 (1951), pp. 549–554. Reprinted by permission of the author and of *Philosophy and Phenomenological Research*.

"Eternity and Sempiternity" by Martha Kneale, from *Proceedings of the Aristotelian Society* 69 (1968–69), pp. 223–238. Reprinted by courtesy of the Editor of the Aristotelian Society. © 1969 The Aristotelian Society.

Other volumes in the Modern Studies in Philosophy Series:

CONTENTS

The following abbreviations have been used in the footnotes:

Cogitata metaphysica: C.m.
Renati Des Cartes Principiorum Philosophiae Pars I et Pars II: Desc.
  Princ. Phil.
Epistolae: Ep.
Ethica: E.
Korte Verhandling van God, de Mensch en des Zelfs Welstand: K.V.
Tractatus de Intellectus Emendatione: TdIE.
Tractatus Theologico-Politicus: Tr. Theol.-Pol.

References are to parts, chapters, or sections, as appropriate for each work, references to TdIE being to Bruder sections. The letters are referred to by number as in the Gebhardt editions. Where page references are given they are to the Gebhardt edition, which is indicated as G. For details, see the Bibliography.

INTRODUCTION

In his British Academy lecture, which opens Part Three of this collection, Stuart Hampshire remarks of traditional interpretations of Spinoza:

> All these masks have been fitted on him and each of them does to some extent fit. But they remain masks, and not the living face. They do not show the moving tensions and unresolved conflicts in Spinoza's *Ethics*.[1]

An anthology of papers on Spinoza may perhaps fare a little better in this respect than any single interpretation. Through the very plurality of its perspectives it will at least exhibit indirectly some of the "tensions" and "conflicts" to which Mr. Hampshire refers. Even if each were still "imposed from outside"—and I believe that some of them, including Hampshire's own essay, are not so—they would give some indication of the richness of Spinoza's thought. Is Spinoza a "nominalist" eluding his own nominalism in the general terms he uses (Savan) or has he developed a theory of intuitive knowledge which he can legitimately express in his own argument despite its nominalistic interpretation of some misuses of language (Fløistad, with Parkinson taking a position somewhere between these two extremes)? Is he a rigid determinist who celebrates freedom in defiance of his own metaphysic (Kolakowski) or in seeing freedom "positively" as self-understanding does he evade a literal question of "determinism" or its opposite and indeed stand "nearer to the truth at certain points than any other philosopher has ever been" (Hampshire)? A similar tension appears to the student of Spinoza's political theory: a tension between the rigorous demands of the rational life and the practical bent of his concrete political directives (Gildin). And in the interpretation of his metaphysic itself, on which all else depends, recurrent puzzles have returned to plague successive generations of his critics. Are the infinite attributes through which we are to understand God or nature mere "as-ifs" through which we approach an ultimately unintelligible ground of being, are they almost independent entities in their own right, or can we effect some synthesis of these opposing views? (See Professor Donagan's first essay.) Is

1. See below, p. 297.

the eternity of the mind irrelevant to time, as it is usually interpreted as being, or did Spinoza believe in its everlasting duration (Kneale, and Donagan's second paper)? Or is duration for Spinoza in fact a derivative and even distortive aspect of reality, so that finite modes are themselves eternal in the nontemporal sense, and "enduring," or striving to endure, only as they betray their origin in the eternal order of infinite substance (Hallett)? Each interpretation conflicts with some other, yet each interprets reasonably some aspect of the text.

In fact the very form of the *Ethics* provides at first sight the most glaring conflict of all. Spinoza claimed to write "by the geometrical method," stating sets of axioms, definitions, and proofs which should lead us time and again to a perspicuous "Q.E.D." But still the conclusions he has "demonstrated," which should be, in his own phrase, "as clear as noonday light," give rise to the controversies we have noticed and many more. Why, the impatient reader may ask, should we concern ourselves with a text so full of "unresolved conflicts," and in particular so inconsistent with its own alleged aim? If an axiomatized system—and that is what the *Ethics* looks like—provides neither intelligible premises nor conclusions reached by logically rigorous methods, has it not failed? Should we take it more seriously than any other failure of intellectual history, like the attempt to square the circle?

Indeed we should. For the "unresolved conflicts" in the *Ethics* are also the "moving tensions" which make it so rewarding a text to study.

To take first the question of literary form: the "geometric method" permitted Spinoza to condense into a more compelling shape what was in fact a debate with his forebears and his contemporaries on the fundamental problems of God, nature, and man. The late-comer therefore needs, as Professor Wolfson shows in the first essay below (the first chapter of his by now classic *Philosophy of Spinoza*), to "unpack" the geometrical method and learn to listen to the controversies to which it responds. Admittedly, the major aim of the contributors to this volume is not to perform this kind of historical research, valuable though it is. Although in some contexts, as for example in Professor Donagan's first paper, they do set Spinoza's argument into its place in contemporary, rather than, like Wolfson, medieval, history of thought, they chiefly seek, as philosophers, to understand *what* Spinoza is saying, rather than *why*, in historical terms, he happened to say it. Nevertheless, the method of "unpacking" proposed in Wolfson's chapter is an indispensable tool for the student of the *Ethics*. Using it, he can at least remove his uneasiness about the form of the work: he can read the *Ethics* as the series of answers in a language game for which the questions must be inferred.

Still the substantive puzzles remain—and the reader may still wish to express his impatience: why study a work which even its admirers describe as "full of unresolved conflicts"? What does it mean to say that the "unresolved conflicts" in the work are the "moving tensions" which continue to fascinate its devotees? It means that the philosophy of Spinoza, in particular the *Ethics* of Spinoza, permits, and indeed demands, an indefinite range of interpretations, each of which may illuminate, yet none of which exhausts, the meaning of the text. This maxim is defensible on many grounds.

First, it is true of all great works of art, including literature, and *a fortiori* of philosophical literature. Nor do I mean here philosophical works which happen to be "literary" as well as "philosophical"—as some would hold of Plato's *Symposium*. No; as much as the *Symposium* or the *Republic,* the *Critique of Pure Reason,* the central books of the *Metaphysics,* the *Ethics* are great works of philosophical literature, however cramped or elegant their style, however abstract or concrete their method of presentation. As insistently as poetry, philosophical thought demands its own expression. Or, as Schlegel put it, it is like music in that "it must create a text for itself." Like a musical composition, moreover, as Schlegel continues, a philosophical work, in the series of meditations through which it treats its object, "develops, substantiates, varies, and contrasts" its theme. True, this is no identity; philosophy is neither poetry nor music; it develops thoughts, not sounds, arguments, not images. But my point here is only that great philosophical texts constitute a subset of great works of art, and share with their cousins the possibility, and the need, for perpetual interpretation and reinterpretation in an unending series of readings, any of which may be competent but none of which can be final. A great work of music, it is plain, is never presented once for all. Any performance, or the interpretation of any given performer, presents one aspect of the work, as one Leibnizian monad mirrors the universe, while the universe is the infinite sum total of all monadic perspectives—or, better, in this context: as each finite mode expresses the nature of substance in one determinate fashion under one attribute, while substance is the totality, and more than the totality, of its infinite range of expressions under infinite attributes. That we can, and must, always return to the *Ethics* for yet another reading is a mark, not of its incoherence, but of its inexhaustible life.

If this is true of transcendent works of art in general, and of literature in particular, moreover, it is true of philosophical texts also for a special reason, and that is the nature of philosophical reflection. For philosophy is the discipline which reflects systematically on what is otherwise taken for granted, whether in the practice of some art or science or in some aspect of everyday life, like perception or moral choice. Such reflection is inexhaustible, partly perhaps because of the inexhaustibility of its object, partly, however, because of the self-proliferation of reflection itself. Sartre complains about the possible infinite regress of thoughts about thoughts about thoughts and proposes to cut off this danger with his *pre-reflective cogito*. Yet the possibility always remains, unless the process can come to rest in what Sartre calls "pure reflection" (which I believe his own premises forbid his achieving) or perhaps, indeed, as in Part Five of the *Ethics,* in the intellectual love of God. Even if Spinoza achieved the peace of mind he there describes, however, his readers can only glimpse and try to understand it. For most of us, reflection continues to be open. It contains on principle the possibility of "going further" which prevents the philosophical development of a fundamental concept, or the interpreter's understanding of such a concept, from coming definitively to a close.

This is especially true for readers of Spinoza, further, because of the scope and grandeur of his philosophical theme. The *Leitmotif* of the *Ethics* is the grounding of our finitude in the Infinite (see in particular Hallett and Gueroult). We are to learn to understand our destiny as finite expressions of Infinite Substance by turning from our ordinary inadequate ideas, from our tattered imaginings of this and that, to the grasp of Substance itself, infinite and indeterminate, as the rational foundation of this finite and for the most part confused existence. To relate human finitude to divine infinity is never easy; witness, for example, the tortuousness of Kierkegaard's method of "indirect communication" which would have as its main issue the recognition by the finite creature of his debt to his infinite creator. But Spinoza's task is much more difficult than Kierkegaard's. For it is precisely the Christian sense of distance from God, the contradiction between finite and infinite, that he hopes to overcome. "Everything that is, is in God, and nothing can be or be conceived without God" (*E.,* I, xv): that is both the ultimate issue of the Judaeo-

Christian tradition and its absolute denial. God is the unique Being whose essence entails existence (see Hallett, and Earle's papers on the ontological argument); on the other hand, we, like all finite things, exist only dependently on *His* essence, not our own. We strive to exist forever, on and on indefinitely; that is, paradoxically, the "essence" of the finite. Yet our striving cannot alone bring us into being nor yet keep us there. My essence, the essence of any finite mode, is determined by its relation, in the divine intellect, to other essences, and I exist, as any finite mode exists, only in my due place in an infinite nature—so to speak, by His permission. How then can we, finite existences, cast out of essence, as it were, be "in" God? Or if I am "in" God, is not my existence too the consequence of my essence, as God's existence is of His essence, since I must exist "in the order of things" at that precise place in the infinite interconnections of finite modes at which my "essence" comes "in the order of thought"? Yet Spinoza insists that for finite things essence and existence *are* separate, as they are not for God. He speaks, for example, in *E.,* II, viii, of the way in which the essences of nonexistent things are in the mind of God (a point touched on in Professor Donagan's second paper), and this seems to provide an asymmetry for finite modes between their essences (which are "forever") and their existences (which are only "at some determinate time"). But this asymmetry fits only uneasily on the parallelism of ideas and motions, or thoughts and things. If thought and extension are really parallel— and surely Spinoza insists they are—how, again, can my essence (= my idea = my mind) be anything but my necessary existence (= myself as extended thing = my body) at just this place in the infinite concatenation of finite modes? So it seems I not only express the divine nature in some determinate way but *am* a piece of it. Yet this is certainly not what Spinoza meant, even though his enemies took him to mean it. What he did mean is perhaps what is expressed in more fashionable, though, it seems to me, in less intelligibly rigorous form, in Heidegger's "ontological difference": the fact that we have to approach Being through the difference between beings and Being which is essential to the Being-in-the-world that is our way of being. We come to Being only *through* this difference and so never reach it definitively, yet it is *Being* we have to come to in order to understand the difference itself. But there is a clarity, an intellectual purity, in Spinoza's rendering of this thesis that is missing in Heidegger, and that makes Spinoza recurrently worthy of debate, while Heidegger, it seems, must be believed with adulation or not at all.

Spinoza's explication of finitude through its grounding in the Infinite, it should be noticed further, not only presents a philosophical argument worth persistent and repeated study; it is, as few philosophical texts can claim to be, the apotheosis of a certain kind of human vision, which itself recurs, if in different vocabularies, throughout the centuries. John Scotus Eriugena's *De Divisione Naturae* is in some ways a pre-echoing of Spinoza's theme. God for him is beyond Being, as for Spinoza *Natura Naturans* transcends the *Natura Naturata* with which it is yet somehow identical. Or again, for Eriugena the traditional categories reduce to motion and rest, much as for Spinoza motion-and-rest is the immediate infinite mode of substance under the attribute of extension. Again in our time—as David Hawkins has also pointed out—David Bohm's reflections at the hand of physics strangely re-echo Spinoza's *Ethics,* not in terms of influence, but of a pure convergence.[2] As atomism, the effort to explain the whole of reality through its least parts, recurs from time to time as a style of metaphysical thinking, so, if more rarely, does Spinozism, the effort to understand the parts of reality in terms of the ultimate nature of the whole. Thus the *Ethics* represents, as few texts do, a permanent possibility of human vision, one of the possible ultimates of philosophical reflection. Many philosophies, like Descartes's, Locke's, perhaps even Kant's, speak to the problems of a given age; Spinoza speaks to the speculative daring of any age. If it were not for the distinction between appearances and things in themselves, Kant said, we would all be Spinozists. But the distinction between appearances and things in themselves is at best an uneasy one; there is in any speculative thinker a strand of Spinozism, a move toward understanding through and in the whole, a tendency which has received its supreme expression in the *Ethics* itself.

Nevertheless, to say that is not really to take the *Ethics* out of history. For philosophy is historical in a sense more immediate or more essential than the historicity of works of art, or of other kinds of works of art. Philosophy in the west is a conversation that has

2. Professor Hawkins (*The Language of Nature,* Garden City, N.Y.: Doubleday, 1967, p. 162 n.) refers to Bohm's *Causality and Determinism in Modern Physics;* see, more recently, his "Some Remarks on the Notion of Order," and "Further Remarks on Order," in C. H. Waddington, *Theoretical Biology,* Vol. II (Edinburgh: Edinburgh University Press, 1969), p. 18–60.

gone on since Thales, a conversation in which each philosophical thinker, however profound or original, must take his place. No single interlude, however beautifully developed, can wholly shut off further conversation. This holds of Spinoza in a number of respects. He must be read, not only as in conversation with the medievals or the Cartesians, but as the culminating thinker in the tradition of substance metaphysics that goes back to Aristotle, or rather as one of two such culminating thinkers, for substance metaphysics reaches its culmination, and its *coup de grâce,* in Spinoza on the one hand and on the other in Hume. Yet, secondly, as the case of Bohm indicates, Spinozism is also a philosophy that can be expressed in the language of more than one age: in terms of process rather than of substance, of a world emergent into ever higher forms of order (or orders of order, as Bohm puts it) rather than of an eternal or atemporal reality. At any juncture in the continuing conversation that is philosophy, then, this particular vision may become apposite, not only for a certain kind of thinker, but for thinkers in a certain kind of time, perhaps especially in a "needy time" like ours.

More than this: particular problems, the issue of freedom or of "identity theory," for example, may come to be discussed in terms to which the Spinozistic formulations appear especially pertinent. With these special applications to current academic discussion the present collection has not for the most part been directly concerned, although part of Professor Jonas's paper does summarize the nub of Spinoza's view of the mind-body problem, and of course Mr. Hampshire's essay is itself an application of Spinozistic perspectives to problems in the philosophy of mind and action. I have tried, however, to include some discussions of Spinoza's "philosophical psychology" (Blair, Wartofsky), as well as of his "meta-ethics" (Curley's second paper), which also resonates to contemporary thinking. But much has been omitted, both of important parts of Spinoza's thought, in particular, for example, his treatment of religion, and of important aspects of his influence or of his contemporary relevance, say, in the literature of Marxist philosophy or in connection with psycho-analysis (see Hampshire and Blair, however) or in evolutionary biology (see reference to Rensch in the bibliography). The major aim of this anthology, in short, is to assist the reader toward an understanding of Spinoza's metaphysics, and hence of the epistemological method (Curley's first paper) and the ethical theory which ultimately depend on it, in the belief that special problems like those of "philosophical psychology" can best be dealt with on that ground.

I am grateful to Professor Amelie Rorty, as well as to some of the contributors, especially Professor Alan Donagan and Dr. E. M. Curley, for their advice, to Mrs. Kathleen McLaughlin and Mr. Oscar Swan for their translations of Gueroult and Kolakowski respectively, and to Mrs. Susan Denning and Miss Janet Setzer for their efficient and devoted help in the preparation of the manuscript. For the interest which motivated the collection of this anthology I am indebted to my students at Davis, but also and above all to a great teacher, the late D. W. Prall, under whose guidance I first read the *Ethics* all but forty years ago.

Acknowledgments of permission to reprint previously published material are made in each case on the first page of the essay in question.

MARJORIE GRENE

University of California, Davis
June 1972

I am grateful to Miss Robin Harrod for her help in reading the galleys.

M.G.

Göttingen
June 1973

PART ONE
Spinoza's Method

Behind the Geometrical Method

H. A. WOLFSON

In discussing once with a group of friends the importance of philology and of bookish learning in general for the study of the history of philosophy, I happened to remark that philosophers, after all, see the universe which they try to explain as already interpreted to them in books, with the only possible exception, perhaps, of the first recorded philosopher, and all he could see was water. "How about Spinoza?" challenged one of the listeners. "Was he also a bookish philosopher?" Without stopping to think, I took up the challenge. "As for Spinoza," I said, "if we could cut up all the philosophic literature available to him into slips of paper, toss them up into the air, and let them fall back to the ground, then out of these scattered slips of paper we could reconstruct his *Ethics*."

Not long after that I found myself reconstructing the *Ethics* out of scattered slips of paper figuratively cut out of the philosophic literature available to Spinoza. The problem before us, as I discovered, was like that of a jig-saw puzzle. Suppose we have a box of pieces out of which we are to construct a certain picture. But the pieces contained in the box are more than can be used, and from among them we have to select those which are needed for our purpose. Furthermore, the pieces do not fit together, and they have to be reshaped. Finally, many necessary pieces are missing, and we have to supply them ourselves. But to offset all these difficulties, we have an outline of the picture which we are to construct.

The picture which we have to construct in our own jig-saw puzzle is the *Ethics* as it was originally formed in the mind of Spinoza, of which the present *Ethics* in its geometrical form is only a bare outline.[1] Since, however, we do not know nor can we ascertain exactly what books Spinoza had actually read, what quotations he had come across in the course of his readings, or what casual information he

H. A. Wolfson, *The Philosophy of Spinoza* (Cambridge, Mass.: Harvard University Press, 1934), Vol. I, Chapter I, pp. 3–31. Reprinted by permission of the author and of Harvard University Press.

1. Cf. H. Wolfson, *The Philosophy of Spinoza* (Cambridge, Mass.: Harvard University Press, 1934), I, 59.

had gathered from conversations with friends, we must take as our box of pieces the entire philosophic literature available at the time of Spinoza and out of this make our necessary selections. Furthermore, since philosophic texts and ideas are the most plastic of material, capable of assuming a variety of meanings with different philosophers, we must reshape our pieces in the form which we have reason to believe they assumed in the mind of Spinoza. Finally, since the *Ethics* before us is not the result of a syncretism of traditional philosophy but rather the result of criticism, and since this criticism, though implied, is not explicitly expressed, we shall have to supply it ourselves.

In our study of the *Ethics* we must try to follow the same method that Spinoza followed in writing it. Spinoza did not start out with classified lists of bibliographies, outlines, abstracts, quotations, and all the elaborate equipment with which methodical scholarship of today prepares itself for the writing of an informative work of reference. He started out with a certain fund of knowledge acquired through miscellaneous reading which in his mind formed itself into a composite picture of the salient features of traditional philosophy. In this composite mental picture, we may assume, the problems of philosophy presented themselves in a certain order, each problem modelled after a certain pattern and expressed in a certain terminology. Tagged on to this picture, underneath its surface, and deep down into the recesses of Spinoza's consciousness, we may further assume, there was an aggregation of notes swarming with references to sources of texts, to parentages of ideas, to conflicts of opinions, and to diversities of interpretations, all of them ready to come up to the surface, whenever the occasion arose, and take their place in the picture. In our endeavor to retrace the steps of Spinoza's reasoning, we must, therefore, first of all, equip ourselves with a similar fund of knowledge, or philosophical mass of apperception, as it may be called.

With such an apperceptive mass as our equipment we begin to read the *Ethics*. Without forcing ourselves to understand the book, we let its propositions penetrate into our amassed fund of knowledge and by the natural process of association and attraction become encrusted with terms, phrases, and ideas out of the storehouse of our memory. At first these encrustations are indistinguishable and shapeless clumps, clinging to the propositions as bits of scrap-iron cling to a magnet. But then we let our mind play upon them—to scrutinize them and to study them. By the catalytic action of the mind these indistinguishable and shapeless clumps begin to dissolve; they begin to group themselves, to solidify themselves into larger units, to become differentiated from each other, to assume form, and ultimately to crystallize themselves into distinct topics of recognizable historical problems of philosophy. Thus at the very outset of the *Ethics,* Proposition I, together with Definitions III and V and Axioms I and II upon which it is based, emerges as a distinct topic by itself, which we label the definition of substance and mode. The next five propositions, II–VI, crystallize themselves into a discussion of the unity of substance, made up of two historical problems, the unity of God and creation. Propositions VII–X and XII–XIII shape themselves into a discussion of three closely related topics under the general heading of the Simplicity of Substance, and wedged in between them is Proposition XI, where the term "substance" gives way to the term "God"; this is easily recognized as a discussion of the traditional proofs of the existence of God. Next follow two propositions, XIV and XV, which deal with the attributes of extension and thought, and a Scholium, which deals with the infinity of extension. The remaining propositions of the First Part of the *Ethics* readily group themselves into discussions of the various meanings of the causality of God, among which Spinoza dwells especially upon the immanence, freedom, necessity, and purposelessness of God's causality. In the Second Part of the *Ethics* the propositions fall into the traditional outline of the discussion of the soul, dealing in the conventional order and manner with the definition of the soul, its relation to the body, and the classification of its faculties. The last three parts of the *Ethics* deal with what is traditionally known as practical philosophy as contrasted with the theoretical philosophy of the first two parts, dealing successively with the problems of the emotions, virtues, and the final happiness of man. As our mind scrutinizes still further these groups of propositions it discovers that they follow one upon the other according to a certain order of sequence, which is at once intrinsically logical and extrinsically in conformity with historical patterns. With this, the first stage in our study of the *Ethics* comes to an end.

Then the next stage in our investigation is to find a certain coherence within each group of propositions. The data upon which we have to work are twofold. On the one hand, there are the problems of philosophy as they unfold themselves before us in all their variety of forms in the vast literature that was available to Spinoza. On the other hand, there are the utterances of Spinoza in the *Ethics,* elliptical, fragmentary, disjointed, and oftentimes, if we are to admit the truth to ourselves, enigmatic and unintelligible. Between these two extremes we expect to find the problems as they must have formulated themselves in the mind of Spinoza, the doubts which he must have raised against accepted views, and his own solutions of these doubts which he must have meant to express in his uttered statements in the *Ethics.* The task before us, then, is to reconstruct the process of Spinoza's reasoning in all its dialectical niceties and in all its fulness of detail so that it will lead us to a thorough understanding of the statements which confront us in the *Ethics.* By the method of trial and error we experiment with one conjecture after another, until we finally arrive at a result which seems to us satisfactory. Thus, for instance, at the very outset of the *Ethics,* in Proposition I and its underlying Definitions III and V and Axioms I and II, which we have already set apart as a topic by itself, dealing with definition of substance and mode, we reconstruct out of the material scattered in the literature of philosophy the problem as we assume it presented itself to the mind of Spinoza—the division of being, the definition of substance and accident, the classification of substances, and so on. Again, out of direct internal discussions of these problems which occur in the philosophic literature of the past, or indirectly out of certain suggestions and hints, and sometimes even without these direct or indirect aids, we reconstruct a criticism of these traditional definitions as we assume it formulated itself in the mind of Spinoza. As a result we are enabled to integrate these Axioms, Definitions, and Proposition I into a coherent chapter, containing a logically formed argument.[2] We follow the same method in our study of the next group of propositions, Propositions II–VI, which we have found to reflect two historical problems, the unity of God and creation, and which we have subsumed under the heading of the Unity of Substance. Here our task is somewhat more difficult, for we have to deal here not with one single proposition, as is the case in Proposition I, but with five propositions, each of which is followed by a demonstration, and between which there seems to be no unity and transition. Again, by the method of trial and error we ultimately succeed in reconstructing the thought of Spinoza so that in the light

2. Cf. *ibid.,* I, 61 ff.

of it these five propositions form a connected logical syllogism.[3] And so we go through the entire *Ethics,* and by the use of different devices we succeed in bringing unity, coherence, and harmony within each group of propositions. With this, the second stage of our investigation comes to an end.

Then we take up the third and last stage of our investigation, that of documenting our findings so that we may convince others of the truth of our statements and reasoning. Here, too, we must follow the same method that Spinoza would have followed, had he documented his *Ethics.* We feel that it would not be enough to quote from books which we happen to know, or which happen to be generally known. We must ask ourselves what works Spinoza himself would have used if he had chosen to document his writings. To answer this question we must determine, even though only in a general way, the extent and variety of the philosophic literature available to Spinoza.

Two philosophic literatures were open to Spinoza, the Hebrew and the Latin. His knowledge of Hebrew he had acquired in a school where he had studied it systematically under the guidance of competent teachers probably from the age of seven to the age of eighteen (1639–1650).[4] Latin he began to study later, at first not in a school but privately. His systematic study of that language under the tutorage of Francis van den Enden did not begin until 1652, when he was already twenty years old. Though he had also a knowledge of several modern languages, Spanish, Portuguese, Dutch, French, and possibly also Italian, German, and Flemish,[5] the philosophic material in these languages was negligible. Hebrew made accessible to him not only the works of Jewish philosophers but also the works of Arabic philosophers, the works of Aristotle, mostly as incorporated in the commentaries of Averroes, the works of some of the Greek commentators on Aristotle, and also the works of some of the Latin scholastic philosophers. Latin similarly opened to him not only the original

3. Cf. *ibid.,* I, 85 ff.

4. As for the years of Spinoza's entering and leaving the Hebrew School *'Ez Hayyim,* see Dunin-Borkowski, *Der junge De Spinoza,* 1910, p. 103, and Freudenthal, *Spinoza Leben und Lehre,* ed. Gebhardt (Heidelberg: C. Winter, 1927), I, 31.

5. As for Spinoza's knowledge of languages, see *Ep.,* 19 (G., IV, 95, lines 12–15); *Ep.,* 26 (G., IV, 159, line 16); Lucas' *La Vie de feu Monsieur de Spinoza* in A. Wolf, *The Oldest Biography of Spinoza* (London: G. Allen & Unwin, 1927), pp. 51–52 and 104.

Latin writings of the philosophers of the Roman period, of mediaeval scholasticism, and of the Renaissance, but also translations from the Greek, Arabic, and Hebrew. In Hebrew the most important works of Jewish philosophers, whether those translated from the Arabic or those written originally in Hebrew, were already accessible to him in printed form, some of them in several editions; but the translations from non-Jewish authors, with but a few slight exceptions, were accessible to him only in manuscript form. Manuscripts, however, at that time were not yet gathered up and stored away in a few closely guarded central libraries; they were still widely scattered among individual owners and freely circulated, especially in Amsterdam, where Hebrew scholarship and Hebrew printing presses flourished and where privately owned collections of Hebrew manuscripts must have existed. Furthermore, the student of Hebrew philosophic texts could gain a thorough knowledge of the contents of the unpublished Hebrew translations of Arabic and Greek authors through the numerous and extensive quotations from their works as well as through the elaborate discussions of their views which were to be found in Hebrew works already published. In Latin the proportion of printed works in philosophy was greater than in Hebrew, even of works which were translated into Latin from the Hebrew. Thus, for instance, the bulk of Averroes' commentaries on Aristotle, which were translated into Latin from the Hebrew, existed in many printed editions in Latin, whereas in Hebrew they existed only in manuscript form.

To Spinoza these three literatures, Hebrew, Latin, and Arabic, represented a common tradition. Whatever differences he noticed between them, they concerned only problems of a purely theological and dogmatic nature; the philosophic basis of all such problems, and especially the discussion of problems of a purely philosophic nature, he could not fail to see, were all of a common origin. They were all based upon Greek philosophy, at the centre of which stood Aristotle. The same Greek terminology lay behind the Arabic, Hebrew, and Latin terminology, and the same scientific and philosophic conceptions formed the intellectual background of all those who philosophized in Arabic, Hebrew, or Latin. The three philosophic literatures were in fact one philosophy expressed in different languages, translatable almost literally into one another. And within each of these philosophic literatures numerous works existed which were encyclopaedic in nature, covering as they did the entire range of philosophy, containing the same roster of problems, the same analyses of those problems, the same definitions of terms, the same metaphysical brocards, the same clash of contrasting views, the same arguments in support or in refutation of each view, and, barring certain individual differences of emphasis or of interpretation, arriving also at the same conclusions. A reader who had mastered any of these books in one of these three languages found himself treading upon familiar ground when he came to read any book in the other languages.

We do not know exactly in what language Spinoza would have written his books had the choice of language been determined by him on the basis of the ease with which he could express himself in it rather than on the basis of the linguistic equipment of the readers whom he wished to reach. Had Spinoza lived in the land of his forefathers, Spain or Portugal, before the expulsion, or in any other European country where Jewish philosophy was cultivated, such as Southern France or Italy, he would have undoubtedly written in Hebrew, for Hebrew had been the exclusive medium of expression of Jewish philosophers and scientists throughout Europe ever since the disappearance of Jewish life in Southern Spain under Moslem rule with the coming of the Almohades in the twelfth century. The particular attitude of an author toward the problems of religion was no deterrent to his use of Hebrew, for every shade of opinion, from extreme adherence to tradition to the most daring adventures into freedom of thought, found expression in Hebrew literature. In the intellectual autonomy which the Jews enjoyed during the Middle Ages, with the systematic pursuit of the study of philosophy and the sciences in Jewish schools out of Hebrew books, Jewish thinkers were always assured of appreciative as well as critical readers among their own people of whatever views they chose to express in Hebrew. But toward the end of the fifteenth century there appeared Jewish philosophers who, though brought up on Hebrew philosophic literature and themselves writing in Hebrew, wrote books in non-Jewish languages for non-Jewish readers. Elijah Delmedigo, better known as Helias Hebraeus Cretensis (1460–1497), wrote his *Quaestiones Tres* and his *Adnotationes in Dictis Averrois super Libros Physicorum*[6] in Latin, and Judah Abrabanel, better known as Leo He-

6. These two works are printed together with Joannes de Janduno's *Quaestiones in Libros Physicorum*, 1501, and other editions.

braeus (d. 1535), wrote his *Dialoghi d'Amore* in Italian.[7] In Spinoza's own time and in the community in which he was born, Hebrew was still used extensively by his own teachers and schoolmates in their literary works, but use was also made by some of them of Spanish and Latin. His teacher Manasseh ben Israel wrote on theological problems in Hebrew, Latin, Spanish, and Portuguese. Under these circumstances, what language Spinoza would have used if he had chosen that in which self-expression was the easiest for him can be only conjectured. That it would not have been Latin or Dutch, in which his books happen to be written, is quite evident by his own confession. At the time of the publication of his *Principia Philosophiae Cartesianae* and *Cogitata Metaphysica* (1663) he still felt the deficiency of his Latin, and before allowing his friends to publish these works he stipulated that one of them should, in his presence, "clothe them in more elegant style."[8] In 1665, in one of his letters to Blyenbergh,[9] he intimates that he could express his thoughts in Spanish, "the language in which I was brought up," better than in Dutch. Whether Hebrew was with him, as it was with many Jewish authors of his time and place, a more natural vehicle of literary expression is uncertain.

But it is quite certain that Hebrew literature was the primary source of his knowledge of philosophy and the main stock upon which all the other philosophic knowledge which he later acquired was grafted. He had become familiar with Hebrew philosophic literature before he began to read philosophy in Latin. His nascent philosophic doubt arose as a reaction against the philosophy which he read in Hebrew. With the exception of the new sciences, his readings in Latin supplied him merely with a new vocabulary for old ideas. Throughout his discussions of philosophical problems, especially those bordering upon theology, Hebrew sources appear as the matrix in which the general outline of ideas was formed. Other sources appear as insets. It is Hebrew sources, too, upon which he draws for his casual illustrations. An outstanding example of this is

7. It is quite possible, however, that the *Dialoghi d'Amore* was written originally in Hebrew. Cf. I. Sonne, *Lishe'elat ha-Lashon ha-Mekorit shel Wikkuhe ha-Ahahab li-Yehudah Abarbanel,* in *Ziyyunim,* Berlin, 1929, pp. 142–148. For new evidence that it was originally written in Hebrew, see Wolfson, *op. cit.,* II, 14.

8. *Ep.,* 13 (G., IV, 63, lines 10–22).

9. *Ep.,* 19 (G., IV, 95, lines 12–15).

to be found in his discussion in Chapter XV of the *Tractatus Theologico-Politicus* of the two contrasting attitudes shown by philosophers towards the problem of the relation of faith to philosophy or of theology to reason. The problem was an old one, and it had been discussed in Mohammedanism, Christianity, and Judaism alike. In each of these three religions, the two contrasting attitudes had their exponents. In Mohammedanism, such exponents, to mention but two, were Algazali and Averroes. In Christianity, two typical exponents of these attitudes could be found in Bernard of Clairvaux and Abelard. Spinoza, however, mentions none of these. He takes Alpakhar and Maimonides as his examples of typical representatives of these two contrasting views, and he does so simply because these were the two men through whose works he first became acquainted with the nature of the problem. He did not even feel the need, writing as he did in Latin for non-Jewish readers, to substitute two corresponding Christian authors for these two Jewish authors, for in Spinoza's time Jewish philosophy had not yet been eliminated from European philosophy and relegated to the esoteric field of oriental wisdom. From the thirteenth century down through the seventeenth century it was quite fashionable for theologians and philosophers to quote Hebrew authorities by the side of Greek authorities, and those who followed the habit of quoting Greek sources in the original Greek also quoted Hebrew sources in the original Hebrew. The only concession that Spinoza seems to have made to his non-Jewish readers is that he referred to his Hebrew authorities with the aloofness of an outsider.

Following this principle, we go first to Hebrew philosophic literature for our documents. It is not any particular author that we go to, but the field of literature as a whole. If one particular author, Maimonides for instance, happens to be resorted to more often than others, it is not because he has been especially selected for our purpose, but because Spinoza himself would have selected him, for his work is the most excellent depository of mediaeval philosophic lore, where one can find the most incisive analyses of philosophic problems, the most complete summaries of philosophic opinions, the clearest definitions of terms, and all these couched in happy and quotable phrases. But we always try to give sufficient parallels from other Hebrew authors so as not to create the erroneous impression that we are trying to draw parallels between one single Hebrew author and Spinoza. In like manner, in order not to create the erroneous impression that the material drawn upon is unique in Hebrew philosophic literature, we quote, or refer to, similar passages in the works of Arabic or scholastic authors. When the occasion demands, scholastic sources are resorted to in preference to the Hebrew. Furthermore, in order not to create the erroneous impression that there is something peculiarly "mediaeval" about the views we quote from the various mediaeval sources, we trace their origin to Aristotle's works. Frequently we string together a list of names from the various linguistic groups of philosophy in order to indicate that the views under discussion are a common philosophic heritage. Before quoting a passage from a certain book we do not stop to ask ourselves whether that book was known to Spinoza. In several instances we rather suspect that the book in question was unknown to him. But that makes no difference to us. Provided the idea expressed in the passage under consideration is not uncommon, we assume that it was known to Spinoza, even though for the time being we do not know exactly the immediate literary source of his knowledge. In such instances, only one who would arrogate to himself divine omniscience could assert with certainty that the idea could not be found in any source available to Spinoza. The burden of proof is always upon the negative.

But very often certain passages are identified as being the direct and immediate sources of Spinoza. As a rule Spinoza does not quote sources literally, even when he mentions them. In a letter to Meyer, for instance, he introduces his reproduction of Crescas' proof of the existence of God by the words "it reads as follows" (*sic sonat*),[10] and yet the passage which follows is not an exact quotation. But in many instances the evidence points to certain passages as directly underlying the utterances of Spinoza. In determining these direct sources it is not the similarity of single terms or even of single phrases that guides us, for in the history of philosophy terms and phrases, no less than the ideas which they express, have a certain persistency about them and they survive intact throughout their winding transmigrations. It is always a term or a phrase as imbedded in a certain context, and that context by its internal structure and by a combination of enveloping circumstances, that help us to determine direct literary relationships. When we feel that we are in a position, for

10. *Ep.*, 12 (G., IV, 6, line 18).

instance, to affirm with reasonable certainty that it is Thomas Aquinas from whom Spinoza has taken over in the Scholium to Proposition XXIX of *Ethics,* I, the distinction of *natura naturans* and *natura naturata* it is not because these phrases happen to occur in his works, for as phrases they happen to occur also in the works of other authors; it is only because Spinoza's description of these two phrases seems to be a modification of the description given by Thomas Aquinas, and also because the reason for the modification of the description by Spinoza can be adequately accounted for.[11] When, again, we are in a position to affirm with reasonable certainty that it is Crescas from whom Spinoza has taken over in the Scholium to Proposition XV of *Ethics,* I, the three "examples" by which his "opponents" prove the impossibility of an infinite extension and in refutation of them the three "distinctions" which he mentions in Epistola XII to Meyer, it is not because these "examples" and "distinctions" are to be found in Crescas, for as individual "examples" and "distinctions" they are to be found also in other authors; it is only because these three "distinctions" are used by Crescas as refutations of three arguments which correspond respectively to the three "examples" of Spinoza.[12] Finally, to take but one more example, when we are in a position to affirm with reasonable certainty that Spinoza's discussion of the highest good, of human society, and of the virtues in Propositions XIX–LXXIII of *Ethics,* IV, is based upon Aristotle's *Nicomachean Ethics* it is not because we discover in them certain similarities in individual terms or phrases; it is only because we discover in them definite literary similarities in the construction of the arguments.[13] It is by such methods that direct literary relationship has been established between Spinoza and many of the authors quoted in this work.

A list of passages quoted or referred to in this work from various authors will be found in the Index of References, and an analysis of topics of each of these authors will be found in the Index of Subjects and Names. The works quoted or referred to, it will be noticed, are drawn indiscriminately from the various linguistic groups of philosophic literature—Greek, Latin, Hebrew, and Arabic. Conspicuously absent among them, with the exception of a few references, mostly of ancillary importance, to Meir ibn Gabbai, Moses Cor-

---

11. Cf. Wolfson, *op. cit.,* I, 254 ff.
12. Cf. *ibid.,* I, 264 ff.
13. Cf. *ibid.,* II, 233 ff.

dovero, and Abraham Herrera,[14] is the Cabalistic literature, which from earliest time has been considered a source of Spinoza's philosophy. This exclusion was unintentional; it merely happened that in our search for documentation we had no occasion to resort to the Cabalistic literature for source material. Not that the Cabalistic literature could not have furnished us with apt illustrative material, but there is nothing in the Cabalistic literature which could be used for our purpose the like of which we did not find in philosophic literature, for, as has been said by one of the leading Cabalists, Moses Cordovero: "Know that in matters metaphysical oftentimes the true masters of Cabala will be found to agree with the philosophers."[15] "To follow" would perhaps have been a more accurate term than "to agree."

The list of passages is by no means exhaustive. Had we thought it necessary, we could have added innumerable parallels to every passage quoted; but our purpose was not to compile a complete catena of parallel passages. A complete Index of mediaeval philosophy, Latin, Hebrew, and Arabic, is indeed one of the desiderata of scholarship, but that will have to be done independently of any study of Spinoza. Nor are the passages quoted or referred to by us irreplaceable by similar passages from other works, though we have always tried to select passages which are most suitable for our purpose. It would be quite possible to rewrite considerable portions of this work by substituting other quotations for those used by us, without necessarily changing our present analysis and interpretation of the *Ethics,* for the passages quoted are only representative of common views which were current in the philosophic literature of the past. Had we thought it desirable, then instead of writing one single book on the *Ethics,* we could have written a series of papers bearing such titles as "Aristotle and Spinoza," "Seneca and Spinoza," "Averroes and Spinoza," "Maimonides and Spinoza," "Thomas Aquinas and Spinoza," "Leo Hebraeus and Spinoza," "Descartes and Spinoza," and many other correlations of Spinoza with names of authors who are quoted in this work or who could have been quoted. But our purpose was only to draw upon these authors for material in building up our interpretation of Spinoza and not to establish analo-

14. Two of the references to Herrera, however, seem to point to a direct literary connection and are of special significance. Cf. *ibid.,* I, 245 and 314.

15. *Elimah Rabbati,* I, 16.

gies, and we were especially careful to avoid the extension of analogies beyond the limits of what the actual facts warranted, and also to avoid the suggestion of influences when no direct literary relationship could be established. Had we thought it advisable we could have eliminated all the quotations from our texts, either by omitting them altogether or by giving them in paraphrase form. But the interpretation of texts is an essential part of our work, and since texts had to be used, no paraphrase, however felicitous, could take the place of an exact quotation. Probably the most logical literary form for this work would have been that of a commentary upon the *Ethics* preceded by a few general chapters of introduction. But we chose our present method because our purpose was not to comment upon single and isolated passages of the *Ethics,* but to show the unity, continuity, and logical order that runs throughout the work, and withal to present the philosophy of Spinoza as a systematic whole. Of all the authors quoted or referred to in this work, it is only Maimonides and Descartes, and indirectly through them, and quite as often directly through his own works, also Aristotle,[16] that can be said to have had a dominant influence upon the philosophic training of Spinoza and to have guided him in the formation of his own philosophy. It would indeed have been possible, within certain limits, to depict the philosophy of Spinoza against the simple background of any one of these three philosophers, except for the fact that that would not have been a true presentation of the genesis of his thought, for it had a more complex origin. All the other authors quoted in this work, however helpful they may have been in our reconstruction of the *Ethics,* can be said to have had a direct influence only upon single passages in the *Ethics,* or upon single propositions, or at most upon certain groups of propositions. To go beyond that and to attempt to build up an extended analogy between the philosophic systems of any of these authors and Spinoza, on the mere basis of such isolated parallels of expressions or passages, even when a direct

16. For lists of authors in relation to whom Spinoza has been studied, see Ueberweg-Frischeisen-Kohler-Moog, *Die Philosophie der Neuzeit bis zum Ende des XVIII. Jahrhunderts* (12th ed.; 1924), pp. 668 ff.; R. McKeon, *The Philosophy of Spinoza* (New York: Longmans, Green, 1928), pp. 322 ff. Among all the studies listed, no less than five on Spinoza and Maimonides and no less than sixteen on Spinoza and Descartes, there is only the following one which deals with Spinoza's relation to Aristotle: Julius Guttmann, "Spinozas Zusammenhang mit dem Aristotelismus," in *Judaica, Festschrift zu Hermann Cohens siebzigstem Geburtstage,* Berlin, 1912, pp. 515–534.

literary relationship between them could be established, would only mean the inflation of footnotes into essays or monographs.

But whether direct or indirect, the sources of Spinoza are more important for us as a means of establishing the meaning of his text and philosophy than as a means of establishing an analogy or priority of doctrine. The text of his *Ethics* is not a mosaic of quoted or paraphrased passages. Nor has his philosophy developed as a rash out of the infection of certain heretical or mystical phrases. It has grown out of the very philosophy which he discards, and this by his relentless driving of its own internal criticism of itself to its ultimate logical conclusion. In our endeavor to reconstruct the processes of Spinoza's reasoning, therefore, it is not phrases that we are to deal with but the thought and the history that lie behind them and the use that he makes of them. When he says, for instance, that God is the immanent cause of all things, it is not enough for us to find some one who had called God an immanent cause. We have to study the meaning of the term "immanent" in its complicated historical development and the particular use made of it by Spinoza throughout his writings. We shall then discover that he means by it something quite different from what we should ordinarily take it to mean.[17] Not that we are to assume that Spinoza had actually gone through all the steps of the investigation which we are to trudge through in discovering the meaning of such terms—for that was not necessary for him. He lived in an age when the traditions of philosophy were still alive, and what we nowadays have to discover by the painstaking methods of research came to him naturally as the heritage of a living tradition.

Studied against the rich background of tradition, even the most colorless of terms and expressions may become invested with technical significance of the utmost importance. A case in point is the special significance which may be discovered in Spinoza's choice of the terms "attribute," "created things," and "actuality" in his definition of duration,[18] and of the terms "first thing," "actual," "human mind," "idea," "individual thing," and "actually existing" in his definition of mind.[19] Even when Spinoza is obviously merely restating well-known sources our task is not completed by merely supplying the perfunctory references. We must again study the meaning of the sources quoted and their implications and all the possible uses he

17. Cf. Wolfson, *op. cit.*, I, 323 ff.
18. Cf. *ibid.*, I, 347 ff.
19. Cf. *ibid.*, II, 42 ff.

could have made of them. We shall often find that what at first sight appears merely as a repetition of what others have said is in reality a criticism of what they have said. For despite Spinoza's expressed aversion toward openly criticizing his opponents,[20] and perhaps because of it, his *Ethics* is primarily an implied criticism of his opponents. Thus, for instance, when he enumerates the various meanings of cause and asserts that God is a universal, efficient, essential, and first cause, it is not enough merely to identify the immediate source of his statement. We must study the implications of these terms, and we shall then find that instead of merely repeating what his predecessors have said, Spinoza is really challenging their right of saying what they have said and of applying to their God the term "cause" in all these senses.[21] And so throughout the *Ethics,* from his opening definition of substance to his concluding description of the religion of reason, we shall find that behind every positive statement there is lurking a negative criticism. With every one of his positive assertions we seem to hear Spinoza's challenge to his opponents: I accept your own definitions of terms, but I use them with greater consistency than you. I am not unwilling to use your own descriptions of God, but they are logically more applicable to my God than to yours. I see no reason why I should not use your own formulae, but I must give them an interpretation of my own. It is quite possible for me to adopt with some reservation one of your views, but I must reject all the others which you consider of equal probability.

That the *Ethics* in its literary form is a peculiar piece of writing is quite apparent. But its peculiarity does not consist in the obvious fact that it is divided into propositions and demonstrations instead of chapters and sections. It consists in the fact, which becomes obvious only after a careful study of the work, that the manner in which it makes use of language is rather peculiar. It uses language not as a means of expression but as a system of mnemonic symbols. Words do not stand for simple ideas but for complicated trains of thought. Arguments are not fully unfolded but are merely hinted at by suggestion. Statements are not significant for what they actually affirm but for the denials which they imply. Now, the mere use of the geometrical method cannot explain that, for even within the geometrical

20. Cf. *ibid.,* I, 58.
21. Cf. *ibid.,* I, 304 ff.

method Spinoza could have been clearer and more expatiative. To some extent it may be explained, perhaps, by the cloistered atmosphere in which the *Ethics* was conceived and written. No challenging questions of inquiring students or friends guided Spinoza in the manner of its exposition or goaded him into a fuller expansion of its statements. Despite the fact that he allowed himself to enter into the discussion of problems which troubled the minds of his correspondents, he never communicated to them the fulness of his own thought or discussed with them the philosophic problems which troubled his own mind. The congenial group of merchants, booksellers, medical students, and holders of public office which formed the immediate circle of Spinoza's friends had a layman's interest in the general problems of philosophy, but they could hardly serve as effective sounding-boards for his views during the experimental stages of his thinking. They seem to have had a more vigorous grasp of the problems of theology, in which they were the liberals of their day, but with all the adventuresomeness of their spirit they were just beginning to approach the liberalism of the mediaeval writings of Jewish rationalists read by Spinoza in his early youth, which he had long outgrown. Spinoza was welcomed by them as an exotic genius to whose occasional expression of shocking views they could listen indulgently because they could dismiss them from their minds as a sort of outlandish heresy. In this strange environment, to which externally he seems to have fully adjusted himself, Spinoza never felt himself quite free to speak his mind; and he who among his own people never hesitated to speak out with boldness became cautious, hesitant, and reserved. It was a caution which sprang not from fear but from an inner sense of decorum which inevitably enforces itself on one in the presence of strangers, especially strangers who are kind. Quite early in his new career among his newly found friends he showed evidence of this cautious and guarded attitude, and when on one occasion he became conscious of it, in the case of Casearius, he deluded himself into the belief that it was due to the faults of the latter arising from his youth and immaturity.[22] Little did he understand the real cause of his own behavior, and little did he know to what extent it stamped his general attitude towards all the others who had not the faults of youth and immaturity. So long had the thoughts of this book been simmering in his uncommunicative mind

22. *Ep.,* 9 (G., IV, 42, lines 19–26).

that it was boiled down to a concentrated essence, and it is this concentrated essence that we are served in the form of propositions. The *Ethics* is not a communication to the world; it is Spinoza's communication with himself.

In its concentrated form of exposition and in the baffling allusiveness and ellipticalness of its style, the *Ethics* may be compared to the Talmudic and rabbinic writings upon which Spinoza was brought up, and it is in that spirit in which the old rabbinic scholars approach the study of their standard texts that we must approach the study of the *Ethics*. We must assume that the *Ethics* is a carefully written book, in which there is order and sequence and continuity, and in which every term and expression is chosen with care and used with precision. We must try to find out not only what is within it, but also what is behind it. We must try to understand not only what the author says, but also what he omits to say, and why he omits it. We must constantly ask ourselves, with regard to every statement he makes, what is the reason? What does he intend to let us hear? What is his authority? Does he reproduce his authority correctly or not? If not, why does he depart from it? What are the differences between certain statements, and can such differences be reduced to other differences, so as to discover in them a common underlying principle? In order to understand Spinoza in full and to understand him well, we must familiarize ourselves with his entire literary background. We must place ourselves in the position of students, who, having done the reading assigned in advance, come to sit at his feet and listen to his comments thereon. Every nod and wink and allusion of his will then become intelligible. Words previously quite unimportant will become charged with meaning. Abrupt transitions will receive an adequate explanation; repetitions will be accounted for. We shall know more of Spinoza's thought than what is merely expressed in his utterances. We shall know what he wished to say and what he would have said had we been able to question him and elicit further information.

But a question may now naturally come up. How do we know that our interpretation is correct? After all, what we have done is to construct an imaginary setting to fit the *Ethics*. How do we know, then, that the setting is not a mere figment of the imagination? Even if it is admitted that the setting is constructed out of historical material and that the *Ethics* seems to fit snugly in it, still it may be argued that the plot of a historical novel may be similarly constructed out of historical material, the individual incidents may be all historically authenticated, and the personages of the novel may all act in their true historical character, and yet the work as a whole be nothing but an artificial and fictitious production.

In answer to this question we may say, in the first place, that the validity of our interpretation of the *Ethics* rests upon its workability and universal applicability. If there is anything arbitrary in our interpretation it is the initial assumption that Spinoza thought out his philosophy in a logical, orderly, and coherent manner, and that he wrote it down in a work which is logical, orderly, and coherent, and in a language which is self-explanatory. But having started out with this assumption and finding that the *Ethics* is far from being a book which is logical, orderly, and coherent, and that the language in which it is written is far from being self-explanatory, we have a right to believe that any interpretation, historically substantiated, that will help to explain the entire *Ethics* as a logically, orderly, coherently, and intelligibly written book is not fictitious like the plot of a historical novel. It is more like the plot of a work of true historical research in which a meagre and sketchy account of certain historical events preserved in a single fragmentary document is presented in a new reconstructed form by the filling in of gaps, by the supplying of details, and by the explaining of causes and motives, all on the basis of other authentic records. Historical research in philosophy, no less than in literature or politics, is justified in claiming the same test of certainty as the hypotheses of the natural scientists, namely, the test of workability and of universal applicability as a description of all the phenomena that come under observation.

The analogy of our study of the *Ethics* to the scientific method of research holds true in still another respect—in the employment of a method which may be considered as a modified form of what is called in science control-experiment. Invariably in the writings of Spinoza several texts are to be found in which the same problems are dealt with. In our study of Spinoza we have always treated these parallel texts as the scientific experimenter would treat his guinea-pigs, performing our experimental interpretation on some of them and using the others as a control. Thus in working on any problem, instead of collecting at once all the parallel texts and ancillary material in the writings of Spinoza and working on all of them at the same time, we confined our investigations to some particular texts, and then tested our conclusions by the other texts. Thus, for instance, in the problem of the unity of substance,[23] for which Propositions II–VI of *Ethics,* I, Chapter II of *Short Treatise,* I, and Appendix I of the *Short Treatise* are parallel texts, or in the problem of the relation of mind and body,[24] for which Proposition X of *Ethics,* II, Preface to *Short Treatise,* II, and Appendix II of the *Short Treatise* are parallel texts, the problem was fully worked out first in connection with one of these sets of texts and then tested and checked up by the others.

Then also, again in analogy to the method of research in the sciences, our investigation was not merely a matter of classifying data; it consisted mainly in discovering problems, stating them, and solving them; and the solution, as a rule, started with a conjecture which was afterwards verified by a method which in scholarship may be said to correspond to the method of experiment and prediction in science. One problem with which to start our investigation always presented itself to us, and that was the problem of linking together apparently disconnected propositions into a coherent argument. To solve this problem it was required to find the missing links which in the original form in which the *Ethics* was conceived in the mind of Spinoza and before it was broken up into geometric propositions supplied a logical transition between the disconnected statements which we now have before us. Now sometimes these missing links could be forged out of material which we happened already to have at our disposal, but most often they had to be invented imaginatively out of material which we only assumed to exist and the corroborative evidence was to be discovered afterwards. And, as a rule, it was discovered. But problems of still greater difficulty presented themselves to us on frequent occasions, such, for instance, as apparent misuse of terms on the part of Spinoza, or apparent contradictions in his own statements, or apparent misrepresentations of the views of others. Invariably in the solution of such problems we set up some distinction in the use of the term which Spinoza seemed to misuse, or we discerned some new aspect in the statement of the idea in which Spinoza seemed to contradict himself, or we assumed the possibility of some new interpretation of the view in which Spinoza seemed to misrepresent others. Here, again, most often these new

23. Cf. Wolfson, *op. cit.,* I, 79 ff.
24. Cf. *ibid.,* II, 33 ff.

distinctions, aspects, and interpretations were invented *ad hoc,* merely for the purpose of solving a certain difficulty, and the evidence corroborating them was discovered afterwards. This is the method which we have followed throughout our investigation, though it is not the method which we have adopted in the presentation of the results. In the final form which this work has assumed, for the sake of clearness and brevity, the order of exposition has had to be the reverse of the order of discovery, and sources, which in the actual process of investigation were evidence by which *a priori* conjectures were corroborated, have had to be presented as data from which conclusions were drawn. The material dealt with in this work did not seem to us to possess sufficient elements of human interest to justify our attempting to intrigue the reader by presenting each problem in the form of a mystery story.

A typical illustration of this kind of proof by experiment or prediction may be found in Spinoza's discussion of the problem of infinite extension. This is one of the discussions in which Spinoza makes reference to his opponents, restating their views and criticizing them. He finds that one of the reasons why his opponents denied the existence of an infinite extension was their belief in the divisibility of extension, and therefore concludes that inasmuch as matter is not divisible an infinite extension does exist. From the context of his discussion it appears that by divisibility he means divisibility into indivisible parts or atoms and that by indivisibility he means indivisibility in the same sense as a point is said to be indivisible. Having identified his opponents, we found that that kind of divisibility of extension which he seems to ascribe to them is explicitly denied by them. Furthermore, we found that Spinoza, in maintaining the existence of an infinite extension which is indivisible, uses the term "infinite" in a sense which is explicitly rejected by his opponents. Spinoza thus seems to misrepresent his opponents and to commit the fallacy of equivocation. This was the difficulty which confronted us. Now, of course, we could have dismissed this difficulty by assuming either that Spinoza purposely misrepresented his opponents in order to be able to refute them, or that out of sheer ignorance he attributed to them views of which they did not approve. But we preferred to believe that Spinoza was both intellectually honest and accurately informed. We therefore tried to find whether it would not be possible for us to interpret his utterances in such a way as would remove our difficulty. We made several vain attempts, until we finally hit upon a possible distinction in the use of the term "indivisible" and correspondingly in that of the term "divisible." By assuming that Spinoza had used these terms according to this new distinction which we invented *ad hoc,* we were able to explain his statements about his opponents in a fully satisfactory manner. We therefore adopted this as a tentative hypothesis, for the truth of which we had no evidence except the internal criterion of its workability. But then, after we had satisfied ourselves as to the workability of our hypothesis, we began to ask ourselves whether it would not be possible to find some external corroboration of it in the form of a statement by some author, mediaeval or ancient, where that distinction in the use of the terms "indivisible" and "divisible" was made. After some search, we found that this distinction in the use of the term "indivisible" is made by Aristotle and Thomas Aquinas.[25]

Or, to take another illustration. In Spinoza's classification of the stages of knowledge, we traced the history of the classification itself as well as of the terms used in it to Aristotle. Then when Spinoza evaluates these orders of knowledge and says that "knowledge of the first kind alone is the cause of falsity; knowledge of the second and third orders is necessarily true,"[26] we likewise traced this evaluation to Aristotle. But here we were faced with a difficulty. Aristotle makes use of four terms, naturally in Greek. Two of these terms correspond exactly to the two terms which Spinoza describes elsewhere as the second and third kinds of knowledge, but the other two terms used by Aristotle usually mean in Greek just the opposite of the two Latin terms which are used by Spinoza in his first kind of knowledge. But inasmuch as all the evidence pointed to this Aristotelian origin of Spinoza's evaluation of knowledge, we assumed that somewhere in the history of the transmission of Aristotle's writings from the Greek into Latin the two terms in question were somehow translated or interpreted in a sense corresponding to the two terms used by Spinoza. Then, after we had completed the chapter on the Stages of Knowledge, we began to ask ourselves whether it would not be possible for us to find some work accessible to Spinoza where that unusual translation or interpretation of the two Aristotelian terms in question actually occurred. After some search, we found that in two

25. Cf. *ibid.,* II, 270 and 282 ff.
26. *E.,* II, xli.

Latin translations made from the Hebrew of Averroes' Arabic Long Commentary on Aristotle's *Analytica Posteriora* these two Aristotelian terms are translated exactly as they are found in Spinoza.[27]

And so in innumerable instances external corroborative evidence was found for previously conceived conjectures. This gave us a sense of assurance that it was not merely an artificial structure that we were setting up for the *Ethics,* but that to some extent we had succeeded in penetrating into the mind of Spinoza and were able to see its workings, to sense its direction, to anticipate its movements, and to be guided to its goal. In order to understand another we must completely identify ourselves with that other, living through imaginatively his experience and thinking through rationally his thoughts. There must be a union of minds, like the union of our mind with the Active Intellect which the mediaevals discuss as a possibility and of which Spinoza speaks as a certainty.

27. Cf. Wolfson, *op. cit.,* II, 146 and 151.

Experience in Spinoza's Theory of Knowledge[1]

E. M. CURLEY

My concern in this paper is with the question, whether Spinoza was, in one tolerably precise and common sense of the term, a rationalist. By rationalism I understand here a certain view of the ideal nature of science.[2] A rationalist is a person who has a program for science according to which it aspires to the condition of mathematics, where mathematics is conceived as a purely *a priori* discipline, which reasons deductively from self-evident premises to substantive conclusions about the nature of things. Experience, for the rationalist, plays no fundamental role, either in the discovery or in the verification of scientific truth. The scientist may appeal to experience to illustrate his doctrines, but he will not appeal to experience to establish them. Where a proposition is either self-evident or deduced from self-evident premises, it would be superfluous to require experimental verification.

Some may reject my question out of hand on the ground that its answer is obviously yes. Others, fewer in number, but better informed, may reject it because they think its answer is obviously no. It has been objected to me that none of the "Continental Rationalists" ever held the view of science this sort of rationalism requires. I have no doubt that is true. But though there are more or less satisfactory treatments of this question in connection with Descartes, and to a lesser extent, with Leibniz,[3] I know of none in connection with Spi-

---

This essay was written especially for this volume.

1. This is a revised version of a paper read to the Australian Association of Philosophy in Melbourne in August 1968.

2. Much, of course, depends on definitions. There are senses of the term in which Spinoza was unequivocally a rationalist. Cf. M. Gueroult, *Spinoza*, I, 9–13 and my *Spinoza's Metaphysics* (Cambridge, Mass.: Harvard University Press, 1969), p. 157. But the sense in question here is probably more common. See, e.g. Bernard Williams' article on rationalism in *The Encyclopedia of Philosophy*, ed. P. Edwards (New York: The Macmillan Co. and The Free Press, 1967), VII.

3. E.g., R. M. Blake, "The Role of Experience in Descartes' Theory of Method," *Philosophical Review*, 38 (1929), 125–143, 201–218 (reprinted in *Theories of Scientific Method: The Renaissance Through the Nineteenth Century*, ed. E. H. Madden (Seattle: University of Washington Press, 1960),

noza.[4] And I think that approaching Spinoza in this way may help to bring to light important features of his real theory of knowledge.

The view that Spinoza was a rationalist, in the sense we are concerned with, is not just mildly inaccurate, it is wildly inaccurate. Experience has a much greater role to play in Spinoza's theory of knowledge than this view can allow for. To see why this is so we need to discuss Spinoza's doctrine of the three kinds of knowledge. For the view that Spinoza was a rationalist tends to rest on a natural but mistaken interpretation of that doctrine.

We start with the fact that Spinoza divided knowledge into three kinds: imagination, reason, and intuition. That much is not contentious. But how are these three kinds of knowledge supposed by Spinoza to differ from one another, to be like one another, to be related to one another? Are they entirely independent of one another? Or does one of them provide the basis for one or more of the others? What, precisely, did Spinoza intend to include under each of his three headings? These are fundamental questions about Spinoza's doctrine. And they are, as we shall see, very difficult to answer uncontentiously.

Much of the obscurity of the division stems from Spinoza's characteristic brevity. But some arises from the fact that there are three different versions of the division (in the *Short Treatise,* the *Treatise,* and the *Ethics*). While the three versions are similar, there are differences between them which may indicate changes in Spinoza's conception of his three kinds of knowledge. We shall have to keep this possibility in mind as we discuss the question of how the division is to be taken.

A. Gewirth, "Experience and the Non-mathematical in the Cartesian Method," *Journal of the History of Ideas,* 2 (1941), 183–210; E. Denisoff, *Descartes, premier théoricien de la physique mathématique* (Louvain: Nauwelarts, 1970); G. Buchdahl, "Descartes' Anticipation of a Logic of Scientific Discovery," in *Scientific Change,* ed. A. C. Crombie (New York: Basic Books, Inc., 1963); J. J. MacIntosh, "Leibniz and Berkeley." *Proc. Arist. Soc.,* 71 (1970–71), 147–163. See also Buchdahl's *Metaphysics and the Philosophy of Science* (Cambridge, Mass.: M.I.T. Press, 1969).

4. So though McKeon begins well, with an extended description of Spinoza's lively interest in experimental science, he goes on to give an account of Spinoza's epistemology which makes that interest unintelligible (*The Philosophy of Spinoza,* New York: Longmans, Green & Co., 1928, pp. 130–157). Parkinson, though he thinks Spinoza ought to have granted an important role to experience, is content to discount the evidence that he did and to treat him as conforming to the stereotype of rationalism (*Spinoza's Theory of Knowledge,* Oxford: Clarendon Press, 1954. See particularly pp. 12–15 and 157–162).

There is one feature of Spinoza's division which is preserved with little variation in each version: the use of an example from mathematics. Three numbers, *a, b,* and *c,* are given, and we are asked to find a fourth number, *d,* which is in the same ratio to *c* as *b* is to *a.* We may come to know what number *d* is in any one of four ways.

First, we may have been taught by someone to employ the following rule: multiply *b* and *c,* then divide their product by *a* to find *d.* If we simply apply this rule because this is what we have been told to do to solve this sort of problem, without having been given any reason for doing so, then our knowledge is what Spinoza calls knowledge from report or signs. This is one subkind of the first kind of knowledge, one variety of imagination.

If, on the other hand, we have tested the rule by performing calculations with it in simple cases where the answer is obvious, or if our teacher has done this for us, or if we have discovered the rule ourselves by generalizing from such simple cases, then our knowledge is what Spinoza calls knowledge from vagrant experience. This is the second subkind of the first kind of knowledge, another variety of imagination.

We have the second kind of knowledge, reason, if our knowledge is based on the proof of Proposition 19 in the Seventh Book of Euclid's *Elements.* Then, Spinoza says, we know what sort of numbers are proportional because we know the nature and property of proportion. We understand the common property of all proportionals. But we do not, if our knowledge is of this kind, "see the adequate proportionality of the given numbers."

When we do see *that,* then we have knowledge of the third kind, intuitive science. This is something which involves no process of reasoning. We simply see, in one intuition, what the ratio of *a* to *b* is, and see what number *d* must be.[5]

Such is the example Spinoza repeats each time he discusses the three kinds of knowledge. Sometimes he uses other examples as well. And always he gives a different general description of the three kinds of knowledge. But because this example is so often repeated, because it lends itself so easily to rationalistic interpretation, and because it has a deceptive familiarity about it, we may profitably use it to introduce the interpretation under discussion.

5. Here I blur some differences in Spinoza's various presentations of the mathematical example. See Joachim, *Spinoza's Tractatus de Intellectus Emendatione* (Oxford: Clarendon Press, 1940), p. 33, n. 1 and p. 31, n. 2.

The rationalistic interpretation of this doctrine would run along the following lines: (i) imagination, the first and least valuable of Spinoza's three kinds of knowledge, corresponds to ordinary empirical knowledge; it would include whatever is known by observation or inference from observation; since it has this empirical basis, it is highly fallible; it need not always be mistaken, but it very often is; consequently, though it may be very important for practical purposes, it is lacking in certainty, and does not constitute genuine scientific knowledge; (ii) reason, the second kind of knowledge, is infallible and does constitute scientific knowledge; but it is inferior to intuition, since it does not involve a direct insight into the truth of what is known; on the contrary, it is essentially derivative from intuition; for it always requires an inference from premises; the ultimate premises for things known by reason could not be supplied by the imagination, since the imagination is fallible; they must therefore be supplied by intuition; (iii) intuition, the third and best kind of knowledge, is like reason in being infallible and certain, but unlike reason in that it is noninferential and does involve a direct insight into the truth of what is known; it is the basis for all genuine scientific knowledge.

This is what I have in mind when I speak of the rationalistic interpretation of Spinoza's division of knowledge. I think the best way to bring out the difficulties faced by the rationalistic interpretation will be, first, to make some general comments on Spinoza's mathematical example, and then to discuss each of the three kinds of knowledge in turn, taking up the other examples Spinoza gives and reflecting on his different descriptions of the three kinds of knowledge.

General comment first. The Platonic overtones of this division of knowledge are evident, particularly in the *Short Treatise,* where the three kinds of knowledge are called, not imagination, reason, and intuition, but opinion, true belief, and clear knowledge. But the parallel is imperfect in one rather interesting respect. The four stages of cognition in the *Republic* are distinguished from one another primarily by a difference in their objects. There may also be a difference in the state of mind of the knower. *Dianoia,* for example, may be distinguished from *noesis* not only by its being concerned with mathematical objects rather than forms, but also by its involving a process of reasoning as opposed to an immediate apprehension of its object. But the differences in the objects of cognition are fundamental. The principal difference between *eikasia* and *pistis* is that the objects of the former are mere likenesses of the living things, the works of nature and of human hands, which are the objects of *pistis*.

In Spinoza's division, however, unless the oft-repeated mathematical example is misleading, there need be no difference in the object of cognition. Each of the three kinds of knowledge is presented as a different way of solving the same problem. *Prima facie,* what is known need not vary from one kind of knowledge to another. Even the eternal truths of mathematics can be known, albeit inadequately, by imagination.

Unless the mathematical example is misleading, the different kinds of knowledge need not have different kinds of object. But the mathematical example may be misleading. It is well known that Spinoza regularly uses mathematical examples to illustrate various points in his philosophy. But it is not always recognized that, on his view of the status of mathematical entities, there is something odd about this procedure. Mathematical entities, for Spinoza, are entities of reason, abstractions which exist only in the intellect and not in reality. On at least one occasion Spinoza explicitly reminds us of this when he is giving a mathematical example. This occurs in the *Treatise* in connection with the doctrine that a perfect definition must explain the essence of the thing and not use its properties. Spinoza writes,

> To explain this, I shall omit other examples, lest I seem to wish to lay bare the errors of others, and shall bring up only an example of something abstract, which is the same however it may be defined, e.g., a circle. If this be defined as any figure in which lines drawn from the center to the circumference are equal, no one fails to see that such a definition does not in the least explain the essence of a circle, but only one of its properties.[6] And though, as I have said, this does not make much difference where it is a question of defining figures and other entities of reason, still it does matter greatly when the things are physical and real.[7]

It is puzzling that Spinoza should say both that abstract entities are the same however they may be defined and that the traditional Euclidean definition of a circle does not give its essence. One thing, however, is clear, and that is that Spinoza is somewhat diffident about using a mathematical example because he thinks that the definitions of mathematical entities provide only a partial analogy with the kind of definitions he is most interested in—definitions of real things. And

6. Cf. Hobbes's use of the same example in *De Corpore,* I, 5.
7. *TdIE,* par. 95 (G., II, 34–35).

this suggests that perhaps we ought not to press his mathematical examples too far. It may be that the different kinds of mathematical knowledge provide only a partial analogy with the different kinds of knowledge of real things. And it may be that where knowledge of real things is concerned, the different kinds of knowledge do have different kinds of object. At this point it must be an open question whether or not they do. The mathematical example gives some ground for thinking that they don't. As we proceed, we shall discover some ground for thinking that they do. And we shall also see that in other respects the mathematical example is very tricky.

I

So much for general remarks. I want now to take up each of the three kinds of knowledge in turn, beginning with the first subdivision of imagination. I have called this knowledge "from report," which renders Spinoza's phrase "ex auditu." The phrase is usually translated "by hearing" or "by hearsay." But "auditu" can mean "report" and "report" seems preferable at least in that it does not suggest a limitation to things heard as opposed to things read. What it does suggest —rightly or wrongly—is that the belief is based on the authority of the reporter. Given Spinoza's description of his mathematical example, that suggestion seems a proper one:

> Merchants will say, carelessly, that they know what must be done to find the fourth number, because, of course, they have not forgotten the procedure which, undefended, without any demonstration, they heard from their teachers.[8]

It would still, presumably, be knowledge *ex auditu* if the merchants had read the instruction in a manual. On the other hand, if the teacher had given an appropriate defense of the procedure, this, we may suppose, might have converted knowledge *ex auditu* into some other kind of knowledge. The essential thing in knowledge *ex auditu* seems to be that the person believes that *p* simply because someone else has said that *p*.

The mathematical example suggests that knowledge from report can be converted into some other kind of knowledge by giving reasons for belief. Spinoza's other examples, however, appear to indicate that this will not always be possible. "Only from report," he says, "do I know on what day I was born, and who my parents were,

8. *TdIE,* par. 23 (G., II, 11).

and similar things which I have never doubted."[9] It is difficult to see how Spinoza could know on what day he was born or who his parents were in any other way than by report.

So the mathematical example is *prima facie* misleading in suggesting that knowledge from report can be converted into some one—or any one—of the other kinds of knowledge. Still, we might say—even though *I* can know only by report who my parents were or what day I was born on, *someone* must know, or have known, these things in some other way. And we might wish to say that in general this must be the case: that wherever one person knows that *p* by report, someone must know that *p* in some other way. If we are to call knowledge by report *knowledge,* then we want to know how the reporter knows. If he is only the proximate link in an infinite chain of reporters, each of whom knows only by report, then we should be very reluctant to call this knowledge. If, on the other hand, the chain of reporters terminates somewhere, then we want to know how the ultimate reporter knows. By hypothesis, he must know in some other way than by report—from vagrant experience, reason, or intuition. The result is that knowledge from report either is not knowledge at all, or is, in the end, derivative from some other kind of knowledge.

I suspect that this is a conclusion which Spinoza would accept. In classifying knowledge from report as a kind of knowledge, Spinoza does not seem to intend that the term "knowledge" be taken as a honorific one. In the *Short Treatise* he remarks that the man who makes his calculations on the authority of someone else, without taking into account the possibility that the man may be lying,

> has no more knowledge of the Rule of Three than a blind man has of color. Whatever he may have said about it, he simply repeated as a parrot repeats what it has been taught.[10]

Clearly, this kind of knowledge does not get very high marks, and is only called "knowledge" in a sense of that term which does not imply anything about the truth or falsity of what is believed. This is quite consistent with the way in which the division is introduced. In the *Short Treatise* it is introduced as a classification of the modes of which man consists, which are "certain ideas." In the *Treatise,* Spinoza speaks of reviewing "all the ways of perceiving which I have hitherto used to affirm or deny anything without doubt." And in the *Ethics* he appears to regard it as a division of the ways in which we

9. *TdIE,* par. 20 (G., II, 10).
10. *K.V.,* II, 1 (G., I, 54).

"perceive . . . things and form universal notions." So we need to take this division as a classification of the ways in which we come to have ideas or beliefs. There is no implication in speaking of *knowledge* from report that we have here something worthy of the name, and consequently there is no reason to suppose that it *must* in the end depend on some other kind of knowledge.

Consider now the various descriptions Spinoza gives of knowledge from report. It is not clear that he always conceived of it in the same way. In his earliest work, the *Short Treatise,* Spinoza describes this kind of knowledge simply as knowledge from report (assuming that *hooren zeggen* translates *auditu*). In the *Treatise* he characterizes it as perception we have from report (*ex auditu*) or from some conventional sign (*ex aliquo signo quod vocant ad placitum*).[11] And finally, in the *Ethics,* Spinoza describes it as knowledge,

> from signs, i.e. from the fact that, having heard or read certain words, we recall things and form certain ideas of things which are like them and through which we imagine the things.[12]

So we have a shift from describing the first subdivision of imagination as knowledge *ex auditu*—to knowledge *ex auditu aut signis*—to knowledge *ex signis*. Corresponding to this shift in the description we also have—or seem to have—at least a partial shift in the kind of example given. Of course Spinoza continues to use the mathematical example —in the *Ethics* that is practically the only example he does give—but at the end of the passage just quoted Spinoza refers us to a passage earlier in the *Ethics, E.,* II, xviii, S. The relevant passage seems to be the following one:

> . . . we can clearly understand how it is that the mind from the thought of one thing turns at once to the thought of another thing which is not in any way like it. For example, from the thought of the word *pomum* a Roman turned immediately to the thought of the fruit, which has no resemblance to the articulate sound *pomum* nor anything in common with it, except that the body of the man was often affected by the thing and the sound, that is, he often heard the word *pomum* when he saw the fruit.

This is the sort of process Spinoza has in mind when he speaks, later in the *Ethics,* of the fact that "having heard or read certain words, we recall things and form ideas of them . . ."

11. On this phrase, see Joachim, *op. cit.,* p. 26, n. 1. Cf. *TdIE,* pars. 88–89 (G., II, 33).

12. *E.,* II, xl, S.

The difficulty here lies in seeing how there could be anything in common between the sort of process described in xviii, S. and the sort which is presumably involved in Spinoza's earlier examples of knowledge *ex auditu*. When my parents tell me that I was born on a certain day, they use language—conventional signs—to do this. But their words do not recall the thing to me. However traumatic the experience of birth may be, it is not the sort of thing that we can observe and later remember in the way that we can observe and later remember an apple. More importantly, the process whereby a word which has become associated with a thing brings the thing to mind does not look like a very plausible candidate for a kind of knowledge at all. When my mother tells me that a certain man was my father, then, if I am a wise child, I may know that he was my father. But what does the Roman know when he hears the word *pomum?*

This apparent change in Spinoza's description and examples of the first subdivision of knowledge might suggest that Spinoza gradually broadened his conception of it to include not only things accepted on the authority of another person, but also anything communicated through language. Some such broad construction of knowledge *ex auditu aut signis* seems to be behind David Savan's claim that Spinoza regarded language as inevitably inadequate for the expression of philosophic truth. But this interpretation is quite untenable.[13] Spinoza's classification of knowledge *ex signis* as one of the varieties of imagination does not entail any radical thesis about the inadequacy of language to express clear and distinct ideas, whether in philosophy or in other areas.

Still the question remains: What did Spinoza intend to include under the heading of knowledge *ex auditu aut signis?* What similarity is there, if there is any, between the early examples and the later example?

The problem can be partially resolved by recalling that knowledge *ex auditu aut signis* is not knowledge in any honorific sense of the term. The proper question is not: What does the Roman know when he hears the word *pomum?* but: What does the Roman affirm or deny when he hears the word *pomum?* Spinoza will not be inconsistent

13. See Savan, "Spinoza and Language," pp. 60–72 in this volume. Savan argues not only from the necessarily imaginative character of language, but also from the numerous contradictions he finds in Spinoza's philosophy. I find Parkinson's rebuttal of Savan (p. 73 in this volume) thoroughly convincing. The most decisive evidence occurs in Spinoza's discussion of language in *Tr. Theol.-Pol.*, ch. vii (G., III, 111).

with his earlier examples if he says that the Roman does not, strictly speaking, know anything. But he must, to be consistent with his earlier examples, maintain that the Roman thinks something, that he affirms or denies something.

And once we put the matter like that, we can see that Spinoza would maintain this. For it is one of his distinctive doctrines that every idea involves an element of affirmation or negation. In opposition to Descartes, Spinoza holds that there is no such thing as having an idea without affirming or denying something about the object of the idea. Whatever the merits of this controversy between Descartes and Spinoza may be,[14] its application to the present case is clear. When our Roman hears the word *pomum* and forms an idea of an apple, he is making a judgment about the apple. Other things being equal, he is judging that there is an apple present to him, or as Spinoza says, contemplating it as present to him.

So there is not so great a difference as there first appears to be between Spinoza's earlier and later examples of knowledge "from report." And I think that reflection on this later example may help us to correct something I said in the beginning. I have spoken—naturally, but misleadingly—of knowledge from report as believing that *p* because someone, who is taken to be an authority, has said that *p*. The mathematical example tends to suggest this, but wrongly. Knowledge from report is believing that *p* because someone—who may or may not be taken to be an authority—has said something—which may or may not be that *p,* but which makes us think that *p*. It is, as the comparison with the parrot might have told us, a very simple stimulus-response situation. Indeed, I suspect that once you introduce the notion of authority you get something which is not knowledge "from report" at all. For to say that the reporter is taken to be an authority implies a judgment on his reliability as a truth-teller. If this judgment is supported by evidence—if we take the reporter's word because we have found him, or people like him, to be trustworthy in similar situations in the past—then I think Spinoza might want to classify this as knowledge from vagrant experience. It is difficult from his sketchy remarks to say with any certainty how the classification would go. But if my suspicions are correct, then it

14. I have discussed this issue in some detail in an article to appear in a collection of essays on Spinoza entitled "Descartes, Spinoza and the Ethics of Belief," in *Spinoza: Essays in Interpretation,* ed. Freeman and Mandelbaum, Open Court, 1973.

might after all be possible to convert some of the seemingly recalcitrant cases of knowledge from report into some other kind of knowledge. I might be able to know from vagrant experience, for example, what day I was born on.

If this discussion of knowledge from report has accomplished nothing else, at least we have seen, in a more or less noncontroversial case, how hard it is to know from Spinoza's descriptions and examples just what he had in mind. I pass now to knowledge from vagrant experience. "Vagrant experience" renders Spinoza's "experientia vaga." This phrase is usually translated "mere experience" (Elwes), which has nothing to recommend it, or "vague experience" (White), which has at least etymology to recommend it. But "vagrant" has the same etymological root, is closer to the probable meaning of the Latin, and conveys more accurately the spirit of the passage in Bacon's *Novum Organum* which is usually identified as the source of this phrase:

> But not only must we seek and procure a greater abundance of experiments, of a kind different from any done heretofore, we must also introduce an entirely different method, order and process of continuing and advancing experience. For when experience wanders aimlessly, following only itself . . . it is mere groping, and stupefies rather than instructs. But when experience proceeds according to a definite law, in order and continuously, then it will be able to hope for something better in the sciences.[15]

It is worth preserving some echo of this origin, for it may be that Spinoza, in speaking of *experientia vaga,* intended to include only a certain kind of experience. Bacon, in the passage just quoted and quite generally, wanted to make a distinction between what we might call a casual and haphazard use of experience and what we might call a systematic use of experience. For all that he was the father of modern empiricism, he had little use for the empiricists of his day;[16] but he also thought that there was a more sophisticated way of being an empiricist.

I don't wish, at this stage, to assert flatly that Spinoza would have agreed. I only wish to suggest that possibility and to point out that there is nothing in Spinoza's descriptions of knowledge from vagrant experience which would rule it out. In the *Treatise,* for example,

15. Bacon, *Novum Organum,* I, 100.
16. See e.g., *ibid.,* I, 64.

Spinoza's own gloss on "experientia vaga" is that it is "experience not determined by the intellect." It is difficult to know quite how to take this. Is the qualification an explicative one, implying that it is a general characteristic of experience as such that it is not determined by the intellect? Or is it a restrictive qualification implying that some experiences are determined by the intellect, that others are not, and that only the latter come under the heading of vagrant experience? It is hard to tell just what Spinoza had in mind.[17]

Such speculations put a different perspective on Spinoza's low evaluation of knowledge from vagrant experience. It is clear that Spinoza viewed the imagination as the only source of error. Reason and intuition are infallible. But what, precisely, did Spinoza include under the headings of imagination, reason, and intuition? Could he have had higher hopes for a use of experience which "proceeds according to a definite law"?

We cannot answer that question now—we can only ask it. Hopefully the answer will emerge as we go forward. Right now I should like to direct attention to Spinoza's examples of knowledge from vagrant experience, to see what can be gleaned from them.

To begin with the mathematical example, the first thing to notice is that there is a certain ambiguity in Spinoza's description of it. In the *Short Treatise,* and less definitely in the *Ethics,* our knowledge from vagrant experience of the Rule of Three seems to be described as a case of what would nowadays be called hypothetico-deductive testing. Someone tells us that the fourth proportional is given by the formula $d = \dfrac{bc}{a}$. We are unwilling to take his word for it, so we try the formula out in some simple cases where the answer is obvious. Finding that it works in these cases, we accept the general rule.

In the *Treatise* the process seems to be induction by simple enumeration. Others, Spinoza says,

17. A similar ambiguity infects the description given in the *Ethics.* Is the knowledge that we have through our senses of singular things necessarily mutilated, confused, and without order? Or did Spinoza envisage a kind of knowledge gained through the senses that would still be orderly? Cf. *TdIE,* par. 84 (G., II, 32). Joachim glosses *experientia vaga* as *knowledge by uncritical experience,* and when he abbreviates this to *empirical knowledge* characteristically uses scare-quotes (Joachim, *op. cit.,* pp. 27–28). For a passage which plainly implies that experience can be understood clearly and distinctly, see *Tr. Theol.-Pol.,* ch. v (G., III, 76–77).

will form a universal axiom from their experience with simpler cases where the fourth number is evident—as with 2, 4, 3 and 6, where they find that multiplying the second and third numbers and dividing their product by the first gives 6 as a quotient. Since they see that the number is produced which, without this procedure, they already knew to be proportional, they then conclude that the procedure is always good for finding the fourth proportional.[18]

Here it sounds as though—instead of testing a rule which has been suggested to us prior to our investigations of particular cases—we are constructing the rule directly from those cases without any antecedent hypothesis. But though the descriptions vary in this way, it does not appear that Spinoza would have allowed that there was any relevant difference between hypothetico-deductive testing and induction by simple enumeration. Even in the *Short Treatise,* where what he is describing is pretty clearly the former rather than the latter, he remarks that the person who comes by his belief in this way is also subject to error, "For how can he be sure that the experience of a few particulars can give him a rule for all?"

The next point is this. What we know immediately from our induction or our testing is a general proposition, a:b = c:d if and only if $d = \frac{bc}{a}$. What we know ultimately, however, is a singular proposition —say, that where a, b, and c are 5, 7, and 25, d = 35. This is implicit in the way Spinoza has set up his example. We are given three numbers and asked to find the fourth proportional. Where we have knowledge from vagrant experience, we know the answer in the particular case because we have come to know a relevant general proposition by induction or by some equivalent procedure. Where we have knowledge by reason, we know the answer in the particular case because we have come to know a relevant general proposition by deduction. But where we have intuition we know the answer in the particular case without needing to know any general proposition. This seems to be a crucial difference between the three kinds of knowledge— at least as far as the mathematical example goes. So what we know, when we know something by vagrant experience, may be either a general proposition or a singular one.

A further point is this. In the mathematical example, our knowledge from vagrant experience—whether of the general rule or of the

18. *TdIE,* par. 23 (G., II, 12).

answer in the particular case—is going to rest on a number of singular propositions. We infer the general rule that where a:b = c:d, $d = \dfrac{bc}{a}$ from premises like

$$2:3 = 4:6 \text{ and } 6 = \frac{3 \times 4}{2}$$

$$1:3 = 2:6 \text{ and } 6 = \frac{3 \times 2}{1}$$

and so on.

In the particular case where a, b, and c are 5, 7, and 25, we need in addition to know that

$$\frac{7 \times 25}{5} = 35$$

And Spinoza apparently thinks that at least some of these premises will be known, not by vagrant experience, but by intuition, for he says that we arrive at the Rule of Three by considering simple cases "where the fourth number is evident." If our knowledge from vagrant experience of the Rule of Three were typical in this respect, then knowledge from vagrant experience would depend on intuition.

Spinoza's other examples of knowledge from vagrant experience indicate that the mathematical example is not typical in this respect. In the *Short Treatise,* when he is illustrating his thesis that the passions depend on knowledge of the first kind, he says that surprise is found in someone who has that kind of knowledge,

> for since, from a few particulars, he draws a general conclusion, he is astonished when he sees something which goes against his conclusion—like someone who, having seen only sheep with short tails, is surprised by those from Morocco that have long ones.[19]

Clearly the premises of the inference here are going to be known by observation. And this appears to be the case with most of the examples Spinoza gives of knowledge from vagrant experience. He says that we know in this way that oil feeds fire, that water extinguishes it, that the dog is a barking animal, and man a rational one. He seems to think of all of these as known through induction by simple enumeration, where the premises are known by observation—though he points out in the *Short Treatise* that we need not be conscious of having gone through any process of inference.

I have spoken of the premises of these inductions as being known by observation. I take it that this kind of knowledge—knowledge of

19. *K.V.,* II, 3 (G., I, 56).

a singular proposition through (simple) observation—would be one species of knowledge from vagrant experience, though most of the examples Spinoza gives of knowledge from vagrant experience when he is classifying the different kinds of knowledge are general propositions. In the *Ethics,* when he wants to discuss the problem of error, which can only arise in the first kind of knowledge, Spinoza gives as an example the judgment, which rustics are supposed to make, that the sun is only about 200 feet away from us. What is involved here, on Spinoza's theory of perception, is that the rustic is aware of a certain modification of his body which has been caused by the sun. His awareness of this modification is or contains implicitly a judgment that the modification is of a kind that has a certain kind of cause. There is nothing, Spinoza thinks, erroneous in that judgment taken by itself. The error consists in the fact that the rustic does not also make a further judgment about the true distance of the sun and the true cause of this particular modification of our body. When we later come to know that the sun is much farther away, we still imagine it as near, i.e. judge that it is the kind of modification that typically has a certain kind of cause, but then we also understand why we imagine it as near when in fact it isn't.

Part of what is going on here is that Spinoza is assimilating cases of ordinary perception to cases of induction by simple enumeration. After saying in the *Treatise* that knowledge from vagrant experience is perception from experience "not determined by the intellect," Spinoza goes on to explain that

> it is only so called because it happens thus by chance and we have no other experience which opposes it. Therefore it stays with us unshaken.[20]

The remark inevitably recalls Bacon's complaint that

> the induction of which the logicians speak, which proceeds by simple enumeration, is a puerile thing, concludes at hazard, is always liable to be upset by contradictory instances, takes into account only what is known and ordinary, and leads to no result.[21]

But though we naturally think of the man who, having seen a number of sheep with short tails and none with long tails, instinctively assumes that all sheep have short tails, Spinoza's explanation seems

20. *TdIE,* par. 19 (G., II, 10).
21. *The Works of Francis Bacon,* ed. J. Spedding, R. Ellis, and D. Heath (London: Longman & Co., 1857), IV, 25.

also to be intended to cover the case of the man who, having a certain sense experience and none to the contrary, instinctively assumes that the sun is only 200 feet away.

To sum up, knowledge from vagrant experience may be of singular or of general propositions, may or may not involve sense experience, may or may not be inferential, and may or may not depend on some other kind of knowledge. I have not gone into the general question of whether knowledge from vagrant experience can be converted into some other kind of knowledge. But I have suggested that Spinoza's descriptions of knowledge from vagrant experience leave open the possibility of a use of sense experience which is in some way purified and reliable. If there turns out to be positive evidence that Spinoza did envisage such a use of sense experience, that will be a mark against the rationalistic interpretation of Spinoza, for that interpretation supposed that any knowledge that had an empirical basis came under the heading of imagination.

II

I turn now to reason. The rationalistic interpretation of Spinoza here would have it that this kind of knowledge always involves a deductive inference from self-evident premises known by intuition. This interpretation receives its strongest support from the mathematical example. What seems to be essential to our knowing through reason that $d = 35$, where a, b, and c are 5, 7, and 25, is that we have come to know Proposition 19 of Book VII of Euclid's *Elements* by deducing it from the self-evident axioms and definitions of that work and that we have inferred our singular conclusion from that general truth of mathematics, with the help no doubt of certain singular mathematical truths (such as

$$\frac{7 \times 25}{5} = 35).$$

Unfortunately Spinoza's descriptions of reason in the *Treatise* and the *Ethics* and his other examples of reason do not support such an interpretation. (I ignore the *Short Treatise* here because it gives no examples of reason other than the mathematical one and its description of reason is too vague to be of use to anyone.)

In the *Treatise,* Spinoza characterizes reason as the kind of perception we have "where we infer the essence of one thing from another, but not adequately." He distinguishes two species of this. One occurs "when we infer the cause from some effect"; the other "when something is inferred from some universal which some property always accompanies."[22]

The mathematical example seems to fall under the second of these two species of reason. We know, from Euclid's definition of proportion, the nature of a universal, namely, proportionality. This we may suppose to be known by intuition. We deduce from that definition a certain property of proportional numbers, namely, that the product of the means always equals the product of the extremes. And we use that property to discover the fourth proportional in the particular case, with the help, we must add, of some other mathematical knowledge that we have. So the mathematical example accords quite neatly with the rationalistic interpretation.

But Spinoza also gives, in the *Treatise,* another example of this species of reason which does not. "I have come," he says,

> to know the nature of vision and at the same time that it has the property that at a great distance we see one and the same thing as smaller than when we look at it close at hand. From this I infer that the sun is larger than it appears to be, and other similar conclusions.[23]

This example will repay close attention. If it were strictly parallel to the mathematical example, then it might be spelled out in the following way. Once we come to know the nature or definition of vision by intuition we are able to deduce from this definition a property of vision—namely that things seen at a distance look smaller than they do when seen close at hand. And from this property of vision we deduce that the sun is larger than it appears to be.

Now I want first to raise some questions about the definition of vision which is fundamental to this account: Where do we go to find our definition of vision? What does it look like when we find it? In the mathematical case we know, or think we know, where to go to find it. We look at the definitions at the beginning of Book VII of Euclid's *Elements* and there it is: "Numbers are proportional when the first is the same multiple, or the same part, or the same parts of the second that the third is of the fourth." Perhaps Spinoza would not have regarded this definition as really adequate, on the same grounds on which he rejected the Euclidean definition of a circle. But at any rate, when it is a question of the definition of proportionality, we have some idea of how to proceed.

22. Cf. Joachim, *op. cit.,* p. 30.
23. *TdIE,* par. 21 (G., II, 11).

Where do we look for a definition or statement of the nature of vision? Well, first of all, not in the dictionary. The kind of definition Spinoza is after is not going to be a statement about the correct use of language. Probably we look for it in a work like Descartes's *Dioptrique*. And what we find given there as an account of the nature of vision is not a simple statement which comes at the beginning of the investigation, but a complex theoretical explanation of the process by which we see things. It takes Descartes six chapters to state the nature of vision. He begins by making certain assumptions about the nature of light and its rays. We are to consider it "as nothing else, in the bodies that we call luminous, than a certain movement or action, very rapid and lively, which passes towards our eyes through the medium of the air and other transparent bodies."[24] In terms of this hypothesis about the nature of light—and Descartes makes it very explicit that it is a hypothesis—he goes on to explain various properties of light—e.g. such laws of geometrical optics as the law of reflection and Snell's law of refraction. Then he gives a description of the structure of the eye, explains how the light rays coming from the object are focused on the retina of the eye and the impulses received there transmitted through the optic nerve to the brain by the animal spirits. At this point the story gets a bit murky and we encounter obscure references to the pineal gland and to the ultimate agency of the mind in perception. At any rate, though, Descartes purports to account, in terms of this picture of the visual process, for quite a number of different properties of vision—and in particular for the fact that things seen at a distance appear to be smaller than the same things seen from close up.

Whether or not this is a good explanation of the nature of vision does not matter. The point is that this is surely the kind of story Spinoza has in mind when he speaks of our coming to know the nature of vision. We can see this if we look at the requirements he lays down in the *Treatise* for a good definition of a created thing. The principal ones are that it should give the proximate cause of the thing and that it should suffice for deducing all the properties of the thing. Clearly these are conditions which the Cartesian causal account of vision is at least intended to satisfy, so that it has some claim to being a good definition.

It is because Spinoza has these requirements for a good definition

24. Descartes, *Discourse on Method, Optics, Geometry and Meteorology*, ed. and trans. P. Olscamp (New York: Bobbs-Merrill, 1965), p. 67.

that he rejects the Euclidean definition of a circle. It does not even attempt to give the proximate cause of the circle and would not, Spinoza thinks, suffice for deducing its properties. Presumably he would reject the Euclidean definition of proportionality on the same ground.

As an alternative which would meet his requirements, Spinoza suggests that a circle might be defined as that figure which is described by any line of which one end is fixed and the other moving. This definition gives the proximate cause and from it we can deduce the properties of the circle—e.g. such facts as that all the lines drawn from the center to the circumference are equal. The causal definition of the circle gives you its essence, not just a property. And similarly, the Cartesian causal account of vision, if it is correct, gives you the essence or nature of vision.

It would be easy to infer from this that Spinoza envisaged replacing Euclidean geometry by a reformed geometry, constructed on Spinozistic principles from genetic definitions. Easy, but, I think, mistaken. For in the same passage where Spinoza was complaining that the Euclidean definition of a circle did not give its essence he also said that it did not really matter how entities of reason are defined, that they are "the same however they are defined." This seemed a puzzling conjunction of views.

But it becomes intelligible, I suggest, if we advert to the discussion of definition which arises in Spinoza's correspondence with Simon de Vries.[25] De Vries writes to Spinoza asking him to choose between two conceptions of definition: the first, that of Borelli, a more or less orthodox Aristotelian, for whom definitions must be true, primary, clearly known to us, and essential, since they are needed as premises in demonstrations; the second, that of Clavius, according to whom definitions are formulas of human construction, which need not be justified so long as we do not affirm the thing defined of anything which we have not first shown to possess the defining characteristic. On this second view, a definition need not be true, primary, or best known to us.

Spinoza replies that there are two different kinds of definition which have two different kinds of requirement: (i) those which explain a thing as it exists outside the intellect; these must give a true description of their object and do not differ fundamentally from

25. *Ep.*, 8–10.

propositions or axioms; (ii) those which explain a thing as we conceive it or can conceive it; these are not appropriately characterized as true or false, nor are they susceptible of proof—to ask someone to prove such a definition would involve the absurdity of asking him to prove that he has conceived what he has conceived; the only requirement to be made here is that definitions which explain a thing as we conceive it be conceivable, i.e. that they not involve a contradiction.

I take it that the definition of a real thing, which is exemplified by the Cartesian account of vision, would be a definition which explains a thing as it exists outside the intellect. It would, therefore, have to give a true description of its object. We can consider shortly how we are supposed to tell whether or not it does this.

But the definition of an entity of reason, such as a circle, would be a definition which explains a thing as we conceive it or can conceive it. Such definitions are quite arbitrary for Spinoza since there is no object external to the intellect which they can describe or fail to describe.

This, I suspect, is why Spinoza says in the *Treatise* that it does not matter how entities of reason are defined. Provided it is consistent, any definition which purports only to explain a thing as it exists in the intellect is automatically a good definition, for it creates its own object. This is why we should not think of Spinoza as envisaging the replacement of Euclidean geometry by a reformed geometry constructed on Spinozistic principles from genetic definitions. There is nothing wrong with Euclidean geometry as it stands. Its definitions meet the only test that definitions of entities of reason are required to face—consistency. The point of criticizing the Euclidean definition of a circle is merely to illustrate, in what is of necessity a noncontroversial case, how a definition might fail to meet the requirements that definitions of real things must meet.

We now have some idea, I hope, of *what* Spinoza thinks we know when we know the nature of vision. Now the question is: how does Spinoza think we come to know it? Descartes plainly regards his theory of vision as an hypothesis which is well established because it explains a wide range of phenomena.[26] We want to know whether

26. "Not having here any other occasion to speak of light than to explain how its rays enter into the eye and how they can be deflected by the different bodies that they encounter, I need not undertake to explain its true nature. And I believe that it will suffice that I make use of two or three comparisons which

or not Spinoza would have agreed. Unfortunately he does not often or in detail discuss the epistemological status of definitions. But there are remarks Spinoza makes in various places which we can appeal to for clarification. In the *Theological-Political Treatise,* Spinoza writes that

> the method of interpreting nature consists chiefly in arranging systematically the history of nature, from which, seeing that certain things are given, we infer the definitions of natural things.[27]

And a bit farther on he adds that

> Nature does not give us definitions of natural things . . . the definitions of natural things must be inferred from the diverse actions of nature.[28]

These passages certainly suggest strongly that Spinoza would have agreed with Descartes that our knowledge of the nature of vision is empirically based. And there is a passage in the correspondence with de Vries which I think needs to be read as being in agreement with this. After receiving the letter in which Spinoza had drawn his distinction between two kinds of definition, de Vries apparently wrote, in a letter now lost, to ask whether we ever needed experience to know whether the definition of any attribute is true. Spinoza replied that

> We never need experience except for those things which cannot be inferred from the definition of the thing, e.g. the existence of modes, for this cannot be inferred from the definition of the thing. But experience is not needed for those things whose existence is not distinguished from their essence and therefore is inferred from their definition. Indeed no experience will ever be able to teach us this. For *experience teaches us no essences of things,* but the most it can do is to determine our mind to think only of certain essences of

---

help to conceive it in the manner which to me seems the most convenient to explain all those of its properties that experience acquaints us with, and to deduce afterwards all the others which cannot be so easily observed, imitating in this the Astronomers, who, although their assumptions are almost all false or uncertain, nevertheless, because these assumptions refer to different observations which they have made, never cease to draw many very true and well-assured conclusions from them." Descartes, *op. cit.,* pp. 66–67. I don't think we need to take *too* seriously Descartes's suggestion that his hypothesis may not "explain the true nature" of light. Cf. Descartes, *Principles,* IV, 204–207.

27. *Tr. Theol.-Pol.,* ch. vii (G., III, 98).
28. *Tr. Theol.-Pol.,* ch. vii (G., III, 99).

things. Therefore, since the existence of attributes does not differ from their essence, no experience can ever cause us to grasp it.[29]

This is not an easy passage to understand, and the clause underlined is often quoted without its surrounding context in support of a rationalistic interpretation of Spinoza. But I take it that Spinoza's main point here is that, if we are inquiring whether or not a definition is true, i.e. whether or not there is something in nature answering to it, then we do not need experience to answer this query *if* the definition is the definition of an attribute. For an adequate definition of an uncreated thing must leave no question as to whether or not the thing exists.[30] But if the definition is the definition of a mode, a thing whose essence or definition does not involve existence, then we will need experience to know whether or not it is true, i.e. whether it describes something existing *in rerum natura*. When Spinoza says that experience teaches us no essences of things, I understand him to mean that experience is not required in order for us to know whether a definition represents a possible kind of entity. We can know *a priori* what the possible causes of a thing are. To know what the actual causes are (determine our minds to think only of certain essences of things) we require experience.

Thus insofar as our knowledge through reason that the sun is larger than it appears to be presupposes our knowing the nature of vision, it presupposes our knowing something through our observation of nature. Experience enters here in another way also. In the mathematical case it is not enough just to know the common property of proportional numbers. To get the answer in the particular case we need also to know that $\frac{7 \times 25}{5} = 35$. Analogously, in the case where we know that the sun is larger than it appears to be, it is not enough just to know that a large object will appear much smaller at a great distance. We need to know as well that the sun is much farther away than it appears to be. Spinoza could scarcely have been unaware of the need for such a premise. In the *Dioptrique* Descartes made the point quite explicitly. And as we have seen, one of Spinoza's examples of error was the judgment of the untutored imagination that the sun is only about 200 feet away. Moreover Spinoza's description of the true judgment which replaces this error—that the distance of the

29. *Ep.*, 10.
30. *TdIE,* par. 97 (G., II, 35).

sun is more than 600 times the diameter of the earth—certainly suggests that Spinoza was familiar with the empirical methods used by astronomers to determine this distance. So our knowledge through reason that the sun is larger than it appears to be presupposes empirical knowledge in at least two different ways.

That concludes what I have to say about the vision example, which is given by Spinoza to illustrate knowledge which we have from some universal which some property always accompanies. In the *Treatise,* Spinoza recognizes one other species of reason, or inferring inadequately the essence of one thing from another—namely inferring the cause from some effect. And he gives one example of this species of reason:

> after we have perceived clearly that we feel a certain body, and no other, from that, I say, we clearly infer that the mind is united to the body, the union being the cause of the sensation. But from this we cannot understand absolutely what that sensation and union are.[31]

The premises here are presumably the sort of facts which Descartes appealed to in support of the same conclusion in the Sixth Meditation. Descartes writes there that

> it was not without some reason that I believed that this body (which by a certain special right I called mine) belonged to me more properly and more strictly than any other; for in fact I could never be separated from it as from other bodies; I experienced in it and on account of it all my appetites and affections, and finally I was touched by the feelings of pleasure and pain in its parts and not in the parts of the other bodies which are separated from it.[32]

In other words, when you prick *this* body, *it* bleeds and *I* feel pain. When you prick *that* body, it also bleeds, but *I* don't feel pain. Such are the premises from which we seem to be working here. What we infer is a causal explanation—that the mind and the body are united. But we don't, Spinoza thinks, adequately understand either the nature of the union or the effect which it causes. He remarks in a note that "we understand nothing concerning the cause beyond what we contemplate in the effect . . . the cause would only be explained in the most general terms." Again, in another note, he says that

31. *TdIE,* par. 21 (G., II, 11).
32. Descartes, *Oeuvres et lettres,* ed. A. Bridoux (Paris: Gallimard, 1966), p. 321.

such a conclusion, although certain, is still not sufficiently safe, except for those who take the greatest care. For unless we are very much on guard, we will immediately fall into error. Where we conceive a thing so very abstractly, and not through its true essence, we are at once confused by the imagination. What is, in itself, one, we imagine to be many.

This last looks like a gibe at Descartes, who had still thought of mind and body as distinct entities, in spite of holding that they were "united."

This example of reason in operation is as embarrassing for me as it is for someone who wants to maintain a rationalistic interpretation of Spinoza. For the premises from which the inference proceeds appear to be, not just propositions which are known through experience, but propositions known through a rather uncritical sort of experience. In the case where we were said to know, through reason, that the sun is much larger than it seems to be, we had the correction of a naïve judgment of experience in the light of other sense perceptions and a scientific theory supported by a great body of critically sifted experience. The present case does not appear to involve anything anywhere near so complicated. I find it difficult to see what Spinoza thought the two cases had in common. I can see how the astronomical case is an instance of coming to know something through knowing some universal and its associated property. And I can see how the mind-body case is an instance of inferring a cause from its effect. What these are supposed to have in common is that they are both instances of "inferring the essence of one thing from another, but not adequately." That general description looks all right for the mind-body case. It is, for Spinoza, of the essence of the mind that it be united to the body. So what we are coming to know is the essence of the mind through something else—viz. its effects, certain sensations. The essence is not conceived adequately because the effects do not give us any clear idea of the nature of the union. I read this as a comment on Descartes and I think I understand it.

The general description does not look all right for the astronomical case. What is inferred—i.e. that the sun has a certain size—is something which is clearly conceived. But the size of the sun is not of its essence. Spinoza says so explicitly in a footnote.

I come then to the conclusion that Spinoza's doctrine of reason—as it is expounded in the *Treatise*—is confused. It does not seem to

be consistently thought out.[33] And I suspect that we may attach
some significance to the fact that he gives a very different characterization of reason in the *Ethics*. But we can say this—that as reason is
conceived in the *Treatise,* however confused the account may be, it
does seem to be essentially inferential (and so far forth the rationalistic interpretation is confirmed), but it does not seem to be
based always on premises known by intuition. Sometimes, at least,
the premises appear to be known by a combination of observation
and inference based on observation (and to that extent the rationalistic interpretation is in trouble). I am not sure it follows from this
that reason is sometimes dependent on intuition, sometimes dependent on imagination. But if we are to resist that conclusion, we shall
need, at some stage, to say how those inferences from experience
which do not belong to the imagination differ from those which do.

In the *Ethics,* reason is said to be that kind of knowledge which
we have "from the fact that we have common notions and adequate
ideas of properties." The Dutch translation of the *Ethics* which appeared contemporaneously with the *Opera Posthuma* reads "universal notions" for "common notions."

One's first impression of this, coming to it from the *Treatise,* is
that this is just the second species of reason over again, except that
the *Treatise's* first species of reason (knowing a cause through its
effects) has been dropped so that the second species now includes
everything which is said to be known through reason. Probably first
impressions are roughly right here. But not entirely so. This description does introduce a new concept—the concept of common notions,
which is of considerable significance in the mature theory of the
Ethics. What it means is indicated in the passage to which Spinoza
refers—*E.,* II, xxxviii, C. He has just proven that those things which
are common to everything and equally in the part and in the whole
can only be adequately conceived. From this, he claims,

> it follows that some ideas or notions exist which are common to all
> men, for all bodies agree in some things, which must be adequately,
> that is, clearly and distinctly perceived by all.

So this is what the common notions are—they are ideas clearly perceived by everyone of things in which all bodies agree. There is a
contrast here between those ideas which are common to and clearly

33. I claim no originality for this conclusion. Cf. Joachim, *op. cit.,* pp. 28–
32. But I cannot, of course, accept his interpretation of the mind-body example.

perceived by all men and those ideas which are not common to and clearly perceived by all men. The latter group includes traditional examples of universals. There is no such thing, strictly speaking, as the idea of Man or Horse or Dog, because the ideas that different men have of these species will differ from one another.[34] But the common notions do *not* vary from one person to another; they are formed by everyone in the same way. And the reason why they do not vary is that they have as their objects properties which cannot be inadequately perceived, properties which all bodies agree in possessing. It is a property of all bodies that they are extended, that they are either in motion or at rest, that sometimes they move more rapidly and sometimes more slowly.[35] Since these properties of extension and motion and rest are present in all bodies, they are present in all our experience of bodies. From this Spinoza thinks it follows that they can only be adequately conceived,[36] i.e. that our ideas of extension and motion and rest must necessarily be adequate.

So when Spinoza describes reason in the *Ethics* as involving knowledge of the common notions, this means that it does involve knowledge of a universal (and to that extent we have agreement with the second species of reason in the *Treatise*), but knowledge of a universal of a very special sort—one which is common to all bodies (and to that extent we seem to have a shift from the *Treatise*). I might add that not only does reason, in the *Ethics,* involve knowledge of the common notions, but the common notions are said[37] to be the foundations of our reasoning.

Since there is a shift in Spinoza's description of reason here, it is natural to ask how his former examples of reason would fare under the new description. Could they plausibly be interpreted to be examples of reason under the new description? In the mind-body case, the answer seems to be "no." From the fact that I feel a certain body and no other, I infer that my mind is united to my body. This does not appear to involve my having ideas of any properties common to all bodies, except insofar as I must have some idea of what a body is to be able to make the judgment "I feel this body" or "I feel pain when you prick this body." And that could hardly be a sufficient condition for this to count as an instance of reason. If it were, any judgment

34. *E.,* II, xl, S. 1 (G., II, 121).
35. *E.,* II, Lem. 2 (G., II, 98).
36. *E.,* II, xxxviii.
37. *E.,* II, xl, S. 1.

about bodies would be an instance of reason. Nor is it very surprising that our knowledge in this way of the union of mind and body should not, in the *Ethics,* be classed as an example of reason. As suggested earlier, there seems to be little that would distinguish this knowledge from the inadequate knowledge we have from vagrant experience of the ability of water to extinguish fire.

In the astronomical case, the answer seems clearly to be "yes." There we are supposed to have come to know the nature and properties of vision—and we infer from this that the sun is larger than it appears to be. And although vision is not a property common to all bodies, and our idea of it, therefore, is not a common notion, our knowledge of the nature of vision does presuppose our knowledge of the common notions. For on the Cartesian account of vision, to know how vision works requires knowing the laws of motion. It is an essential part of the Cartesian hypothesis about the nature of vision that light be thought of as an action or tendency toward movement which "follows the same laws as does movement." E.g. by construing the situation in which a ray of light strikes a smooth, flat surface as analogous to that in which a body traveling at a constant velocity strikes a flat and perfectly hard surface, Descartes purports to explain the law of reflection. We know how a moving body would behave under these admittedly ideal conditions. Knowing this, and assuming light to be a tendency toward movement, we come to understand a law of optics. I take it that the laws of motion would be examples of common notions. Motion-and-rest is a universal property of bodies; our idea of motion, therefore, will be a common notion; and on Spinoza's theory that every idea involves an element of affirmation, our common idea of motion will involve a series of affirmations about things which possess this property—i.e. it will involve the laws of motion.

This interpretation is borne out by what Spinoza says of method in that section of the *Theological-Political Treatise* quoted earlier. When, in the examination of natural things, we proceed from the history of nature to its interpretation, Spinoza contends, "we must first try to investigate those most universal things which are common to the whole of nature, namely, motion and rest, and their laws and rules, which nature always observes and by which she necessarily acts. From them we can come by degrees to those other things which are less universal."[38] Spinoza is here subscribing to the mechanistic

38. *Tr. Theol.-Pol.,* ch. vii (G., III, 102).

ideal which permeated the science of his time—the ideal of explaining all the phenomena of nature in terms of the actions of bodies in motion. Since the Cartesian explanation of vision was such a mechanistic theory, any knowledge which presupposes it—as our knowledge in the astronomical case does—would presuppose our possession of the common notions.

Before leaving the topic of reason we need to say something about the epistemological status of these common notions, which constitute the foundations of our reasoning. The first point to note is that they are not supposed by Spinoza to be known through intuition. When Spinoza introduces the doctrine of intuitive knowledge in *E.,* II, xl, S. 2, he says:

> In addition to these two kinds of knowledge [i.e. imagination and reason], there is, *as I shall show in what follows,* a third kind, which we shall call intuitive science.

Since at this point in the *Ethics* Spinoza has already discussed the common notions and explained why they must be adequately conceived, I think we may infer that he does not regard our knowledge of the common notions themselves as intuitive. So reason would include not only cases where our knowledge of something presupposes knowledge of the common notions, but also our knowledge of the common notions themselves.

But although our knowledge of the common notions is rational knowledge and not, in Spinoza's sense of that term, intuitive knowledge, it does not follow that he would not regard these principles as "evident." I think he would regard at least some of them as "evident." In the *Ethics*[39] he professes to give an *a priori* proof of the law of inertia—or at least of a form of that law—and after having demonstrated it he remarks that the law is "evident" (or, more literally, known *per se*). The law of inertia would be an example of a common notion, so some of the common notions would be regarded by Spinoza as "evident."

It is not clear to me just what the force of saying this is. Can Spinoza suppose that a proposition which is known *per se* will be seen immediately to be true by anyone who considers it and understands its terms? When Descartes put forward the law of inertia in his *Principles of Philosophy* he plainly regarded it as a proposition which most people would immediately think false:

39. *E.,* II, Lem. 3, C.

Because we live on the Earth, whose constitution is such that all
the movements which occur near us stop in a short time, and often
for reasons which are hidden from our senses, we have judged from
the beginning of our lives, that the movements which stop in this
way, for reasons unknown to us, stop of themselves. And we still
have a strong inclination to believe that all other movements in the
world are like this—that they naturally come to an end of themselves, because it seems to us that this is what we have experienced
many times.[40]

We will see that the law of inertia is true only after we have divested
ourselves of these childhood prejudices. To help us do this, Descartes brings forward a mixture of *a priori* and *a posteriori* arguments. First he contends that the law must be true because "rest is
the opposite of motion and nothing can by its own nature tend toward its opposite." He then goes on to argue that the law is confirmed by what we observe in projectile motion:

There is no reason why projectiles continue to move when they have
left the hand that throws them except that, according to the laws of
nature, every body which moves continues to move until its motion
is arrested by other bodies. It is evident that the air and other fluid
bodies among which we see these things moving, gradually diminish
the speed of their movement; for we can even feel from our hand
the resistance of the air if we beat it quickly enough with an extended
fan.[41]

So in Descartes the status of the law as a fundamental principle does
not entail that it will be immediately obvious and does not exclude
the need for arguments, which may sometimes be empirical.

Whether or not Spinoza would have agreed with this Cartesian
approach is not clear. There is some reason to think he might have.
Descartes' description of the grounds for our Aristotelian prejudices
about motion conforms closely to Spinoza's description of knowledge from vagrant experience. Because we happen to live on the earth
and the earth has a certain constitution, our experience of bodies in
motion has been of a certain sort. So far we are like the man living
in Holland who has seen only sheep with short tails. Having had no
contrary experience, we generalize hastily. But when we try to work
out a consistent and general theory of motion, covering projectiles as

40. Descartes, *Principles*, II, 37 (Bridoux, pp. 633–634). Cf. Spinoza's treatment in *Desc. Princ. Phil.*, II, 14–15 (G., I, 201–203).
41. Descartes, *Principles*, II, 38 (Bridoux, p. 634).

well as rolling stones, we find it impossible to conceive of motion in Aristotelian terms. The fact that we are here trying to give a coherent explanation of a set of apparently contradictory experiences might well have raised this process beyond the level of imagination and onto the level of reason.

On the other hand, I cannot see how Spinoza could have accepted this and remained consistent with his views about the common notions. For it is supposed to be impossible to perceive them inadequately precisely because they are ideas of properties common to all objects we experience. So the partiality and unrepresentativeness which characterizes vagrant experience is apparently ruled out in their case. It is not that they are apprehended by a special faculty, but that their pervasiveness in experience precludes error. How Spinoza might have reconciled this view with the fact that people did, for many centuries, have inadequate ideas about motion, I do not know.

III

In the *Treatise,* Spinoza defines intuitive knowledge as "perception where a thing is perceived either through its own essence or through knowledge of its proximate cause." He gives the following examples:

> A thing is perceived through its essence alone, when from the fact that I know something I know what it is to know something, or when from the fact that I know the essence of the mind, I know that it is united to the body. By the same kind of knowledge we know that two and three are five and that two lines parallel to a third line are parallel to each other . . .

Later he adds the example of seeing what the fourth proportional is.

I shall not undertake a detailed discussion of these examples. But I should like to call attention to a curious remark Spinoza makes at the end of his list. He says that "so far the things which I have been able to understand by this kind of knowledge are very few." This has often puzzled Spinoza's commentators, to whom it has seemed that mathematics ought to provide a great many examples of intuitive knowledge. The explanation, I think, is that mathematical knowledge doesn't really count, since it is knowledge, not of real things, but of entities of reason.

From Spinoza's general description of intuition, there appear to be two species of intuition: (i) knowing a thing through its essence, and (ii) knowing it through knowledge of its proximate cause. Now it might be argued that this is misleading. On Spinoza's understanding of the term "essence," the essence *is* the proximate cause.[42] So what we have is, not two species of intuition, but two equivalent ways of describing intuition. The function of the word "or" in the definition is not to suggest that there are two different kinds of intuitive knowledge but to indicate that the one kind of intuitive knowledge may be described in various ways.

But I think that is wrong. Later in the *Treatise,* Spinoza takes up the question of intuitive knowledge again and his discussion there makes it quite plain that there are two species:

> Our ultimate goal requires that things be conceived either through their essence alone, or through their proximate cause. That is, if a thing exists in itself, or as is commonly said, is its own cause, then it will have to be understood through its essence alone. If, on the other hand, the thing does not exist in itself, but requires a cause in order to exist, then it must be understood through its proximate cause.[43]

So there are two kinds of intuition in the *Treatise* and the distinction between them corresponds to a fundamental distinction in Spinoza's metaphysics, the distinction between things which exist in themselves and things which don't. I take it that the things which exist in themselves are the attributes of God—e.g. extension and thought—while the things which don't exist in themselves are the modes, both finite and infinite.[44]

In line with this division of intuition into two species, Spinoza goes on in the passage just quoted to suggest that there are two distinct kinds of definition with two distinct kinds of requirement. The definitions of created things, i.e. things which do not exist in themselves, i.e. modes, are supposed to give the proximate cause of the thing and to suffice for deducing its properties. The definitions of uncreated things, i.e. things which do exist in themselves, i.e. at-

42. Cf. *E.,* II, Def. 2.
43. *TdIE,* par. 92 (G., II, 34).
44. Cf. *K.V.,* I, 7 (G., I, 46–47).

tributes, are supposed, first, to show that the thing needs no cause, second, to make clear that it must exist, and third, to suffice for deducing the thing's properties.

If what I said earlier is correct, the Cartesian account of the nature of vision would probably be an example of one sort of thing Spinoza has in mind in speaking of the definition of a created thing. Spinoza would clearly class vision as a mode. Similarly an adequate account of the nature of motion and rest—which is explicitly named as an infinite mode—would also be an example of a definition of a created thing. But an adequate account of extension, which is an attribute, would be a definition of an uncreated thing.

This is somewhat speculative, but it at least makes a bit more intelligible Spinoza's remark that so far he has been able to understand very few things by intuition. And it also fits in well with what Spinoza wrote to de Vries in response to his question "Do we need experience to know whether or not a definition is true?" The answer was—no, if it is the definition of an attribute; yes, if it is the definition of a mode. It seems to me that we are on the right track here—at least insofar as the doctrine of intuition in the *Treatise* is concerned. And it will be sufficiently obvious, I think, that, if this is correct, empirical knowledge will be required for one species of intuition.

I come, finally, to the doctrine of intuition as it occurs in the *Ethics.* "This kind of knowing," Spinoza says there, "proceeds from an adequate idea of the formal essence of certain attributes of God to adequate knowledge of the essence of things."[45] We are left pretty much to our own devices in interpreting this. The only example Spinoza gives is that of seeing the fourth proportional and it is exceedingly difficult to see how that fits the general description. But there is a key remark in Part V of the *Ethics,* where Spinoza speaks of intuitive knowledge as knowledge of singular things, in opposition to the second kind of knowledge, which is described as universal.[46]

Let me just suggest very briefly what I think Spinoza may have had in mind here by comparing the *Ethics* with the *Treatise.* In the *Treatise* the primary contrast between reason and intuition seemed to be that, whereas reason involved an inadequate, because inferential, knowledge of the essences of things, intuition involved an adequate and immediate knowledge of their essences. And there were

45. *E.,* II, xl, S. 2.
46. *E.,* V, xxxvi, C., S.

two species of intuition—one exemplified by knowledge of the essence or definition of an attribute, the other exemplified by knowledge of the essence or definition of a mode. (This seems correct, provided that we qualify it by saying that Spinoza did, inconsistently, include under the heading of reason some cases where the object of knowledge was not an essence.)

In the *Ethics,* intuition seems to be conceived more narrowly. It includes adequate knowledge of the essences of singular things, i.e. finite modes, but it does not include adequate knowledge of the essences of the divine attributes. Knowledge of the nature of an attribute, such as extension, is knowledge of something universal, of something common to all bodies. In the *Ethics,* though not in the *Treatise,* this kind of knowledge is classified under the heading of reason. I suspect (but this is conjecture) that the same would be true of the infinite modes, such as motion and rest. In the *Ethics,* but not in the *Treatise,* knowledge of the nature of motion and rest, of its laws and rules, is rational knowledge, not intuitive knowledge.

So there is, in the end, a difference in the kind of object which the two highest kinds of knowledge have. Reason is knowledge of the essences of those things that in the *Treatise* are described as fixed and eternal things—the attributes and infinite modes of the *Ethics.* Intuition is knowledge of the essences of those things that in the *Treatise* are described as singular mutable things—the finite modes of the *Ethics.*

If I am right about this and if in the *Ethics* intuition is restricted to knowledge of the essences of finite singular things, then on Spinoza's mature view intuition will always be based on experience of a certain sort—for it is Spinoza's doctrine that only through experience can we come to know the essences of singular things:

> There seems to be no small difficulty in our being able to attain knowledge of these singular things . . . other aids must be sought besides those which we may use to understand the eternal things and their laws. Still this is not the place to discuss those aids, nor indeed is it necessary until after we have acquired sufficient knowledge of the eternal things and their infallible laws and after the nature of the senses has become known to us. Before we make ready for knowledge of singular things, there will be time to treat of those aids which help us to know how to use our senses and to perform, according to definite laws and in order, the experiments which will suffice to determine the thing which is being investigated, so that we may infer

from them by what laws of eternal things it has come to be. Then its intimate nature will become known to us . . .[47]

The view here is that knowledge of the essence of a finite singular thing requires the use of experiments—but the experiments must wait until we have acquired knowledge of the laws of eternal things—i.e. knowledge of the nature of the attributes and the infinite modes—and of the nature of our senses. Since in the *Ethics* this knowledge is classified as rational knowledge, rather than intuitive knowledge, the result is that intuition depends on reason—and not reason on intuition, as the rationalist interpretation would have it. But what is far worse for the rationalistic interpretation is that both reason and intuition depend heavily on experience.

To sum up: The rationalistic interpretation of Spinoza is correct in supposing that Spinoza saw the basic structure of science as being ideally that of a deductive system. And it is also correct in supposing that Spinoza regarded our knowledge of the first principles of this system as being *a priori*. These principles cannot be conceived to be false and are knowable independently of any particular sense experience, for they are present implicitly in every sense experience. That is why the human mind possesses an adequate knowledge of the infinite essence of God.[48] But this is rational knowledge, not intuition.

As we descend from first principles to lower-level principles we arrive at principles whose falsity can be conceived, at least so long as their dependence on first principles is not seen. Even after such a truth has been deduced from first truths, there may be people who will not be convinced by the deduction. Such people suffer from prejudice and to remove the prejudice it may be necessary to appeal to experience. The further we descend from first principles, the more necessary the appeal to experience becomes. Assumptions have to be introduced which are not self-evident and which are justified only

47. *TdIE,* par. 102–103 (G., II, 37). Commenting on Gebhardt's claim that this passage shows the influence of Bacon, Joachim justly remarks that "it may be so . . . But . . . nothing is here said about observation and experiment which Spinoza *could only have derived from Bacon*—which he might not equally have drawn from his knowledge of Descartes, or indeed have originated himself. Nor is it accurate to say . . . 'Whereas hitherto . . . Spinoza has deliberately contrasted his own deductive method with the Baconian method of induction based on experiments, he now, all of a sudden, recognizes the value of the latter as regards knowledge of singular things.'" Joachim, *op. cit.,* p. 218, n. 1.

48. *E.,* II, xlv, xlvii.

by the fact that they account for the phenomena—assumptions like those Descartes made about the nature of light.[49] And when we get to the level of individual cases, to explaining why a particular body behaves in the way it does, it is absolutely essential to have a technique for determining the nature of things by experiment. As I understand Spinoza, he believed that this kind of knowledge, knowledge of "intimate nature" of a finite singular thing—which in the *Ethics* appears to be the only kind of intuitive knowledge—had to wait on our having attained an adequate knowledge of the laws of nature and in particular on our having attained a knowledge of the way in which our senses work. Such knowledge is presumably necessary in order for us to be able to interpret experience. But it is equally necessary, in order for us to attain the highest kind of knowledge, to conduct the experiments which will enable us to determine "by what laws of eternal things" the thing whose nature we are seeking has come to be.

49. Cf. Spinoza's introduction to Part III of *Desc. Princ. Phil.* (G., I, 226–228).

Spinoza and Language[1]

DAVID SAVAN

I

Philosophical analysts have made a number of moves toward a re-assessment of the history of philosophy. It might be expected that such historical studies would consider how the views which philosophers have held on language, mathematics, and logic have affected their thought and its formulation. Any such expectations have so far been largely disappointed.

In his recent and lucid exposition of Spinoza, Mr. Stuart Hampshire points out that Spinoza hoped to emulate the example of the geometers in freeing language of its intimate connection with the imagination so that it might be employed to express clearly and distinctly the ideas of a true philosophy.[2] Spinoza's interest in language and in the bearing of language upon philosophy is, however, considerably more important in the shaping of his thought and writings than Hampshire indicates. It is not just that Spinoza wrote a treatise on a natural language, or that nearly every one of his writings attempts some analysis of language and mathematics. Nor is it just that he experimented with a variety of literary forms in the exposition of his thought, using dialogue, autobiography, aphorism, historical and Biblical criticism, as well as the method of geometrical demonstration. Nor again is it just that he occasionally formulates philosophical theses in syntactical terms. It is also that Spinoza holds that both language and mathematics are fundamentally inadequate to the formulation or direct expression of philosophical truths. Hampshire's view, widely shared—that Spinoza thought words could divorce the imagination in order to marry true philosophy—is, I believe, wrong. I shall argue that Spinoza's views on words and language make it impossible for him to hold that his writings (or anyone else's) can be a

The Philosophical Review 67 (1958), pp. 212–225. Reprinted by permission of the author and of the *Philosophical Review*.

1. A version of this paper was read to the meeting of the American Philosophical Association, Eastern Division, held at Boston University, December 27–29, 1955.

2. Stuart Hampshire, *Spinoza,* pp. 18–20, 23–24, 93.

direct or literal exposition of philosophical truth. I shall conclude with a suggestion as to what Spinoza intended his writings to accomplish and how he thought they could do it.

II

Spinoza states clearly enough that imagination or opinion, knowledge of the first and lowest kind, is of two species: (1) "vague experience," or images proper, and (2) "signs" or "hearsay," as "when we hear or read certain words."[3] His theory of words is in its outlines a familiar one. Words are nothing more than bodily motions. These motions are the responses of the human body to the action upon it of external bodies. The idea of such a motion will be mutilated, confused, and inadequate, since it can be properly understood only in conjunction with the ideas of the external motions which induced it. Since we do not know its cause we will either suppose it to be uncaused or to be induced by some final cause. Bodily motions which have once occurred together will tend to recur together, in company with their attendant circumstances. These attendant circumstances include our purposes, desires, and interests. In this way words arise from experience and refer to experience. They express the constitution of our own body rather than the nature of external bodies. The soldier may connect with the word "horse" the image of a war horse, armored, and in battle, while the farmer will call up the image of a slow and heavy animal plowing the fields.

Further, the limitations of the human body ensure that as a word is associated with a growing number of images the differences among the images will increasingly be overlooked. The number and significance of the differences thus canceled out will vary directly with the number of images with which a word is associated. Such transcendental terms as *being, thing,* and *something* are associated with every image without exception. Hence, in these cases, all differences will be canceled, all images will be conflated, and the terms will be utterly confused. A lesser degree of the same confusion is illustrated by universal terms like *man, horse, dog,* and so forth. In the case of universals the selection of differences to be overlooked and resemblances taken into account will vary from individual to

3. *E.,* II, xl, S. 2. The following account of words is based primarily on Book II of the *Ethics,* but substantially the same views are to be found in the *Improvement of the Understanding.*

individual, according to the desires and interests which each person imagines. So some will imagine man as a featherless biped, some as an animal capable of laughter, and some as a rational animal. Such definitions are not so much true or false as well- or ill-adapted to the purposes of those who frame them.

The imaginative, general, and confused character of words is, in Spinoza's view, not contingent or accidental. It is not the result of ignorance and cannot be eliminated by knowledge. It is rather the necessary consequence of the action of external bodies upon our body. In the same way we necessarily continue to imagine the sun as near even after we know its true distance. No purgative can eliminate the imaginative and confused generality of words.

Hovering in the wings, only just off stage, when Spinoza speaks of words, is the image of sleeping and dreaming. While words are joined through syntax, the material flow of language in speech is conceived by him as a kind of dreaming. Speech, fiction, error, and madness are ranges—perhaps there are others—of a dream continuum. In the lower ranges of this continuum—in madness and dreams proper—we are almost entirely unaware of the external motions which stimulate our own bodily motions and their images. In the upper ranges—in error, fiction, and speech—we are aware of the external motions in a confused way but wrongly attribute our own images to them. It is easiest to fall into the error of supposing our motions and images to be true of the external world when we speak a language which, like Hebrew, tends to treat adjectives as nouns. All languages, however, exhibit this same tendency to some extent, and it is the task of the philosopher to reverse the process as far as possible. To do this properly he must have some knowledge of the factors determining memory and recollection, upon which speech in part depends. Without this knowledge he is like an amanuensis who reproduces a book written in a script and language which he does not understand.[4]

In nearly every important respect, Spinoza opposes true ideas to words. An idea is not an image and does not consist of words. A true idea can neither arise from experience of words and images nor can it be verified through such experience, for experience can give no knowledge of essences.[5] Whereas ideas and their *ideata* are singular and unique,[6] words are inherently general and applicable

4. *Ep.*, 40.
5. *Ep.*, 10 and *TdIE*, par. 26; cf. also *Ep.* 37; *E.*, II, xliii, S.; *E.*, V, xxviii.
6. Although common motions, common notions, and properties are in a sense

to an indefinite multitude. Whereas an idea is certain, words are uncertain. Whereas "that true Word of God which is in the mind . . . can never be depraved or corrupted,"[7] words are corruptible. And whereas it is of the nature of reason to consider things as necessary and under a certain form of eternity, words are connected with contingency and time.

So sharply does Spinoza separate words from adequate ideas that it is difficult to make out for language any useful philosophical function at all. It is no more possible for us to discover and express true knowledge through language than it is for a somnambulist to communicate intelligently with the waking world. Spinoza explicitly rejects the semantic theory of truth. If Peter exists and without *knowing* this I happen to assert, "Peter exists," my assertion is not true.[8] Now suppose that Peter exists, that I know that he exists, and that while I am sound asleep I either say, "Peter exists" or dream that I say, "Peter exists." It is clear that on Spinoza's view the sentence "Peter exists" is in these circumstances not true. Now, in this example, substitute "God" for "Peter." This is the situation to which the writings of the philosopher are condemned by the imaginative and dreamlike character which, on Spinoza's view, is necessary to language. It is one thing to know that God exists and quite another to dream that I know, to imagine that I know, or to say that I know that God exists. How then can language represent, express, or formulate the clear and distinct ideas of the true philosophy? After separating the two so radically Spinoza appears to show no interest in explaining how they may be brought together. If he was aware of this situation, then he cannot have intended that the *Ethics* should be a simple and straightforward exposition of his philosophy.[9]

III

Was Spinoza aware that his views made it difficult to accept any verbal account as a direct exposition of the true philosophy? It would

---

general, they are nevertheless either singular modes, whether finite or infinite, or real properties of such modes.

7. *Ep.*, 76. Cf. also *Tr. Theol.-Pol.*, ch. xv.

8. *TdIE*, par. 69. Cf. *Ep.* 40.

9. The inadequacy of Spinoza's theory of language will be obvious to the reader today, and of course the particular difficulty with which I am concerned will not arise in a more adequate theory of language.

be strange if he were not, in view of the evidence of his writings. It should be noted first, however, that this difficulty is hardly a novel one. Its lineage can be traced at least to the *Parmenides* of Plato. The radical inadequacy of words is something which Spinoza points out emphatically and repeatedly in most of his writings.

The most telling evidence that Spinoza was aware of this difficulty is to be found in the contradictions which abound in his *Ethics,* as well as in his other writings. If Spinoza were trying to catch the clear, distinct, and unique ideas of a true philosophy in the net of a language which is inherently vague and general, he would expect contradictory statements to appear in his exposition. Many such statements do occur in the *Ethics,* often in such close proximity to one another that it is hardly believable that so careful a writer as Spinoza was not aware of them. Since he allows the contradictions to stand it is to be presumed that he did not intend the *Ethics* to be a simple exposition of truth.

The contradictions to which I refer may be classified as follows: (a) those arising from the attempt to define in words the nature of the unique entity, substance; (b) those arising from the attempt to define or describe the unique properties of substance; and (c) those arising from attempts to define or describe modes or modal essences.

(a) Are the definitions of substance and God[10] intended by Spinoza as adequate formulations of our knowledge? Yet he disowns the terms used in these definitions. Substance "is in itself and conceived through itself." The term *being,* however, together with the other transcendentals, is called by Spinoza "in the highest degree confused."[11] The term *conceive* is a universal term only somewhat less general and confused than *being.* For by *conceive* he wishes "to express the action of the mind," that is to say, understanding.[12] But, he writes, "In the mind there exists no absolute faculty of understanding, desiring, loving, etc. These and the like faculties, therefore, are either altogether fictitious, or else are nothing but metaphysical or universal entities, which we are in the habit of forming from individual cases."[13] As to being conceived *through itself,* the purity of this notion is at least compromised by Spinoza's repeated

10. *E.,* I, Def. 3, 6.
11. *E.,* II, xl, S. 1.
12. *E.,* II, Def. 3, and *E.,* IV, xxiii ff.
13. *E.,* II, xlviii, S.

attempts to conceive the activity of substance through something else —namely, through geometry.

God is defined as "being absolutely infinite." It has already been pointed out that Spinoza rejects the term *being*. By "infinite," the other important word in this definition, is meant "absolute affirmation of existence of some kind."[14] But he equates existence with the transcendental, *being*. Like *being*, existence is general, abstract, and confused.[15]

It is obvious that Spinoza wishes to refer his readers to a being and an existence which is concrete, singular, and unique. It is clear also, however, that he is willing to use language which he regards as radically inadequate. When he writes that "the reason why we do not possess a knowledge of God as distinct as that which we have of common notions is . . . [that] we have attached the name God to the images of things which we are in the habit of seeing, an error we can hardly avoid,"[16] he is speaking of philosophical as well as of popular uses of the word "God."

(b) A second and more obvious set of contradictions occurs in the discussion of the properties of substance or God. In the *Ethics* unity, love, joy, will, intellect, and perfection, are all both explicitly affirmed and explicitly denied of substance.

The demonstration that God is one—both single and simple—is listed by Spinoza in the Appendix to Book I of the *Ethics* as a major conclusion. Nevertheless, in Book I he also writes that "a definition does not involve or express any certain number of individuals."[17] What this means in regard to substance or God is stated more explicitly in the early *Cogitata metaphysica* as well as in a letter written late in Spinoza's life. "It is certain that he who calls God one or single has no true idea of God, or is speaking of him inappropriately."[18]

Again, he writes that "properly speaking, God loves no one."[19] Yet, a few propositions later, he attempts to demonstrate that "God loves himself," and that "God . . . loves men."[20] Since he has defined love as involving pleasure, he attempts to demonstrate that God

14. *E.*, I, viii, S. 1.
15. *TdIE*, par. 55; cf. *E.*, II, xlv, S.
16. *E.*, II, xlvii, S.
17. *E.*, I, viii, S. 2.
18. *Ep.*, 50, and *C. m.*, I, 6.
19. *E.*, V, xvii, C.
20. *E.*, V, xxxv and xxxvi, C.

"cannot be affected with any affect of joy or sorrow." But he goes on
to contradict himself by writing that "the nature of God delights in
infinite perfection" and that God's love "is joy [granting that it is
allowable to use this word], accompanied with the idea of Himself."[21]

With respect to will and intellect, we are offered a demonstration
that they can no more be ascribed to God than flesh and blood can
be ascribed to the constellation of the Dog. Nevertheless, he continues, and in the same book of the *Ethics,* to speak of God's intellect
and will.[22]

Although Spinoza follows tradition in calling God perfect, when
he discusses the origin and meaning of the word in the Preface to
Book IV of the *Ethics,* he identifies it as only a mode of thought, an
ens rationis formed through the comparison of particular things and
sharing the generality and confusion previously ascribed to "being."
Other properties of God, such as freedom and eternity, are explained
through the notion of existence, already discussed above.

(c) In discussing modes and *natura naturata* Spinoza's theory of
words leads him into two kinds of difficulties. First, he ascribes to
some modes properties previously defined by him as applicable only to
natura naturans. So he speaks of man as free and man's mind as an
"eternal mode of thought." He speaks also of necessary, infinite,
and eternal modes which exist under every attribute of God.[23] Nevertheless, it is evident from the definitions of the words "free,"
"eternal," "infinite," and "necessary," given at the beginning of the
Ethics, that these words can apply only to God as *natura naturans.*
He demonstrates, indeed, that "God alone is a free cause" and that
he differs radically in essence and existence from every mode.[24] To
apply to a mode a term which applies to *natura naturans* is like
expecting the constellation of the Dog to bark.

Second, when Spinoza applies to modes terms which are proper
to *natura naturata* he again contradicts himself. Desire, he states,
is the essence of man, and desire which springs from reason is the
essence of the human mind insofar as it acts. This in turn is nothing
other than the effort to understand.[25] But we have pointed out above

21. *E.,* V, xvii, xxxv, and xxxvi, S.
22. *E.,* I, xvii, S.; *E.,* I, xxxiii, S. 2.
23. *E.,* IV, lxvi ff.; *E.,* V, xl, S.; *E.,* I, xxi–xxiii.
24. *E.,* I, xvii.
25. *E.,* III, ix, S., and Aff., Def. i; *E.,* IV, lix, lxi; *E.,* IV, xxiii, xxvi.

that Spinoza regards desire, understanding, and will as either altogether fictitious or else as metaphysical or universal entities. Furthermore, insofar as they designate characteristics which are common
to a number of modes, they cannot form the essence of any individual mode.[26]

Consider next the word "good." Spinoza speaks of knowledge
of good (and of evil) which is true, adequate, and certain.[27] Nevertheless, he writes also that the notion *good* is an "entity of the
imagination," "indicates nothing positive in things considered in themselves," and is general or universal.[28] In fact, "if men were born
free [and were led by reason alone], they would form no conception
of good and evil."[29]

A similar difficulty arises in Spinoza's discussion of the passions.
Although these are inadequate and confused ideas, we can nonetheless form some clear and distinct conception of them. They follow
with the same natural necessity as do other modes, they may be
understood through their causes and properties, and the method pursued in the discussion of God and the mind is to be applied to them.
It would appear, then, that the discussion of the passions in Book III
of the *Ethics* is a direct statement of our knowledge of the passions.
Spinoza writes, however, that "there are as many kinds of each affect
as there are kinds of objects by which we are affected; . . . men are
affected in different ways by one and the same object . . . ; and,
finally . . . one and the same man is affected in different ways towards
the same object."[30] His analyses and definitions must, therefore,
overlook and confuse together the specific differences among the
actual affects. That is to say, Spinoza's discussion is in terms of
words which are abstract, general, and confused.

Finally, it is to be noted that Spinoza admits that even in his discussion of the third and highest kind of knowledge he must speak
in terms of time and change—that is to say, in terms of the imagination—"in order that what we wish to prove may be more easily explained and better understood."[31] Yet only three propositions earlier
Spinoza had written that "ideas which are clear and distinct in us

26. *E.*, II, xxxvii.
27. *E.*, IV, xiv ff.; *E.*, IV, xxvii ff.
28. *E.*, I, App.; *E.*, IV, Pref.; *E.*, IV, lxii, S.
29. *E.*, IV, lxviii; cf. *E.*, IV, lxiv.
30. *E.*, IV, xxxiii; cf. *E.*, III, li, lvi, lvii.
31. *E.*, V, xxxi, S.

. . . cannot follow from mutilated and confused ideas, which are related to the first kind of knowledge."

In sum, then, in Spinoza's discussions of substance, its properties, and its modes, contradictions and difficulties occur so frequently and so clearly that it is probable that Spinoza was aware of them. He allowed them to stand, I suggest, because his theory of language led him to believe that no simple, direct, precise, and consistent verbal account of the true philosophy was possible.

IV

How is the *Ethics* to be understood? Spinoza's theory of language is inadequate. He is so concerned to associate words and language with imagination that he offers no theoretical account of how words can convey ideas (in his sense of "idea") or of the proper function of language in the communication of philosophical truth. The fact that Spinoza makes no attempt to deal with this question in the *Ethics* is, perhaps, the strongest argument against the thesis of the first part of this paper, that Spinoza was aware of the difficulties in which he was involved through his theory of language.

Be that as it may, I wish to point out briefly that Spinoza does explicitly hold a general theory of *entities of reason* and that it is this theory of *entia rationis* which underlies his method in the *Ethics*.[32]

An entity of reason is "a mode of thought which serves to make what has been understood the more easily retained, explained, and imagined."[33] Such an entity has no existence outside the intellect. Since it has no extramental object which could be clearly and distinctly conceived, Spinoza denies that it is an idea or that it can be called true or false. It is a characteristic error that philosophers, misled by the words associated with entities of reason, hypostatize them and ascribe to them some reality outside of the mind. They are of use to us only if they function as tools or mental aids and are not treated as if they had some independent status.[34]

Entities of reason originate because it is easier for our minds to imagine things abstractly than to conceive things as they are, in their

32. The following account of *entia rationis* is based upon the *Cogitata metaphysica, Ep.* 12, 19, 50, 83 and *E.,* I, App.; *E.,* IV, Pref.

33. *C. m.,* I, 1.

34. Hence *entia rationis* cannot be assimilated to *ratio,* or knowledge of the second kind.

specific connection with substance. So we find it easier to remember things if we can group them together in such classifications as genus and species. So too we imagine extension abstractly—that is, apart from the substance of which it is an attribute—and then try to explain this abstract extension by comparing one part of it with another through the aid of measure and geometrical figures. Or again we may abstract finite modes from the substance, attributes, and infinite modes upon which they depend and then try to explain the resultant images by using factitious instruments like time and numbers to assist us in comparing the images. When these aids are clearly understood to be abstractions, existing only in the intellect—as they are by all good mathematicians—they can assist us to discover and formulate such truth as is proper to the imagination. I shall return to this point in a moment, for it is the clue to the correct understanding of the *Ethics,* as well as of Spinoza's writings on natural science, Hebrew grammar, and Biblical criticism.

Since entities of reason are, like words, functions of the imagination, words have a proper role to play in their formulation. In particular, philosophical entities of reason such as the distinction of God's essence from God's existence, power, and other properties, genus and species, the transcendentals, the modalities, the notions of nonbeing, opposition, order, relation, conjunction, accident, perfection, good, and evil—all these arise through *verbal* comparisons of modes given to us through the imagination. Philosophers have been particularly prone, therefore, to two kinds of error: (a) they have often given unsuitable or misleading verbal descriptions of their entities of reason; (b) even worse, through not distinguishing the imagination from the intellect clearly enough, they have supposed that the words they used were names of entities existing outside the intellect. When he encounters this latter confusion, Spinoza prefers to speak of "entities of the imagination" rather than of "entities of reason." Properly defined and properly understood as abstractions, however, the entities of reason may serve the philosopher (as they do the mathematician) as eyes, as it were, through which the intellect may see more clearly what is presented confusedly in the imagination.

Correctly employed, then, entities of reason may assist the philosopher in at least three ways. (1) When one image is compared with another they may enable the intellect to discover that truth which is resident in imagination. (2) By constructing certain general models or exemplars we may see how a collection of things whose detailed natures we do not understand may nevertheless in general exemplify our adequate ideas of infinite modes and attributes of substance. (3) By recognizing the abstract character of such negative entities of reason as *nonbeing, limit,* and *falsehood* we may hold more firmly to the positive content of the clear ideas which are native to the intellect. We will not then confuse them with the verbal entities and verbal distinctions of the traditional philosophers.

(1) By comparing our experiences, and with the assistance of mathematical and philosophical entities of reason, scientists have discovered the true size and distance of the sun. We are thereby enabled to see that our image of the sun as small and near is our response to external motions and thus a sign of our native strength and power. So too in his discussion of the passions Spinoza compares a variety of experiences in order to show the limitations and the positive strength of the passions. Spinoza's resort to a posteriori argument is not an inconsistency but an integral part of his method.

(2) In the Preface to Book IV of the *Ethics* Spinoza states that he wishes to form an idea of man which can serve as a model or exemplar of human nature. In other places in the *Ethics* Spinoza speaks of this idea of man as universal and of the proofs concerning it as general.[35] In a letter of 1665 he points out that the abstract and general definition of man by which all who have a similar external appearance are classed together is an entity of reason.[36] To construct this universal idea of man he has used such entities of reason as *good* and *evil* and such "metaphysical" entities (i.e., entities of reason) as *understanding, desire,* and *will.*[37] The value of this method, which occupies a major part of the *Ethics,* is that these entities of reason, corresponding to nothing outside the intellect, enable us to use words correctly in comparing the experiences which our imagination provides us. They enable us to see how our adequate ideas of substance, thought, extension, motion and rest, and so on, ideas which are native to the intellect, operate within our experience. This, I would suggest, is what Spinoza means when he writes that "demonstrations are the eyes of the mind by which it sees and observes things."[38] In a letter of 1664 he puts it thus: "We see that

35. *E.,* III, lv, S., and *E.,* V, xxxvi, S.
36. *Ep.,* 19.
37. *E.,* II, xlviii, S.
38. *E.,* V, xxiii, S.

the imagination is also determined to a great extent by the constitution of the soul; for, as we know from experience, in all things it follows the traces of the intellect and concatenates its images and words in a certain order, and interconnects them, just as the intellect does with its demonstrations."[39]

In the Preface to Book IV of the *Ethics* Spinoza also gives a detailed account of the genesis and growth of another entity of reason, *perfection*. He seeks to show how, through the comparison of our experiences and with the mediation of words, we confuse perfection with the final cause of a thing. When we come to see, however, that perfection is an entity of reason, existing nowhere outside the mind, we recognize it as an aid to the consideration of the specific reality, essence, and action of every mode which we experience. Every individual thing, considered in terms of its own essence and activity, is perfect.[40]

(3) Finally, there is a third way in which entities of reason can assist the philosopher. Negation, limitation, determination, and falsehood cannot be ascribed to God, for they are only entities of reason. Without introducing negation or determination in some form, however, we cannot distinguish one substance from another, essence from existence, power from action, or necessity from freedom. Hence God is unique, and in God essence, existence, power, necessity, and freedom are one and the same. They can be distinguished only verbally. As Spinoza puts it, to distinguish God's essence from his existence is to confuse truth with falsehood.[41]

Philosophers and theologians have been confused by words into supposing these distinctions in God's nature to be real. A large part of the task of the *Ethics* is to show the philosophers how many of their errors originate in the confusion of entities of reason with entities existing outside the intellect, that is, in confusing the intellect with the imagination. The positive task of the *Ethics* is to show that once the limitations of language are recognized we can conceive of substance and its modes through their own living ideas. Language may indeed express philosophic truth, just as one may dream of gray elephants as well as of pink elephants. But in order to know what is true and what is false in one's dreams one must first wake and under-

39. *Ep.,* 17.
40. *Ep.,* 19; cf. also *Epp.* 21 and 23, and *E.,* I, xxxiii, S. 2.
41. *E.,* I, viii, S. 2.

stand that dreams have their own laws. They cannot be read as simple, straightforward prose narratives.

The several arguments in demonstration of a single proposition are different ways of deploying the entities of reason. The definitions of *substance* and *mode* do not involve reference to any positive ideas. A comparison of the rules for defining created and uncreated things (given in the *Improvement of the Understanding*) with the definitions of the *Ethics* will show that the latter simply translate the formal rules into the material mode.

It is Spinoza's view, then, that "a thing is understood when it is perceived simply by the mind without words and images."[42] So far is he from supposing that words can be disengaged from the imagination in order to represent true ideas. Spinoza concludes the *Ethics* with the warning that he has shown us a road which is difficult to travel. If, however, anyone "had acquired new ideas in the proper order, according to the standard of the original true idea, he would never have doubted of the truth of his knowledge, inasmuch as truth, as we have shown, makes itself manifest, and all things would flow, as it were, spontaneously toward him."[43]

42. *Tr. Theol.-Pol.*, ch. iv.
43. *TdIE*, par. 44.

Language and Knowledge in Spinoza

G. H. R. PARKINSON

Although Spinoza's views about language have not been neglected by grammarians,[1] they have received relatively little attention from philosophers. It has been argued fairly recently, however, that these views are well worth the philosopher's attention, and that if this is given to them the *Ethics* will appear in quite a new light. This thesis is maintained by Professor D. Savan, in his article "Spinoza and Language."[2] Briefly, Professor Savan argues that Spinoza's views on words and language "make it impossible for him to hold that his writings (or anyone else's) can be a direct or literal exposition of philosophical truth."[3] Professor Savan argues further that not only do Spinoza's views have this consequence, but that Spinoza saw that they did; the language used in the *Ethics,* then, was not meant to be a "literal exposition of philosophical truth," but has some other function, which Professor Savan tries to state. Professor Savan presents this challenging thesis with skill and learning; it will be argued in this paper, however, that his thesis is radically misconceived—that Spinoza's views on language do not have the logical consequences that Professor Savan asserts, and further that Spinoza did not think that they have these consequences. But this paper has more than the merely negative aim of refuting a mistaken view; it also aims at bringing out more clearly some aspects of Spinoza's views about knowledge, and at answering a question which it is Professor Savan's merit to have stated very forcefully—namely, which of the types of knowledge recognized by Spinoza are expressed by the language of the *Ethics.*

Inquiry 12 (1969), pp. 15–40. Reprinted by permission of the author and of *Inquiry*.

1. E.g. J. M. Hillesum, "De spinozistische spraakkunst," *Chronicon Spinozanum,* 1921; N. Porges, "Spinozas Compendium der hebräischen Grammatik," *Chronicon Spinozanum,* 1924–26.
2. In this volume.
3. Savan, "Spinoza and Language," p. 60.

I

Our first task is to state the evidence that can be brought forward to support the idea that Spinoza's views about language have the logical consequence that no writings (Spinoza's included) can be a literal exposition of philosophical truth. Professor Savan refers mainly[4] to Book II of the *Ethics,* but our survey will not be restricted to the evidence that he produces.

(i) The first item of evidence cited by Professor Savan[5] is taken from what Spinoza says in the *Ethics* about what he calls the first kind of knowledge, "imagination." This kind of knowledge is sub-divided by Spinoza[6] into two types. The first is sense-experience of particular things, and is called by Spinoza *cognitio ab experientia vaga;* this is often translated as "knowledge from vague experience," though perhaps *vaga* might be rendered better as "wandering" or "inconstant." The second type is "knowledge from signs" (*cognitio ex signis*), called elsewhere "knowledge from some so-called 'conventional' sign" (*ex aliquo signo, quod vocant ad placitum*).[7] This is the type that concerns us here. Spinoza discusses it in *E.,* II, xviii, S., in which he speaks of what he calls *memoria,* by which he seems to understand, not memory in the usual sense of the term, but the association of ideas. Take, he says, the word *pomum.*

> From thinking of the word *pomum,* a Roman will immediately fall to thinking of the fruit, which has no likeness to that articulate sound, nor anything in common with it, except that the body of one and the same man had often been affected by these two; that is, that the man has often heard the word *pomum* whilst he saw the actual fruit.[8]

There is here, then, an association (Spinoza calls it a *concatenatio,* a "concatenation" or "linking") of ideas. Spinoza makes two points

4. *Ibid.,* p. 61, note 3.

5. *Loc. cit.*

6. *E.,* II, xl, S. 2. Unless otherwise indicated, translations from Spinoza are by the present author.

7. *TdIE,* par. 19 (G., II, 10).

8. A minor point may be noted here. The first phrase in this sentence might suggest someone who is not actually seeing or hearing the word in question. It should be remembered, however, that for Spinoza the attribute of thought covers the various forms of sense-perception, so that what Spinoza says applies equally to someone who hears or reads the word *pomum.*

about this. First, it is an association of ideas which has no explanatory function; it merely *involves* the nature of things that are outside the human body, it does not *explain* their nature. We call certain things "apples" because a certain word was spoken whilst objects of a certain type were affecting our sense-organs; this tells us nothing *about* apples. Second, this linking of ideas occurs in accordance with the "order and concatenation of the affections of the human body," and not in accordance with the order of the intellect, which is the same in all men. Spinoza abandons at this stage his example of the word *pomum,* and notes instead how a soldier who sees a hoof-print will think of war, whereas a farmer will think of the plough; however, he could easily have found cases in which the same word has different associations for different hearers or readers. The upshot of all this seems to be that Spinoza is saying that someone who hears or reads words is not so much thinking, as associating ideas.

(ii) The second piece of evidence cited by Professor Savan[9] is taken from Spinoza's views about "transcendental terms," such as "being," "thing," "something" (*ens, res, aliquid*) and "universal concepts," such as the concepts of man, horse and dog.[10] The context shows that by "term" Spinoza means here, not an idea or concept, but a word which stands for an idea; what he says about universal concepts is also applicable (and is applied by him) to the words that are used for these concepts, e.g. to the word "man" as well as to the concept of man. Such words we will call "universal terms." Spinoza's account of these terms and concepts involves a theory— incidentally only a tentative one[11]—about the physiology of imagination. He asserts that when we perceive some external object, the object perceived affects certain parts of the human body; when this happens repeatedly, the external thing leaves on these parts of the body a kind of trace (*vestigium*),[12] with the result that we can contemplate the thing as if it were present even when it is not.[13] Such a trace Spinoza calls an "image" (*imago*). Now, the human body can at a given time form only a limited number of such images distinctly; if this number is exceeded, the images will begin to be mixed together, and if the number is greatly exceeded, they will be

9. Savan, *op. cit.,* p. 61.
10. *E.,* II, xl, S. 1.
11. *E.,* II, xvii, S.
12. Postulate 5 after *E.,* II, xiii, S.
13. *E.,* II, xvii, C.

completely mixed. Corresponding to a physical state of this last kind, "the mind also will imagine all the bodies confusedly without any distinction, and will as it were comprehend them under one attribute, namely that of being, thing, etc."[14] "Universal concepts" correspond to a physical state in which images are mixed, but not completely mixed; the power of imagining is overwhelmed, not completely, but only to the extent that the mind cannot imagine small differences in individual bodies (e.g. their colour or size) or their precise number. Such concepts are not formed by everyone in the same way, but vary in accordance with the thing by which a body has been most often affected.

> For example, those who have often contemplated with admiration the stature of men will understand by the word "man" an animal of erect stature; those who have been accustomed to contemplate something else will form another common image of men . . . Hence it is not surprising that so many controversies have arisen among philosophers who have wanted to explain natural things by the mere images of things.[15]

In short, Spinoza is saying that words of extreme generality, such as "being," "thing," "something," and words of rather less generality, such as "man" and "horse," all stand for what would now be called generic images. The generic images for which the "transcendental terms" stand are in the highest degree confused, and so (Spinoza implies) are useless for thought, as are the words which stand for them. The generic images for which universal terms stand (Spinoza's "universal concepts") are less confused, but are vitiated by the fact that they vary from person to person, whereas the "order of the intellect" is the same in all men.[16]

(iii) Professor Savan next cites a number of passages to support the thesis that "in nearly every important respect, Spinoza opposes true ideas to words." The argument is short and concentrated, and at this stage it will be most convenient simply to quote the paragraph in question, giving a detailed analysis later.

> An idea is not an image and does not consist of words. A true idea can neither arise from experience of words and images nor can it be verified through such experience, for experience can give no knowledge of essences. Whereas ideas and their *ideata* are singular and

14. *E.*, II, xl, S. 1.
15. *E.*, II, xl, S. 1.
16. *E.*, II, xviii, S. Cf. (i) above.

unique, words are inherently general and applicable to an indefinite multitude. Whereas an idea is certain, words are uncertain. Whereas "that true Word of God which is in the mind . . . can never be depraved or corrupted," words are corruptible. And whereas it is of the nature of reason to consider things as necessary and under a certain form of eternity, words are connected with contingency and time.[17]

Professor Savan is here citing a number of passages from Spinoza: to these we may add another which he cites much later[18] in support of his view that words cannot be "disengaged from the imagination in order to represent true ideas." This is a sentence from the *Tractatus Theologico-Politicus,* Chapter IV, which states that "A thing is understood when it is perceived simply by the mind without words and images" (G., IV, 64–65).

(iv) The last piece of evidence cited by Professor Savan[19] comes from the *De Intellectus Emendatione.*[20] Spinoza asserts that if someone says that (for example) Peter exists, but does not know that Peter exists, that assertion is, as far as the speaker is concerned (*respectu illius*), false—"or, if you prefer, not true"—even if Peter really exists. (It may be noted that Professor Savan says that if I make such a statement, "my assertion is not true." This is not quite what Spinoza would say; he would say that it is not true *for me,* not true *as far as I am concerned*). It follows from this, Professor Savan argues, that if I merely *say* that God exists—e.g. if I utter the words when asleep—what I say is not true. It is, then, "one thing to know that God exists and quite another . . . to say that I know that God exists. How, then, can language represent, express, or formulate the clear and distinct ideas of the true philosophy?" Professor Savan also compares a passage from a letter, in which Spinoza draws a distinction between the shape and arrangement of letters, which can be copied by someone who is ignorant of what they mean, and "the thoughts and meaning which this arrangement expresses."[21]

(v) A further piece of evidence may be found in the *De Intellectus Emendatione.*[22] Here Spinoza says that words are "a part of the

17. Savan, *op. cit.,* p. 62.
18. *Ibid.,* p. 72.
19. *Ibid.,* p. 72.
20. *TdIE,* par. 69 (G., II, 26).
21. *Ep.,* 40 (Wolf tr., p. 234). Cf. also *Desc. Princ. Phil.,* I, Ax. 9 (G., I, 156–57).
22. *TdIE,* pars. 88–89 (G., II, 33).

imagination"; that as we form many concepts "according to the way in which words, from some disposition of the body, are joined in the memory in an erratic way (*vage*)," it follows that words, equally with the imagination, can be a cause of many great errors. What this means is not quite clear, but Spinoza may have in mind the way in which one word sometimes suggests another, the connexion not being one of logic but, e.g., of mere sound. He adds that words have been given their meaning "according to the pleasure, and the understanding, of the multitude, with the result that they are merely signs of things as they are in the imagination, but not as they are in the intellect." Here again, then, a clear distinction seems to be drawn between words and the intellect.

II

Such, then, is the evidence that can be brought to support the view that Spinoza cannot consistently say that language is an adequate medium in which to express philosophical ideas. The cumulative evidence is impressive; Professor Savan clearly has a case. It will be argued here, however, that a closer examination shows that the evidence does not have the implications that he claims.

(i) The passage cited from *E.*, II, xviii, S. shows beyond doubt that Spinoza thought that when a word is heard or read, there may occur an association of ideas which cannot properly be called thinking in the fullest sense; the concatenation of ideas, Spinoza would say, does not occur "according to the order of the intellect." If, on hearing the word "apple," I associate with my hearing of the word a mental image of an apple, this association of ideas has no explanatory function; further, the ideas associated will vary from person to person— e.g. one man may think of a cooking apple, one may think of an eating apple, and one may have a vague generic image, of the kind that Spinoza calls a "universal concept." So much was certainly Spinoza's view; the question is, does it follow from this (as Professor Savan argues) that words are not an adequate medium in which to express philosophical truths? Spinoza does not draw such an inference explicitly in this passage; he speaks only about the hearer or reader of words, and says nothing about the person who *uses* words. However, it would be open to Professor Savan to argue:

(a) Even if someone were to use, say, written words to express genuine thought, yet if everyone who reads words always associates ideas in the way just described, no one will be able to grasp the thought that the writer wishes to convey.

(b) Further, if every hearer or reader of words associates ideas in the way described, how could anyone learn to use words to express thought?

It is clear that the important question here is, *does* Spinoza think that, whenever we hear or read words, we always associate ideas in the way described in *E.,* II, xviii, S.? For example, suppose someone to read the sentence "Two straight lines cannot enclose a space," and suppose that this sentence calls up some mental image; is he associating ideas in essentially the same way as when he has a mental image of a straight line on reading the words "straight line?"

This is the point at which to consider an important passage from Ep. 17 (Wolf trans., p. 140). Spinoza says there that the imagination is determined, not only by the constitution of the body, but also by that of the soul: "For, as we know from experience, in all things it follows the traces of the intellect and concatenates its images and words in a certain order (*ex ordine*), and interconnects them, just as the intellect does with its demonstrations; so much so that there is almost nothing that we can understand of which the imagination does not form some image from the trace thereof." (It will be noticed that Spinoza is here using the word "image" in the sense of a mental image, rather than in the sense of a physical imprint on the body.) In this passage, Spinoza says clearly that it is possible to associate mental images in a way which does not vary from person to person, but which follows what he calls in the *Ethics* the "order of the intellect." Words, too, can be connected in a way which follows the order of the intellect; this seems to imply that someone who understands a subject can express his understanding in words, and also that someone who hears these words and associates with them the appropriate images is in a way following the order of the intellect. What *E.,* II, xviii, S. says about words, therefore, is incomplete, and needs to be supplemented from Ep. 17.

The passage just quoted from Ep. 17 is also interesting in that it implies that Spinoza believed that thought and words are distinct; words *follow* the traces, or tracks (*vestigia*) of the intellect. One would expect him to say, then, that words are the signs of thought, rather than that to think is to use words in a certain way. That this was his view is suggested by a passage from *E.,* II, xl, S. 1: "These terms (sc. 'being,' 'thing,' 'something') stand for ideas which are in the highest degree confused."[23] Confirmatory evidence is provided by a passage from Axiom 9 of Part I of his geometrical version of Descartes's *Principles of Philosophy*. Here Spinoza refers to two books which have been copied out in the same hand, but of which one is by a distinguished philosopher and the other is by some trifler. To attend to the sense of the words, as opposed to their shape, is to attend to them "in so far as they are images of a sort" (*quatenus veluti imagines sunt*)—images, it may be assumed, of the *thoughts* of the philosopher and of the trifler.

This does not mean that Spinoza thought that words refer only to ideas. In *E.*, II, xlix, S., he speaks of "the words by which we refer to things," and in Chapter 5 of his *Compendium of Hebrew Grammar* he seems to relate words to things rather than to ideas when he says that by a noun (*nomen*) he understands a word (*vox*) "by which we signify or indicate something which falls under the intellect"—e.g. things and their attributes, modes and relations, or actions and their modes and relations. This need not be inconsistent with what has been suggested above; Spinoza may have believed that words stand for ideas, and ideas are of things and actions, so that ideas are as it were the medium through which words refer to things.

There is one further point to be made about the passage cited from Ep. 17. It will be noticed that Spinoza does not say that the intellect uses words; what he says is that the imagination uses (more exactly, "concatenates" and "interconnects") words, and that in some cases it follows the tracks of the intellect. It may seem strange that Spinoza should count as examples of the same kind of knowledge, "imagination," both that use of words in which someone states a mathematical axiom or proof, and the association of ideas which is brought about (say) by hearing the word "apple." Perhaps he is influenced by the fact that in each case we are concerned with something that can either be sensed or (in the ordinary sense of the word) imagined, and both of these are covered by his use of the word "imagination." It seems, however, that a distinction should be drawn here, and that it should be recognized that we are dealing with two types of imagination, corresponding to (though not exactly the same as) Kant's distinction between the transcendental imagination, which is concerned with the *a priori* or necessary, and the empirical imagi-

23. Cf. I (ii) above.

nation, whose laws are discovered inductively.[24] The fact that Spinoza does not draw such a distinction may perhaps be due to a certain indifference on his part towards the imagination. Although, as Dr. C. de Deugd has recently stressed,[25] the imagination plays a significant part in his theory of knowledge, Spinoza seems reluctant to admit this, and prefers to stress the dangers of relying on the imagination and disregarding the intellect.[26]

(ii) We turn now to the second piece of evidence cited by Professor Savan: namely, Spinoza's views about transcendental and universal terms (the latter, it will be recalled, are the words which stand for universal concepts). One may at first wonder why Professor Savan should lay any stress on these. He is trying to show that Spinoza's views about language imply that no words can be a suitable medium in which to express philosophical truths; but what Spinoza says in *E.*, II, xl, S. 1 concerns some words only. There seems to be nothing to prevent him from saying, with perfect consistency, that logically proper names, which (as opposed to words like "thing," "man," "horse," etc.) refer to genuine individuals, have a precise and constant reference, and are not systematically misleading. However, to point this out would be to reply only to half of Professor Savan's criticisms; for, as he later observes,[27] Spinoza himself uses transcendental and universal terms in the definitions of the *Ethics*. Thus, substance is said[28] to be "conceived through itself," and Professor Savan asserts that "the term *conceive* is a universal term"[29] (It could be added that the same definition uses the transcendental term "thing," for it says that the concept of substance does not require

---

24. Cf. *Critique of Pure Reason,* A115–125; B80–81, 151–52. In my *Spinoza's Theory of Knowledge* (Oxford: The Clarendon Press, 1954), p. 145, I distinguished between that use of signs "which is a type of imagination and that which is not." In a sense, this is a sharper distinction than Spinoza would draw, for it has been seen above that even when the imagination follows the "order of the intellect" it is still the *imagination*. On the other hand, it is following the order *of the intellect,* so that some distinction from the sort of imagination described in *E.*, II, xviii, S. seems to be required.

25. C. de Deugd, *The Significance of Spinoza's First Kind of Knowledge* (Assen: Van Gorcum, 1966).

26. E.g. *E.*, I, xv, S., I, App., II, xl, S. 1; *Tr. Theol.-Pol.* ch. vi.

27. Savan, *op. cit.,* p. 64.

28. *E.*, I, Def. 3.

29. Savan, *op. cit.,* p. 64. It could be added that the same definition uses the transcendental term "thing," for it says that the concept of substance does not require the concept of another *thing,* from which it must be formed.

the concept of another *thing,* from which concept it must be formed.). Again[30] God is declared to be an "absolutely infinite being," and "being" is a transcendental term. This seems to show that, whether or not Spinoza could operate only with logically proper names, in fact he does not, but uses those same universal and transcendental terms whose adequacy he denies. It is clear that this still does not prove the thesis that Spinoza's views about language imply that no philosophical truth can be expressed adequately in verbal form; all that it could show is that there are occasions when Spinoza, at any rate, did not.[31] However, if Spinoza's definitions really are inadequate by his own standards, this fact is important; it either casts serious doubts on Spinoza's logical competence, or (as Professor Savan prefers to think)[32] it suggests that his writings are not meant to be a literal exposition of philosophical truths. It will be worth while to ask, then, whether Spinoza's definitions really do involve inconsistencies of the kind just described.

The problem reduces to this. Granted that Spinoza thinks that some uses of the words which he calls "transcendental terms," and some uses of what we have called "universal terms," are philosophically objectionable, does he think that all uses of such words are objectionable? Let us take as an example the word "thing." As used in the definition of substance in Book I of the *Ethics,* does this word stand for a generic image of extreme vagueness? It seems much more probable that Spinoza would say that the concept of a thing, as used in this definition, is what he calls a "common notion." According to Spinoza, "those things which are common to all, and are equally in the part and in the whole, can only be conceived adequately";[33] such adequate concepts are what he calls "common notions"[34] and are in part the basis of "reason," his "second kind of knowledge."[35] Now, Spinoza might argue as follows: any finite body is an extended

---

30. *E.,* I, Def. 6.

31. It may be added that Spinoza's definitions, to which Professor Savan refers, are not strictly truths; they are declarations of the intention to use words in certain ways. However, if the definitions are incoherent, a corresponding incoherence will presumably be found in any propositions in the verbal expression of which the defined terms are used.

32. Savan, *op. cit.,* p. 64.

33. *E.,* II, xxxviii.

34. *E.,* II, xxxviii, C.; *E.,* II, xl, S. 1; *E.,* II, xl, S. 2.

35. *E.,* II, xl, S. 2.

thing;[36] God, too, when conceived under the attribute of extension, is an extended thing.[37] But if God, and any finite body, are extended things, they are, *a fortiori,* things. Further, any body is a mode of God or substance,[38] i.e. is a part of God.[39] We may therefore say of the whole (God), and of a part of the whole, that it is a thing; the concept of a thing is therefore a "common notion," and the word "thing" justified in so far as it stands for such a notion.[40]

The argument that Spinoza's definitions contain universal terms of the kind to which he objected can be answered in essentially the same way. It has already been mentioned that Professor Savan points out that in *E.,* I, Def. 3 the word "conceived" occurs, and that he asserts that the word "conceive" is a universal term. It may be noted, incidentally, that Spinoza's examples of universal concepts are the concepts of man, horse, and dog; the corresponding universal terms would be nouns.[41] Perhaps, then, the relevant universal term would be "conceiving" rather than "conceive." Given this, is "conceiving," in the context of *E.,* I, Def. 3, a universal term of the kind that Spinoza condemns—i.e. does it stand for a generic image, which may vary from person to person? It is more likely that Spinoza would say that the concept of conceiving, as he uses it, is a common notion. His reasoning might run as follows. Some ideas are particular, i.e. finite modes of thought;[42] but there is also an infinite idea, the "idea of God in thought."[43] Now, to have an idea is to conceive something;[44]

36. *E.,* II, Ax. 5.
37. *E.,* II, ii.
38. *E.,* II, Def. 1.
39. *E.,* I, xv, S.
40. There may appear to be a logical circle here. It may be thought that the use of the word "thing" has been justified by saying that the concept of a thing is a common notion; but, it may be said, are not common notions themselves justified because deduced (in *E.,* II, xxxviii) from the axioms and definitions of the *Ethics*—in some of which the word "thing" occurs? The answer seems to be that *E.,* II, xxxviii is offered, not as a justification of the axioms and definitions of the *Ethics,* but as a statement of what they involve. Certainly, Spinoza does not think that axioms need justification; in his view, their truth is evident to anyone who understands the words in which they are expressed (cf. *Spinoza's Theory of Knowledge,* pp. 39–40).
41. Cf. *E.,* II, xlviii, S.—the faculties of understanding, desiring, loving, etc. are "universals."
42. *E.,* II, ix and *E.,* II, Def. 7.
43. *E.,* I, xxi.
44. *E.,* II, Def. 3.

conceiving, then, is something that can be predicated both of a finite mode of thought, which is a part of God, and of the whole, God. The concept of conceiving is therefore a common notion, and words like "conceiving" and "conceive" are justified, to the extent that they stand for this common notion.

It may be objected that the reply just made to Professor Savan's arguments is merely an exercise within the logic of Spinoza's system; it does not show that Spinoza had what a modern philosopher would regard as good, or even as intelligible reasons for thinking that universal and transcendental terms are sometimes admissible and sometimes not. To this it may be replied that the logic of Spinoza's system is just what is at issue here; the question is essentially one of self-consistency. However, this may still not satisfy the objector; let us, then, try to rephrase what Spinoza has said in a way that avoids his technical jargon. In effect, *E.,* II, xl, S. 1 is an attack on a kind of empiricism, which is ascribed to certain unnamed philosophers—probably the Scholastics. Such philosophers, Spinoza is saying, proffer as explanatory concepts vague and imprecise notions which are the result of repeated acts of sense-perception. Against this, Spinoza states the claims of a deductive, *a priori* method; the rigorous deduction of consequences from propositions whose truth cannot be doubted by any rational being, and from explicit definitions of terms. Spinoza's criticisms of Scholasticism may be unfair—this point will not be argued here—but they do at least seem to be intelligible.

(iii) It was mentioned in Part I of this paper that Professor Savan cites on p. 62 a number of passages in support of the thesis that "in nearly every important respect, Spinoza opposes true ideas to words." There is a double ambiguity in this remark. First, the word "true" might mean "genuine," as when we speak of "true friendship," or it might mean "agreeing with fact." "Idea" might mean "concept," as when we speak of "the idea of history"; if so, "true" will presumably mean "genuine," since a concept is not said to agree or not to agree with the facts. Professor Savan, however, may have in mind Spinoza's insistence that an idea is a judgement.[45] If so, Professor Savan may mean by "true ideas," genuine judgements; but he may also mean judgements that are true in the sense of agreeing with fact.

45. See, e.g., the references in *TdIE,* par. 62 (G., II, 24), to "a concept, that is, an idea, or [*sive*] the coherence in the mind of subject and predicate." Cf. *E.,* II, xlix and S.

Since his main thesis is about philosophical truth, it may be assumed that in the present context he uses "true idea" in this last sense.

After these preliminary remarks we can discuss in detail the paragraph quoted from Professor Savan.

(a) "An idea is not an image and does not consist of words." No reference is given here, but it seems probable that what is in mind is *E.,* II, xlix, S.: "I warn my readers to distinguish carefully between an idea, i.e. a concept of the mind, and the images of things, which we imagine. Next, it is necessary to distinguish between ideas and the words by which we refer to things (*quibus res significamus*)." The importance for Professor Savan's thesis of the assertion that an idea is not an image is this. He maintains that, for Spinoza, words are restricted to the imagination; consequently, if no image is an idea, no words can express an idea.[46] In examining Professor Savan's argument, we must first look at the context of the passage just cited. This shows clearly that in distinguishing between an idea and "the images of things, which we imagine," Spinoza is drawing attention to a feature of his terminology which was mentioned recently: namely, that an idea is not "like a mute picture on a tablet," but involves affirmation or negation—in other words, it is not simply a mental picture, but is a judgement. This does not imply, nor does Spinoza think, that when we imagine something we are not having an idea. For example, in saying[47] that to "perceive" (sc. to imagine) a winged horse is to affirm wings of a horse, Spinoza must mean that such an act of the imagination involves a judgement, i.e. an idea.[48] Again, when Spinoza says in *E.,* II, xvi, C. 2 that the ideas that we have of external things indicate the constitution of our body rather than the nature of external things, he is clearly speaking of imagination.[49] In sum, in saying that ideas must be distinguished from images, Spinoza does not mean that in no sense can we be said to have ideas when we imagine; what he means is that to imagine is more than just to have a picture in the mind, it is also to affirm or deny. It follows from this

46. It may be noted that Professor Savan here seems to be regarding an image as something mental, although in this same Scholium (*Verborum namque . . .*) Spinoza uses the term "image" in the sense which he usually gives it, namely that of a physical trace.

47. *E.,* II, xlix, S.

48. Cf. *E.,* II, Ax. 3—an idea is involved in all modes of thought.

49. Cf. *E.,* IV, i, S. which refers to this corollary.

that, even if words are restricted to the imagination, this does not imply that they cannot express any ideas.

What is said about "ideas and the words by which we refer to things" in *E.,* II, xlix, S. can be dismissed more briefly. As the context shows, Spinoza has in mind the fact that people can talk deceptively, uttering sentences whose meaning is the opposite of what they really think. This is undoubtedly true; but it does not imply that a judgement cannot be expressed verbally in an undeceptive way.

(b) "A true idea can neither arise from experience of words and images nor can it be verified through such experience, for experience can give no knowledge of essences." Professor Savan cites Ep. 10, in which Spinoza says that experience does not teach us the essence of things; the most that it can do is to determine our mind so that it thinks only of certain essences of things. He also cites *TdIE,* par. 26, in which Spinoza says that it is evident that from "hearsay," which in his view is a kind of imagination, we never perceive the essence of a thing; and as the individual existence of a thing is known only when its essence is known, it follows that no certainty which we derive from hearsay belongs to knowledge. With these Professor Savan compares three other references: the first is Ep. 37, in which Spinoza says that clear and distinct ideas follow only from other clear and distinct ideas which are in us, and have no external cause, from which it follows that we must distinguish between the intellect and the imagination, i.e. between true ideas and the rest. The second is *E.,* II, xliii, S., in which Spinoza says that an idea is "a mode of thinking, namely understanding itself," and the third is *E.,* V, xxviii, which states that the third kind of knowledge cannot follow from the first. It will be noticed that none of these passages refers explicitly to words, but it seems clear how Professor Savan would argue. He would probably say that the reading or hearing of words involves the senses of sight and hearing, or (in the case of the blind) of touch. Now, Spinoza says that no sense-experience can give us knowledge of essences, or (what is the same) give rise to a true idea; therefore he must say that such ideas cannot be obtained through the medium of words. Similarly he must say that we cannot verify a true idea through the medium of words—e.g. by consulting a book.

The important question here is this: granting that, e.g., the sense of sight is involved when one reads something, does Spinoza think that reading is a kind of that experience which, according to him, can give us no knowledge of essences? Let us look first at the context of

the reference to knowledge from hearsay in *TdIE,* par. 26. Spinoza
is saying there that the man who knows how to find a fourth proportional simply because he remembers a rule, given to him without
any proof, has no knowledge of essence; we may put this by saying
that the man does not see why, given that the first three numbers
are 2, 4, and 3, the fourth *must* be 6. This surely does not imply
that no truth, and no proof, can be stated in words. However, this is
not all that Spinoza has in mind when he says that experience does
not teach us the essence of things. He means also that to understand
something is to show how a judgement about it follows necessarily
from propositions the truth of which cannot be denied; and this is
something that cannot be done by experience alone, which is unable to establish any necessary laws.[50] Once again, this does not
seem to imply that no truth can be stated or verified by means of
words; all that Spinoza is saying is that no *a priori* truth can be established by means of sense-experience or by induction, which is a
very different proposition. In sum, the passages just cited do not
imply that Spinoza would be inconsistent in saying that, for example,
by reading the sentence "When we love a thing which is like us, we
try as much as we can to bring it about that it loves us in return"
we can grasp the true idea which this sentence expresses, and that
we can also verify its truth by following the proof of this proposition
written down by Spinoza as *E.,* III, xxxiii.

(c) "Whereas ideas and their *ideata* are singular and unique, words
are inherently general and applicable to an indefinite multitude."
This is somewhat similar to (ii) above, which concerned transcendental and universal terms; here, however, Professor Savan is not
concerned with Spinoza's account of the way in which certain ideas
are formed, but is arguing that words are by their very generality incapable of referring precisely to what is singular and unique. The
answer to this argument has two parts. First, Spinoza would say that
some words are, in his usage, used correctly of one object only. For
example, he argues that the word "God," used as he employs it, is
properly applied to one object only;[51] anyone who says that there is
more than one God has either failed to understand the logical con-

50. Cf. *TdIE,* par. 27, and *E.,* II, xl, S. 2; we do not see *why* the fourth proportional is equal to the product of the second and third numbers, divided by the
first, if we have simply found this to work with small numbers, and have generalized from this.

51. *E.,* I, xiv, C. 1.

sequences of Spinoza's definition, or is using another definition of God. The same can be said of Spinoza's use of the word "substance." There are, then, words which are not "applicable to an indefinite multitude." Second, Spinoza often does not want to restrict what he says to one individual only. He talks, for example, not just about the mind of Spinoza, but about "the human mind." In so doing he is of course using a universal term, which refers to a vast number of entities; the point is, however, that a universal term is perfectly appropriate for what he wants to say. It is true that such a term might be misleading, in that it might tempt us to suppose that there is an object named by the words "the human mind," but Spinoza gives an express warning against temptations of this kind.[52] It is true, also, that Spinoza objects to universal terms; but, as has already been seen, what he objects to are generic images, which vary from person to person, whereas in the *Ethics* the meaning of the term "human mind" is explained precisely.[53]

(d) "Whereas an idea is certain, words are uncertain." Professor Savan does not cite any passage in support of this, but he may be referring to *E.,* II, xliii, S., "A true idea involves the highest certainty." By "certainty" Spinoza does not mean the mere absence of doubt;[54] what he means is that the man who has a true idea—namely, the man who "knows a thing perfectly, i.e. in the best way"[55]—knows that he has a true idea.[56]

In one sense of the words "true idea," what Spinoza has said is plainly false, for it is clear that we can state a proposition which happens to be true without knowing that it is true. This, however, is not what Spinoza has in mind. He accompanies his remark about the certainty that attaches to a true idea with the warning that we must not regard an idea as "something mute, like a picture on a tablet"; rather, an idea is "understanding itself" (*ipsum intelligere*).[57] What he seems to mean is that a true idea, as he understands the term, is not something that we can compare with reality, as we may compare a portrait with the original; rather, to speak of someone as having a true idea of a thing is to say that he understands that thing.

52. *E.,* II, xlviii, S.
53. *E.,* II, xi; *E.,* II, xiii.
54. Cf. *E.,* II, xlix, S.
55. *E.,* II, xliii, S.
56. *E.,* II, xliii.
57. *E.,* II, xliii, S.

As mentioned in (b) above, Spinoza's view is roughly that to understand something is to make a judgement about that thing which is seen to follow deductively from self-evident truths, and Spinoza's argument is that anyone who has understanding of this sort must know that he has it. All this throws some light on Spinoza's theory of knowledge, but one may ask what it has to do with words and their alleged "uncertainty." Plainly, not everything formulated in words is a true idea, as Spinoza understands a true idea; but this does not imply, nor does Spinoza say that it implies, that no true idea is ever formulated in words.

(e) "Whereas 'that true Word of God which is in the mind . . . can never be depraved or corrupted,' words are corruptible." The reference is to Ep. 76 (Wolf trans., pp. 354–55); the "true word of God" of which Spinoza speaks is the reason. Professor Savan also compares *Tr. Theol.-Pol.*, ch. xv; he gives no precise reference, but he may have in mind G., III, 182, where Spinoza says that he finds it amazing that certain theologians "want to submit the reason, the greatest gift to us and the divine light, to dead letters, which could have been corrupted by human wickedness." Spinoza adds that the true word of God is to be found in the mind; the written word is a mere image of this. It is clear that he is here thinking of people who tamper with sacred texts, altering them to suit their purposes; the corruptibility of words of which Professor Savan speaks is presumably wider in scope, covering also changes in the meaning of words, changes which occur gradually and without evil intent. There is no doubt that language is "corruptible" in this way, but it is hard to see how it follows from this that philosophical truths cannot be given adequate linguistic expression. It is obvious that changes in the meanings of words make it difficult to understand something written in a previous era; but such difficulties can be overcome, and in any case they affect the man who wants to understand what another has written rather than the writer himself.

(f) "Whereas it is of the nature of reason to consider things as necessary and under a certain form of eternity, words are connected with contingency and time." The reference to the way that reason considers things, not given by Professor Savan, is *E.*, II, xliv and C. 2. It is not clear what precisely is meant by saying that words are "connected with contingency and time," but it seems likely that Professor Savan has in mind the first corollary to *E.*, II, xliv. This states that "it depends on the imagination alone that we consider things as con-

tingent, with regard both to the future and to the past," and it has
already been seen that, for Spinoza, words are closely connected
with the imagination. If this is what is meant, then a reply has already
been given in (i) above. Let us consider again the sentence mentioned in (i), "Two straight lines cannot enclose a space." The proposition expressed by this sentence would be regarded by Spinoza as
necessarily true, and he would no doubt say that to grasp this truth
is to consider things "under a certain form of eternity." Someone
who reads this sentence is, according to Spinoza, making use of
"imagination," but with the important difference that in this case the
imagination is "following the traces" of the intellect.

(g) We have now completed the examination of the paragraph in
which Professor Savan quotes a number of passages in support of his
view that "in nearly every important respect, Spinoza opposes true
ideas to words." It remains to consider the somewhat similar passage which Professor Savan cites elsewhere, to the effect that "A
thing is understood when it is perceived simply by the mind without
words and images."[58] It has been seen already[59] that Spinoza believes that thought and words are distinct; that thought is imageless
and wordless. Here, however, he seems to be saying rather more,
namely, that images and words are a hindrance to thought, or, that
something is understood only when images and words are absent.
However, attention to the context of this passage shows that this is
not what Spinoza means. He is speaking of the difference between
Christ and the prophets, and is saying that God revealed himself to
the mind of Christ "immediately" (i.e. without media), whereas he
revealed himself to the prophets by "words and images." He has in
mind, for example, God speaking to Moses, or the visions that the
prophets had;[60] he is not thinking, say, of people reading Euclid, or
of people reading Spinoza.

(iv) We come now to the passage from the De Intellectus Emendatione,[61] which states that if a man says that, e.g., Peter exists without knowing that Peter exists, that assertion is false as far as the
speaker is concerned. "The assertion 'Peter exists' is true only with
regard to the man who knows certainly that Peter exists."[62] It is

58. Tr. Theol.-Pol., ch. iv (G., III, 64–65).
59. Cf. the discussion of (i) and (ii) above.
60. Cf. Tr. Theol.-Pol., ch. i (G., III, 17 and 20).
61. TdIE, par. 69 (G., II, 26).
62. TdIE, par. 69 (G., II, 26).

clear that this is closely allied to the view discussed in (iii) (d) above —namely, that for someone to have a "true idea" of a thing he must understand that thing, must know it "perfectly, i.e. in the best way."[63] Professor Savan maintains that what Spinoza says in this paragraph of the *De Intellectus Emendatione* implies that language cannot express the clear and distinct ideas of the true philosophy. But this seems to be a mere *non sequitur*. It may readily be granted that a man can say, e.g., that God exists without knowing that God exists; but it does not follow from this that a man who says that God exists does not know that God exists, or, more generally, that a man who knows a philosophical truth can never express it in words. (v) The final piece of evidence cited also came from the *De Intellectus Emendatione*.[64] Here Spinoza says that words are a part of the imagination, and that they can be the cause of many errors because of the erratic way that they are joined in the memory. Further, the meaning of words has been established by the multitude, so that words are merely the signs of things as they are in the imagination, not as they are in the intellect. This can clearly be seen, Spinoza continues, from the fact that people have used negative terms to refer to what is only in the intellect and not in the imagination—e.g. "incorporeal," "infinite." Indeed, many things which are really affirmative are expressed in negative terms because their contraries are much more easily imagined, and so "occurred first to the first men, and acquired positive names"; such words are "uncreated," "independent," "infinite" and "immortal." In sum, "We affirm and deny many things because the nature of words allows us to affirm and deny it, not the nature of things; and if we do not know this we may easily take something false to be true."

Although Spinoza could be said to be distinguishing here between words and the intellect, it does not follow that he thinks, or should think, that no truth discoverable by the reason can be stated in words. What he objects to here is not the use of words as such, but the uncritical acceptance of common usage as a guide in philosophy. That this does not imply that Spinoza thinks that knowledge cannot be put into words can be seen from the explanation to Definition 20 of the affects in the third book of the *Ethics*. Here, after defining "favour" and "indignation," Spinoza adds:

63. *E.*, II, xliii, S.
64. *TdIE*, pars. 88–89 (G., II, 33).

I know that in common usage these names mean something else. But it is not my intention to explain the meaning of words; it is my intention to explain the nature of things, and to indicate them by words whose usual meaning is not wholly inconsistent with the meaning that I want them to have.

In attacking the idea that the philosopher should accept ordinary usage Spinoza is, of course, at variance with many modern philosophers; but though his views may be challenged, it cannot be said that they are inconsistent.

III

According to Professor Savan, not only do Spinoza's views about language make it "difficult to accept any verbal account as a direct exposition of the true philosophy,"[65] but Spinoza knew that this was so. We have argued that if Spinoza thought so, he was mistaken; but let us see if there is any good reason to suppose that he did think so. "The most telling evidence," Professor Savan says,[66] "is to be found in the contradictions which abound in his *Ethics,* as well as in his other writings." If Spinoza thought that language is an unsuitable medium in which to express philosophical truths, then he would expect contradictory statements to occur when he tried to express such truths in language.

Many such statements do occur in the *Ethics,* often in such close proximity to one another it is hardly believable that so careful a writer as Spinoza was not aware of them. Since he allows the contradictions to stand it is to be presumed that he did not intend the *Ethics* to be a simple exposition of truth.[67]

These contradictions are stated by Professor Savan on pages 64–68 of his article; one of them has been discussed above,[68] where it was maintained that it is not a genuine contradiction. It could be argued that the same can be shown of many of the contradictions listed by Professor Savan, but to develop such arguments here would lengthen this paper considerably. It would, in any case, be unnecessary; for

65. Savan, *op. cit.,* p. 63.
66. *Loc. cit.*
67. *Loc. cit.*
68. Cf. the account, in II (ii), of Spinoza's use of transcendental and universal terms.

even if we grant that Spinoza's writings are as contradictory as Professor Savan claims, it does not follow that Spinoza was aware of this fact, but discounted it as irrelevant. All that we would be entitled to say is that, whatever Spinoza's philosophical virtues may be, consistency is not one of them.[69]

Professor Savan's main argument in support of his view that Spinoza thought that words could not give an adequate exposition of the true philosophy has turned out to be unsound; and it may be added that there are arguments against this view, to some of which at least there seems to be no convincing answer. One argument to which an answer can perhaps be found is to the effect that, if Spinoza did maintain the thesis that Professor Savan ascribes to him, then he would be involved in a self-contradiction. The thesis is that language cannot express philosophical ideas adequately. But this is surely itself a philosophical thesis; now, if this thesis is expressed adequately by the sentence which is used in stating it, then there is after all one philosophical statement that can be made adequately in language, which leads to a contradiction. It may be, however, that the contradiction can be avoided by distinguishing, in a Wittgensteinian manner, between showing and stating. The inadequacy of language, it may be argued, is not so much stated by Spinoza as shown—shown by the contradictions in the *Ethics* itself, which, it might be suggested, is regarded by Spinoza as the most coherent system that can be constructed with words. This seems to be a valid answer, though it will be noted that it implies that the *Ethics* does contain serious contradictions, and that this was recognized by Spinoza.

But there are stronger arguments against Professor Savan's view. As he himself admits,[70] the fact that Spinoza makes no attempt to explain how words can convey true ideas is a strong argument against the thesis that he was aware of the difficulties in which his theory of language involved him. Again, there can be no doubt that Spinoza

69. There may be a temptation to produce another argument in support of the view that a defence of the consistency of the *Ethics* is superfluous in the present context. It might be argued that even if what Spinoza says is consistent, and that he thought it to be so, it does not follow that he thought it to be true; he might simply regard it as a story which is coherent, but false. This, however, is not what Spinoza would say. First, he is concerned to construct a system which is not merely self-consistent, but is such that its truth cannot be denied by any rational being. Second, he would say that any account of reality which is logically possible is also true, since everything possible exists (e.g. *E.*, I, xvi; *E.*, I, xxxv).

70. Savan, *op. cit.*, p. 68.

thinks that the propositions of Euclidean geometry are genuinely known; to be exact, they are examples of the "second kind of knowledge."[71] Now, in Chapter 7 of the *Tractatus Theologico-Politicus*[72] Spinoza says that Euclid, who "wrote nothing but what is extremely simple and in the highest degree intelligible," is easily explained in any language; to comprehend his meaning and to be certain of the true sense of what he says we need only a moderate knowledge of the language in which he wrote. This clearly implies that propositions which are examples of the second kind of knowledge can be expressed in linguistic terms.

It is now time to leave behind the criticism of Professor Savan's thesis, and to try to find an answer to the important question which he poses. The question is this: given that (as we have argued) Spinoza can consistently say that philosophical knowledge can be expressed in words, what are the kinds of knowledge, as Spinoza understands them, that are expressed by the language of the *Ethics?*

It is not difficult to see that one of these is "reason," the second kind of knowledge. In *E.,* II, xl, S. 2 Spinoza defines this kind of knowledge by saying that

> we perceive many things and form universal concepts . . . from the fact that we have common notions and adequate ideas of the properties of things; . . . and this I will call *reason* and *knowledge of the second kind.*

Of itself, this is too condensed to be clear, but Spinoza also refers to *E.,* II, xxxviii, C.; *E.,* II, xxxix and C.; and *E.,* II, xl, which help to explain what is meant. "Common notions" have already been mentioned in this paper.[73] They are, as their name implies, ideas or notions which are common to all men,[74] and so are to be distinguished from those universal concepts which vary from person to person, and which Spinoza relegates to the first kind of knowledge. All bodies, Spinoza says, agree in some things—e.g. they all involve the concept of one and the same attribute, that of extension; they can move now more slowly, now more quickly; and they can now move and now be at rest.[75] Now, these things that are common to

71. Cf. *E.,* II, xl, S. 2.
72. *Tr. Theol-Pol.,* ch. vii (G., III, 111).
73. Cf. the discussion of (ii) in Sect. II.
74. *E.,* II, xxxviii, C.
75. *E.,* II, Lem. 2.

all bodies have their corresponding expressions in the attribute of thought, and these are the "common notions." These ideas are "adequate," i.e. true.[76] An example of what Spinoza has in mind would be the basic concepts and truths of physics, which are true of absolutely all bodies. "Adequate ideas of the properties of things" differ from "common notions" in that they are the mental correlate of what is common to the human body and "certain external bodies by which it is customarily affected."[77] Here Spinoza seems to be thinking of the basic truths and concepts of sciences such as physiology, which do not apply to absolutely all physical things. We have spoken so far of basic concepts and truths; reason, however, is also concerned with the propositions which are deduced from these and which, as following from adequate ideas, are themselves adequate.[78] In sum, reason is regarded by Spinoza as deductive knowledge, having as its basis propositions which every man must accept. It has one further feature, which the definition of reason in *E.,* II, xl, S. 2 does not bring out: namely, that it is "universal."[79] By this Spinoza means, not that its propositions are universal truths (although they are), but rather that "the bases of reason are notions which explain those things which are common to all, and which explain the essence of no single thing."[80] What Spinoza seems to mean here is that the science of physics, for example, is concerned with a falling body simply as a falling body, and not as *this* falling body. Again, the science of physiology is concerned with a human heart simply as a human heart, and not as the heart of this particular person.

It is clear that much of what is said in the *Ethics* is of this type. The book has little to say about physics, though the axioms and lemmata after *E.,* II, xiii present in deductive form a few propositions "about the nature of bodies." It does, however, offer a deductive account of the human mind, an account in which the conclusions drawn are general, in the sense that they relate, not to this or that human mind in particular, but rather to *the* human mind. One may indeed be tempted to suppose that the whole of the *Ethics* is an expression in verbal form of knowledge of the second kind. Let us see to what extent this is so.

76. *E.,* II, xxxviii.
77. *E.,* II, xxxix.
78. *E.,* II, xl.
79. *E.,* V, xxxvi, S.
80. *E.,* II, xliv, C. 2; cf. *E.,* II, xxxvii.

It might be thought that what Spinoza calls "imagination" has no place in the *Ethics*. By "imagination" he means, not only what would now be called imagination, but sense-experience and induction also. These have in common the fact that they do not provide us with necessary truths, and this, it might seem, debars the imagination from playing any part in the *Ethics*. There, Spinoza is concerned to establish necessary truths; he is not, for example, interested in establishing such propositions as "Hatred is seldom good"; rather, he wants to prove that hatred *can never* be good[81]—i.e. that it is impossible for hatred to be good. Despite this, imagination has a part to play in the argument of the *Ethics;* not a major part, certainly, but at any rate a supporting role.

(a) Spinoza appeals to experience in support of postulates which, although logically possible, are not regarded by him as self-evident. An example of this is to be found in *E.,* II, xvii, S. After Spinoza has given an explanation of how we can "contemplate things that do not exist as if they were present," he adds that this could happen through other causes, but that it is sufficient for him to have shown one way in which it *could* happen. He then says:

> However, I do not think that I have strayed far from the true cause, since all the postulates that I have assumed contain hardly anything that does not agree with experience, of which we may not doubt, after we have shown that the human body exists as we sense it.

There is much that might be discussed here. First, one might comment on the *a priori* nature of Spinoza's approach to science—his readiness to be satisfied with an explanation which is logically possible, whether or not it is the right one. Second, one might ask why exactly we "may not doubt" of experience—the answer perhaps being that Spinoza is in effect appealing to a causal theory of perception, and is saying that our perceptions give us reliable information about the external world in that they are the mental aspect of the human body, which is causally affected by external objects. What matters here, however, is a third point: namely, that Spinoza is prepared to accept the testimony of experience. He does not state here the conditions under which he is prepared to do this. For example, if someone were to say that substance is divided, because we experience it as divided, Spinoza would deny that this follows;[82] why, then, should

81. *E.,* IV, xlv.
82. *E.,* I, xv, S.

he accept the testimony of experience in certain other cases? The answer seems to be that to say that substance is divided conflicts with reason, and therefore must be false; to say that the postulates mentioned in *E.*, II, xvii, S. are true does not, and so the fact that experience shows what these postulates state may be regarded as confirming them.

Spinoza also appeals to experience in the *Ethics* when arguing against a thesis. In *E.*, IV, xxxix, S. he says that he does not assert that the body dies, in the sense of radically changing its nature, only when it becomes a corpse, and adds that "experience itself seems to teach the contrary." (He is referring to a case of complete loss of memory.) In this Scholium, Spinoza makes explicit what is only implied in the passage quoted in the last paragraph—namely, that the testimony of experience is acceptable in so far as there is no deductive reason (*nulla ratio me cogit*) to suppose the contrary.

(b) A more common use of the testimony of experience in the *Ethics* is to support conclusions that have been established deductively; not that Spinoza thinks that there is any *logical* need for such support, but that he wants to be more persuasive. A good example is to be found in *E.*, III, ii, S. Here, after proving that the body cannot determine the mind to thought, nor the mind determine the body to motion or rest, Spinoza says: "But although the situation is such that no reason for doubt remains, I hardly believe that men can be induced to consider these matters calmly unless I prove them by experience," and proceeds to give a number of such proofs. Other passages in which experience is used to support deductive proofs are *E.*, III, xxxii, S.; *E.*, III, Def. 27 of the affects; *E.*, IV, xxxv, S.; *E.*, V, vi, S. The need to use experience in this way is also discussed in Chapter 5 of the *Tractatus Theologico-Politicus.*

We have now spoken of the part played in the *Ethics* by reason and by imagination; it remains to be asked if any part is played by "intuitive knowledge," the "third kind of knowledge." Although Spinoza says much in the fifth book about the effects of intuitive knowledge, the nature of such knowledge has long been a source of perplexity. There is no room for an adequate discussion here, but at least some points can be made which relate to the question whether the *Ethics* contains, or could contain, any examples of intuitive knowledge which are formulated in words.

Some readers of Spinoza, impressed by the close connexion between intuitive knowledge and what Spinoza calls "the intellectual love of God," think that intuitive knowledge is some kind of mystical vision, inexpressible in words. This would certainly explain Spinoza's failure to give a clear account of the third kind of knowledge; however, there seems to be no real evidence for this view. If Spinoza thought that intuitive knowledge cannot be expressed adequately in words, so that any account of it is at best analogical, then one would expect him to say so; and he does not. When intuitive knowledge is defined in *E.*, II, xl, S. 2 no hint is given that this definition is in any way less literal than those of the second and third kinds of knowledge.

The definition just mentioned says of intuitive knowledge that it "proceeds from an adequate idea of the formal essence of certain of the attributes of God to an adequate knowledge of the essence of things." Spinoza contrasts it with reason, which, as mentioned earlier in this section, has as its basis "notions which explain those things which are common to all, and which explain the essence of no single thing."[83] This contrast may suggest that the second and third kinds of knowledge can be interpreted in Hegelian terms. Reason, it may be thought, is abstract, and because of this abstractness the propositions established by reason are not wholly true. Intuitive knowledge, on the other hand, is concrete, and anything known by it is true. To complete the Hegelian analogy it would have to be said that what is known by intuitive knowledge is *one* truth, *the* truth—the complete systematic whole of which reason and imagination grasp only fragments—and it has indeed been argued that Spinoza argued, or tended to argue, in this way.[84] On this interpretation, the *Ethics* would not contain an example of intuitive knowledge, since the complete system of knowledge has not yet been constructed.

Such an interpretation, however, is not supported by the evidence. Spinoza does not say that only what is known by the third kind of knowledge is true; on the contrary, *E.*, II, xli says expressly that both the second and third kinds of knowledge are true, and *E.*, V, xxxvi, S., after proving by the third kind of knowledge a proposition which can also be proved by the second, says of the latter demonstration that it is "legitimate and placed beyond the possibility of doubt."[85]

83. *E.*, II, xliv, C. 2.

84. See, e.g. H. H. Joachim, *Spinoza's Tractatus de Intellectus Emendatione* (Oxford: Clarendon Press, 1940), p. 99.

85. This also tells against an interpretation of the second and third kinds of knowledge put forward by a Marxist philosopher, L. Kolakowski. His view is that Spinoza believed that the intellect cannot give genuine knowledge because

As to the idea that there is only one truth, which is grasped by the third kind of knowledge, this finds no support in the text of Spinoza. For example, *E.*, II, xl, S. 2 offers as an example of intuitive knowledge the solution of a problem about a fourth proportional. The problem, it will be recalled, is this: given three numbers, to find a fourth which shall be to the third as the second is to the first. Spinoza shows how this can be solved by the imagination and by reason, and then says that when the numbers are simple we can use intuitive knowledge.

> For example, given the numbers 1, 2 and 3, everyone sees that the fourth proportional is 6; and this is seen much the more clearly, because from the very ratio which we see (with one intuition) that the first has to the second, we conclude the fourth.

Clearly, knowledge of this kind is far from being knowledge of the one "systematic whole" of which Hegelians speak; one may also cite the *De Intellectus Emendatione*,[86] in which Spinoza says that he has not yet been able to grasp many things by intuitive knowledge, whereas on the Hegelian interpretation he should have said that he has been unable to grasp anything by it.

The argument so far has been that there is no reason to believe that Spinoza thought that intuitive knowledge is ineffable, or that he at any rate was unable to give an example of it. We have said already that the question of the precise nature of intuitive knowledge is too big to be discussed in this paper; what can be said here is that, however it is to be explained, Spinoza thought that examples of it are to be found in the *Ethics*. The problem of the fourth proportional, which has already been mentioned, might fairly be said to be merely illustrative, and not to form an integral part of the deductive system of the *Ethics*. However, in the Scholium to *E.*, V, xxxvi Spinoza gives an example of intuitive knowledge which is an integral part of his system. In *E.*, V, xxxvi he has said that the intellectual love of the mind towards God is that very love of God by which God loves himself, not in so far as he is infinite, but in so far as he can be explained through the essence of the human mind, considered under

---

it is conditioned by its everyday practical activity; only intuitive knowledge is free from such distortions. (See "Marx and the Classical Definition of Truth," cited in *Revisionism: Essays on the History of Marxist Ideas,* ed. L. Labedz, New York: Praeger, 1962, p. 182).

86. *TdIE,* par. 22 (G., II, 11).

the aspect of eternity. It seems to be this that Spinoza has in mind when he says:[87]

> Then, since the essence of our mind consists in knowledge alone, of which the principle and foundation is God (by *E.*, I, xv and *E.*, II, xlvii, S.), from this it becomes clear to us how and in what way our mind follows in respect of essence and existence from the divine nature, and continually depends upon God. I thought it worth while to note this here, so that I might show by this example how much power is possessed by the knowledge of single things, which I have called "intuitive" or "of the third kind."[88]

Spinoza goes on to say, as noted earlier, that he has already proved by the second kind of knowledge that everything (and therefore the human mind also) depends upon God in respect of essence and existence, but that this proof, though valid, "does not so affect our mind as when the very same thing is concluded from the essence itself of each single thing, which we declare to depend on God." The precise interpretation of this passage is difficult; but there is surely no doubt that Spinoza is here claiming to state, in words, and as an integral part of his argument, an example of the third kind of knowledge.

87. *E.*, V, xxxvi, S.
88. *E.*, II, xl, S. 2.

Spinoza's Theory of Knowledge in the Ethics

GUTTORM FLØISTAD

Spinoza claims in the *Ethics* to have shown that there are altogether three ways of knowing or forming ideas of things, that is, three kinds of knowledge, knowledge by imagination (first kind), by reason (second kind), and by intuition (third kind).[1] It follows that Spinoza must himself be using one or two or all three kinds in developing his own system in the *Ethics,* including the propositions in which he is talking *about* the kinds of knowledge themselves. The question is, which? This essay is devoted to a discussion of this problem.

The problem is raised by Professor D. Savan in connection with his discussion of Spinoza's view on words and language,[2] and discussed further by G. H. R. Parkinson in his reply to Savan in this volume.[3] According to Savan, Spinoza's view on words and language is such that his writings cannot be, nor were intended by Spinoza to be, "a direct or literal exposition of philosophical truth."[4] Since in an important sense we have access to the propositions (or knowledge) of the *Ethics* only via its "words and language," this presumably means that our problem is extremely difficult, if at all possible, to solve. At any rate Savan provides no solution to it.

Parkinson argues that Savan's interpretation of Spinoza's view on words and language is "radically misconceived";[5] Spinoza's view does not have the logical implications stated by Savan. In particular, there is nothing in Spinoza's view from which it follows that language is in principle unsuitable for expressing true knowledge. From this, Parkinson then goes on to discuss the problem of which kinds of knowledge are to be found in the *Ethics*. The bulk of the propositions, he thinks, belong to knowledge of reason, or the second kind. However, instances of knowledge of imagination, or the first kind, and of intuition, or the third kind, do occur. Difficulties may arise as to

---

Inquiry 12 (1969), pp. 41–65. Reprinted by permission of the author and of *Inquiry*.

1. Cf. *E.,* II, xl, S. 2.
2. D. Savan, "Spinoza and Language," pp. 60–72 in this volume.
3. G. H. R. Parkinson, "Language and Knowledge in Spinoza."
4. Savan, *op. cit.,* pp. 60–61.
5. Parkinson, *op. cit.,* p. 73.

the correct interpretation of the passages exemplifying the various kinds of knowledge. The point, however, is that we may safely assume that Spinoza would have claimed to have stated adequately, in words, the examples he gives of the three kinds of knowledge.[6]

In the following I shall argue in part against, in part in agreement with Parkinson. I wish to hold (1) that no instances of knowledge of the first kind occur in the *Ethics,* nor are allowed to enter into its system, (2) that the major part of the propositions of the *Ethics,* with some qualifications, belong to the second kind of knowledge, and (3) that knowledge of the third kind occurs much more frequently and plays a more significant role in the *Ethics* than Parkinson seems to maintain. I shall enter only briefly into the controversy between Savan and Parkinson as to whether or not true knowledge may be adequately expressed in language. This is not to say that I regard this problem as irrelevant to the present case, nor as being in any way exhaustively discussed by the two participants; rather a discussion of which kinds of knowledge Spinoza himself uses in the *Ethics* presupposes a solution of the "expression-problem," to the effect that knowledge may somehow be adequately expressed in language. This seems to be Parkinson's position, too, and Savan would presumably agree. "Language may indeed express philosophical truth," he says.[7] He merely differs from Parkinson in his explanation of how this is achieved. Given, then, *that* true knowledge may somehow be expressed adequately in words, the problem as to which kinds of ideas or knowledge do occur in the *Ethics* may, as I shall try to show, be argued, at least to a large extent, independently of any explanation of how such knowledge can be expressed.

I

1. Does the *Ethics* contain instances of inadequate ideas? A few premises may yield a preliminary answer: Knowledge or ideas of imagination are inadequate and false, whereas knowledge or ideas of reason and of intuition are adequate and true. And, adequate and true ideas cannot follow from inadequate and false ones, nor themselves give rise to other than adequate and true ideas.[8] As the *Ethics* presumably must be said to contain some true propositions, and if,

6. Cf. *Ibid.,* pp. 94–100.
7. Savan, *op. cit.,* p. 71.
8. Cf. *E.,* II, xl; *E.,* V, xxviii, Dem.

furthermore, it is regarded as a structured whole, that is, as a system of coherent propositions, it would seem to follow that no inadequate or false idea can occur in the *Ethics*. Spinoza's treatment of inadequate ideas, including the so-called passive emotions[9] present no difficulty here: hate of someone, for instance, is based upon and involves an inadequate and false idea; an idea or, as one may also say, a description of one person hating another may itself perfectly well be adequate and true. Or in general, ideas or descriptions of inadequate and false ideas may be adequate and true. Since a true idea is the "standard of itself and falsity"[10] we may even say that ideas of other ideas being false, are necessarily true. It is logically impossible to know something to be false unless this knowledge itself is adequate and true.[11]

The weak premiss in this argument is of course the assumption that the *Ethics* is a coherent system of propositions. Many or even most writers on the subject are inclined to see a number of incoherences in the *Ethics*. Savan is one of them. To decide exactly where incoherences in fact lie is notoriously difficult. Hardly any two writers are in complete agreement. Thus Parkinson rejects most of the incoherences detected by Savan. I shall, in the course of this paper, suggest some possible incoherences, and, indirectly also suggest why it is so notoriously difficult to decide what is and what is not incoherent. At present it suffices to say that if but one incoherence is admitted the above argument is likely to be worthless.

Parkinson points to a similar general argument against the occurrence of ideas of imagination in the *Ethics*. Spinoza, he rightly says, is "concerned in the *Ethics* to establish necessary truths." This means, for example, that "he is not . . . interested in establishing such propositions as 'Hatred is seldom good'; rather, he wants to prove that hatred *can never* be good."[12] Imagination, which Parkinson takes to involve sense-experience and induction, "do not provide us with necessary truths, and this, it might seem, debars the imagination from playing any part in the *Ethics*." He adds, however, that despite this, "imagination has a part to play in the argument of the *Ethics;* not a major part, certainly, but at any rate a supporting role."[13]

9. Cf. *E.,* III, Aff., Gen. Def.
10. *E.,* II, xliii, S.
11. Cf. *E.,* II, xlii, Dem.
12. Parkinson, *op. cit.,* p. 96.
13. *Loc. cit.*

Parkinson then proceeds to point out various "supporting roles" for experience. He mentions *E.*, II, xvii, S., where Spinoza talks about all the (true) postulates which contain hardly anything "that does not agree with experience" (*quod non constet experientia*). A second "more common use of the testimony of the experience in the *Ethics* is to support conclusions that have been established deductively."[14] Thus Spinoza says in *E.*, III, ii, S. that he wants to prove these conclusions "by experience" (*experientia comprobavero*). Incidentally, in the same scholium, and in many other places, he also uses the phrase "experience teaches (us)" (*experientia docet*).

There is no need here to go into further details. The problem is clear enough: Do these (and similar) occurrences of the term "experience" in the *Ethics* justify the conclusion that experience, that is, imagination in the sense of inadequate ideas, plays a "supporting role" in the *Ethics?*

Parkinson's affirmative answer is difficult to accept. The trouble lies with the meaning of "supporting role," that is, according to the instances quoted above, with the meaning of "agreeing with," "prove by" and "teach." The affirmative answer says that adequate ideas may be supported by, that is, agree with, or be proved by, or taught to us by inadequate ideas. On a very plausible interpretation this means that adequate ideas (postulates, deductively proved propositions) may somehow follow from inadequate ones. And this contradicts the statement that adequate ideas cannot follow from inadequate ideas.

However, a closer look indicates that the interpretation of the various expressions (agreeing with, etc.) for the "following from" is incorrect or at least imprecise. If we were to describe what happens when experience is taken to support, in various ways, an adequate idea, we should have to say something like this: The ideas of experience are not inadequate ideas in the usual sense. They do not, strictly speaking, occur in a sequence of inadequate ideas, but rather, somehow, in a sequence of adequate ideas. The starting-point is not experience itself alone, but the adequate idea, which experience is taken to support. Experience is hence regarded from the viewpoint of, or within the frame of, the adequate idea. That this is so may even be taken as a condition for grasping the supporting role of experience. Thus experience in no way stands on its own feet. It enters into a

14. *Ibid.*, p. 97.

sequence of adequate ideas by way of its supporting role, that is, because of the preceding adequate idea to be supported. Or, more precisely, experience enters into a sequence of adequate ideas because of the (presumably adequate) idea that an adequate idea (a postulate, a deductively proved proposition) may be supported by (seen to agree with, or proved by) experience.

For this reason it is incorrect or imprecise to say that it is a matter of an adequate idea following from an inadequate idea of experience. Primarily, we may say that the idea formed on the basis of experience or imagination *follows from* the adequate idea in question, together with the idea of experience supporting this adequate idea. It is only on the basis of such a preceding "following from" that we may turn round, as it were, and say that the adequate idea follows from or is supported by, or agrees with, or is proved by experience.

2. It is admittedly difficult to grasp exactly how our knowledge or understanding operates in the "supporting-relation" between an adequate idea and experience. The above description, no doubt incomplete, may therefore perhaps be made more intelligible by way of an example. Let us take the deductively established proposition that "every individual thing, or whatever thing that is finite and has a determined existence, cannot exist or be determined for action unless it is determined for action and existence by another cause which is also finite and has a determined existence."[15] Or in short, roughly, every individual thing (bodies, ideas, actions) has a cause. This is a "common property" on account of which "we can have only a very inadequate knowledge (that is, by imagination or experience) of individual things which are outside us."[16]

Ideas of common properties are ideas of reason.[17] In *E.*, I, xxviii we therefore have an instance of the second kind of knowledge. Spinoza does not directly set out to prove this deductively established proposition by experience. In a sense he rather uses experience as counting against the proposition. In *E.*, III, ii, S., where he proceeds to give a number of proofs by experience in favour of *E.*, III, ii, he says: ". . . experience teaches as clearly as reason that men think themselves free on account of this alone, that they are conscious of their actions and ignorant of the causes of them." This is in many ways an interesting statement with regard to our problem. Strictly

15. *E.*, I, xxviii.
16. *E.*, II, xxxi, Dem.
17. Cf. *E.*, II, xl, S. 2; *E.*, II, xxxix, Dem.

speaking, experience is not said here to count against the truth of the idea of the common property; experience is merely said to show the failure of man to recognize the common property. However, it is just this use of "experience," I think, that can illuminate what Spinoza has in mind when, in various ways, he talks about the "supporting role" of experience. "Experience" in the quotation clearly does not denote the experience or imagination characteristic of the person who inadequately thinks himself free because he knows no cause of his actions. Such a person would not possibly admit nor understand that "experience teaches as clearly as reason . . ." etc. What Spinoza has in mind is rather the experience of the philosopher who *beforehand* knows the truth of the principles that every individual (his actions, etc.) has a cause. This knowledge is, so far as I can see, simply to be regarded as a necessary condition for saying, that is, stating in words, that "experience teaches as clearly as reason that men think themselves free on account of this alone, that they are conscious of their actions and ignorant of the causes of them." Particularly the use of the phrase "ignorant of the causes" shows clearly that the case is viewed from the point of view of some "deeper," adequate insight. The person who thinks himself free is unlikely to admit any ignorance lying behind his "freedom." In view of this the beginning of the quotation (". . . experience teaches as clearly as reason . . .") becomes understandable. Experience is clear and it is as clear as reason. Spinoza could not have said this unless experience had to do with clear and distinct, that is, adequate ideas.

We may ask whether experience and reason, or, more precisely, whether the adequate idea of experience and reason, are in this case one and the same or different. The question is difficult to decide. The fact that they teach us "clearly" the same state of affairs suggests that both cases concern one and the same adequate idea (the idea, namely, that men think themselves free . . . etc.). This adequate idea, it may be said, results as an application of the adequate idea of the common property expressed in *E.,* I, xxviii to how men commonly think about their freedom. In this application, then, experience and reason apparently count as equal. However, they can hardly be said to be the same. The idea of the common property in *E.,* I, xxviii applied to "men" is undoubtedly an idea not of experience, but of reason. What experience may be said to do then is to confront this idea of reason with "actual life," that is, with particular individuals in general. But this experience, or imagination, does not descend, as it were, to the level of inadequate ideas characteristic of men who unjustifiably think themselves free. Experience must all along have regard for the common property in its concern with particular instances in general. This regard for the common property is presumably the reason why Spinoza is able to align experience with reason, and moreover, to say that experience may in various ways support propositions deductively established by reason.

3. Whatever the right interpretation of the supporting role of experience may be, it is fairly clear that experience, or imagination, may involve adequate ideas and hence that ideas of reason may agree with or be proved by or in a sense follow from experience. The *Ethics* contains some evidence of the adequacy of experience or imagination. Thus a statement in *E.,* II, xlvii, S. runs: "But that men have knowledge not so clear of God as they have of common notions arises from the fact that they cannot imagine God as they do bodies." Spinoza seems here to be saying that men owe at least some of the clarity of their knowledge of common notions (to which belongs knowledge of common properties[18]) to the fact that they can imagine bodies. The question arises as to whether "imagine bodies" here means "imagine bodies as particulars" or "imagine the common properties of bodies." Since the clarity has reference to common notions or properties, it presumably means the latter. This answer is suggested in *E.,* V, vii, Dem., where Spinoza talks about "common properties of things, which we always regard as present and which we always imagine in the same manner." These common properties are presumably what Spinoza has in mind when now and then he talks about things which we may imagine clearly and distinctly[19] and also when suggesting the possibility of imagining things "to be necessary."[20]

It follows from these considerations that we shall have to distinguish between two kinds of imagination, or for that matter, of experience, in the *Ethics*. On the one hand, imagination designates a kind of knowledge, namely the first kind, which is throughout inadequate and false. On the other hand, it refers to what may be called an adequate use of a certain faculty of mind. In the latter case imagination agrees "with the laws of human reason"[21] or as Spinoza also

18. Cf. *E.,* II, xxxix and *E.,* II, xl, S. 1.
19. E.g. *E.,* III, liii; *E.,* V, vi, S.
20. *E.,* IV, xi, Dem.
21. *E.,* IV, xviii, S.

puts it, it is "united to true thoughts."[22] As such, imagination or experience may consistently be said to support deductively established propositions.[23]

Parkinson, consequently, is right in saying that experience has a supporting role in the *Ethics*. He is wrong, however, in thinking that the experience in question involves inadequate ideas or knowledge of the first kind. And since these are the only instances of inadequate ideas he is able to point to, the conclusion seems to be that no instance of such ideas actually occurs in, nor for that matter, is allowed to enter into the system of the *Ethics*. In other words, Spinoza in the *Ethics* is at most employing knowledge of reason and intuition only. This appears to be Spinoza's own view as well when he says that true ideas only are allowed to occur in philosophical speculation.[24]

II

1. Knowledge by reason consists in having and forming "common notions and adequate ideas of the properties of things."[25] As common notions Spinoza mentions the notions of the attribute of extension and of motion and rest.[26] Properties are that which is common to the human body and certain external bodies by which the human body "is used to be affected."[27] Ideas of such properties are hence also common, though in a restricted sense, and are in fact sometimes

22. *E.*, V, iv, C., S. Strictly speaking, Spinoza is here talking about emotions which agree with "the laws of human reason" and an emotion which is "united to true thoughts." However, that "imagination" here may be substituted for "emotion" is clear from *E.*, III, Aff., Gen. Def. Cf. also *E.*, IV, ix, Dem. Concerning the distinction between an emotion and an idea (e.g. of imagination) cf. *E.*, IV, viii, Dem.; *E.*, V, iii, Dem.

23. Parkinson distinguishes also between "two types of imagination, corresponding to (though not exactly the same as) Kant's distinction between the transcendental imagination which is concerned with the *a priori* or necessary, and the empirical imagination whose laws are discovered inductively" (pp. 80–81). I don't feel at all certain as to the validity of drawing this distinction within Spinoza's view on imagination. I would rather prefer to classify his use of imagination in all cases as empirical. However, there is no need to decide this question for the point I want to make. Parkinson is clearly discussing the supporting role of the empirical type of imagination (in his sense of "empirical").

24. Cf. e.g. *Ep.*, 56.

25. Cf. *E.*, II, xl, S. 2.

26. Cf. *E.*, II, xxxviii, C.; *E.*, II, Lem. 2.

27. *E.*, II, xxxix.

so called by Spinoza himself.[28] To adequate ideas of reason belongs, furthermore, "what we may deduce" from the ideas of the common properties.[29] Hence reason is or involves deductive knowledge. A further characteristic of ideas of reason is to be found in *E.*, II, xl, S. 2 and *E.*, V, xxxvi, S.: they are universal.

What does this mean? Parkinson suggests as instances of common properties the basic truths and concepts of science such as physiology.[30] To knowledge by reason belongs also knowledge derived from such basic truths and concepts. The universal character of this kind of knowledge may be explained, according to Parkinson, by saying that "the science of physics, for example, is concerned with a falling body simply as a falling body, and not as *this* falling body." And the science of physiology is universal in the sense that it "is concerned with a human heart simply as a human heart, and not as the heart of this particular person."[31]

This account may very well be true. However, the question at present is whether or to what extent Spinoza's views on the second kind of knowledge apply to his own procedure in the *Ethics*. The question is, in other words, whether or to what extent the *Ethics* itself is an expression, in verbal form, of the second kind of knowledge.

Parkinson feels tempted to suppose, according to his interpretation of Spinoza's view on reason, that with a few exceptions "the whole of the *Ethics* is an expression in verbal form of the knowledge of the second kind."[32] The exceptions are instances of imagination and of intuition. According to the above argument against the occurrence of the first kind of knowledge in the *Ethics,* the exceptions should be even fewer.

There are good arguments for this position. It is clear that the *Ethics* has throughout a kind of deductive form. The propositions are derived from basic definitions, axioms and postulates. This applies to Spinoza's treatment of ontology in Part I, as well as to his short treatment of bodies after *E.*, II, xiii, and to what is his main concern in the *Ethics:* the explanation of the human mind. The deductive procedure is perhaps most obvious in the theory of emotions: desire (*cupiditas, conatus*), pleasure (*laetitia*) and pain (*tristitia*) are the

28. Cf. e.g. *E.*, II, xl, S. 1.
29. Cf. e.g. *E.*, V, xii, Dem.
30. Parkinson, *op. cit.,* p. 95.
31. *Loc. cit.*
32. *Loc. cit.*

three basic emotions, from which all others are derived. Most propositions of the *Ethics* clearly also fulfil the requirement of universality:
they are, for instance, about finite entities, about the mind and body
and about desire, pleasure and pain, etc. *in general.*

The position, however, is not as straightforward as this account
may suggest. In fact it is complicated by at least three factors: (i)
by Spinoza's view on language, (ii) by his account of the second
kind of knowledge itself, and (iii) by his account of the third kind
of knowledge. Parkinson discusses (i) fairly extensively in his reply
to Savan: he seems to encounter little or no difficulty concerning (ii),
and leaves (iii), that is, possible consequences of occurrences of the
third kind of knowledge for occurrences of the second kind, entirely
out of consideration. I shall comment on (i) and (ii) in turn, and
then say a few things about (iii) in connection with a discussion
of the role played by the third kind of knowledge in the *Ethics*.

2. The main difficulty in Spinoza's theory of language with respect
to the present problem arises from his view on the so-called transcendental terms (such as "being," "thing," "something") and on universal or general terms and notions (such as "man," "dog," "horse").
According to Spinoza these terms and notions belong to imagination
or the first kind of knowledge and are consequently inadequate for
the expression of true knowledge. Savan then makes the valid observation that these terms and notions do, nevertheless, frequently occur
in the *Ethics,* the effect in his view being that the *Ethics* abounds
in contradictions. This, then, becomes a major premiss in his conclusions that language, as viewed by Spinoza, cannot be, nor can have
been intended by Spinoza to be, a direct or literal exposition of philosophical truth.

Parkinson attempts to solve the problem by arguing for the view
that even if Spinoza thought some uses of the objectionable terms
and notions to be inadequate, it does not follow from this that he
thought all uses of these terms and notions objectionable. Most of
Spinoza's own statements on transcendental and universal terms may
in fact be so interpreted as to accord with reason. God and also any
finite thing as a part of God, Parkinson says, may very well, according
to Spinoza, be called a thing. In this case "thing," therefore, stands
for a common notion. And similarly, "to conceive," or rather "conceiving," as a universal or general term may be predicated both of
God and of a finite mode of thought. Hence "the concept of conceiving is . . . a common notion, and words like 'conceiving' and 'con-

ceive' are justified, to the extent that they stand for this common notion."[33]

Parkinson's conclusion with respect to the use of transcendental terms and terms for universal notions, and also with respect to the use of language in general, is, I think, true: language may adequately express true knowledge. To show this is his chief concern in refuting Savan's view. It is interesting, however, to notice another significant conclusion which is clearly contained in his way of arguing. This is the conclusion that the question of whether or not a certain term may adequately express a true idea does not depend on the term itself, but on the idea (or knowledge) to be expressed by the term. Thus the first step in his argument is throughout to point to some adequate idea, particularly common notions, and he then goes on to say, for instance, that words like "thing" and "conceiving" are justified *in so far as* (*or to the extent that*) they stand for such notions. He knows well, in other words, that terms such as "thing" and "conceiving" may stand for or express intuitive knowledge, for instance when used to denote the "essence of things."[34] In Parkinson's account of the supporting role of experience or imagination, the terms "thing" and "conceiving," as actually used in the *Ethics,* may occasionally stand for inadequate ideas ("thing") involving an inadequate or partial thinking activity ("conceiving").[35] (Since "conceiving" is used in the *Ethics* to cover the activity of thinking in general, including imagining or imagination, it is conceivable, in Parkinson's view that Spinoza occasionally uses "conceiving" to signify a way of thinking in which he only partially or inadequately knows what he is saying.)

With respect to this dependence-relation between language and knowledge, Parkinson's view (indirectly expressed) is in agreement with that of Savan.[36] This view I take to represent Spinoza's main contribution to a theory of language. The theory concerns the non-linguistic, epistemological conditions both for expressing true (and for that matter, also false) knowledge adequately in language, and for language being able to express and thus communicate true (and false) knowledge adequately to some hearer or reader. His thesis, generally formulated, would run something like this: Whether or not language may adequately express knowledge by imagination,

33. *Ibid.,* pp. 83–84.
34. Cf. *E.,* II, xl, S. 2 and Sect. III below.
35. Cf. *E.,* III, Def. 1 and III, Def. 2.
36. Cf. Sect. I above.

reason, and intuition depends not only on language, i.e. the right application of words,[37] but also on the kind of knowledge or way of knowing things which one is exercising or is able to exercise.

The thesis has a number of implications, particularly in the field of communication. To work them out in any detail is a major task in itself and one which exceeds the scope of this essay. I shall therefore merely indicate some of those which are important for the present communication problem: to decide from a reading of the *Ethics* which kinds of knowledge are expressed in the language of the *Ethics* itself.

First, the thesis makes it conceivable that one and the same term or formula may be used to express each of the different kinds of knowledge. Thus the term "God" as used in the *Ethics* may apparently stand for an adequate idea of both the second and third kinds,[38] and also for some inadequate idea when used by people labouring under a misconception of God.[39] Secondly, it is conceivable that a certain term or formula used to express a certain kind of knowledge may be taken by some reader or hearer to express a different kind of knowledge, depending upon the kind of knowledge or way of knowing things he is able to exercise in connection with the term or formula in question. Thus the term "God" or "substance," when used by Spinoza to stand for an idea of intuition, may be taken to stand for an idea of reason or of imagination.

Thirdly, it is conceivable—and this is a concession to the significance of the right application of language—that certain terms or formulae, or set of terms or formulae, are more suitable for expressing one kind of knowledge than for expressing another. The term "God" again provides an example, likewise expressions for characterizations of God, such as "God is the cause of himself." However, the third implication is presumably subject to qualification, particularly in terms of the second implication above. For even if certain terms or formulae, or set of such, are more suitable for expressing one kind of knowledge than for expressing another, one has still somehow to understand these terms or formulae, that is, the idea expressed by them, in order to see that this is so. Since every idea, on Spinoza's account, is of necessity causally connected with other ideas, this means that the decision

37. Cf. *E.*, II, xlvii, S.
38. Cf. Sect. III below.
39. Cf. e.g. *E.*, I, xv, S.

concerning the third implication (and hence also the second implication) requires consideration of context.

These implications pose an important problem for our discussion: Does the recognition of the occurrence of a certain kind of knowledge or way of knowing things as expressed in the language of the *Ethics* require that one actually be in possession of that kind of knowledge oneself? This question is difficult to answer. If one were to classify all ideas in the *Ethics,* the answer would presumably have to be yes, particularly due to the first and second implication above. This, however, is evidently tantamount to saying that one would have to share Spinoza's total world view. And a modern interpreter, or at any rate most of them, would obviously find themselves in a difficult position.

The task at present, however, is the more general and therefore more modest one of deciding upon the kind or kinds of knowledge employed by Spinoza in the *Ethics.* And this task, on account of the third implication in particular, can presumably be undertaken without committing oneself (at least not entirely) to the ideas taken into account. The fact, however, that the third implication is subject to qualification in terms of the second implication above, inevitably yields for the analysis an element of uncertainty.

3. In accounting for knowledge by reason Spinoza, so far as I can see, mentions as objects of this kind of knowledge the attribute and (finite and infinite) modes of extension only. It is of these objects that reason is said to form "notions which are called common and which are the fundamental principles of our ratiocination."[40] Applied to the *Ethics* this account of reason encounters two difficulties. The first arises from the fact that Spinoza's chief (or rather sole) purpose in the *Ethics* is to explain the human mind, and not objects of extension,[41] and the second arises in view of the principles, that is, the definitions and axioms, actually forming the basis of his own "reasoning" in the *Ethics.* It is in no way self-evident that these principles belong to the second kind of knowledge. I shall remark on the two difficulties in turn.

The discrepancy between the account of the objects of reason and the subject actually dealt with in the *Ethics* could in general be taken to suggest that Spinoza does not, at least not explicitly, have his own propositions of the *Ethics* in mind when dealing with knowledge by

40. *E.,* II, xl, S. 1.
41. Cf. e.g. *E.,* III, iii, S.

reason. He is rather thinking of sciences such as physiology and physics (as suggested by Parkinson), which, presumably, are to be developed on the basis of his account of knowledge by reason and presumably also within the frame of his short treatment of bodies inserted after *E.*, II, xiii. However, even if this is so, it does not follow that his account of reason is not applicable to the *Ethics* itself, that is, to the analysis of the human mind. There is in fact ample evidence that it is, so ample indeed that Parkinson apparently finds it superfluous to adduce it. He merely assumes "conceiving" to be a possible common notion, characteristic of knowledge by reason. In the context of the present discussion the evidence may nonetheless be worth considering, even if it should merely confirm Parkinson's procedure.

4. The problem may in general be conceived as one of translating ideas of extended or physical objects into ideas of the mind. I shall first consider the necessity of such a translation in Spinoza's theory of the mind, and then secondly its possibility.

The necessary character of the translation is stated in *E.*, II, xix, xxiii, and xxvi. It follows from these propositions that the mind can have no knowledge of itself unless it perceives (conceives, forms ideas of) modes of extension, more precisely, the modification of its body as affected by external bodies. I shall leave aside the problem of what "modification" or "affection" means here. The important thing at present is the view that the mind's knowledge of modes of extension is a necessary condition for a theory of the mind. It would seem then that Spinoza, in dealing with knowledge by reason in *E.*, II, xl, S. 2, according to himself at any rate, is doing the right thing.

As to the possibility of the translation there seems to be but one answer: Every idea of a physical object is translated already into the mind's knowledge of itself. The meaning of this somewhat peculiar saying may perhaps be brought out in the following way. An idea of a physical object (i.e. a modification of the body by some other body or bodies) is primarily an idea of *the object*. But it is evidently also an *idea* of the object. One cannot have the one without the other. Or, an object can only be an object to us in so far as it modifies or affects us, that is, in so far as we have conceived or formed an idea of it. In still other words, we have no access to an object except by having formed an idea of it.[42] However, that an idea of an object

42. Cf. *E.*, II, xxvi.

is an *idea* of the object is not brought out in the idea of *the object*. A higher-order reflection is called for in the sense that one has to form an idea of *the idea* of the physical object. In this way the mind comes to know itself explicitly, that is, its ideas of objects, a self-knowledge which is present in an implicit manner in the idea of an object.[43]

If we ask how the mind's self-knowledge or its higher-order reflection is brought about, Spinoza has little to say. To him (as, incidentally, to many other philosophers) it is a given capacity of the mind, a capacity which notably is always exercised in one way or another. That is to say, in having an idea of some physical object, the mind also has an idea of this idea and thus of itself.[44] However, problems connected with the transformation of the mind's knowledge of physical objects into its self-knowledge need not detain us here. What matters is *that* knowledge of physical objects necessarily is or involves the mind's knowledge of itself, and that this is made possible in virtue of two facts, (1) that an idea of an *object* is an *idea* of an object, and (2) that this is brought out by the given capacity of the mind to reflect upon its knowledge of physical objects, that is, to form an idea of its ideas of such objects.

The Self to be known by the mind, then, consists of ideas of modes of extension (i.e. of modification of the body by some other mode of extension).[45] They may be termed first-order ideas. And knowledge of this Self consists in ideas of such ideas. They are second-order ideas. This state of affairs explains and justifies a significant trend of Spinoza's theory of man. Although primarily (or solely) meant to be a theory of the human mind, Spinoza, as mentioned above, finds it necessary to give at least a brief account of modes of extension in general and of the human body in particular. Of equal significance is the fact that most propositions in the *Ethics* are about, or contain a reference to, the human body and thereby indirectly (on account of *E., II, xix*) to modes of extension in general. In other words, most propositions in the *Ethics* are, or contain, first-order ideas. On the other hand, most propositions are also about the human mind, that is, they consist of second-order ideas. Thus in Spinoza's theory of the human mind ideas of the two orders frequently occur

43. For a further discussion of this problem cf. G. Fløistad, *The Problem of Understanding in Spinoza's Ethics,* Doctoral dissertation (mimeo), University of London, 1967, to be published.

44. Cf. e.g. *E., II, xvii, S.*

45. Cf. *E., II, xiii* and *II, xv.*

side by side. Or, more precisely, in arguing his case Spinoza frequently switches from ideas of the first order to those of the second, and vice versa. Spinoza's view of the genesis of the mind's self-knowledge, and hence also of the theory of the mind, may be taken to explain the significance of, and to justify, this procedure.

If we asked for further explanation of, and justification for, this procedure, Spinoza would undoubtedly refer us to what may be called the thesis of identity of thought and extension. This thesis may in fact be identified as one of the major premisses for the proposition concerning the genesis of the mind's knowledge of itself.[46] The thesis says, as is well known, that thought and extension are one and the same thing, but expressed in two manners. The thesis applies to the attributes as well as to the modes: the attributes of thought and extension (or thinking and extended substance) "are one and the same substance which is now comprehended through this and now through that attribute." And similarly, "a mode of extension and the idea of that mode are one and the same thing but expressed in two manners."[47] Since the human mind consists of ideas of which the body, or its modifications by other modes of extension, are the objects, the same holds good for the mind and body.[48] Spinoza here apparently has only finite modes in mind, but he is certainly committed to holding the same view as to the infinite modes.

In short, we may say that whatever goes for the attribute and modes of extension goes, respectively, for the attribute and modes of thought. It is this thesis that forms, if not a sufficient, at least a necessary condition for the possibility of transforming knowledge of the body and physical objects in general into knowledge of the mind. The thesis may now assist us in deciding the role played by the second kind of knowledge in the *Ethics*.

5. The common notions said to be granted common to all men (i.e. the notion of the attribute of extension and of motion and rest)[49] present no problem. On account of the identity thesis they are readily translated into the corresponding common notions of thought, the notion of the attribute of thought, and the notion of absolutely infinite understanding. Both pairs of notions may perfectly well be said to

46. *E.,* II, xxiii.
47. Cf. *E.,* II, vii, S.
48. Cf. *E.,* II, xxi, S.
49. Cf. *E.,* II, xxxviii, C.

belong to the fundamental principles of our ratiocination[50] or, more precisely, to be *the* basis of reason.[51] The former pair, being first-order notions, are the basis, we shall have to say, of our reasoning about modes of extension, whereas the latter, being second-order notions, are the basis of our reasoning in matters of thought, e.g. about the mind and its ideas.

In what sense, then, can these notions possibly be said to be the basis for the propositions of the *Ethics* and thus help to decide the kind of knowledge expressed in these propositions? In trying to provide an answer to this question I shall follow Spinoza's own procedure and focus on the role played by the attributes, leaving the infinite modes out of consideration.

The *Ethics* itself allows of various interpretations. A minimum interpretation, as one may call it, is suggested in *E.,* II, xlv: Every idea of every body or individual thing actually existing involves the eternal and infinite essence of God, that is, the conception of the attribute of extension.[52] In other words, whenever Spinoza is presenting ideas of modes of extension, these ideas involve and express[53] the conception of the attribute of extension. The same ideas, however, being finite modes of thought, necessarily involve and express the conception of the attribute of thought. This is, or rather may be, made explicit in second-order ideas (which of course themselves involve and express the attribute of thought).

I shall not enter into a discussion here of difficulties connected with a first-order idea being an expression of the attributes of extension and thought alike, nor of those connected with the possibility of a second-order idea being an expression of the attribute of thought only.[54] The question at present is whether the interpretation of common notions as the basis of reason in terms of involvement or expression may help to decide our initial problem. The answer, I think, must be no. One cannot on this interpretation decide whether propositions about modes of extension, or about ideas of such modes, belong to the second kind of knowledge. For one thing, one cannot, for instance, on the basis of Spinoza's use of the term "body" or "idea" or "mind" in certain propositions, decide whether these propositions

50. *E.,* II, xl, S. 1.
51. Cf. *E.,* II, xliv, C. 2, Dem.
52. Cf. *E.,* II, xlv, Dem.
53. Cf. *E.,* I, xxv, C.
54. Cf. *E.,* II, xvii, S.

involve and express and are thus based on the notion of the attribute of extension and thought as common notions characteristic of reason. The use of certain *terms* is here in principle insufficient. It is perfectly conceivable that propositions concerning modes of extension and thought express knowledge of the third kind.[55] Presumably one is entitled at most to say that an (implicit or explicit) use of the *distinction* between modes of extension and thought (e.g. between the mind and body or between an idea and its object) is a necessary condition for a proposition expressing knowledge of reason. This is suggested by the account of knowledge of reason itself, and also, though indirectly, in Spinoza's account of intuitive knowledge.[56]

Other interpretations of the common notions as the basis of reason appear to be more promising. In the statement that "the bases of reason are the notions which explain these things which are common to all . . . ,"[57] "explain" may be taken to refer to propositions concerning the attributes. Thus an attribute is said, for instance, to be "that which the intellect perceives as constituting the essence of a substance"[58] and (therefore) to be in itself conceived through itself, to be eternal and exist of necessity, and to be the cause of the modes, i.e. its modifications.[59]

Does this mean that all propositions in the *Ethics* which are deduced from, or proved by, these propositions explaining common notions belong to the second kind of knowledge? If there were propositions exclusively proved by such propositions explaining the common notions it would be tempting to answer in the affirmative. The trouble is that Spinoza's actual procedure in the *Ethics* makes it extremely difficult to decide whether there are any such propositions. A closer examination shows in fact that propositions concerning God or Substance somehow enter into the premisses of almost every proposition, and certainly into the premisses of those propositions explaining the common notions themselves. And although God, or Substance, may in a sense be the object of reason (namely in so far as he is conceived in terms of an attribute), he is no doubt, on Spinoza's account, primarily the object of intuition.[60]

55. Cf. Sect. II, 2 above.
56. Cf. Sect. III below.
57. *E.*, II, xliv, C. 2, Dem.
58. *E.*, I, Def. 4.
59. Cf. *E.*, I, vii, x, xi, and xvi.
60. Cf. Sect. III below.

This is of course not to say that knowledge by reason is not employed by Spinoza in the *Ethics*. It merely suggests (i) that it is difficult to decide whether a proposition belongs to knowledge by reason by considering the common notions forming the basis of this kind of knowledge, and (ii) that possible occurrences of knowledge by reason in the end depend on knowledge by intuition.

6. In order to decide whether the "bulk of the propositions" in the *Ethics* belong to the second kind of knowledge, another, more adequate, criterion is called for. The only one offered by Spinoza, as mentioned earlier, is found in *E.,* II, xxxix, Dem. in the idea of properties common to "the human body and certain external bodies by which the human body is used to be affected."[61] This idea is apparently not basic to reason in the same sense as, say, the notion of the attributes; it belongs, however, together with the basic common notions, to the fundamental principles of our ratiocination. It is this criterion or idea of common properties that underlies Parkinson's conclusion concerning the occurrence of the second kind of knowledge in the *Ethics*.

There is much to be discussed here. First of all there is the problem of translating (first-order) ideas of common properties into the corresponding (second-order) ideas of common ideas or notions, and then, secondly, the problem of applying this part of Spinoza's account of the second kind of knowledge to his own procedure in the *Ethics*. The latter problem is a twofold one, due to the distinction between mind and body. However, any satisfactory treatment of these problems would take us too far for present purposes. I shall have to confine myself instead to pointing out briefly certain difficulties connected with the translation and application of the account of reason in question, in particular certain difficulties which indicate the need to take account of intuitive knowledge.

7. The solution of the translation problem is in principle suggested in 4 above. Spinoza in fact performs the translation himself when he calls ideas of common properties "common."[62] We should note, of course, that in the present case we are concerned with ideas of properties[63] common to a (more or less) limited range of individuals, and that a first-order idea of such a common property is to be regarded as an expression of this common property as well as of the

61. Cf. Sect. II, 1, above.
62. Cf. *E.,* II, xl, S. 1.
63. Cf. *E.,* II, xxxix, C.

attribute of extension (being common to *all* modes of extension), and (indirectly) also of the attribute of thought (being common to all ideas or modes of thought).

The more immediately relevant problems arise, however, when we attempt to apply the idea of common properties, and its translation into common notions, to the propositions of the *Ethics*. An example may be helpful, and the most natural choice is *E.,* II, xxxix itself, where Spinoza presents his view on common notions: "That which is common to and a property of the human body, and certain external bodies by which the human body is used to be affected, and which is equally in the part and whole of these, has an adequate idea in the mind."

To Parkinson this proposition, presumably, is a common notion and belongs as such to knowledge by reason. In one sense the proposition undoubtedly is or represents a common notion: it explains what commonly has an adequate idea in the mind. Our question, however, is whether the proposition is common in the sense which it itself prescribes. In other words, can *E.,* II, xxxix be interpreted as concerning itself?

The case may presumably be argued in various ways. One way is this. The proposition clearly opens with a first-order idea ("That which is common to . . ."), and it says about the object of this idea that the idea of it is adequate. Thus the proposition ends up with saying something about an idea, that is, it ends up by itself being a second-order idea. It is not an idea of an idea of a *certain* common property. It is rather a second-order idea of *the adequacy* of such ideas and their objects *in general*. In other words, *E.,* II, xxxix is a generalization concerning the adequate character of certain notions. And the concept of being such a generalization is certainly different from the concept of being common, applying to the object of the generalizing propositions. It would seem, then, that *E.,* II, xxxix is not, at least not immediately, applicable to itself.

Despite this, *E.,* II, xxxix may still in a sense be regarded as a common proposition or notion. Its common character concerns the adequacy of a certain type of ideas. The point is merely that this common character is not accounted for in *E.,* II, xxxix itself. And it is even hard to see how it can be accounted for in a way similar to the account given of a common notion in *E.,* II, xxxix. The concept of adequacy of ideas seems, for instance, to have no reference to modes of extension as have ordinary common notions. Adequacy of ideas seems to be a purely mental phenomenon, which cannot be arrived at by any translation of common properties of modes of extension into common notions. The theory of knowledge of reason presented in *E.,* II, xxxix will therefore have to be supplemented if this theory is itself to belong to knowledge by reason. The way to supplement the theory is already suggested in the above argument. One has merely to postulate the capacity of the mind to reflect upon and form common notions of its ideas of common properties of things. To Spinoza such a postulate appears to be a matter of course.[64] And it is this capacity which is tacitly exercised in *E.,* II, xxxix as well as in most other propositions of the *Ethics,* including those, for instance, in which "conceiving" explicitly occurs as a common notion.

In view of this the above interpretation of *E.,* II, xxiii concerning the genesis of the mind's self-knowledge, if it does not break down, at least will have to be modified. The mind may perfectly well have no knowledge of itself save in so far as it perceives the ideas of the modifications of the body. But this self-knowledge, we shall have to say, is not restricted to second order ideas merely corresponding to particular first order ideas. It also comprises second order ideas whose objects are first order ideas in general. If this is correct the mind seems to occupy a position superior to that of the body within the system of the *Ethics.* And the thesis of identity of the mind and body consequently does not hold good in general.

8. Other propositions in the *Ethics* present difficulties of a different kind. Take for instance *E.,* II, xli: "Knowledge of the first kind is the only cause of falsity; knowledge of the second and third kind is necessarily true."

This proposition, in which Spinoza offers a general characterization of the three kinds of knowledge, may also perfectly well be conceived of as a (complex) common notion. It states, for instance, that it is a common character of the first kind of knowledge to be the only cause of falsity. Again it is hard to see how this common (or general) character is taken care of in the account of reason in *E.,* II, xxxix. This, however, is not our present concern. Granted that the proposition belongs to knowledge by reason, we are faced with the problem of how an idea of reason can have all three kinds of knowledge as its objects.

That we may have a common and adequate idea of the concept of

64. Cf. e.g. *E.,* II, xxi, S.; *TdIE,* G. II, p. 14 f.

the first kind of knowledge is perhaps not so peculiar. The concept of the first kind of knowledge being false is itself an adequate idea, at least of the second kind. This follows from the statement that "knowledge of the second and third kinds and not of the first kind teaches us to distinguish the true from the false."[65] In other words, in *E.*, II, xli the reasoning activity of the mind is, as far as the first kind of knowledge is concerned, simply reflecting upon an idea produced by itself. The occurrence of the concept of the second kind of knowledge is even less peculiar. Here reason is simply reflecting upon, or forming, an idea of itself in general (the idea namely that the common notions produced by it are necessarily true).

What is not a matter of course, to the reader at least, is how the concept of the third kind of knowledge may occur as an object of reason. This means that reason in *E.*, II, xli is said to reflect upon intuition, not upon any particular intuitive idea, but upon intuitive ideas or the intuitive way of knowing things in general. And why is this a difficulty? Above all because of the thesis of identity between an idea and its object, here applied to the relation between first and second order ideas.[66] The object is the idea of intuitive knowledge being true. If *E.*, II, xli is regarded as an idea of reason, this means, in view of the identity thesis, that an idea of (i.e. about) intuitive knowledge may be translated into, and is the same as, an idea of reason. In the case of the concepts of the first and the second kind of knowledge occurring in *E.*, II, xli this difficulty does not arise. The concepts of both kinds of knowledge belong to, or may belong to, knowledge of reason and are consequently translatable into a higher order idea of reason. In view of the occurrence of the concept of intuitive knowledge, the possibility of such a translation, advocated by the identity-thesis, seems to break down.

To this problem there seem to be two possible solutions. It is first of all tempting to apply the distinction between "use" and "mention" to *E.*, II, xli and to say that in this proposition Spinoza is not actually using but merely mentioning the third kind of knowledge. He is saying something *about* it. And this is surely possible without exercising intuition. In this case the difficulty just mentioned appears to be wholly fictitious. The idea about the third kind of knowledge in *E.*, II, xli is an idea *of* a property common to all intuitive ideas and hence (possibly) an idea of reason.

65. *E.*, II, xlii.
66. Cf. *E.*, II, xxi, S.

However, I do not feel at all sure as to whether the use-mention distinction *necessarily* applies to *E.,* II, xli (or, for that matter, to a number of similar propositions) as *used* by Spinoza. Is it in principle impossible for an idea about a certain kind of knowledge to belong to that kind of knowledge itself? It is certainly possible in the case where the object of the idea is the concept of the first and the second kind of knowledge. And why should not an idea about intuition itself be or at least involve an intuitive idea?

One reason for holding this view I find in the fact that Spinoza could not possibly have used the concept of the third kind of knowledge in *E.,* II, xli unless he had previously exercised the intuitive way of knowing things. It may even be said that the concept of the second kind of knowledge in the context of the *Ethics* presupposes the concept of the third kind. The second kind of knowledge is second in the *Ethics* not only in relation to the first kind but also to the third. And in view of the great importance attached to intuitive knowledge, particularly in Part V of the *Ethics,* it is hard to see how Spinoza (presumably unlike his readers or hearers), while using the concept of intuition could wholly have dispensed with that kind of knowledge itself.

Granted, then, in view of these in no way conclusive reasons, that the idea about intuitive knowledge as used in *E.,* II, xli may itself possibly be, or involve, an intuitive idea, the difficulty we are concerned with is a genuine one. And in view of the identity thesis concerning an idea and its object, there appears to be only one way of solving the problem: we shall have to question the assumption that *E.,* II, xli (and similar propositions) is an expression of the second kind of knowledge only. For it may, at least in part, be an expression of intuitive knowledge.

It is time to consider, briefly, the third kind of knowledge and its relation to the second kind.

III

1. Intuitive knowledge is said to proceed "from an adequate idea of the formal essence of certain attributes of God to the adequate knowledge of the essence of things."[67] I shall first explain some aspects of this account of intuition and then try to show its relevance to our problem.

67. *E.,* II, xl, S. 2.

We may begin by considering the meaning of "proceeds." Now a most reasonable interpretation seems to be in terms of a process of increasing knowledge. That is to say, "proceeds" signifies that the mind comes to know more and more by intuition. Intuitive knowledge of the essence of things is thus more advanced than intuitive knowledge of the formal essence of certain attributes of God. How, then, is this possible? How can knowledge of the essence of finite modes rank higher than knowledge of the attributes? A natural answer to this question is suggested by asking: What is there to be known over and above the formal essence of the attributes, that is, the essence of each attribute considered separately (this is what "formal" means)? The natural answer is: the attributes in their relation to one another, more precisely, in their unity. And knowledge of the unity of the attribute in God is undoubtedly a far more genuine knowledge of God than knowledge of him in terms of one of the attributes alone.

That knowledge of the essence of things is knowledge of God is clear from a number of propositions in Part V.[68] That this knowledge is of God as a unity of thought and extension (of mind and body, of an idea and its object) is not explicitly stated in these propositions themselves. Here Spinoza makes rather frequent use of the mind–body distinction. This may be interpreted in two ways. He is either, for the most part, discussing the initial stages of intuitive knowledge only, or, in addition to this, he is also accounting, in an indirect manner, for the more advanced "unity-directed" stages of intuitive knowledge. "Indirect" here refers to the fact that the unity of thought and extension, on Spinoza's account, is a phenomenon of thought. This follows, e.g., from the statement that a (second-order) idea of the mind (of its first-order ideas) is united to the mind in the same manner as the mind (or its first-order ideas) is united to the body (or the extended or physical objects of the first-order ideas). It follows that whenever Spinoza uses the concept of the mind (or an idea) in Part V (and for that matter in all previous parts) he *may have* the unity of thought and extension "in mind."

The above interpretation of "proceeds" in terms of a process of knowing in which the mind finally comes to know ("intuit") the unity of thought and extension, may thus still hold good. Apart from that, however, a similar interpretation of the account of intuitive

68. E.g. *E.*, V, xxiv; *E.*, V, xxv, Dem.

knowledge in *E.*, II, xl, S. 2 is called for if this account is to cover a number of basic statements in the *Ethics*. What I have in mind are, first of all, statements concerning God in Part I, such as that he "is one alone"[69] and that he is "a being absolutely infinite, that is, a substance consisting of infinite attributes . . ."[70] The point is that statements such as these are an expression of a kind of knowledge that clearly goes beyond any knowledge of attributes, be it of the second or the third kind.[71]

The presumed intuitive knowledge expressed in such statements may, I think, be detected in one way or another in a large number of cases. Most definitions, as well as some of the axioms and quite a few propositions of Part I, in fact make explicit use of the concept of God as being something, or someone over and above an attribute and its modifications. This applies to the very definition of an attribute itself.[72] The implicit occurrences are even more frequent. In using expressions such as "being the cause of itself,"[73] "being in itself" and "being conceived through itself"[74] Spinoza no doubt has God as an absolutely infinite being primarily in mind (and not the attributes to which the expressions also apply). As premisses of propositions, the same "highest level" notion of God occurs throughout the *Ethics*—as suggested above, because in the proof of most propositions Spinoza makes use of premisses which in the end go back to definitions, axioms and propositions explaining this notion of God. It is presumably for this reason that nothing, and in the present context that means no proposition of the *Ethics,* can exist or be conceived without God.[75]

2. This yields a unique position to the intuitive knowledge in the *Ethics*. And we may ask whether this position invalidates the view that most propositions in the *Ethics* belong to knowledge by reason. Not necessarily, but it certainly calls for a qualification of this view, particularly in terms of an account of the relation between the second and third kinds of knowledge. I shall here suggest but one step in direction of such a qualification.

69. *E.*, I, xiv, Dem., C.
70. *E.*, I, vi.
71. The problem is discussed in detail in Fløistad, *op. cit.*
72. *E.*, I, Def. 4.
73. *E.*, I, Def. 1.
74. *E.*, I, Def. 3; *E.*, I, Ax. 1; *E.*, I, Ax. 2.
75. Cf. *E.*, I, xv.

Consider the structure of the *Ethics*. In Part I it offers an account of God and of what follows "from his essence." This account, apparently, has no purpose in itself. It merely provides a basis for Spinoza's main concern in the *Ethics,* to explain the human mind. The explanation is centred around the idea of the liberation of the mind towards its "consummate blessedness."[76] This is a matter of knowledge, that is, of the way of knowing or understanding things. The more the mind is able to know things by the second and third kinds of knowledge, the more liberated it becomes, and the more lasting is the satisfaction it enjoys.[77] Intuitive knowledge is here far more advanced and powerful than the second kind.[78] From the third kind of knowledge "the greatest possible mental satisfaction arises."[79]

In the context of this idea of liberation Spinoza now says that "the endeavour or desire of knowing things according to the third class of knowledge [can] arise from . . . the second class of knowledge."[80] In other words, the thinking activity characteristic of intuition may arise from the thinking activity involved in ideas of reason. Or, ideas of reason may give rise to ideas of intuition.

To explain exactly how this transition actually takes place is a difficult task. But the account given in *E.,* II, xl, S. 2 of reason and intuition makes it perfectly conceivable. As it appears from this account, both reason and intuition (in its initial stage) have as their object the attribute of extension. The difference is that to reason the attribute is a common notion, whereas intuition is able to form an idea of its formal essence. The transition may hence be conceived of as a transition from a common notion of the attribute of extension to a notion of the formal essence of the same attribute. Due to their "common" object, the two notions, the one being the "end" of reason, the other the beginning of intuition, are obviously closely related.

However, the point I want to make at present does not so much concern the possible and exact character of the transition as the mere saying itself that ideas of intuition may arise or follow from ideas of reason. To say this obviously presupposes the concept of intuition. It presupposes that one knows what intuition is about. The

76. Cf. *E.,* II, Pref.
77. Cf. e.g. *E.,* V, xx, S.
78. Cf. *E.,* V, xxxvi, S.
79. *E.,* V, xxvii.
80. Cf. *E.,* V, xxviii.

position of the author of *E.,* V, xxviii concerning the transition is hence different from the position of the mind talked about. The latter is presumably able to exercise reason only, and the proposition says about him that he, on the basis of this ability, may come to know things intuitively.

If we ask for the source of this knowledge expressed in *E.,* V, xxviii, we shall, I think, have to go back to the procedure in Part I to find an answer. Here Spinoza appears to go exactly the opposite way to that prescribed to the mind in *E.,* V, xxviii (and in other propositions in Part V). He begins with an intuitive knowledge of God as an absolutely infinite being and opens the way to the lower-level knowledge by intuition, and also to knowledge by reason by defining an attribute and its modes. The relation to God as an absolutely infinite being is all along taken care of, particularly in the definition of an attribute. Knowledge by reason expressed in later propositions thus appears to be derived from knowledge by intuition. For this reason, presumably, Spinoza is able to say in Part V that knowledge by reason may give rise to the intuitive way of knowing things.

Where does this take us? Not very far, I am afraid. The account merely suggests that the highest-level knowledge of intuition is the basic knowledge expressed in the *Ethics,* and that this knowledge, to Spinoza at any rate, is somehow present and thus expressed in every proposition of the *Ethics,* including those classified as knowledge by reason. How this is possible would require an extensive discussion of the relation between the third and the second kind of knowledge. The clue to a proper understanding of this relation is not, I think, to be found primarily in the theory of knowledge summarized in *E.,* II, xl, S. 2, nor in the account of the liberation of the mind in Part V, but in Spinoza's own deductive procedure in Part I.

At present we may rest content by stressing once more the unique position of intuitive knowledge in the *Ethics.* Its significance is perhaps best brought out by saying that the ability to exercise intuition is a necessary condition for framing the ontology as well as the epistemology, psychology and moral and social philosophy characteristic of the *Ethics.* In other words, without possessing the intuitive way of knowing things, Spinoza could not possibly have written the *Ethics.*

PART TWO
Metaphysics

Substance and Its Modes

H. F. HALLETT

"CAUSE OF ITSELF"

I. Causation as Action

The conception of causation is fundamental in the philosophy of Spinoza; but it is causation conceived as action, and not as the mere regular sequence of inactive events. For by "action" here is meant not change of motion or rest, of content or quality, among spatio-temporal objects, nor of mode or content among mental ideas; on the contrary, mere uniform temporal change is essentially the ideal limit of the privation of action. This at the least was established by Hume. By "action" is signified the distinction in unity of "potency" and its "actuality." For to say that something is "actual" is to imply that it is the determinate actuality of some potency-in-act. Agency involves both a power of act*ing* and the expression of that power in something enact*ed,* a doing and a deed, and in action *par excellence* that which is enacted is the exhaustive expression of the potency, without inhibition or frustration, by which agency may otherwise be reduced to durational effort more or less effective. Action is thus originally and essentially eternal, and becomes durational only by limitation and modification. Mere uniform temporal sequence can be styled "causality" only by way of paradox—*lucus a non lucendo.*

Spinoza's philosophical intention, therefore, is to derive all things from a primordial infinite power or indeterminate potency self-actualized in an infinite and exhaustively determinate eternal universe; and it is thus that he conceives that "infinite beings follow in infinite ways from the divine nature,"[1] i.e. from the self-actualizing creative potency-in-act. The further derivation of the durational world of common experience and science, composed of things that in their order and status are imperfectly active, or conative, thus becomes an essential problem, the solution of which constitutes the

---

H. F. Hallett, *Benedict de Spinoza,* London: The Athlone Press, 1957, Chapters I–III, pp. 9–43. Reprinted by permission of the Athlone Press.

1. *E.,* I, xvi.

chief value of Spinoza's theory—affording as it does the clue to that reversal of human privation that constitutes the essential character of morality.

It follows that all interpretations of the doctrine of Spinoza that fail to take due note of its *activism,* and interpret causation in terms of the confessedly impotent categories of positivistic theory are thereby hamstrung from the start, and can only proceed to further and more mischievous misunderstandings which seem to involve him in fallacies so futile and obvious as to lie beyond the possible stupidity of the merest tiro.

Part I of the *Ethics* is chiefly devoted to the clarification of the principles governing the nature and existence of the eternal self-actualizing potency, and to the deduction of the formal character-istics of this primordial agent. The essential nature of this being is laid down in the first definition: "By *cause of itself* I understand that the essence of which involves existence." Such a being is wholly in-dependent of the operation or existence of what is other than itself, and is thus real *sans phrase.* That alone is primordially real that realizes itself as potency-in-act, subject to no alien contingency.

This primordial being is thus at once both cause and effect, and critics unable to divest themselves of the common notion of "cause" have often poured scorn upon the conception. Martineau,[2] for ex-ample, claims that in the phrase *causa sui* the *causa* cancels the *sui,* and the *sui* cancels the *causa,* and Pollock that the definition "leaves causation wholly out of account" and "implies that the use of the word cause in this sense is really inappropriate."[3] Whether the com-mon use of the term "cause" as implying temporal production or conditioning is in any degree defensible, and if so how, and in what degree, need not now be canvassed; suffice it to emphasize once more that it is anachronistic as attributed to Spinoza. For him cau-sation is the actualization of potency, not the mere sequence of pas-sive "events," or even the relation of "sign" and "thing signified," but rather what Berkeley distinguished as "real causality," involving real power to generate or produce. Essentially it is not that the cause *has* the power, but that it *is* the power, and if that power is ab-solute its actuality (or effect) is, with it, self-existent.

2. James Martineau, *A Study of Spinoza* (London: Macmillan, 1882), pp. 117–119, 224–225.

3. Sir Frederick Pollock, *Spinoza, His Life and Philosophy* (London: Duck-worth, 1899), 2nd ed., p. 149.

The primordial Real, then, is the duality in unity of cause or potency and effect or actuality. Spinoza has several ways of expressing this ultimate nature: as a distinction in identity of (1) "Substance" and "mode"; (2) "Creator" and "creature"; (3) *"Natura naturans"* and *"Natura naturata";* (4) "Essence" and "expression." Let us briefly examine these variant modes of expression *seriatim.*

1. *Substance and Mode.* Formal definitions of these terms are given at the beginning of *Part I* of the *Ethics,* and there is therefore no valid excuse to be offered by those who carelessly substitute other uses of them derived from alien sources. Substance does not stand for "matter" either in its commonsense or its Lockian interpretation. It is not a supposed underlying somewhat in which qualities inhere, but "that which is in itself and is conceived through itself: that is, that the conception of which does not require the conception of anything other from which it must be formed."[4] It is self-existent and self-manifest being, self-actualizing and self-certifying being or potency-in-act. The definition of Mode of Substance at once contrasts it with Substance while maintaining their asymmetrical relation: "By Mode I understand the *affectiones* of Substance, or that which is in another, through which also it is conceived."[5] Here the interpretation to be placed on the term *"affectio,"* and what it means to be "in another," and to be conceived "through another" must be considered.

"In another" is evidently used by way of contrast with the "in itself" of the definition of substance. Whereas substance is self-existent and self-manifest, what is modal depends for its existence on what transcends, or lies beyond, its own proper nature, and can be conceived only as so related. But this does not mean (as has too often been supposed), at least not primarily and essentially, dependence on extrinsic co-ordinate modes (e.g. on things spatio-temporally other) as things are supposed to depend on their "natural causes"— a man on his parents, or a tree on the soil and atmosphere, for existence or sustenance. The mode's original "other" is substance itself as the potency-in-act of which the mode is the actual being thence derived. It is in this sense that Spinoza speaks of certain "immediate" and "mediate" infinite and eternal modes of substance[6] (e.g.

4. *E.,* I, Def. 3.
5. *E.,* I, Def. 5.
6. *E.,* I, xxi, xxii. Cf. also *Ep.,* 64.

"infinite intellect," eternal "motion and rest," and the idea and "make of the whole universe"), which are the primordial and generically perfect actualizations of divine potency; and here there can be no dependence on extrinsic co-ordinate modes. With the finite modes this dependence on substance entails a *derived* dependence on other finite modes, however, and these function as the *proximate* others of the finite mode under consideration. It is this derived dependence that remains in evidence in the spatio-temporal order which, as we shall see, privatively expresses the eternal order of actualities.

Originally, then, a mode is "in another" because it is a mode *of substance* which, because the relation of mode and substance is asymmetrical, is for it an "other." Yet substance and mode are not symmetrically and mutually other, for the mode is the actuality of the potency-in-act which is substance: it is an *affectio* of substance. But this, again, does not mean that substance is "affected," or acted upon, by something other than itself, but that it takes a nature by way of self-expression. The meaning lies nearer to our use of the term "affect" when we say that a man "affects the aristocrat" than when we say that he is "affected by the climate"—though there is, of course, no suggestion of pretence: substance actualizes and manifests itself in the mode—it is the active cause, and the mode its enacted effect. Self-actualizing and self-manifesting substance is thus essentially real and intelligible as "cause of itself," i.e. as creating its own actuality, exhaustively and eternally. The primordial Real is substance as infinite indeterminate potency eternally actualized as exhaustively determinate mode, and is thus self-existent, self-manifest, *causa sui*.

Finally, it is of first importance to remember that just as the "substance" of Spinoza must not be confused with the "substances" of other philosophies or of common sense, so also his "mode" must not be identified with the individual things of temporal human experience. Many, if not most, expositors and critics of Spinoza have suffered shipwreck on this rock. The sense and manner in which such things are "modes" will, I hope, become clear as we proceed; but here, and in all strictness universally, "mode" must be taken *au pied de la lettre* of the formal definition: as contrasted with, yet essentially related to, substance. Modes derive their existence from the creative action that is substance; substance realizes itself in the creation of modes, for there is no action without deed. Its existence is necessary by reason of its essence as free action creatively enacting its own expression. For it "essence" and "existence," though distinct, are identical.

2. *Creator and Creature.* Substance as cause is thus absolutely free action or creation: it is not a "thing" but self-realizing and self-manifesting *agency*. Modes as effects of that agency are created beings actualizing the potency of their cause. The notion, sometimes entertained, that Spinoza's substance is a *totum* of which its modes are the parts is too jejune to merit refutation. But again, in using the terms "creator" and "creature," with their long association with theology, popular and otherwise (though I do not suppose that theologians of intellectual merit are likely to fall into these errors), we must not be led to think of the modes or created beings as precipitated "out of nothing" to constitute a world *existentially* divorced from its creator (though deriving its essence from the exercise of his will). We are concerned, not with magic, but with metaphysics. Creative substance did not precede the created modal world in time, and produce it by a dated *fiat* of its ungrounded "will." The otherness of the creator is not existential, for the creator exists only as creating. Creation is eternal, and no temporal being is fully "created." The emergence of time, and its relation to eternity belong to a later stage of our analysis.

It was, perhaps, because of the danger of misinterpretation by minds ill-trained in theology that Spinoza almost entirely excluded from the *Ethics* this terminology which he had not hesitated to adopt and define in his earlier works, the *Cogitata Metaphysica* and the *Short Treatise*. But I do not think that this indicates any radical change in his view. Nor is the exclusion complete.[7]

I have said that creation is an eternal action, and that therefore created things are eternal. This implies that durational beings are not, as such, "creatures" in the full sense. It will be well, therefore, to postpone further discussion of this mode of expression until the mode of egression of such beings comes to be considered.

3. "Natura naturans" *and* "Natura naturata". Spinoza also expounds the primordial nature of the Real by the use of the medieval conceptions thus expressed. The significance of the terms *"Natura naturans"* and *"Natura naturata"* may be traced as far back as the

7. Cf. *E.*, I, App.

great Greek philosophers: but here it may suffice to say that beginning at least with Plato the distinction makes inchoate appearance in the Aristotelian discrimination of the "unmoved mover" and "that which is moved." This was utilized by Augustine, and developed by Scotus Eriugena into a distinction and identification of God and the world. "Nature" as creative potency-in-act is God—Nature as creating a nature for itself: Nature "naturing itself"; Nature regarded as a determinate totality of determinate being—as having received a nature—is the world or Nature "natured." This mode of expression and thought was further developed by the Arabian philosopher Averroës, and it reappeared in the thought of the Renaissance philosopher-poet Giordano Bruno. Whether it reached Spinoza from this source, or from earlier or intermediate sources, Jewish or otherwise, we have no certain knowledge. Spinoza expressly defines his use of the terms in *E.,* I, xxix, S.: "By *Natura naturans* we must understand that which is in itself and is conceived through itself, or those attributes of substance which express eternal and infinite essence, that is, God in so far as he is considered as a free cause. By *Natura naturata* I understand all that follows from the necessity of God's nature, or of any one of God's attributes, that is, all the modes of the attributes of God in so far as they are considered as things which are in God, and which without God can neither be nor be conceived." This definitely identifies the distinction with that of Substance and Mode as the integral *termini* of creation. Nature, the primordial real, is a unity of agency and deed, and is thus asymmetrically bipolar: as infinite indeterminate potency-in-act it is *Natura naturans:* as *actus,* i.e. the exhaustively determinate actuality, of this potency it is *Natura naturata.* Genetically God is prior to the world; ontologically they are identical as indeterminately infinite and infinitely determinate. It is in this sense that Spinoza speaks of "God or Nature"—for though in all strictness God is *Natura naturans,* the identity of this with *Natura naturata* validates the phrase. But, of course, *Natura naturata* is not to be identified with the durational world of common experience—the "common order of nature," which is temporal, multiplex, and divided—it is the eternal "make of the whole universe," infinite, one, and indivisible, of which the durational world is but a privation. The common objections to the identification of God and Nature thus collapse, since the durational world with its manifold imperfections is not, by Spinoza, regarded as being incorrigibly divine or fully created.

4. *Essence and Expression.* Spinoza sometimes speaks of the primordial causality which is the essential constitution of "God or Nature" as the "expression" of its essence in existence.[8] This is, perhaps, a somewhat less happy mode of statement, because we are apt to think of "expression" under the analogy of the fashioning of something physical—characters, sounds, or artistic and other artificial products—in accordance with ideas or mental conceptions. But Spinoza must not be taken as conceiving creative action on the analogy of such verbal or artistic "expression" of ideas in another medium. For Substance, *Natura naturans,* or God is not exclusively mental; nor is modal being, *Natura naturata,* or the eternal universe exclusively non-mental. These are not two beings having the same form, or having different forms conventionally associated, in different materials. We have yet to deal with the distinction of the mental and the physical, and their relation, as it is understood by Spinoza, but they are certainly not to be identified with those of creator and creature. Undoubtedly, for Spinoza the eternal extended universe which is the actuality of Substance as "extension" may be regarded as an "expression" of Substance as "thought," but equally the eternal psychical universe which is its actuality as "thought" may be regarded as an "expression" of Substance as "extension." This does but emphasize the identity of "extension" and "thought" as "attributes" of Substance. Their distinction is intellectual, i.e. with *respect* to intellect; and it is because philosophy is an intellectual discipline that the creative actualization of potency comes to be conceived as "expression." Danger, however, lurks in this usage, viz. that of exclusive "intellectualism" which forgets that intellect, which for man as philosopher is basic, is but a modal being—and not the exclusive actuality of Substance.

II. Substance and Attribute

We are thus led next to a consideration of the nature of the Attributes of Substance, their interrelation, and status with respect to "God or Nature." Spinoza's formal definition of "Attribute" indicates clearly enough that the term is not to be taken in the vulgar sense of a characteristic or quality related to Substance as, e.g., sobriety is related to Peter, or redness to a rose: "By attribute I under-

8. In this connexion see F. Kaufmann, "Spinoza's System as Theory of Expression," *Philos. and Phenomenol. Research,* 1 (1940), 83–97.

stand that which the intellect perceives of substance as constituting its essence."[9] The attributes of Substance, then, are the essence of Substance as apprehended, and truly, by intellect: they do not *inhere* in it, but *constitute* its essence. This is further emphasized by Spinoza in *Epistola ix:* "By substance I mean that which is in itself, and is conceived through itself. *I mean the same by attribute* except that it is called 'attribute' with respect to intellect which attributes such and such a nature to substance."[10] It is equally important, however, not to place an illegitimate emphasis on the relation with intellect as many expositors have done under the influence of idealistic developments from which Spinoza was entirely free. No Kantian or idealistic significance is to be attached to Spinoza's words: intellect does not necessarily condemn itself to phenomenalism by merely imputing the Attributes to Substance that as a "thing-in-itself" is devoid of them. Nor on the other hand, is the Real limited by intellect whether human or divine. What intellect perceives it perceives truly, for that is the nature of intellect: imagination and its modes are *privations* of intellect. Yet human intellect, circumscribed as it is in its range of objects (though essentially self-transcendent), though it suffers no privation such as to lead it to error, is nevertheless imperfect and, as Spinoza says, differs from infinite intellect "as the Dog in the heavens differs from the barking animal."[11] The Attributes of Substance are thus neither qualities or characteristics of Substance nor its phenomenal appearances due to the relativity of human intellect. The Attribute *is* the Substance under the determining scrutiny of intellect. In the letter from which I have already quoted, Spinoza offered his correspondent two examples to illustrate the kind of distinction he had in mind: (1) the third patriarch, Israel, was also called Jacob (i.e. supplanter) because he seized his brother's heel; again (2) a plane surface is one that reflects all rays of light without any other change—it is called "white" in relation to a man observing it. What both examples bring home is evidently the notion of "respect": what distinguishes an Attribute from Substance is that it is the same but in a different respect; and we know from the definition of "Attribute" that this respect is respect to *intellect*. Now intellect is not extrinsic to Nature, like a spectator at the games, but is involved in it. Nor is it as such substantial (for substance is

9. *E.,* I, Def. 4.
10. My italics.
11. *E.,* I, xvii, S.

indeterminate). It is therefore a mode or actualization of Substance. Thus the respect by which an Attribute is distinguished from Substance is intrinsic—not like that of Jacob to Isaac, or the plane surface to the observer; and the Attribute is Substance with respect to one of its own actualizations. Substance, we have seen, is infinite and eternal potency-in-act, and as such absolutely indeterminate; its actualization consists in its exhaustive determination. But what in itself is absolutely indeterminate must, with respect to its determinate actualizations be a *determining* agency, and thus *reflectively determinate*. As actualizing the determinate its indeterminacy is specified, i.e. intellect as an actual determination of Substance perceives the essence of Substance as a potency-in-act whence flow the specific determinations involved in or essential to intellect. Thus *human* intellect perceives Substance as infinite and eternal *thinking* potency-in-act and as infinite and eternal *"extension"* or physical potency-in-act.

This is the root of the distinction both of the Attributes and of Substance and Attributes. Though Substance in itself is absolutely indeterminate, with respect to its determinate actualizations it is generically determinate—"generically," because as infinite and eternal only the universal properties of finite modes can be unconditionally imputed to Substance. Why, then, it may be asked, does Spinoza single out *intellect* as the referent by which Attributes are distinguished from Substance? The answer is simple enough: because the purpose of philosophy is to make Nature *intelligible,* so that this respect to intellect must be, for it, central.

Further, though *human* intellect thus perceives Substance as thinking and physical potency-in-act, in so far as these potencies are reflectively determinate the nature of Substance in itself cannot be confined to these Attributes. An absolutely indeterminate potency cannot be the source merely of determinate psychical and physical actuality, for thus it would not be indeterminate but psycho-physical potency-in-act. Its absolute indeterminacy necessitates the inference to infinite Attributes; for only the infinitely determinate can exhaustively actualize the absolutely indeterminate.

The *conceived* (and truly conceived) distinctions of the infinite Attributes of Substance is thus with respect to the actualization of one of them, viz. Thought. Substance as such suffers no such distinction, nevertheless these distinctions are valid since from its very nature as potency-in-act Substance exists only as self-actualizing—as producing infinite things "in infinite ways." It may be objected that it is paradoxical to say that Substance is both absolutely indeterminate and also "consists of infinite Attributes"—and indeed it would be so if the nature of Substance provided no "logical room" for this disparity, if, for example, Substance were a "thing" and not an *agent*. The apparent contradiction is "dialectical" or self-resolved in the conception of creative agency.

For philosophy, then, i.e. for intellect, the primordial Real or Substance actively functioning as creator consists of infinite Attributes "each of which expresses eternal and infinite essence." This is "God or Nature."

"GOD OR NATURE"

In the foregoing account of Substance, its Modes, and its Attributes, I have trespassed somewhat beyond the account given by Spinoza himself in the Definitions and first ten Propositions of *Part I* of the *Ethics*. In these he is primarily concerned with the conceptions alone, without reference to their precise application to the primordial and consequent Real. It is only in *Proposition xi* that he turns explicitly to metaphysical assertion, and identifies the Real with "Substance consisting of infinite Attributes each of which expresses eternal and infinite essence"; and we have to wait until *Proposition xvi* before learning that the Modes of this Substance are "infinite beings flowing in infinite ways" from the necessity of its nature.

Reality, we have seen, means agency, not mere objective givenness, and in agency we discern potency-in-act and actuality—or, in other words, essence and existence.

I. Essence or Potency-in-Act

"God or Nature," Spinoza repeatedly affirms, is "infinite, one, and indivisible." It will be convenient to consider these essential properties in the reverse order:

1. *Indivisible*. "Substance absolutely infinite is indivisible":[12] the infinity of the Attributes of Substance does not entail multiplicity of essences. This follows from the nature of an Attribute, which

12. *E.*, I, xiii.

has already been considered. An Attribute is the determi*ning* nature of Substance with respect to some *determinatum* (e.g. intellect) of its absolutely indeterminate potency-in-act. For it is of the nature of creation that absolutely indeterminate potency is actualized in determinate beings of every conceivable kind, and it is with respect to these universal kinds that Substance is generically determinate to infinity, i.e. "consists of infinite Attributes," *each* of which (and not the *aggregate* of which) constitutes the essence of Substance. For to say that its Attributes are infinite *in number* is but to deny that they are numerable. In Substance as such the Attributes are neither one nor many, but infinite—for Substance is absolutely indeterminate, though infinitely determining. It is true that the human intellect, e.g., enumerates the Attributes that fall within its cognizance, viz. Thought and Extension, but as thus imputing duality to the divine essence man's knowledge of that essence, though formally adequate, remains clouded by a determinacy that must be transcended in Substance—hence the insistence on the infinity of the Attributes in spite of human limitations. Not that for man Thought and Extension are wholly unrelated and disjoined: they are united in the epistemic, or subject and object, relation of "experience" in which alone they are discerned. But it is the limitation of human nature as a mode of Thought and Extension alone that renders them discernible, though undivided and infinite in potency. For man Extension is at once essential to Thought as its primary object, and Thought to the discernment of Extension, the character of each being revealed by contrast with the other. Thus in "experience" Thought and Extension are at once realized and discerned as *epistemically* indivisible. Yet "experience," too, has a determinate character which (*pace* the "Experience-philosophers") disqualifies it for identification with Substance; and the substantial nature of Thought, or of Extension, or of any of the infinite Attributes of Substance, is realized only in the absolute "unity" of Substance—a unity infinitely more intimate than the epistemic unity of "experience." As so united, *substantial* Thought is identical with *substantial* Extension, *substantial* X, etc. For the determinacy of each Attribute in the modal perspective is but the obfuscation of its own implicit negativity qualified by the clarity explicit by its discernment from another with which it is epistemically, or otherwise, united and indivisible. It is thus that the divine intellect, which is the actuality of *substantial* Thought, infinitely transcends the human intellect, which is but the actuality of Thought as an Attribute epistemically united with Extension alone in determinate "experience." "If intellect pertains to the divine nature it cannot, like ours, follow the things which are its objects (as many suppose), nor can it be simultaneous in its nature with them, since God is prior to all things in causality, but on the contrary, the truth and formal essence of things is what it is because as such it exists by way of knowledge in God's intellect. Therefore the intellect of God, in so far as it is conceived as constituting his essence" (i.e. as potency-in-act) "is in truth the cause of things, both of their essence and of their existence."[13] But this is not a peculiarity of Thought, for *mutatis mutandis* the same may be asserted of all the Attributes which in Substance are indivisible.[14]

2. *Unique.* God, or Substance consisting of infinite Attributes, is not one among many but beside it no substance can be or be conceived.[15] This follows from the definition of God as "Substance consisting of infinite Attributes": for thus all Attributes are attributed to it, and substances with the same attribute are not discernible or distinct.[16] Spinoza takes occasion in both *E.,* I, xiv, C. 2 and xv, S. to deal with the conventional view (entertained by Descartes) that extended substance is created, and additional to the creative Substance or God, pointing out that the arguments adduced in favour of this arise from the misconstruing of the nature of extended substance. He allows that God is not "corporeal" in the sense of possessing a "body" determined in length, breadth and depth. Such a conception of Extension, whether taken to be a substance or an Attribute, is erroneous: all "bodies" are but its finite modes or actualizations: Extension as such is extensional potency-in-act.[17] But

13. *E.,* I, xvii, S.

14. Here we have confined attention to Substance, or God as *Natura naturans;* but it may be added that no ground for the imputation of divisibility to this can be drawn from the multiplicity inherent in *Natura Naturata,* or the finite modes of Substance, to be considered in the next chapter; for even here the multiplicity is fully integral when we consider "the whole order of nature." *Natura naturata* as it actualizes *Natura naturans,* is "infinite, unique, and indivisible"; for each individual part focalizes the whole which is thus immanent in each. *Natura naturata* is not an aggregate of parts but a macrocosm of microcosms to infinity.

15. *E.,* I, xiv.

16. *E.,* I, v.

17. The alternative interpretation of Extension as empty three-dimensional space is, of course, equally improper.

this being so, and all potency being proper to "God or Nature," Extension, though substantial, can be no substance distinct from the infinite creative Substance.[18]

A word is perhaps required concerning Spinoza's distinction of "unity" or "singleness" as applied to "God or Nature" and its "uniqueness"—the former description being regarded by him as "very improper." "A thing can only be said to be one or single in respect of its existence and not of its essence: for we do not conceive things under numbers until they have been brought under a common genus. . . . Hence it is clear that nothing can be called one or single unless some other thing has been conceived which agrees with it."[19] Thus, the uniqueness of "God or Nature" follows from its indeterminate infinity as essence or potency-in-act which excludes the possibility of another.

3. *Infinite.* In his *Letter on the Nature of the Infinite*[20] Spinoza distinguishes between "infinite by nature or definition," "limitless," and "innumerable." Now Substance, the primordial potency-in-act, is by nature indivisible, and hence its infinity cannot mean limitless multiplicity of parts. Again, since it is unique its infinity cannot mean the indefinite remoteness of extrinsic limits, or, indeed, the mere absence of limits. Its infinity (in spite of the negative suggestion of the term itself) is "by nature or definition"; and this has application not only to its nature as "substance" (for "every substance is necessarily infinite"),[21] but also to its special nature as "consisting of infinite Attributes each of which expresses . . . infinite essence."[22] The Attributes are infinite *in number* only with respect to the intellect by which they are distinguished. Substance is infinite as potency-in-act, potency being, as such, by nature indeterminate, i.e. involving no negation, either intrinsic (for it is indivisible) or extrinsic (for it is unique). It is only when Substance is conceived as modally actual that the infinity of "God or Nature" can be interpreted as limitlessness or innumerability, and that a "part" of *Natura naturata* (such

18. It must be admitted that the Cartesian phrase "extend*ed* Substance" is misleading and, indeed, paradoxical. The comparable phrase, "think*ing* Substance" is more correct. And the same applies to the Spinozistic phrases *"res extensa"* and *"res cogit*ans."

19. *Ep.,* 50.

20. *Ep.,* 12.

21. *E.,* I, viii.

22. *E.,* I, xi.

as a man) can be regarded as *"Deus quatenus finitus est,"*[23] and the Attributes which it expresses as numerable, e.g. Thought and Extension. And even so the finiteness of the "part," and the numerability of the Attributes involved, are not absolute, but must be qualified by essential relation with a complement, and by the limitless numerability of the Attributes, respectively.

Thus, Substance, "God," or *Natura naturans,* is infinite by nature or definition, and can in no wise be *conceived* as finite (though we may attempt so to *imagine* it). But *Natura naturata,* abstractedly conceived is infinite in virtue of its cause, viz. *Natura naturans,* and can be divided into parts, and viewed as an indefinitely great assemblage of such parts. Yet this is to conceive it as merely "given," as "actual" but not "enacted," after the fashion of the empiricists. For *Natura naturata* is only properly conceived as eternally flowing from the primordial potency-in-act; and as so conceived it, too, is infinite by nature or definition. And so again, its finite "parts" are not mere *sectors* of the "whole," but exist only in relation with their complement, and thus as "microcosms" or "finite-infinites." This is a topic to which we must presently return.

II. Existence or Actuality

"God or Nature" exists or is actual as *Natura naturata* exhaustively and determinately realizing the infinite, indeterminate potency-in-act that is *Natura naturans.* This self-actualization is neither a mere possibility, nor is it contingent, but necessary. Thus the actual world is the only possible world.[24]

1. *Possibility, Contingency, and Necessity.* Spinoza had had conversations with Leibniz, and it is conceivable and perhaps even probable that *E.,* I, xxxiii was directly aimed at the Leibnizian conception of infinite possible worlds in the mind of God, from which he chose the best for creation. The idea is anthropomorphic, interpreting creation as a sort of artistic production *ex nihilo.* It fails by reason of the

23. Cf. *E.,* II, ix, xi, C. As difficulties have been raised by some commentators concerning this doctrine of the relation of man and God (cf. H. Barker, "Notes on the Second Part of Spinoza's *Ethics," Mind,* N.S., xlvii, pp. 437 *et passim*) it may be well to say here that Spinoza does not equate the human mind as durationally extant with *"Deus quatenus humanae mentis essentiam constituit,"* but only as thinking adequately.

24. *E.,* I, xxxiii.

paradoxical nature of the being which must be imputed to the un-created possible worlds which are at once "ideally" actual and also merely possible. For nothing can be said to be *merely* possible if "possible" is distinguished from "contingent," that being contingent that is known to issue from a cause the existence of which remains in doubt.[25] Now all that exists or is actual is the actuality of potency-in-act original or derived, and it is thus that actual existence is necessary though not extrinsically compelled. Necessity, rightly under-stood, is true freedom or potency-in-act. This is not to deny that *durational* things are authentically contingent in so far as the occur-rence of durational causes cannot be certainly foretold by durational minds. But, as we shall see, durational things are privations of eternal beings, and their contingency is concomitant with their privativity. As referred to this or that finite "part" of *Natura naturata* they may be authentically contingent, but as referred to God they are certainly necessary.

Now, when we consider "God or Nature" as *causa sui* no such distinction of certain necessity and authentic contingency can be en-tertained, much less any notion of its being merely possible; for *Natura naturata* is the very exhaustively determinate actuality of the infinite indeterminate primordial potency-in-act that is *Natura naturans*. Because that potency is infinite, unique and indivisible, its actuality is perfect and necessary. For a "potency" not "in-act" is no potency at all.

2. *Proofs of the Existence of God.* Those who thus far have fol-lowed the development of Spinoza's doctrine will notice with no sur-prise that he concludes the real existence of God in a laconic inference occupying but three lines of the text: "If it be denied, conceive that God does not exist. Then his essence does not involve existence; which is absurd."[26] That he also deigns to add two or three other proofs, *a priori* or *a posteriori* in form, implies no recog-

25. It should not be necessary to point out that *mere possibility* must be dis-tinguished from *potentiality* (though even philosophers of high repute have sometimes failed to discern them, and rejected the one on the ground of the vacuity of the other). A block of marble "has the possibility" of becoming an Apollo (or many another statue), but not the potentiality, even in the sense in which an acorn "has the potentiality" of becoming an oak tree (and no other) —though even here the potency is not wholly intrinsic or immanent (as with the *causa sui* or an eternal *creatum*).

26. *E.,* I, xi.

nition of dissatisfaction with this essential proof, which indeed is involved in all of them as *conditio sine qua non*.

The first additional proof proceeds from the principle that what exists or is actual is so by reason of a cause or potency-in-act, and what does not exist fails to exist by reason of the opposition of some cause or potency-in-act. This cause of existence or non-existence must lie either in the nature of the thing itself or beyond it: in its nature when it is necessary or impossible; beyond it when it is contingent. That for which there is nothing, intrinsic or extrinsic, that can prevent existence, exists necessarily (the main proof); thus "God or Nature," which is "absolutely infinite and consummately perfect" so exists.

The second additional proof is *a posteriori* in form, proceeding from the existence of "ourselves." This existence implies a "power to exist" possessed by such finite beings; and if God did not exist the power of these beings to exist would exceed that of a being absolutely infinite; which is absurd. Thus either nothing exists or God exists necessarily.

But as he says in the *Scholium* that follows: "In this last demonstration I wished to prove the existence of God *a posteriori*, not because it does not follow *a priori* from the same premisses, but in order that the proof might be more easily understood." He then gives the *a priori* form of this *a posteriori* proof (forming a third additional proof): To be able to exist is a potency, and it follows that the greater the potency the greater the ability to exist. Now "God or Nature" is defined as absolutely infinite in potency, and therefore exists necessarily. Here the point is, of course, that power to exist is not an extrinsic power imputed to God but God's very essence from which existence or actuality flows.

It needs little acuity of perception to recognize the equivalence or dependence of all these proofs upon the same principle, viz. that expressed in the main proof, commonly called the "ontological proof." I say "equivalence with" or "dependence upon," for a distinction may be drawn according as the proofs are, in Cartesian phrase, "analytic" or "synthetic" in method. The "ontological proof" is, of course, as such "synthetic," proceeding from essence to existence, from potency-in-act to actuality; the additional proofs, especially the *a posteriori* one, involve "analytic" procedure from existences, taken to be authentic, by the emendation of essences to an actuality certified by perfect essence or potency-in-act. But the emendation of imperfect essences taken as authentically actual itself proceeds only in the light of the "ontological principle" of the dependence of actuality or existence upon potency or essence.

This "analytic" form of proof, though allied with that which Kant oddly styled the "cosmological proof," and rejected, must carefully be distinguished from it. It does not argue from existences "contingent" in the sense of caused wholly extrinsically, and thus fortuitous, to a being necessarily existent as the ground of such being taken as authentic or "given." To be wholly dependent on extrinsic potency is to be nothing at all; every authentic existent must in part at least actualize its own potency-in-act, and the argument runs that dependence on extrinsic potency is a measure of finiteness and imperfection not suffered by "God or Nature." Nor can it be validly supposed that the authentic existence of anything (which the proof assumes as starting point) can be merely hypothetical—depending on an infinite regression of causes, all hypothetical. It is not (as Spinoza points out in *Epistola xii*) that such a regression is impossible, but that the authentic existence of any part of the series requires a passage beyond hypothesis, i.e. to a being dependent on no extrinsic cause, the existence of which actualizes its own intrinsic potency-in-act. If anything exists, *a fortiori* self-dependent being exists.

The "ontological proof," properly so called, is the "synthetic" form of the argument, which moves, not from imperfect to perfect being, but from perfect essence to necessary existence, from infinite indeterminate potency-in-act to exhaustively determinate actuality or existence. For the divine essence is not the mere conception of God to which existence must be superadded, but the infinite potency-in-act which necessarily actualizes itself.

The "ontological proof" has often been subjected to destructive criticism—sometimes validly, when it has been advanced in eccentric form. Kant is often said to have given it its final *quietus* in his celebrated figure of the "hundred thalers." Real existence, he argued, is not a "predicate" which by mere predication precipitates a concept into the real world. To think of a hundred thalers as existing is not the same as to add them to one's bank balance. Similarly, we can gain no assurance of the real existence of God from merely thinking of him as existing. What is truly astonishing is that a thinker of Kant's unquestionable acuity and authority should have supposed that such a refutation has any impact on the genuine ontological proof. Even Descartes had realized that the mere thought of existence is no ground for its certain attribution, and that the nerve of the argument lies in the principle that "in the concept or idea of everything that is clearly and distinctly conceived" existence is "contained," existence possible or necessary, such a concept or idea being "true."[27] And Hegel ridiculed the suggestion that God can rightly be conceived as in this matter comparable with "every wretched form of existence."[28] What is at the root of the general dissatisfaction with the ontological proof is a false opinion about the nature ascribable to God, and derivatively about the natures of all authentic existents, viz. that "reality" means mere objective "givenness" and not *agency*—existence being related to essence as actuality to potency-in-act. The actuality of Kant's hundred thalers stems from extrinsic potency-in-act, whereas that of God from infinite intrinsic potency-in-act. Thus the one is contingent on the actuality of that from which it stems, the other is necessary.

III. Essence and Existence

Finally, the relations and distinction of essence and existence in "God or Nature," i.e. of the infinite indeterminate primordial potency-in-act and its infinitely determinate enactment or actuality, serve to determine Spinoza's account of the divine causality as *free* and as *immanent,* and being both free and immanent, as *eternal.* With "God or Nature" essence and existence are at once identical and distinct as the indeterminate is identical with and distinct from its exhaustive determinations—a complex relation which is generally expressed by Spinoza in the form: "The essence of God *involves* existence."

1. *Identical: Causality and Freedom.*   Because the actuality of the divine potency-in-act is its exhaustively determinate expression, it follows that the divine action or causality is self-originated and in accordance with its own laws, uncompelled and uninhibited. "God alone is a free cause; for God alone exists and acts from the necessity alone of his own nature."[29] The unique necessity of his creative

27. Cf. *Meditationes, Resp. ad Obj. 1.*
28. Hegel, *Lectures on the Philosophy of Religion,* trans. Spiers and Sanderson (New York: Humanities Press, 1962), iii, 363.
29. *E.,* I, xvii, C. 2.

action is identical with perfect or absolute freedom, for God necessarily creates all that his infinite potency involves. To suppose that God would be more free if he could "bring it about that those things that follow from his nature should not be" is to suppose that he would be more perfect if he lacked a potency which is his (for a potency not "in-act" is no potency)—a palpable absurdity. To suppose, again, that God's "freedom" is elective is to deny his omnipotency. For election entails inhibition of potency, i.e. its negation. For the divine nature altogether transcends that of durational man who can be conceived as perfecting himself by the exercise of elective freedom, thus offsetting the privation concomitant with durationality. With "God or Nature," not to create all within his power is not to increase, but to limit, perfection.

2. *Distinct: Causality and Immanence.* Again, because the divine actuality, i.e. all the beings created by the divine potency-in-act, is exhaustively determinate while that potency is absolutely indeterminate, it follows that the distinction of creator and creature must be so maintained as to define their relation as *causal,* yet without recession from the identity of power and act. It is thus that the causality of God must be conceived as *immanent* in all actual beings, and not as transeunt or agency terminating in some alien actuality.[30] Divine causality is causality *par excellence,* and all relations that can in any sense or degree be called "causal" are framed on its analogy. Causality, according to Spinoza, is not a temporal relation, not such as was destructively analysed by Hume and defended by Kant; it consists not in regularity of temporal sequence but in agency immanent in deed. Empirical transeunt causes, in so far as they are authentic, possess something of this real power, though in a privative and derivative form (a point obscurely expounded even by Kant); but so far as they are transeunt, so that the effect lies beyond the cause, they are evidently devoid of it. The causality of God suffers no such defect, and his effects, therefore, are integral with their cause, which is immanent in them. The two poles of divine creation, *Natura naturans* and *Natura naturata* are indiscerptible, though not co-ordinate, transeunt, or alternative. *Natura naturata* is dependent upon and subordinate to *Natura naturans,* which in turn necessarily actualizes itself as *Natura naturata.*

30. *E.,* I, xviii.

3. *Eternal*.   It follows that "God or Nature" is eternal.[31] Here we must recall the definition of "eternity": it is "existence itself in so far as it is conceived as following necessarily from the essence of the thing"[32]—and Spinoza adds the *Explanation* that "it cannot be explicated by duration or time, not even if this be conceived as without beginning or end." Eternity is not duration "from eternity" "to eternity" (though in time it is *always* available). But neither is it "timelessness," but a form of *existence* transcending duration. He speaks of it as an "infinite existence,"[33] as distinct from duration which is a form of existence conceived as indefinite continuance in actual being.[34] Durational existence involves *conatus* operative against opposing powers;[35] eternal existence is action, free and creative. For action *par excellence* is freedom, but as qualified by opposing agency is constricted to endeavour. And this is the field of elective freedom, but eternity of free necessity. Thus the existence of "God or Nature" is no struggling continuance through time, but an eternal "enjoyment." Nor can the nature of this "infinite existence" be apprehended on any analogy of transition in time, though we make some rough approach to apprehension in the contemplation of our naïve experience of "acting" that defines what we appropriately call the "specious present" (for the "present" is the "moment" of action), and inadequately express as the permeation of the future by the past within a small tract of time. Yet this is but a "rough approach" because our "action" remains durational endeavour rather than creativity or free necessity. It is in pure thought alone that we have experience of eternity, in rational intellection or in intellectual intuition; for "demonstrations are the eyes of the mind by which it sees and observes things"[36]—and by "demonstrations," as we shall see in due course, Spinoza does not mean timeless formal syllogisms, but the real self-generation of concepts. Indeed, in intellectual intuition alone, because it is love rather than perception of objects, community rather than contemplation, is eternal life "enjoyed"; rational intellection apprehends things only *"sub* quadam specie *aeternitatis."*

31. *E.,* I, xix.

32. *E.,* I, Def. 8.

33. *C.m.,* II, 1.

34. *E.,* II, Def. 5.

35. See H. F. Hallett, *Benedict de Spinoza* (University of London: Athlone Press, 1957), ch. IV.

36. *E.,* V, 23, S.

The existence of "God or Nature" is the eternal enjoyment of creativity, uncompelled and uninhibited.

THE MODES OF SUBSTANCE

The modal actuality of the divine potency-in-act, or Substance, as it flows thence is infinite and eternal, and like it unique and indivisible. But unlike it, it is exhaustively determinate: "From the necessity of the divine nature there must follow infinite beings in infinite ways"[37]—yet all so as to form a unique and indivisible universe. It follows that *Natura naturata* is itself eternal, and contains nothing that is not eternal. For the divine potency-in-act is uninhibited and can be actualized in no durational being, whether durational as a whole or durational in its parts. Nor can an eternal whole be conceived as the integration of durational parts.

Spinoza distinguishes modes which are infinite, constituting the whole of nature, and modes which are finite parts of nature; and since these raise difficulties of different kinds we shall do well to give them separate consideration.

I. "Infinite and Eternal Modes"

Natura naturata is evidently an infinite and eternal mode of Substance or *Natura naturans* of which it is the exhaustive actuality; but a more precise delineation requires consideration of the nature of Substance as "consisting of infinite Attributes"—for though these are only intellectually discerptible, philosophy in which we are engaged is an intellectual discipline. It is in the light of the distinctions of the Attributes that Spinoza draws a further distinction between "immediate" and "mediate" infinite and eternal modes of Substance. For when we consider Substance as *thinking* potency-in-act (i.e. the Attribute of Thought), its *immediate* actuality is that which Thought as such accomplishes, viz. understanding (*intellectus*); and it is as such that understanding is an infinite and eternal mode of Substance and finds expression as the exhaustive idea of thinking Nature (*infinita idea Dei*), which thus becomes the *mediate* infinite and eternal mode of Substance *qua* Thought. So again, when we consider Substance as *extensional* potency-in-act (i.e. the Attribute of Exten-

37. *E.,* I, xvi.

sion), its *immediate* actuality is the "motion and rest"[38] inherent in the act of "extending"; and it is as such that "motion and rest" is an infinite and eternal mode of Substance and finds expression in the "fashion or make of the whole universe" (*facies totius universi*),[39] which thus becomes the *mediate* infinite and eternal mode of Substance *qua* Extension.

II. Determination and Individuation

Next, we must turn to the nature and status of the finite modes of Substance which, as I have said, must be distinguished from finite durational beings, empirical or scientific—being necessarily eternal as pertaining to the actuality of Substance. Potency *qua* potency is indeterminate; its actuality *qua* actuality is determinate; potency-in-act is determination. It follows that an infinite potency is actualized as infinitely determinate, involving every kind and range of existence—yet remaining unique and indivisible.

38. "Motion and rest" as the immediate actuality of extensional potency-in-act is thus not to be identified, or confused, with mere spatio-temporal passage and stillness. But neither is the phrase a portmanteau expression for motion recognized as being essentially relative to conventional axes, and thus only electively determinate. Descartes had defined the "proper motion" of a body as its "transference from the vicinity of contiguous bodies taken to be at rest" (*Principles of Philosophy* II, 24–26) and claimed that this is neither spatially absolute nor relative merely to conventional axes, but "a mode of the mobile body" —its mode (let us say) of "attachment" to whatsoever body may be contiguous with it: its intrinsic restlessness. Similarly, its "proper rest" must be its quiescence with respect to whatsoever body may be contiguous with it; its intrinsic inertia. A body's "proper motion and rest" remains unchanged through all vicissitudes, while the body itself remains identical, though its speed and direction of motion are subject to variation under impact. It is but a short step from this account to the view of "motion and rest" as modes of physical agency rather than passive spatio-temporal transference and stillness, absolute or conventional. And if this conception is delimited, "motion and rest" as the immediate infinite and eternal mode of Substance *qua* Extension must be conceived as the actuality of extensional potency-in-act inseparably issuing therefrom.

39. This phrase, naïvely translated as "the *face* of the whole universe," has usually been taken as referring to the spatio-temporal world of experience, the "visible universe," i.e. what Spinoza calls "the common order of nature." This is certainly an error, and the translation of "*facies*" by "fashion or make" (*facio*) is to be recommended. Extensional *Natura naturata* is not imaginationally quantitative and temporal, but infinite and eternal. The phrase is used in *Ep.*, 54.

We have seen already that this is the source of the distinctions of the infinite Attributes of Substance in the reflective modal perspective of "intellect." But the infinite determination of actual Nature is not to be limited to the generic distinctions of the Attributes: it is *exhaustively* determinate. "From the necessity of the divine nature infinite beings must follow in infinite ways, i.e. everything that can be conceived by infinite intellect";[40] or as it is expressed even more vigorously in the *Appendix* to *Part I* of the *Ethics:* To God "material was not lacking for the creation of everything, from the highest to the very lowest grade of perfection; or, to speak more properly, . . . the laws of his nature were so ample that they sufficed for the production of everything conceivable by infinite intellect." Not only is "God or Nature" actual in infinite sorts of existence, cognitive, extensional, "X-ian," but also in infinite grades or ranges under each generic head, from the infinite immediate and mediate modes down to the very least spark of near-non-being, through all degrees of finiteness. Yet in each the primordial potency-in-act is expressed in appropriate form, and in the whole is undivided. In the phrase of Bruno, it is "wholly in the whole, and wholly in every part of the whole."[41]

It has often been claimed that a whole of parts must be divisible, and that if Nature is truly indivisible finite individuals can have no place in it. Spinoza must thus be either atheist or acosmist. This curious error arises from the interpretation of "being" as "thing" rather than as "agent." For the individuality of "things" rests on exclusion, whereas that of "agents" is enriched by mutuality, and in the end by it constituted. The manner of this constitution will become clear as we proceed.

Natura naturata, the actuality of Substantial potency-in-act is thus infinitely individuated, yet without division: it is an Individual of individuals to infinity. Here I must again enter a *caveat* against the common assumption that the finite modes of Substance are to be simply identified with the finite individuals of durational experience that come into being, endure, and pass away serially and contemporaneously "from eternity to eternity." For eternal *Natura naturata* can be no integration of such a stream of durational beings, nor these its differentiated parts. Thus, the problem that has gravelled so many of Spinoza's expositors and critics, as to how an eternal causality

---

40. *E.,* I, xvi.
41. *De la causa, principio et uno, Dial. II.*

can, without self-limitation in the creator (which Spinoza denies, as entailing imperfection), give birth to durational effects, does not arise. The finite modes that are subordinate individuals in *Natura naturata* are themselves eternal as its constituents. Durational finite conators are still far ahead in our exposition—though it must be allowed that Spinoza's own exposition in the *Ethics,* with its moralistic bias, does not sufficiently emphasize the essential gap. Here we are concerned with the eternal individuation of the mediate infinite and eternal mode of Substance, which must be conceived as an eternal macrocosm constituted hierarchically of microcosms to infinity, all of which are eternal as thus embedded.

Further, this individuation of the Individual is not *subdivision* or *section,* for thus *Natura naturata* would not be "infinite, unique, and indivisible" but indefinite, multiplex, and aggregate. Nor would its parts be actualizations of Substance, or analogues of Nature. Thus, our problem is set: the mediate infinite and eternal mode of Substance is the exhaustive actuality of the infinite, indeterminate, potency-in-act, fully determinate and individual; also it is constituted of infinite finite beings of all grades of perfection, each in its own measure actualizing the divine potency: under what *schema* is such a set of relations intelligible?

III. Macrocosm and Microcosms

It must be admitted that Spinoza presents no formal unified account of the relations holding between *Natura naturata* and its finite "parts." Nor are suggestive terms such as "macrocosm" and "microcosm" much in evidence to yield a clue. Formal expression being lacking, his views must be sought out, and with a "speculative eye." Nor are the reasons for this *laches* far to seek: Spinoza is sometimes represented as among the purest of metaphysicians, for whom human values are only of secondary importance, but in fact his ethical interests are far too prominent to allow of such a characterization—though he is certainly a metaphysical moralist. Thus the *Ethics* contains much discussion of the nature, status, and moral relations of durational "man," but all too little of "man" as eternal *creatum*—and that little mainly, though far from exclusively to the perceptive reader, in the latter portion of *Part V* where, consequently, it has often seemed to the impercipient to be a superimposed and largely alien mystical efflorescence. But indeed, the nature of "man" as perfect finite *creatum* (i.e. "as referred to God") lies, as we shall see, at the very root of Spinoza's ethical doctrine, and he would have done better to have given distinct consideration to "man's" eternal nature, not as a mere "eternal part"[42] of the mind, but as its essential nature, and formally related the eternal natures of finite modes in general to the "infinite, unique, and indivisible" nature of the divine actuality, passing thence to its variant immanence in the privative nature of durational beings. Even his moral doctrine might thus have been more acceptable to plain men.

But though we may regret Spinoza's "moralism," we are not left wholly without guidance in our search for his metaphysical *schemata*. With the moralism there is very naturally coupled a one-sided emphasis on the human mind (and Spinoza expressly excludes from the *Ethics* the discussion of physical nature as such—beyond what is advanced in the physical *Lemmata* of *Part II*, and which concerns the nature and degrees of physical individuality, rather than the mode of integration of those degrees). It is therefore to the mental nature of "man" (and his physical nature only as it is epistemologically involved in this), and its relation to "God or Nature," that we have to look for the most promising clues. The human mind, he affirms, is the idea of the human body "and nothing else";[43] yet also it can have adequate knowledge of the eternal and infinite essence of God;[44] and these propositions plainly imply that the nature of God is involved in human nature, and can be sought from it by some valid metaphysical procedure. "God or Nature" is immanent in human nature.

But further, though the human mind is the idea of the human body, yet it can only know its nature, and even that it exists, in so far as it is "affected" by other bodies;[45] and the natures and existence of those other bodies are known by the mind only in so far as they "affect" its body.[46] From these propositions it follows that man's idea of the world of bodies is the idea of the "affections" of his own body by all those other bodies; so that man's knowledge of

42. *E.,* V, xxxix.
43. *E.,* II, xiii.
44. *E.,* II, xlvii.
45. *E.,* II, xix. For *"affectio"* see above, p. 134.
46. *E.,* II, xvi.

nature depends on the capacity of his body to be "affected" by its complement in nature, and the resulting idea is inadequate in so far as it confuses the natures of the body and its bodily complement. Yet this confusion results only in so far as the body and its bodily complement are different in nature—not wholly different (for thus the body could not be "affected" by its complement). In so far as they have "common properties"[47] there can be no confusion; but in so far as their natures differ confusion is inevitable.[48] Thus the inadequacy of man's idea of nature is remediable, not by any process of analysing these confused "affections" (for *ex hypothesi,* in separation neither body nor complement can be perceived by the mind), but only by the resolution of the differences in a full community of body and bodily complement in the *"facies totius universi"*: "he who possesses a body adapted to many things, possesses a mind the greater part of which is eternal."[49]

It is thus full community of each finite being, up to the limits of its finiteness, with infinite *Natura naturata* that constitutes its eternal nature as *creatum,* and the eternal relation of the finite and the infinite is to be conceived, not as the resolution or absorption of the individual in a *totum* on the analogy of mere objective "things"— man is no "bubble of the foam" of Deity—but as congruent reciprocity on the analogy of co-operating agents. The finite *creatum* is an eternal agent or finite individualization of the eternal actuality of the divine agency—an active microcosm of the infinite active macrocosm, which is the hierarchical integration[50] of infinite such microcosmic agents, each of which is framed on the analogy of the whole. Yet because the macrocosm is infinite, and the microcosm only finite, the latter can only be framed on the *analogy* of the former, and the microcosm is an actualization of divine potency, not in so far as this is infinite and indeterminate, but only in so far as it is also actualized and self-determined in another finite agent—which also has reference to a third, and so to infinity.[51]

Let this brief sketch suffice to indicate the relations of finite and

47. *E.,* II, xxxviii, xxxix.
48. See H. F. Hallett, *Benedict de Spinoza* (University of London: Athlone Press, 1957), pp. 74–75.
49. *E.,* V, xxxix.
50. See *E.,* II, Lem. 7, S.
51. Cf. *E.,* II, ix.

infinite active being as conceived by Spinoza. It remains to generalize it and set it forth in what seems the simplest and most telling way, viz. by means of a symbolic exposition. As this device is to be used merely as a clarification of relations already conceived, and not as involving inference, even those who are not accustomed to place much confidence in symbolic procedures as means of attaining truth may find some advantage from its laconicism. Its simplicity, again, should reconcile those who do not work with ease in such a medium.

Let N stand for *Natura naturata* in its infinite integrity. Here we may ignore the distinctions of the Attributes as affecting the modes since individuation proceeds *pari passu* under all of them.

N is the infinite Individual composed of infinite finite individuals of every grade of perfection, so interwoven as to exclude all division from the whole. Let . . . , M_{n-2}, M_{n-1}, M_n, M_{n+1}, M_{n+2}, . . . stand for these finite individuals.

Consider the nature of any one of these finite individuals: it is not a "part" of N in the sense of a "sector"—for so, either it would be no "individual," or N would be a mere aggregate. It is a finite expression of N, reproducing its infinite nature in some finite degree. Thus it is composed of "parts" corresponding with the "parts" of N. Let $M_n m_{n+1}$ stand for that "part" of M_n that corresponds with M_{n-1}, etc., etc.

Then we have:

$$N = \int_0^\infty \left\{ \begin{array}{l} \infty \\[4pt] \cdots\cdots\cdots\cdots\cdots\cdots\cdots\cdots\cdots\cdots \\[6pt] M_{n-2} = \int_0^\infty \ldots, M_{n-3}m_{n-2}, M_{n-2}m_{n-1}, M_{n-2}m_n, M_{n-2}m_{n+1}, \ldots\ldots \\[6pt] M_{n-1} = \int_0^\infty \ldots, M_{n-1}m_{n-2}, M_{n-1}m_{n-1}, M_{n-1}m_n, M_{n-1}m_{n+1}, \ldots\ldots \\[6pt] M_n = \int_0^\infty \ldots, M_n m_{n-2}, M_n m_{n-1}, M_n m_n, M_n m_{n+1}, M_n m_{n+2}, \ldots \\[6pt] M_{n+1} = \int_0^\infty \ldots, M_{n+1}m_{n-2}, M_{n+1}m_{n-1}, M_{n+1}m_n, M_{n+1}m_{n+1}, \ldots\ldots \\[6pt] M_{n+2} = \int_0^\infty \ldots, M_{n+2}m_{n-2}, M_{n+2}m_{n-1}, M_{n+2}m_n, M_{n+2}m_{n+1}, \ldots\ldots \\[6pt] \cdots\cdots\cdots\cdots\cdots\cdots\cdots\cdots\cdots\cdots \\[4pt] 0 \end{array} \right.$$

Consider next the relation between the "part" of M_n that corresponds with M_{n-1} (viz. $M_n m_{n-1}$), and the "part" of M_{n-1} that corresponds with M_n (viz. $M_{n-1} m_n$). Though these are evidently distinct (being "parts" of individual agents of different grades of perfection) they are, within their diverse scopes, in active agreement; for as "parts" of M_n and M_{n-1} analogous with M_{n-1} and M_n respectively, they share a common nature or "property." They are differentiated actualizations of an identical potency-in-act—and thus constitute nodes in the community of *Natura*. This may be symbolically illustrated if we abstract M_n (say) and its relatives in other "parts" of N in our general picture, so as to indicate how it subsists by active community with its complement in *Natura naturata*. Thus:

$$
\begin{aligned}
&M_{n-2} \rightarrow \cdots \cdots \cdots \cdots, M_{n-2}\,m_n, \cdots \cdots \cdots \cdots \\
&M_{n-1} \rightarrow \cdots \cdots \cdots \cdots, M_{n-1}\,m_n, \cdots \cdots \cdots \cdots \\
&M_n \rightarrow \cdots M_n\,m_{n+2}, M_n m_{n-1}, M_n m_n, M_n m_{n+1}, M_n m_{n+2}, \cdots \cdots \cdots \\
&M_{n+1} \rightarrow \cdots \cdots \cdots \cdots, M_{n+1}\,m_n, \cdots \cdots \cdots \cdots \\
&M_{n+3} \rightarrow \cdots \cdots \cdots \cdots, M_{n+2}\,m_n, \cdots \cdots \cdots \cdots
\end{aligned}
$$

Each "part," therefore, of N is the actuality of a grade of divine potency-in-act, so that it stands in community with all other "parts" similarly defined. By this community alone, *as an agent and no mere "thing,"* it maintains, and not loses by mergence, its individual being.[52] And the "texture" of *Natura naturata* may thus be symbolized as an infinite "web" or "lattice" of which the infinite finite agents are the "nodes" operating so as to form the indivisible integrity of the "whole." Thus, let $m_n^{n-1}{}_{-2}$ stand for the community or coaptitude of M_{n-1} and M_{n-2}, then we have:

52. It has often been urged against Spinoza that the integrity of eternal *Natura* leaves no room for finite individuality, all finite modes being merged, without distinction, in the infinite whole. This is the inevitable result of the common failure to take due account of his explicit *activism*. Coapt *agents,* in proportion to their coaptitude, *maintain* their individuality, which is *constituted* by their community. *Natura* is not a "thing," and its "parts" are not *sectors* of a thing, but *microcosms* which, as finite expressions of the macrocosm, live by community with their congruent complement in the macrocosm. Thus, their integrity enhances, not destroys, their individuality.

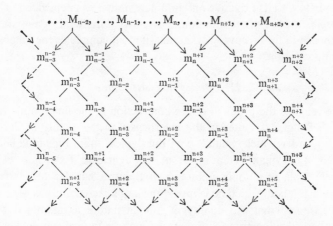

We have thus in *Natura* infinite hierarchical individuation of the perfect Individual—a macrocosm of microcosms to infinity. With Spinoza I have called the microcosms "parts" of *Natura naturata* (as indeed, they are), yet each is nothing save as embedded in the whole which is undivided. When, therefore, we call the "parts" finite (and I speak of the *eternal* "parts") this does not deny to them all tincture of infinity. For each in perfect community with its congruent complement[53] in *Natura naturata,* in its degree expresses the infinite substantial potency-in-act; it is the actuality, not of God in so far as he is infinite, but in so far as he is considered as being "affected" by its complement.[54]

Such, then, is the constitution of *Natura naturata* as it eternally actualizes the primordial potency-in-act, *Natura naturans:* "infinite, unique, and indivisible," yet exhaustively differentiated in hierarchical order "from highest to lowest." It is this that forms the subject-matter of *Part I* of the *Ethics,* and the early propositions of *Part II.* It is to this also that Spinoza returns in the later propositions of *Part V.* Any failure to note that in these portions of his exposition Spinoza is dealing with eternal individuals in their constitutive community as they issue from the eternal potency or Substance, can produce nothing but confusion and futile misinterpretation. *Part II* is mainly concerned with the sources and status of the human mind as durational, *Part V* with its emendation towards eternity, and *Parts*

53. See H. F. Hallett, *op. cit.,* p. 48, note*.
54. *E.,* II, ix.

III and *IV* with its privative and impotent nature as unemended. Thus, he begins with eternal creation, passes to durational "emanation," and thence to that recovery of eternal life that completes the "dialectic of finite creation."

IV. Modes and Attributes

There remains the problem of the contraction in the finite mode from the infinity of Attributes in the macrocosm to the duality of the Attributes under which "man," e.g., our typical finite individual, finds himself. For "man" is a mode of Thought and Extension exclusively.[55] This is a topic upon which Spinoza has far too little to say, though about which he is most pregnantly laconic. It has generally been assumed that the duality of human nature as animated body or embodied mind was for Spinoza a mere empirical *datum,* the infinity of the Attributes of Substance being the result of purely speculative "principle-riding." It is true, of course, that man's knowledge of his own nature as psychophysical is empirical, and not deduced from the nature of Substance, but his limitation to two Attributes, of which he is a duality in unity, is no mere *datum* but issues from the very nature and status of the Attributes which, as we have seen, are relative to "intellect." In Substance the Attributes are identical; in the perspective of intellect they are absolutely diverse, and each must be conceived through itself[56] as constituting the perceived essence of Substance. This being so, it follows that the modes of Substance which, for intellect, are discernible as determinations of diverse Attributes, are, as flowing from their substantial source, not separated under these Attributes but united; so that, e.g., man as mind and man as body are one man, not two living in miraculous harmony. If, now, it is thought that each mode of Substance should by intellect be discernible as a determination of all the infinite Attributes of Substance, and that therefore man cannot be limited to two Attributes, the error arises from failure to take due account of the nature and status of the Attributes. We are fortunate in having Spinoza's own answer to this problem (raised by his very acute correspondent von Tschirnhaus):[57] how does it come about that though each mode is expressed in infinite Attributes, the mode that is the human being

55. *E.,* II, xiii, and C. and S.
56. *E.,* I, x.
57. *Ep.,* 65.

knows only two of these—Thought as expressed in his mind, and Extension as expressed in his body. Spinoza's reply is brief and pointed: "Although each thing is expressed in infinite ways in the infinite intellect of God, yet the infinite ideas by which it is expressed cannot constitute one and the same mind of a singular thing, but an infinity of minds: seeing that each of these infinite ideas *has no connexion with the others.*"[58]

Thus, (1) because the Attributes are wholly diverse in the perspective of intellect (a mode of one of them), one and the same mind must be united with *not more than one* other expression—since the remaining expressions cannot be intellectually incorporated; and (2) because the Attributes are relative to intellect there can be no mind that is *not* united with some other expression—for the mind knows itself only in the act of knowing something other than itself. For mind is not a "thing" to which knowledge is superadded, but a *knowing agent,* and it must first be engaged in knowing something if it is to exist or be actual, and hence knowable. Nay, when the mind knows itself as knowing the body, it knows itself, not as a separate being, but as united with the body; and the union of mind and body is, from the standpoint of mind, *epistemic.* And this is the modal expression of the identity of the Attributes in Substance, and their relativity to intellect.

It has often been claimed that in the system of Spinoza the Attribute of Thought is given a place pre-eminent among the infinite Attributes, in that it corresponds with *all* of them, and not, like the others, with *each* other. This is an objection that is hardly to be met by what has already been said about the union of minds with modes of other Attributes. Yet this pre-eminence of the Attribute of Thought is not to be wondered at in view of the relativity of the Attributes to intellect (which is a mode of Thought), and for philosophy (a human *intellectual* discipline) it is but an expression of the distinction of truth and reality. Here there is no idealistic evading of the paradox that though knowledge is *of* the real, the real transcends knowledge. But this intellectual pre-eminence of Thought affords no ground for an assertion of its *real* pre-eminence. In Substance the Attributes are indiscerptible, and the distinction of union with *all* and with *each* other disappears. It is thus that the divine "intellect," the actuality of substantial Thought (which is not other than substantial Extension,

58. *Ep.,* 66 (my italics).

substantial X, etc.) "resembles ours in nothing but in name. There could be no further likeness than that between the Dog in the heavens and the barking animal. . . . If intellect pertains to the divine nature it cannot, like our intellect, follow, nor be simultaneous with, the things that are its objects . . . but, on the contrary, the truth and real essence of things is what it is because as such it exists by way of knowledge in God's intellect."[59]

59. *E.,* I, xvii, S. The scope of this book precludes a fuller discussion of the difficulties inherent in Spinoza's doctrine of the infinite Attributes of Substance, and of the restriction of human nature to two only of them, for in view of his laconic treatment of them any such discussion must place a greater reliance on rational speculation than is desirable in such an introduction. Nevertheless, for the sake of the more advanced, or more apt, reader, I will add the following remarks by way of clue.

The Attributes are distinct for intellect, but not in Substance itself, i.e. they form no infinite collection, but are discernible without falsification through the nature of modal intellect. Thus, on the one hand, to each true mode of Thought there is united a mode of Substance involving *every* Attribute, and on the other hand, since the Attributes, with their modes, are wholly distinct, and cannot be united to form a single systematic whole, to each true mode of Thought a mode of *one* Attribute only can be united. Addicts of "the Yea and Nay of Elea" are apt to take this as constituting an irreconcilable contradiction. But this is to overlook the substantial, non-collective, unity of the Attributes, and, in particular, to misrepresent the manner in which such a unity must receive modal expression. The human intellect, e.g. is united with "the body and nothing else," i.e. with a mode of Extension alone, and this is the manner in which the indeterminate unity of Substance is modally expressed in human nature. This modal union of Thought and Extension is thus in its way an expression of *all* the infinite Attributes, though a *positive* determination of two only. For determination is negation, the Attributes forming no *collection,* but the nature of each must be conceived, not as contrary to all others, but as their *inversion;* its determination *is* their negation. A rough analogy may be helpful to some readers (but must be used with great discretion): when white light falls on a thing that we perceive as red, the thing absorbs all the constituents of the white light except the red, which it reflects. The thing, therefore, is characterised, *in one way or another,* by all the constituents—its redness being a determination of whiteness involving, and made possible by, the absorption of the other constituents. In so far as white light is not a mere collection of coloured constituents, each colour may be regarded as the inverse of the remainder or complement. The analogy, of course, halts, but we may say that each Attribute of Substance is intellectually discernible from all others because its determinate nature is the inverse of the remainder. Now Thought is, for intellect, *other than* Extension, but it is not its *inverse,* for their union has a determinate character which is the inverse of a remainder. Thus a being uniting a mode of Thought with a mode of some Attribute other than Extension, could not be called a "man," though it might express the same substantial potency under variant inversion, and therefore determination. For the primordial indeterminate substantial potency must be actualized, not merely in every possible way and finite degree, but in every possible concrete form or inversion. The question *why* man is limited to two Attributes only cannot, therefore, arise. For it is such a limited being that we call "man," and the limitation is intrinsic, not extrinsic. Determination not merely *implies* or *involves* negation, it *is* negation.

Essence and the Distinction of Attributes in Spinoza's Metaphysics

ALAN DONAGAN

Writing to Spinoza on February 24, 1663, that *iuvenis doctissimus,* Simon de Vries, propounded a difficulty that has disquieted students of Spinozist metaphysics ever since. He quoted a passage from "the third scholium of prop. 8" in an early version of the first part of the *Ethics,* namely:

> From the foregoing it is plain that, although two really distinct attributes may be conceived (that is, one without the help of the other) they do not on that account constitute two beings (*entia*) or two diverse (*diversas*) substances. The reason is that it is of the nature of a substance that all its attributes, I mean each one, be conceived through itself, since they were all simultaneously in it.[1]

Against this, de Vries protested:

> the author (*Dominus*) seems to suppose that the nature of a substance is so constituted that it can have many attributes, which he has not yet proved, unless he is referring to the fifth definition—of absolutely infinite substance, or God; otherwise, if I may say [so], each substance has only one attribute, and were I to have the idea of two attributes, I should be able rightly to conclude that where two diverse attributes [were], there two diverse substances would be . . .[2]

This argument, I shall contend, is a generalization of Descartes's proof of a real distinction between *res cogitans* and *res extensa.*

De Vries's letter and Spinoza's reply show that even in the early drafts of the *Ethics,* Spinoza used the word "attribute" as a synonym for what Descartes had called "principal attribute" (*"attributum*

This essay was written especially for this volume.

1. *Ep.,* 8 (G., IV, 41). All references to the writings and correspondence of Spinoza are to *Spinoza Opera,* 4 vols., ed. Carl Gebhardt (Heidelberg, 1925). English translations from this work are mine, unless otherwise stated. In this passage and in similar contexts elsewhere, I have rendered *"diversa"* as "diverse," because Spinoza appears to use it technically, as a synonym for *"realiter distincta."*

2. *Ep.,* 8 (G., IV, 41).

praecipuum") : namely, "the one principal property of each substance which constitutes its nature and essence, and to which all others are referred."[3] In the final version of the *Ethics,* Spinoza expressed this in the well-known definition, "By 'attribute' I mean that which the intellect perceives of a substance, as constituting its essence."[4] In the version before de Vries, Spinoza wrote, according to his own quotation, "I mean by 'attribute' the same [as I mean by 'substance'], except that 'attribute' is used with regard to the intellect ascribing such and such a nature to a substance."[5] No property or quality is an attribute, in this sense, unless it constitutes the nature or essence of its substance. When does a property or quality do that? Descartes's answer appears to have been that a property or quality of a substance constitutes its essence, provided that it does not presuppose (*praesupponit*) any other property or quality.[6] By "presuppose another" he appears to have meant what Spinoza was to express by the phrase "cannot be conceived without the help of another" (*"sine ope alterius concipi non posse"*).[7] Thus the property *having a shape* cannot be a principal attribute, because it presupposes the property *being extended in length, breadth, and depth;* whereas the property *being extended in length, breadth, and depth* is a principal attribute, and constitutes the essence of a substance, because it presupposes no other.

A few months after replying to de Vries, Spinoza himself was to restate the Cartesian argument de Vries had generalized—in his *Renati Des Cartes Principiorum Philosophiae Pars I et II More Geometrico Demonstratae,* Part I of which he wrote in two weeks, during a visit to Amsterdam between April and June 1663.

In Spinoza's version, Descartes's argument runs as follows. Mind (*mens*) may be defined as substance the essence of which is constituted by the attribute *cogitatio,* and matter (*corpus*) as substance the essence of which is constituted by the attribute *extensio.*[8] Two premises may now be laid down.

---

3. Descartes, *Principia Philosophiae* I, 53 (Adam and Tannery (eds.), *Oeuvres de Descartes,* VIII, 25). The translation is mine.

4. *E.,* I, Def. 4 (G., II, 45).

5. *Ep.,* 9 (G., IV, 46).

6. Descartes, *Principia Philosophiae* I, 53 (Adam and Tannery, VIII, 25).

7. Cf. *E.,* I, x, S. (G., II, 52).

8. *Desc. Princ. Phil.,* I, Defs. 6, 7 (G., I, 150).

(i) [*Desc. Princ. Phil.,* I, 8, Dem.] "We clearly perceive mind, that is (by Def. 6) *substantia cogitans,* without matter, that is, without any *substantia extensa* (by Props. 3 and 4); and *vice versa* matter without mind (as everybody readily concedes)."[9]

The argument which (in Props. 3 and 4) Spinoza presented Descartes as offering for this premise is that given in *Meditation* II and *Principia Philosophiae* I, 8: that mind is conceived as distinct from matter because it can be known to exist when the existence of matter is in doubt. This argument, which has recently been both attacked and defended,[10] may here be disregarded; for in the *Ethics* Spinoza rejected it, while accepting Descartes's premise as obvious.[11]

(ii) [*Desc. Princ. Phil.,* I, 7, C.] "God can bring about everything that we clearly perceive, exactly as we perceive it."[12]

From these premises it follows that

(iii) [*Desc. Princ. Phil.,* I, 8, Dem.] "through the divine power, mind can exist without matter, and matter without mind."[13]

But Descartes gave the following definition of real distinction between substances:

(iv) [*Desc. Princ. Phil.,* I, Def. 10] "two substances are said to be really distinct (*realiter distinguuntur*) when each one of them can exist without the other."[14]

This conception of real distinction is technical, and derives from a threefold Cartesian classification, which in *C.m.,* II, 5 Spinoza expounded as follows. A *distinctio realis,* which may obtain between substances or parts of the same substance, is recognized by the fact

9. *Desc. Princ. Phil.,* I, 8, Dem. (G., I, 167).

10. Cf. Anthony Kenny, *Descartes* (New York: Random House, 1968), pp. 79–88; George W. Roberts, "Some Questions in Epistemology," *Proc. Arist. Soc.,* 70 (1969–70), 37–60; Saul Kripke, "Identity and Necessity," in *Identity and Individuation,* ed. Milton K. Munitz (New York: New York University Press, 1971), pp. 163*n*–164*n*.

11. That *extensio* and *cogitatio* are distinct attributes is presupposed in *E.,* II, Def. 1 and Ax. 2, 3. That our ideas of these attributes are adequate, being *propria communia,* is clear from *E.,* II, xxxviii–xl. Cf. H. F. Hallett, *Aeternitas* (Oxford: Clarendon Press, 1930), pp. 100–101.

12. *Desc. Princ. Phil.,* I, 7, C. (G., I, 166).

13. *Desc. Princ. Phil.,* I, 8, Dem. (G., I, 167).

14. *Desc. Princ. Phil.,* I, Def. 10 (G., I, 151).

that each of the *diversa* can be conceived without the help of the other, and consequently can exist without it. A *distinctio modalis* may obtain either between a substance and one of its modes, when it is recognized by the fact that, although the mode cannot be conceived without its substance, the substance can be conceived without the mode; or between two modes of the same substance, when it is recognized by the fact that, although neither can be conceived without the substance, each can be conceived without the help of the other. Finally, a *distinctio rationis* obtains between two things distinguished intellectually, of which neither can be conceived without the other: as between a substance and its attribute, or between duration and extension. This classification is much simpler than the elaborate late scholastic theories of distinction, which Spinoza followed Descartes in contemptuously dismissing: *"Peripateticorum distinctionum farraginem non curamus."*[15] As we shall see, Spinoza's own theory of distinction is simply a corrected version of Descartes's.

From (iii) and (iv) it follows at once that

(v) [*Desc. Princ. Phil.*, I, 8] "mind and matter are really distinct."[16]

I think it is evident that in his letter of February 24, 1663, de Vries simply generalized this argument. Take any two attributes, *F* and *G,* that are really distinct by Descartes's definition, that is, are such that one can be conceived without the help of the other, and it will follow from Descartes's proposition about the divine power, that the substances whose essences are constituted by *F* and *G* can each exist without the other, and hence that they too are really distinct. And if that is so, then Spinoza's doctrine that the same substance may have more than one attribute must be false. Anything that appears to be a substance having really distinct attributes can at best be what Descartes thought a man is: a union of really distinct substances.

In the letter in which he replied to de Vries, Spinoza missed the point. He had been asked for a "clearer explanation" of how the same substance could have more than one attribute.[17] But, after replying to a question about his definition of substance and attribute by simply declaring that his definition was clear, he went on as follows.

15. Cf. *C.m.*, II, 5 (G., I, 257–59).
16. *Desc. Princ. Phil.*, I, 8 (G., I, 167).
17. *Ep.*, 8 (G., IV, 41).

Yet you wish, what there is very little need of, that I should explain by an example how one and the same thing can be designated by two names. Well, lest I seem grudging, I shall provide two. First, I say that by "Israel" the third Patriarch is meant; I mean the same by "Jacob," the name "Jacob" having been given to him as well, because he had grasped his brother's heel. Secondly, by "plane" I mean that which reflects all the rays of light without any change; I mean the same by "white," except that "white" is used with regard to a man looking at the plane.[18]

Unfortunately, neither de Vries nor Descartes had evinced the slightest difficulty in understanding how the same thing could be designated by different names, when those names designated different modes of it. Yet in both Spinoza's examples, his different names designate modes, not attributes. In the first, being the third Patriarch, and grasping his brother's heel, are different modes of the man called "Israel" and "Jacob," and not attributes constituting his essence. The second example is in even worse case. For, taking *plane* as a mode of matter, and *white* as a mode of a perceiving mind, the names "plane" and "white" cannot be supposed to designate even modes of the same substance, except by begging the Cartesian question de Vries raised.

That Spinoza came to recognize the inadequacy of his reply to de Vries is at least suggested by the final text of the *Ethics*. The passage quoted by de Vries from "the third scholium of prop. 8" in the early version reappears in *E., I, x, S.,* polished a little, and with a useful gloss which I italicize.

From the foregoing it is plain that, although two really distinct attributes may be conceived, that is, one without the help of the other, we cannot thence conclude that they constitute two beings or two diverse substances; for it is of the nature of a substance that each one of its attributes is conceived through itself; because all the attributes that it has were always simultaneously in it, *nor can one of them be produced by another, but each one expresses the reality or existence* (esse) *of the substance.*[19]

At this point, however, Spinoza went on to give an explanation, which de Vries's objection shows not to have been in the earlier version:

It is therefore far from absurd to attribute to one substance many attributes; for nothing in nature is clearer than that each being

18. *Ep.,* 9 (G., IV, 46).
19. *E., I, x, S.* (G., II, 52).

(*ens*) must be conceived under some attribute, and that, the more reality or existence (*esse*) it has, the more attributes it has which express both necessity or eternity, and infinity; and consequently nothing is also clearer than that an absolutely infinite being (*ens*) is to be defined (as we have done in Def. 6) as a being which consists in infinite attributes, of which each one expresses a certain eternal and infinite essence.[20]

De Vries had wondered whether Spinoza might defend his view that the same substance may have more than one attribute, by appealing to his definition of God. Why was he not content to do that? Well, his definition was not traditional. So, instead of merely citing it, Spinoza counterattacked his Cartesian adversaries by deriving it from the traditional theology they themselves endorsed. Did they not acknowledge God to be an absolutely infinite being? And did they not also acknowledge that no attribute that expresses an eternal and infinite essence can be denied to God? For no being the concept of which is restricted or limited to only some attributes which express an eternal and infinite essence can equal in reality or existence a being that is not so restricted or limited. If this be acknowledged, then it would appear to follow that de Vries's Cartesian principle, "Where two different attributes are, there two different substances must be,"[21] breaks down in the case of God, the infinite substance. And Spinoza's position is that God is the only substance.[22]

What might a Cartesian reply?

The orthodox theory of the divine attributes was complex. Maimonides, insisting that "there cannot be any belief in the unity of God except by admitting that He is one simple substance, without any composition or plurality of elements,"[23] had concluded that God cannot have a plurality of really distinct attributes. Every attributive expression predicated of God in the *Torah* either denotes the quality of a divine action, but not of the divine essence, or, although "indeed intended to convey some idea of the Divine Being itself," denotes the negation of what is opposite to his essence.[24] "All we understand is the fact that He exists, that He is a being to whom none of His

---

20. *E.*, I, x, S. (G., II, 52).

21. *Ep.*, 8 (G., IV, 41).

22. *E.*, I, xiv (G., II, 56).

23. Moses Maimonides, *The Guide for the Perplexed*, tr. M. Friedlaender (London: G. Routledge & Sons, 1904), 2nd ed., I, 51 (p. 69).

24. Maimonides, *op. cit.*, I, 58 (p. 83).

creatures is similar, who has nothing in common with them, who does not include plurality, who is never too feeble to produce other beings, and whose relation to the universe is that of a steersman to a boat; and even this is not a real relation, a real simile, but serves only to convey to us the idea that God rules the universe; that is, that He gives it its duration, and preserves its necessary arrangement."[25]

The sophisticated theories of distinction of the later Christian scholastics, who were for the most part less rigorous than Maimonides in following the *via negativa,* enabled them to hold that the distinction between the divine attributes might be less than a *distinctio realis,* but more than a *distinctio rationis.*[26] The Cartesians, with Spinoza's approval, repudiated these subtleties.[27] In consequence, their position, as Spinoza described it, was very like that of Maimonides: namely, that "all distinctions which we draw between the attributes of God are nothing but [*distinctiones*] *rationis,* nor are those attributes in reality (*revera*) distinguished from one another."[28]

A Cartesian, then, might reply to Spinoza's argument that no attribute which expresses an eternal and infinite essence may be denied to God, by protesting that between any two attributes that express such an essence, there can be no more than a *distinctio rationis.* There can no more be a real plurality of divine attributes than there can be a real plurality of divine essences. This theological position is philosophically so attractive that those who follow H. A. Wolfson in thinking of Spinoza as "the last of the Medievals"[29] are tempted also to follow him in believing that Spinoza held it. Wolfson goes so far as to read the scholium to *E.,* I, x as implying that, while the attributes of God appear to be really distinct, in reality they are one and identical with the divine substance: they "are only different words expressing the same reality and being of substance."[30] In the same fashion, he

25. *Loc. cit.*

26. The most celebrated of these "Peripatetic" theories is Duns Scotus' theory of *distinctio formalis,* for which and for related positions see Maurice J. Grajewski, O.F.M., *The Formal Distinction of Duns Scotus* (Washington, D.C.: The Catholic University of America, 1944). Diane Steinberg has explored some of these views in relation to Spinoza in *Spinoza's Theory of the Divine Attributes* (M.A. thesis, University of Illinois, Urbana, 1970).

27. *C.m.,* II, 5 (G., I, 259).

28. *C.m.,* II, 5 (G., I, 259).

29. Harry Austryn Wolfson, *The Philosophy of Spinoza* (Cambridge, Mass.: Harvard University Press, 1934), 2 vols., I, ix.

30. Wolfson, *op. cit.,* I, 156.

interprets *E.,* I, xii ("No attribute of substance, from which it follows that substance can be divided, can be truly conceived") as complementing the definitions of substance and attribute: "While the definition of attribute states affirmatively the subjective nature of attributes by declaring that they are only perceived by the mind, the proposition denies any independent reality to attributes by which the simplicity of the substance would be endangered."[31]

However, it is as certain as anything disputed in Spinoza's *Ethics* can be, that Wolfson's interpretation of these passages is mistaken.[32] This is most clearly shown in the early *Short Treatise,* written in 1660–1661,[33] in which Spinoza sharply distinguished the conception of the divine attributes in traditional philosophical theology from his own unmistakably post-Cartesian conception. In that work, he divided into three groups what the "Philosophers," scholastic or Cartesian, recognized as divine attributes:

(i) *"propria* or properties which do, indeed, belong to a thing, but never explain what the thing is": for example, *"self-subsisting, being the cause of all things, highest good, eternal and immutable."*[34] These are evidently Maimonides' negative attributes.

(ii) "[T]hings which they ascribe to God, and which do not, however, pertain to him, such as *omniscient, merciful, wise,* and so forth, which things . . . are only certain modes of the thinking thing."[35] These appear to correspond to Maimonides' qualities of divine action.

(iii) "Lastly, they call him the *highest good;* but if they understand by it something different from what they have already said, that God is *immutable and a cause of all things,* then they have become entangled in their own thought, or are unable to understand themselves."[36] The Cartesians are certainly among the "Philosophers"

31. *Loc. cit.*

32. For a decisive criticism of Wolfson's interpretation see Martial Gueroult, *Spinoza,* I, *Spinoza: I, Dieu* (Paris: Aubier 1968), pp. 441–47: "Obsession with the 'Jewish literature' has hindered the commentator from perceiving the words of the text, and has made him read others in it, put there by his prejudice" (p. 445). This and subsequent translations from Gueroult's book are mine. Cf. also E. M. Curley, *Spinoza's Metaphysics* (Cambridge, Mass.: Harvard University Press, 1969), pp. 28–36.

33. *Korte Verhandeling van God de Mensch en des Zelfswelstand* (G., I, 1–121), tr. A. Wolf, *Spinoza's Short Treatise on God, Man, and His Well-Being* (London: Black, 1910), from which all quotations in the text are taken.

34. *K.V.,* I, 7 (G., I, 45; Wolf, 53).

35. *K.V.,* I, 7 (G., I, 45; Wolf, 53).

36. *K.V.,* I, 7 (G., I, 45; Wolf, 54).

referred to here; for they defined God as "a substance which we understand to be through itself perfect in the highest degree (*summe perfectam*)," and maintained that this definition was not to be taken as negative (as Maimonides took it).[37]

Of the attributes recognized by the "Philosophers," then, those of the third group (which include the Cartesian attribute of highest perfection, conceived as positive) are mere chimeras; and those of the first two groups (negative attributes, and modes of the divine activity) are not attributes in the strict sense, because they do not express the divine essence. In sum, Spinoza did not dispute the doctrine of the scholastic and Cartesian philosophers that between such divine attributes as they recognized there are only *distinctiones rationis*. His objection was that neither scholastic nor Cartesian philosophical theology had correctly identified a single genuine divine attribute—an attribute, that is, which expresses an eternal and infinite essence. Such attributes, he remarked in the *Short Treatise,* "need no genus, or anything, through which they might be better understood or explained: for since they exist as attributes of a self-subsisting being, they also become known through themselves."[38]

The clue to Spinoza's position is provided by what he recognized as expressing an eternal and infinite essence. Here, where he was most original, he owed most to Descartes. His revolutionary idea was that the two attributes which Descartes had taken to express distinct finite essences, in fact each express an eternal and infinite essence. That the divine essence and the divine intellect were identical was of course common scholastic doctrine; and some medieval thinkers, notably Crescas, had speculated that God might be the place of the world.[39] Such ideas no doubt encouraged Spinoza. But the concepts he worked with were Cartesian. He took *extensio* and *cogitatio,* as Descartes had expounded them in his theory of the created universe, and argued that each of them is conceived through itself, and admits neither external limitation nor internal division. Each therefore expresses an eternal and infinite essence. Moreover, nothing else known to us does. As he wrote in a note to *K.V.*, I, 7, "up to the present, only two of these infinites [i.e. the attributes of which God consists] are known to us through their own essence; and these are thought

37. *Desc. Princ. Phil.,* I, Def. 8; 5, S.; 6, S. (G., I, 150, 158–159, 160).
38. *K.V.,* I. 7 (G., I, 46–47; Wolf, 55).
39. Cf. Wolfson, *op. cit.,* I, Ch. 7.

and extension. All else that is commonly ascribed to God is not any attribute of his . . ."[40]

Wolfson's interpretation of Spinoza's theory of the divine simplicity must be false, because it is irreconcilable with the two facts

(i) that Spinoza followed Descartes in holding that the attributes *cogitatio* and *extensio* are really distinct, that is, that one may be conceived without the help of the other—our ideas of both being, as *propria communia*, adequate and therefore true; and

(ii) that Spinoza reached the revolutionary conclusion that, since *cogitatio* and *extensio* each express a certain eternal and infinite essence, each of them must be one of the attributes in which God, the absolutely infinite being, consists.

From these two facts it follows that Spinoza was committed to the position that God, the absolutely infinite substance, has really distinct attributes. And *prima facie,* this position furnished him with a conditional answer to de Vries's implicit question, "How can the nature of a substance be so constituted that it can have many attributes?" If the classical assumption be accepted that no attribute expressing an eternal and infinite essence can be denied to God, then it follows from the fact that the really distinct attributes *cogitatio* and *extensio* each express such an essence, that a divine or absolutely infinite substance must be so constituted as to have many attributes.

Yet this conditional answer to de Vries invites a reply which, however repugnant it might have been to de Vries himself, would captivate many philosophers today: namely that it is simply false that an *ens realissimum* exists, to which no attribute expressing an eternal and infinite essence may be denied. The force of de Vries's Cartesian argument is that if it is logically possible that a being divide into independently existing substances, then, even though not so divided, it must nevertheless be composed of really distinct substances. A de Vries who lacked the seventeenth-century respect for classical theology might therefore argue as follows. If there are really distinct attributes each expressing an eternal and infinite essence, then it is logically possible that a being consisting in several such attributes should divide into several independently existing substances. So, even if a single infinite being were to consist in both infinite *extensio* and infinite *cogitatio,* it would not be a single substance, but a

40. *K.V.,* I, 7 (G., I, 44; Wolf, 52).

union of two really distinct substances, as Descartes believed a man to be.

This line of thought is persuasive in itself, and it ought not to surprise us that philosophers like Martial Gueroult, reacting against Wolfson's interpretation of Spinoza's theology as Maimonidean, should have attributed it to Spinoza himself, and have turned Spinoza's God into something very like an infinite counterpart of a Cartesian man.[41]

Gueroult has demurred to this charge. While acknowledging that, according to his interpretation, "the problem of the union of soul and body arises in Descartes in terms analogous to those of the union of attributes in Spinoza," he maintains that this analogy is innocuous. "The union of the *diversa* in Descartes is conditionally necessary, because it is only asserted on the supposition of a contingent fact attested by experience: knowledge of the existence of man. In Spinoza it is absolutely necessary *a priori,* because it is affirmed under the constraint of an eternal truth imposed by pure understanding, knowledge of the absolutely necessary existence of God."[42]

This, while correct, poses a problem. It is true that the union of attributes in Spinoza's God is absolutely necessary, and in a Cartesian man only conditionally necessary; but does Gueroult provide a coherent account of Spinoza's God according to which the union of his attributes is absolutely necessary?

Gueroult's interpretation may be summed up as follows. Each of the divine attributes expresses an essence that is not only eternal and infinite, but also really distinct from that expressed by any other. Hence the essences expressed by the divine attributes must not be confounded with the divine essence itself, which must consist in an infinity of infinite essences. Unlike the essence of God, the essence expressed by a divine attribute is not absolutely infinite, but infinite in its kind.[43] However, it is the essence of a substance: not of a substance absolutely infinite, but of a substance infinite in its kind.

41. The fullest development of this line of thought known to me is in Martial Gueroult's *Spinoza.* However, Gueroult's notes make clear that a similar line is followed in a book I have not seen, Lewis Robinson's *Kommentar zu Spinozas Ethik* (Leipzig, 1928). H. F. Hallett has described Robinson as holding "that the Attributes are the real substances, and Substance but a single order that prevails in them all" (*Creation, Emanation, and Salvation: A Spinozistic Study* (The Hague: M. Nijhoff, 1962), p. 46).

42. Gueroult, *Spinoza,* I, 232.

43. *Ibid.,* pp. 67–74.

Such a substance Gueroult calls "a substance constituted of one attribute" or "a substance of one attribute"; and he takes Spinoza to have considered such substances to be really distinct from each other, self-caused, and self-existent.[44]

Spinoza's God, according to Gueroult, is a union of substances of one attribute, and not a mere aggregation. A set of substances of one attribute, each infinite in its kind, would be a mere aggregate unless their modes were in correspondence. And it is a fundamental tenet of Spinoza's metaphysics that the correspondence between God as thinking and God as extended which is affirmed in the theorem, "The order and connexion of ideas is the same as the order and connexion of things,"[45] holds between the modes, infinite and finite, of any two of the attributes of God.

Yet not even correspondence between the modes of the various attributes of God suffices to unify them into one substance: the correspondence must be absolutely necessary. As Descartes conceived man, it is true by definition that states of a man's consciousness correspond to certain states of his pineal gland,[46] but this correspondence is only conditionally necessary, not absolutely necessary. If the consciousness and pineal gland in question are as a matter of contingent fact those of the same man, then their states must correspond; but if not, they need not.

Gueroult, of course, reminds us that the substances of one attribute united in God exist necessarily, unlike the mind and body united in a Cartesian man. There seem to be two possibilities here. (1) According to classical natural theology, the modes of a necessary existent are not necessitated by its essence: thus God, a necessary existent, freely acts in ways not deducible from his essence. On such a view, the substances of one attribute which constitute God might necessarily exist, and yet the correspondence of their modes be only conditionally necessary, like the correspondence of states of consciousness and states of the pineal gland in a Cartesian man. A union of this kind, being only conditionally necessary, would not satisfy Spinoza's conditions for substantial, or absolutely necessary, unity. (2) According to Spinoza himself, the classical theological

44. E.g. *ibid.,* pp. 51–55, 141.

45. *E.,* II, vii (G., I, 89). For our present purposes, it is unfortunate that Spinoza's proof of this theorem rests on an axiom about knowledge of effects, and cannot be directly generalized to apply to all the attributes.

46. Descartes, *Les Passions de l'Âme,* I, 31–39.

position is incoherent. The essence of a necessary existent necessarily determines each and every one of its modes. Consequently, if the modes of two substances of one attribute correspond, then that correspondence is necessitated by the essences of those substances. Nor can we stop at this point. If the correspondence between the modes of all the substances of one attribute is grounded in their essences, we must ask what is the nature of that ground.

The only answer I have found in Gueroult is this.

> Finally, let us consider the divine substance itself: it is clear that . . . the attributes will be things absolutely different as to their essence but absolutely identical as to the cause (i.e. the causal act) by which each produces itself and produces all its modes. And so the identity of the *causa sui* in each is that by which they constitute one and the same self-existent substance. There is no mere juxtaposition of attributes, because they are identical as to their causal act; no more is there a fusion between them, because they remain irreducible as to their essences.[47]

The objection to this is that it divides the causal act of a substance from its essence in a way utterly foreign to Spinoza. His very definition of *causa sui,* namely, "by '*causa sui*' I mean that of which the essence involves existence . . ."[48] implies that in a self-existent being, which Gueroult takes a substance of one attribute to be, it is indifferent whether it or its essence is said to cause its existence. If the infinite substances of one attribute are really distinct, then their *causae* are really distinct also.

Gueroult is clearly right in taking Spinoza to hold that the identity of the divine substance derives from the causal act by which it necessarily exists. He has overlooked that if there is only one causal act by which all the attributes of God exist, then there is only one essence which involves their existence. And, since each attribute expresses the essence of a self-existent being, that is, the essence which involves that being's existence, if there is only one essence which involves the existence of all the attributes, then that essence is what each and every attribute expresses. God is unified by the fact that all his really distinct attributes express the same essence.

This conclusion can also be derived directly from *E.,* I, Defs. 4 and 6. *E.,* I, Def. 6 lays it down that each one of the divine attributes

---

47. Gueroult, *op. cit.,* p. 238.
48. *E.,* I, Def. 1 (G., II, 45).

expresses an eternal and infinite essence.[49] And in *E.*, I, Def. 4, an attribute (*attribut*um, not *attribut*a) is defined as "that which the intellect perceives of a substance, as constituting *its* essence."[50] This implies that every single divine attribute is perceived by the intellect as constituting *God*'s essence. Hence, since God has only one essence, the eternal and infinite essences which (by *E.*, I, Def. 6) God's diverse attributes express must all be identical with that essence, and therefore with one another. This is confirmed by the way in which Spinoza refers to *E.*, I, Def. 4 in his proofs of *E.*, I, xix and xx. For example:

> Next, by the attributes of God we must understand that which (by Def. 4) expresses the essence of the divine substance.[51]

Gueroult's interpretation of the phrase "the attributes of God" as here equivalent to "the totality of the infinite attributes of God"[52] is refuted by Spinoza's citation of *E.*, I, Def. 4, which is about any single attribute of any substance. Since nothing follows from that definition about anything but what each single attribute of a substance expresses, Spinoza here implies that each divine attribute expresses the essence of the divine substance.

We are now in a deadlock. On the one hand, it has been established that Wolfson was mistaken in denying that the divine attributes are really distinct, and in conceiving Spinoza's God as a Maimonidean *ens simplicissimum;* on the other, Gueroult's proposal has also been found wanting, that the divine attributes each constitute the essence of a distinct substance of one attribute, so that the essence of the divine substance is constituted by an infinity of essences of substances each infinite in its kind. Spinoza's position is *both* that the divine attributes are really distinct, *and* that they each express the same divine essence. Classical metaphysics puts down such a conjunction as impossible, self-contradictory.

H. F. Hallett has made a suggestion for reconciling Spinoza's position with classical metaphysics, which I record largely in his words,

49. *E.*, I, Def. 6 (G., II, 45).
50. *E.*, I, Def. 4 (G., II, 45). My italics.
51. *E.*, I, xix, Dem. (G., II, 64).
52. Cf. Gueroult, *op. cit.*, pp. 302–303, 305–306. Spinoza's use of the phrase *"Deus, sive omnia Dei attributa"* in the enunciation of *E.*, I, xix, simply reflects the definition of God as "consisting in infinite attributes." It implies nothing about whether those attributes express one essence or many.

for fear I have misunderstood him. He agrees that Spinoza holds both that the divine attributes are really distinct, and that they express the same essence. And, he describes that essence, the essence of the divine substance, as that of an absolutely indeterminate infinite potency-in-act.

> [W]hy [he asks] should not an identical infinite potency be truly conceived as having infinite equivalent forms? Why should not that which in and for itself is indeterminate be discernible by intellect as involving infinite determination?

To this, he gives the obvious answer,

> Doubtless, it will be said that this . . . involves a plain contradiction . . .

which he proposes to resolve as follows:

> What Spinoza asserts . . . is not that the infinite forms of potency [i.e. the attributes] are indiscernible . . . but that originally, and in themselves, they are equivalent, so that the primordial potency is absolutely indeterminate. Yet intellect is not thus involved in error: the discernible equivalent forms of potency are not intellectual figments.[53]

There is a fatal objection to such a resolution. On the supposition that the infinite substance is "in and for itself indeterminate," if the intellect "discerns" that substance as "involving infinite determination," then the intellect must discern falsely. But in Spinoza's view, it is at least an extrinsic characteristic of a true idea that it corresponds with its *ideatum*.[54]

Despite their differences, Gueroult and Hallett are agreed that Spinoza's God is a unity as cause, and that the plurality of the divine attributes is a plurality of effects. But this must be wrong. It is true that, as *natura naturans,* absolutely infinite substance is cause, and as *natura naturata* effect; and it is also true that *natura naturata* is the entire system of divine modes, infinite and finite. But the point of Spinoza's doctrine that God is *causa sui* is that *natura naturans* and *natura naturata* are not *really* distinct. In his Cartesian terminology, the distinctions between absolutely infinite substance and its modes, and between any one of its modes and any other, are *modal*, not *real*. Yet, although the plurality of *natura naturata* is *modal*,

---

53. Hallett, *Creation, Emanation and Salvation,* p. 46.
54. *E.*, II, Def. 4, Expl. (G., II, 85).

Spinoza expressly declared the plurality of the divine attributes to be *real*. Hence the distinction between the divine attributes is not the modal one found in *natura naturata* but not in *natura naturans:* it is a real one found equally in both. This becomes evident when the divine attributes are considered in isolation: for example, *extensio*. God as an infinite extended substance, containing motion and rest, is not an effect of some unextended infinite cause. As cause of himself as extended, God is *extended*.

Does a description of a coherent Spinozist theory of substance and attribute emerge from these conflicting exegeses and objections? A few things about Spinoza's position have become reasonably clear. Two principles lie at its heart: his revolutionary principle that there are at least two really distinct attributes, each of which expresses an eternal and infinite essence; and the classical theological principle that there is an *ens realissimum*. As Gueroult has made plain, Spinoza saw that he could only retain both these principles by abandoning the classical conception of God as an *ens simplicissimum:* the fullness of the divine being cannot be a fullness of simplicity. It consists in diversity of attributes—in the impossibility of denying to God any attribute expressing an eternal and infinite essence. God, then, is a *causa sui* that is necessarily expressed in an infinity of diverse attributes. Nor is an attribute a mode: it does not exist in God, as an effect modally distinct from its cause. In other words, God must be conceived as *causa sui* under each attribute.

Yet a difficulty remains intractable. It is the same difficulty which, as we have seen, underlay de Vries's original protest, and was to generate Gueroult's interpretation: namely, would Spinoza have had any reply at all to a more radical de Vries, who was prepared to concede that *extensio* and *cogitatio* are really distinct attributes, each expressing an eternal and infinite essence, but who nevertheless found incoherent the concept of a substance whose essence is expressed by a plurality of such attributes? Such a radical de Vries would, of course, be an atheist, having dismissed the traditional concept of an *ens realissimum* as absurd. Why Spinoza did not perceive this difficulty is plain: he could not imagine that any philosopher would question that an *ens realissimum* exists; and he naturally concluded that, since the Cartesians themselves accepted the real distinction of *extensio* and *cogitatio,* all that remained for him to demonstrate was that each expresses an eternal and infinite essence. He was rightly confident of his ability to do that.

Had he been confronted with a radical de Vries, however, I do not think that Spinoza would have taken refuge in dogmatic theism. Once the buried premise of the radical objection had been brought to light, namely, that to every really distinct attribute there corresponds a really distinct essence, he would have had grounds for rejecting it. The attributes with respect to which such a premise is persuasive are attributes constituting the essences of created substances. The Cartesians, perceiving that such essences as those of triangles and men must be defined in terms of the attributes *extensio* and *cogitatio,* simply took it for granted that the essence of any substance, even that of God, is to be defined in terms of that substance's essential attribute. And to twentieth-century philosophers, who have lost the habit of applying their categories to infinite things, the identification of the essence of a thing with its defining attributes has become virtually axiomatic.

Spinoza, as I understand him, repudiated this whole line of thought, together with the concepts of creation and finite substance. Why, he demanded, should the essence of an absolutely infinite substance, a substance that is *causa sui,* be supposed to be definable in terms of any or all of its attributes? Why not think of the essence of such a substance as standing in a unique relation to each of its attributes: a relation neither of definitional identity nor of causality; a relation, moreover, which might reasonably be signified by speaking of each attribute as "constituting" (*"constituens"*) or "expressing" (*"exprimens"*) that essence? A fundamental formal property of this relation would be that two attributes might on the one hand be really distinct, and on the other constitute or express the same essence.

Although Spinoza did not formally define "essence" in the *Ethics,* since anything which constitutes or expresses an essence pertains to it (although the converse is not the case), his definition of "what pertains to an essence" provides a test, but not a conclusive one, of this suggestion. That definition runs as follows.

> I say that that pertains to the essence of something, which being given the thing is necessarily given, and which being taken away the thing is necessarily taken away; or that without which the thing can neither be nor be conceived, and *vice versa* that which without the thing [can neither be nor be conceived].[55]

55. *E.,* II, Def. 2 (G., II, 85).

It is plain that, according to this definition, although each can be conceived without recourse to the other, both the attributes *extensio* and *cogitatio* pertain to the essence of God. *Extensio* being given, an absolutely infinite being is also given; for *extensio* expresses an eternal and infinite essence, and whatever expresses such an essence is an attribute of an absolutely infinite being. Again, if *per impossibile, extensio* were taken away, there could be no absolutely infinite being; for, since *extensio* expresses an eternal and infinite essence, a being lacking *extensio* could not be absolutely infinite. Parallel arguments obviously hold for *cogitatio*. And nothing in this definition implies that, because *extensio* and *cogitatio* both pertain to the same essence, they cannot be really distinct.

Spinoza's theory of the unity and diversity of *Deus sive Natura* was made possible only by his radically new conception of the relation between a substance's essence and its attributes. To those who overlook this radical novelty, his whole system must appear inconsistent. The decision whether it is consistent or not must, in large measure, turn on whether his new conception of the relation of essence and attribute contradicts either itself, or his other fundamental principles.[56]

56. During the past five years, at first by discussion and later by correspondence, my views about Spinoza's metaphysics have been strongly influenced by Mrs. Diane Steinberg; and I desire to express my gratitude.

Spinoza's Letter on the Infinite
(Letter XII, to Louis Meyer)

MARTIAL GUEROULT

I.—The problem of the infinite and of the indivisibility of substance is treated in Book I of the *Ethics*. *Proposition xii* demonstrates infinity; *Proposition xiii*, its *Corollary* and its *Scholium,* and lastly the *Scholium* of *Proposition xv* demonstrate indivisibility. Infinity and indivisibility are two unique properties of substance which derive immediately from its fundamental property: *causa sui*. Indeed, whatever necessarily exists of itself cannot, without contradiction, be deprived of any part whatever of its existence; consequently, it is necessarily infinite and excludes any partitioning. Infinity and indivisibility being two sides of the same property, there results a radical antinomy between the infinite and the divisible. If we affirm one we must deny the other: the dogmatist, affirming divisibility, denies the infinite; Spinoza, affirming the infinite, denies divisibility. This is an irreducible conflict, as long as we ignore the nature of substance, but one that is instantly resolved as soon as we know that substance necessarily exists of itself.

Given this, however, the problem is far from exhausted. The antinomy opposing infinity and divisibility, resolved in the *Ethics* on the level of substance by excluding the divisible, reappears on the level of the mode, where we must affirm infinite divisibility, that is, both the infinite and the divisible. If it is true that the solution to the second part of the problem is included in that of the first part, the *Ethics* did not expressly develop it. It is *Letter XII* to Louis Meyer, called by Spinoza and by his correspondents *Letter on the Infinite,*[1] which, embracing the problem in its entirety, answers this difficulty— as well as many others.

Its character, at once succinct and exhaustive, is emphasized by the author himself: "I have," he wrote toward the end, "briefly ex-

---

Translated by Kathleen McLaughlin from M. Gueroult, *Spinoza,* Vol. I, Paris: Aubier-Montaigne, 1968, Appendix IX, pp. 500–528. By permission of the author and the publisher.

1. "Epistola de Infinito." Cf. *Ep.,* 80 (G., IV, 331, line 10), from Tschirnhaus to Spinoza, and *Ep.,* 81 (G., IV, 332, line 7), from Spinoza to Tschirnhaus.

posed to you . . . the causes (*causas*) of the errors and confusions which have arisen on the subject of this question of the Infinite, and I have explained these errors in such a way that, if I am not mistaken, there no longer remains a single question relative to the Infinite that I have not touched upon, nor one whose solution cannot be quite easily found from what I have said."[2]

We see by these last lines that this letter presents above all a refutative quality, and it owes to this a great part of its obscurity. The doctrine is not directly expounded, but indicated through the errors whose causes are exposed.

These causes are first of all confusions among things, and secondly the reason for such confusions, which is itself also a confusion, but among our cognitions.

* * *

II.—The difficulties relating to the Infinite flow from three kinds of confusions arising from our failure to distinguish between six different cases.

These six cases are divided into three pairs of opposing terms:

First pair:

1. The thing infinite by its essence or by virtue of its definition.[3]

2. The thing without limits, not by virtue of its essence, but by virtue of its cause.[4]

Second pair:

3. The thing infinite insofar as without limits.[5]

4. The thing infinite insofar as its parts, although included within a *maximum* and a *minimum* known to us, cannot be expressed by any number.[6]

Third pair:

5. The things representable by understanding alone and not by imagination.[7]

[2]. *Ep.*, 12 (G., IV, 61, lines 9–13).

[3]. *Ep.*, 12 (G., IV, 53, lines 2–3): *"Id quod sua natura, sive vi suae definitionis sequitur esse infinitum."*

[4]. *Ep.*, 12 (G., IV, 53, lines 3–4): *"Id quod nullos fines habet, non quidem vi suae essentiae, sed vi suae causae."*

[5]. *Ep.*, 12 (G., IV, 53, lines 4–5): *"Quod infinitum dicitur, quia nullos fines habet."*

[6]. *Ep.*, 12 (G., IV, 53, lines 6–8): *"Id cujus partes, quamvis ejus maximum et minimum habeamus, nullo tamen adaequare et explicare possumus."*

[7]. *Ep.*, 12 (G., IV, 53, lines 8–9): *"Id quod solummodo intelligere, non vero imaginari."*

6. The things representable at once by imagination and by understanding.[8]

The confusion between the two cases of each of these pairs has made us unable to understand: *a*) which Infinity cannot be divided into parts and is without parts; *b*) which, on the contrary, is divisible without contradiction; *c*) which can, without difficulty, be conceived as larger than another; *d*) which, on the other hand, cannot be so conceived.[9]

We will examine the different cases in this order, keeping for the end the analysis of the geometrical example on which the discussion of the fourth case is based.

* * *

III.—The preliminary condition for escaping from such confusion is to have in mind this elementary truth, that there exists in Nature nothing other than substance in eternity and modes in duration.[10]

IV.—*Case no. 1: The thing infinite by its essence.*

This case is that of substance.—Existing necessarily by virtue of its essence, substance cannot without contradiction be conceived as finite, because in so doing one would deny that by its essence substance necessarily posited its existence in the entire expanse of its being; nor could it be conceived as divisible, for partitioning implies finitude. Thus, it is by nature absolutely indivisible. It must be the same for eternity, since eternity is defined by existence, necessary in itself;[11] and for magnitude, insofar as it is conceived as the extension of bodies.[12]

V.—*Case no. 2: The thing without limits only by its cause.*

This case is that of the mode.—The mode is not infinite by reason of its essence, since its essence does not necessarily envelop its existence. It cannot then be thought under the concept of eternity.[13] Conceivable without contradiction as not existing, able to begin and to cease to be, its existence is compatible with finitude, appears divisible for this reason, and can be thought only under the concept of duration.[14]

8. *Ep.*, 12 (G., IV, 53, lines 9–10): "*Id quod etiam imaginari possumus.*"
9. *Ep.*, 12 (G., IV, 53, lines 1–16).
10. In *Ep.*, 12, Spinoza most often capitalizes these words: *Substantia, Modi, Aeternitas, Duratio, Tempus, Mensura, Numerus, Intellectus, Imaginatio.*
11. *E.*, I, Def. 8.
12. *Ep.*, 12 (G., IV, 55–56).
13. *E.*, I, Def. 8.
14. *Ep.*, 12 (G., IV, 54–55).

Yet, as it is produced by God, one must say that it is infinite *by reason of its cause*. Indeed, the power of God, insofar as it is made known through the singular essence of a mode, affirms, that is, produces and conserves,[15] the existence of this mode, without the slightest internal restriction. In this way the infinite is enveloped, since infinity is defined as *"the absolute affirmation of the existence of any nature whatever."*[16] As a result, every mode, in relation to its divine cause, must be conceived as "without limits" or as infinite, at least as to the internal force which affirms it.

However, since its essence does not necessarily envelop its existence, it does not make absolute affirmation *necessary*. Thus, it does not invincibly envelop its actual infinity and leaves open the possibility of its affirmation in part only. The infinity of the internal force is thus resolved into a simple *indefinite tendency* to exist and to persevere in being.[17]

If, then, the existence or the duration of the mode can be limited or divided without contradiction, the limits it receives—without being excluded by the nature of the mode—are like accidents foreign to it, contingent and caused by exterior things without which it seems that it would of itself be infinite and indivisible. The thing is not conceived here as unable to have limits, since it can have them; at the same time, however, it is conceived as having nothing in itself which implies that it *must* have limits. This is why it does not radically exclude time, but only finite time, and must thus be said "to envelop an indefinite time."[18] In this way, it is distinguished from the essentially infinite, which "by a consequence of its nature or by virtue of its definition"[19] excludes *a priori* absolutely every limit.

In a sense, it approaches the Cartesian indefinite, which, like it, fails to imply necessarily either the positing or the exclusion of a limit. But, in another sense, it differs from the Cartesian indefinite, for it is objectively indefinite, being such by virtue of the infinity of its cause and the finitude of its essence, while the Cartesian indefinite is eminently subjective, resulting above all from our inability to decide between the finitude or objective infinity of the thing.

15. *E.*, I, xxiv; *E.*, I, xxiv, C.; *E.*, I, xxv, C.
16. *E.*, I, viii, S. 1 (G., II, 49, lines 19–20).
17. *E.*, III, vii and viii.
18. *E.*, III, viii (G., II, 147).
19. *Ep.*, 12 (G., IV, 53, lines 2–3).

It follows from this that duration is presented under a double aspect:

A. If we consider the mode from inside the immanent cause which produces and sustains its existence from within, the duration of its existence appears infinite and indivisible, because, whether its power of existing be actualized or not according to its infinity, the duration always remains inside the mode what it is at its root, namely, affirmation without limit, absolute or infinite. This is why, participating in the eternity of the act by which God creates both himself and all things, its duration is revealed when it is grasped from within that which posits it and constitutes it as an indefinite and indivisible tendency (*conatus*).[20] This is what we experience in lived duration.[21]

B. If we consider the mode, not in the internal cause which in it is the absolute principle of its existence, but in its essence, which, although enveloping the infinite and indivisible power by which it can be advanced to existence, does not at the same time envelop the necessity that this power make it exist, its duration appears finite and divisible. For, just as its future existence cannot be inferred from its present existence, this existence, considered in abstraction from the infinite chain of finite causes which necessarily force it to such and such a place in the universe, appears in itself as contingent, that is, as arbitrarily able to be or not to be, here as easily as there. It is in fact contingent *in relation to the essence of the mode,* that is, not determined by it, that the existence of this mode happens as exterior things necessarily determine it: it is only the universal context, the common order of Nature, which makes it necessary at such and such a point in the series.[22] Because of this contingency in relation to the essence, it follows that "we can posit the existence and the duration (of the mode) as we wish, without thereby in the least impairing our conception of it; we can conceive it larger or smaller

20. Cf. *E.,* I, xxiv, C.

21. *Ep.,* 12 (G., IV, 58, lines 4–11). This notion of *the lived,* which today, particularly in Bergson, is opposed to the intellectual, in Spinoza is experienced by the understanding alone. It is the imagination, and not the intellect, which substitutes the discontinuous for the continuous, cutting duration into fragments; it is the intelligence, on the contrary, which "experiences" continuity and duration through the intuitive idea it has of the procession of all things, and of myself, starting from eternal substance, infinite and indivisible.

22. Cf. *E.,* I, xxxiii, S. 1; *E.,* II, xxxi, C.; *E.,* II, xliv, C. Cf. also the definition of the contingent, *E.,* IV, Def. 3, and M. Gueroult, *Spinoza,* I, 369, note 40.

and divide it into parts"; an operation which it would be contradictory to hope to perform with substance or with eternity, which are of necessity absolutely infinite and indivisible.[23] Duration is thus "abstractly conceived as a kind of quantity."[24]

What holds for the duration of things, holds also for the magnitude of bodies. Insofar as it envelops the divine power that causes it, every singular body carries an internal tendency to persevere in its being; and, as a result, its nature does not embody anything that might limit or divide its existence. Thus it remains identical to itself, and undivided as long as exterior causes do not intervene to limit it, to fragment it or to destroy it. But, because its essence does not necessarily envelop its existence, we can conceive it at will (disregarding the natural order, which necessarily determines from outside the place and the limits of its existence inside the universe of finite things) as able to be or not to be, or to be limited, fragmented, made larger or smaller and divided into parts. Here, magnitude is not perceived as substance, but superficially and abstractly grasped as a property common to all modes of extension.[25] It then appears as an infinitely divisible quantity.

In conclusion, indivisibility and infinity are real in the mode and appear as such as soon as we enter into its interior to see at the heart of its being the primary indivisibility of the eternal and infinite power of God, the immediate cause in it of the immanent force that makes it exist and continue. As for division, this is extrinsic to it, for it befalls the mode, as if by accident, from without. Finally, the infinite divisibility of time and space, determinable *ad libitum,* is only an abstract concept forged by the imagination from the accidental limitation of the internal force, indivisible in itself, which advances and sustains the existence of the mode. It has, however, a real foundation in the finitude of the essence which makes this limitation possible. On the other hand, it has no basis in substance, which, being absolutely infinite and indivisible, radically excludes it.

VI.—*Case no. 3: The thing infinite insofar as without limits.*

In the second case of the preceding pair, the thing was said to be *without limits because infinite* as to its cause (*nullos fines habet vi suae causae*). It is now said to be *infinite because it has no limits* (*infinitum quia nullos habet fines*).

23. *Ep.,* 12 (G., IV, 54–55).
24. *E.,* II, xlv, S. (G., II, 127, lines 15–17).
25. *Ep.,* 12 (G., IV, 54, lines 7–15 and 56, lines 5–12).

The infinite is here conceived, independently of its cause or reason, in terms of what expresses it externally as infinite; and by a reversal of the order of things, its manifestation—its character of being "without limits"—is presented as its reason (*quia,* etc.). In reality, the thing is without limits *because* it is infinite, and it is infinite *because its essence* absolutely excludes any limit (substance), or *because its cause,* insofar as it is infinite, without excluding limits, does not of itself include them in any way (mode). This infinite, insofar as it is viewed externally, outside of its real reason, is the infinite such as imagination perceives it. The imagination in fact considers as infinite anything whose limits it is actually never able to grasp. This is the indefinite, strictly speaking, which results only from our subjective inability to discover a limit. This concept is thus suited to the infinite of abstract magnitude, which is for the imagination a given whose limit is never reached, but one for which we see no reason whatever to affirm that such a limit be impossible.

However, besides this infinite, infinite insofar as without limits, represented for us by the imagination, and which is so only because we evidently can never assign limits to it, there is another infinity, conceived by the understanding, which it posits as being of itself necessarily without limits and as existing in act outside of us, an infinite which, nevertheless, is not that of the thing infinite according to its essence: it is that of the mode, sprung from the absolute nature of God (whether immediately or mediately), which includes the whole of the finite modes, whether of their essences or, like the face of the whole universe (*facies totius universi*), of their existences, an infinity which is just as infinite as that of substance itself. It is so, however, not through itself but through that thing other than itself which is substance; for it is not *its own nature,* but *the nature of substance* which excludes limitation from it. If, indeed, it were limited, part of substance would be deprived of affections and, so, annihilated; for nothingness has no properties; by this partial annihilation, substance would be finite, which contradicts its nature.[26]

26. Cf. *E.,* I, xxi. Here we freely adapt the general principle of *E.,* I, xxi, Dem. 2 to the context of *Ep.,* 12, namely: if the mode produced absolutely by God's nature alone were finite, then God, beyond the limit of this mode, would have to exist without it; which is absurd, since, by hypothesis, God being given, this mode always follows necessarily from it. *E.,* I, xxi, Dem. 1 is less interesting for *Ep.,* 12, its principle being as follows: if the mode which absolutely follows from the nature of substance alone (or of the attribute) were finite, then it would have to be limited by something, which in that substance would be something

The infinity of this mode is thus primarily defined by being *"without limits"* or by immensity. However, as it does not exist by itself, but by another, it is as a result, like any mode, infinitely divisible. Its division does not in reality contradict its nature; and, moreover, its divisibility is not excluded from it by the nature of substance. On the contrary, the latter requires that the mode be *interiorly* divisible to infinity, but at the same time it requires that it never be rendered finite by an ultimate limit which would restrict its immensity.

Finally, its infinity, as immensity, is, just like all other kinds of infinity, an absolute internal affirmation of its existence, since every infinite is the "absolute affirmation of any existence, whatever it be"; but, contrary to what takes place in the case of singular modes, nothing from outside can restrict its actualization, since this is effected uniquely by virtue of the absolute nature of substance.[27] Thus, it is not only infinite by reason of its cause—the power of God—but infinite *itself,* since it is the infinite effect of this infinite cause, in contrast with the singular mode which, infinite because of its cause, is only a finite effect of it.

VII.—*Case no. 4: The thing infinite insofar as its parts, although included within a maximum and a minimum, cannot be expressed by any number.*

Precisely because the definition of the infinite in case no. 3 does not refer only to understanding, but also to imagination, it puts into question the reality of the infinite outside us. It leads us to think that the infinite is only what is *too great (nimia magnitudine)*[28] for us to be able to determine the number of its parts: but what is too great for our capacity to count does not in any way imply that it is infinite in itself. Indeed, it seems evident that, however numerous its parts may be, they have in themselves a number and that, always having "to be inferred from their multitude," such an infinite can only be something very great and not something really infinite. For whatever is totaled by number is necessarily finite. In brief, the parts of this

---

other than the mode, and, contrary to the hypothesis, it would not absolutely follow from the nature of that substance alone. Be that as it may, in these two demonstrations the infinity of the infinite immediate mode is not derived from its own nature, but from the nature of God, insofar as it produces the mode absolutely by itself alone. It is similar for the infinity of the infinite mediate mode. It should be noted that, in the *Ethics,* Spinoza avoids any demonstration founded on the axiom: *nothingness has no properties.*

27. Cf. *E.,* I, xxi and xxii.
28. *Ep.,* 12 (G., IV, 59, line 17).

thing surpass only our ability to assign their number; in themselves they do not surpass all numbers.

But, in truth, this negation of the infinite in favor of number is only an error proceeding from the imagination. And this error is made evident by spaces, which, although contained within the boundaries of a *maximum* and a *minimum* and able to be as small as one wishes, are still each one an Infinite, without being so by virtue of the immensity of their size nor, consequently, by virtue of the exceedingly great multitude of their parts. As a result, it is asserted that no Infinite is explained in terms of the multitude of its parts; and that, if every Infinite escapes number, it is not because it contains too many parts, but because, by nature, it is not expressible by it. This is what is illustrated by a geometrical example which will be examined later.[29]

VIII.—We have given in effect the essential answer to four questions *a, b, c, d:*

a) Incapable of being divided into parts and without parts is the Infinite of substance, which, being such by its essence, can only be always actual, so that any limitation, partition, or division would destroy its nature.

b) Divisible without contradiction is the Infinite of mode, which, being so by virtue of its cause and not by its essence, is not such that limitation and partition destroy its nature.

c) Able to be conceived without difficulty as larger than another is every Infinite which does not exclude divisibility and is included in every singular mode.

d) Unable to be so conceived are: 1) the Infinite of substance, which excludes absolutely all divisibility; 2) the Infinite of the immediate mode of substance or the sum of its finite modes, infinitely divisible in itself, but on which substance, excluding its restriction, imposes immensity.

These replies, however, especially the one concerning question *c*, require further explanation. This supplement will be found in the study of *cases 5* and *6,* which, transporting us from the ontological to the gnoseological level, will permit us to discover in the confusion among our cognitions the reasons or "causes" of the confusions among things which have just been denounced.

* * *

29. *Ep.*, 12 (G., IV, 50–60). On the subject of this example, cf. Gueroult, *op. cit.*, pp. 519 ff.

IX.—*Cases nos. 5 and 6: Things known by the understanding alone, and things known by the understanding and by the imagination.*

In spite of their self-evidence, the above four truths are usually ignored. This fact is explained less by the nature of their objects than by our way of knowing them. It arises, in truth, when we perceive these objects with the *Imagination,* and not with the *Understanding.* So it is important to distinguish these two kinds of knowledge and to elucidate their relation to their objects.

The understanding knows essences; the imagination knows only existences. The understanding knows things as they are in themselves (*ut in se sunt*); the imagination grasps only the affections that they determine in our body. As a result:

1. Substance cannot be known by the imagination, for the latter, confined to the perception of the affections of our body, can only know modes. It can thus be known only by the understanding. Able alone to conceive its inseity and its perseity, the understanding alone can grasp substance as cause of itself, eternal, infinite by essence, that is, necessarily infinite and, hence, indivisible—this absolute indivisibility having therefore to belong to the eternal and to extended substance.

2. Modes are knowable to understanding and to imagination, but confusedly by the latter and rightly by the former.

The imagination perceives modes, since it perceives the affections of the Body, which are modes. But it does not perceive them as *modes of substance,* since it does not know substance. It thus knows them confusedly, for clear and distinct knowledge of modes is possible only in and through that of substance.

The understanding knows modes and perceives them as *modes of substance,* since it knows substance. It knows them rightly, for it knows them in and through substance and sees "how they flow from eternal things."[30] Hence, it truly knows both the nature of their duration, as infinite and indivisible on principle (lived duration), and the nature of bodies and their diverse sizes, which it conceives as the variable and continuous modifications of the same extended substance, in itself absolutely infinite and indivisible.

X.—Accordingly, if one confuses the thing that is conceivable only and not imaginable with the thing that is imaginable, and, in a thing which is both conceivable and imaginable, what in it is imagined with

30. *Ep.,* 12 (G., IV, 56, line 18).

what must be conceived, the knowledge of Nature is perverted from beginning to end. This perversion, which infallibly befalls any mind where the light of understanding is darkened by the imagination, engenders two fundamental errors (one of which is threefold), and from these arise all the inextricable difficulties relative to the Infinite and to the Divisible:

1. Modes are seen by the imagination as independent of one another, since they are united only in and through substance, which is, precisely, what it does not know. Imagination inevitably conceives them as *really separated,* that is, as substances. Thus, it introduces in them the divisibility of the discontinuous (founded on real distinction), instead of the divisibility of the continuous (founded on modal distinction), which is proper to them.

This is the first error.

2. In transforming modes of infinite substance into really separated substances, the imagination breaks substance into as many finite substances as it perceives modes.

This is the second error; and this error is threefold:

a) Divisibility, which belongs only to modes, is conferred on substance, which absolutely excludes it.

b) In addition, this divisibility is the divisibility of the discontinuous, improperly attributed to modes.

c) Finally, every substance is posited as finite, which is just as absurd as to posit a square circle.

Immediately all the traditional difficulties relative to the Infinite and to the Divisible arise; for, as soon as the infinity of substance is reduced to an infinity of finite substances, that is, of absolutely independent beings, we are then forced to conceive it as resulting from the addition of finite things or parts: one must then explain the *absolutely indivisible Infinite* (that of substance) by the divisible, and what is without parts by parts. In a similar manner, one must also explain the *infinitely divisible Infinite* (that of modes) by the addition of these modes to infinity. Accordingly, whether it is a question of the indivisible Infinite of substance or of the divisible Infinite of the mode, the Infinite must everywhere be said "to be inferred from the multitude of its parts." But, this is to claim to explain the Infinite by the finite, an endeavor which is just as senseless as to wish to construct a triangle or a square with circles, or an essence with essences which negate it; from this there result many absurd consequences which can only be avoided by the negation of the Infinite on behalf of the finite.

XI.—From what precedes, it follows that this proposition: "The infinite is inferred from the multitude of its parts," is the common root of two fundamental errors, the one consisting in denying the indivisibility of substance and in thus affirming that it is finite, the other, in denying the infinite divisibility of its modes and in thus affirming that their multitude is finite. We then understand that the refutation of one is *ipso facto* that of the other or, rather, that these two refutations amount to only one, which consists in proving that no Infinite can be inferred from its parts, that is, that discontinuity is a fiction. For example, it is the same to prove that substance is an absolutely indivisible Infinite as to prove that the line is an infinitely divisible Infinity, since in order to claim the contrary, one must, in both cases, postulate the same absurdity, namely, that substance is composed of parts and the line composed of points: "All this jumble of arguments by which philosophers habitually wish to show that extended substance is finite, collapses of itself: all these discourses presuppose a corporeal substance composed of parts. In the same way, other authors, after having persuaded themselves that the line is made up of points, have managed to find many arguments to show that a line is not divisible to infinity."[31]

To prove the continuity (or the infinite divisibility) of modes is to prove the absolute indivisibility of substance, and *vice versa*. Indeed, just as modes, *qua* modes, are conceivable only through substance, and the merely modal distinction which belongs to them only through the identity and the community of their unique substance, so, too, the endless divisibility of the continuous, which is that of modes, is conceivable only through the indestructible subsistence in them of an indivisible absolute, which necessitates that no truly separate part can ever be reached and that the division, since it can never be completed, be absolutely infinite. This absolute indivisibility, which is immanent in the modes, is that of their substance.

But this indivisible substance which the imagination reduces to the aggregate of its modes grasped as separated parts, that is, as discontinuous, is precisely what can be conceived only by the understanding: "This is why, if we consider magnitude as it is for the imagination, which is the most frequent and the easiest case, we find

31. *Ep.*, 12 (G., IV, 55, lines 34 to 56, line 4). Cf. *E.*, I, xv, S. (G., II, 58, lines 3–6).

it to be divisible, finite, composed of parts, and multiple. If, however, we consider it as it is in the understanding, and if the thing is perceived as it is in itself, which is very difficult, then, just as I have sufficiently demonstrated to you earlier, we find it to be infinite, indivisible, and unique."[32]

Accordingly, as soon as the knowledge of substance is introduced by the understanding, the difficulties caused by the simultaneous affirmation of infinity and divisibility disappear. The alternative which is posited between the one and the other, and which the dogmatist decided in favor of the latter, is henceforth resolved in favor of the former: substance, as a result of its necessary infinity, radically excludes all divisibility and casts it outside of itself into the infinity of its modes.

But in modes will we not then rediscover the simultaneous affirmation of the infinite and the divisible? Certainly, but this time legitimately so, and without posing either a problem or an alternative, for now it can no longer be a question of a division into parts that are actually separate. In virtue of the absolute indivisibility of substance, in relation to which modes are conceived, divisibility strictly speaking —that is, the divisibility of the discontinuous—is excluded beforehand in favor of the divisibility of the continuous, where the parts, not being really separate, can never in themselves constitute a determined multitude, a multitude which would be indeterminable only for us, so that we would think ourselves able, theoretically, to infer their totality and consequently to affirm that it is finite. On the contrary, escaping all self-determined totalization, their totality must be affirmed to be an infinity in act. In brief, the divisible and the finite no longer explain the indivisible and the infinite, but, being explained by them, are henceforth reconciled with them. But this is possible because they are conceived under the form of the indivisible and of the infinite, since the continuous denies all real partitioning and all finite partitioning. Henceforth, finite things being conceived as, each one, interiorly infinite, and all together as constituting an infinite, they are only the second aspect or the immediate expression of the absolute indivisibility of what is by nature the Infinite.

XII.—These conclusions support three others.

1. Substance, being by nature absolutely infinite and indivisible and having by nature to produce modes, can only produce an in-

32. *Ep.,* 12 (G., IV, 56, lines 9–15).

finite number of them.[33] Thus, modes could not be discontinuous, since, in this case, they could only be a finite multitude of finite parts.

2. Infinite divisibility is possible only in modes, since it can be conceived only through the modal distinction which defines them.

3. Substance, the principle of infinitely divisible modes, must itself be indivisible, since divisibility is the property of its affections and since it is beyond its own affections. Indeed: *a*) it is anterior to them;[34] *b*) "it can be conceived in its truth and considered as it is in itself only if one disregards them";[35] *c*) it is their cause, and there is nothing in common between the cause as cause and the effect as effect.[36]

XIII.—To say that the infinite divisibility of every mode envelops the absolute indivisibility of substance,[37] is to say that this substance, with regard to its nature, is complete in each mode. Moreover, this conclusion is evident in the very concept of indivisibility, for *what is indivisible by nature can only be complete wherever it is,* that is, "equally in the part and in the whole."[38] Substance is thus, with regard to its nature, equally, that is, entirely, in the totality of its modes as it is in each of them, in each of them as it is in each of their parts, and in each of their parts as in each of the parts of these parts, etc., to infinity. In addition, it is found there in two different manners:

1. Through the attribute which defines its essence. For example, extension, which constitutes the essence of corporeal substance, is complete in all bodies as in each of them, inasmuch as it is the *common property* by which they are identical among themselves and identical to it. Indeed, since the *nature* of extension remains complete, that is, identically what it is, in the least of its particles, it is necessarily *present, with the indivisibility proper to it, in every part of the different bodies.*[39]

2. Through the substance which this essence defines—insofar as substance, which is in each of them the indivisible cause by which they exist, *is found in its entirety, as regards its nature, inside each of*

33. *E.,* I, xvi.
34. *E.,* I, i.
35. *E.,* I, v, Dem.
36. *E.,* I, xvii, S. (G., II, 63, line 17).
37. XI above.
38. *E.,* II, xxxvii, xxxviii, and xlvi.
39. *E.,* II, xxxvii and xxxviii; *E.,* I, xv, S.

them, as a result of which the idea of this substance is enveloped equally in the idea of the whole and in that of the part.[40]

Hence, every mode, whether small or large, envelops within itself the indivisibility of infinite substance, which is completely bestowed upon it, while by virtue of its definition as a finite being, it must admit divisibility. This divisibility is infinite, however, since division will never be able to *really separate* it, either from other modes or from the indivisible substance immanent in it. Thus, in each part (or mode), however small it may be, we rediscover in its integrity the same indivisible infinite which allows it an infinite divisibility in act. In addition, this infinite divisibility along with the indivisible infinite which underlies it being *circumscribed in the sphere of each of the modes,* there are as many different infinitely divisible infinites as there are different modes. So, for the attribute of extension, there are as many infinites of different sizes, each infinitely divisible in its own fashion, as there are modes or bodies of different sizes. And yet, under each of these different infinites there is also always the same identical Infinite, which could not be smaller or larger than another, namely, the Infinite of substance which is equally complete in each of them: "From this, we know which infinite can be known without difficulty as greater than another, and which infinite, on the contrary, cannot be so known." The infinite that is larger or smaller is the infinite of substance, invariable in itself, perceived as contained within the limits of a mode, limits which are more or less restricted according to the different modes. These infinites which are greater or smaller than one another are exhibited by the geometrical example mentioned below.

These conclusions hold, *mutatis mutandis,* for all attributes and their modes and, consequently, for Thought. Since the indivisible thinking substance is bestowed in its completeness, as regards its nature, upon each mode of Thought, the idea of substance and of its modes is equally, that is, in its completeness, in the whole and in the part. In other words, being complete in the infinite understanding, it is also complete in each of the parts of that understanding, in short, in every soul. This is why every soul, knowing the infinite, can know from it, according to their nature, as God knows them—that is, truly—if not all things, at least all those things which its finite nature does not forbid it to deduce from it (that is to say, from

40. *E.,* II, xlvi, Dem.

the infinite), and so to know them adequately. From this we see that the doctrine of the indivisibility of substance and of the infinite divisibility of its modes is fundamental for the theory of knowledge.

XIV.—However, the concept of various actual infinities, some greater than others, is judged absurd by many. These infinites, they object, should contain, each according to its different size, a greater or lesser number of parts; but in each of them, nevertheless, this number should be the same, since in each it should surpass any assignable number, that is, be the largest of all, and the largest of all numbers cannot be more or less large: the concept of infinites, some of which are larger than others, is thus contradictory. Accordingly, what we call infinite is judged to be so only because the multitude of its parts is too great (*nimia magnitudine*)[41] to allow our understanding to assign a number to it.[42] As a result, such a thing is not in itself infinite, but only infinite for us, that is, something *indefinite,* which is, in reality, only a *finite* thing. For every multitude of parts, however great it may be, always constitutes a number, and every number, being determinate, is finite.

XV.—These objections are based on two principles.—According to the first (which we already know), *the infinite is inferred from the multitude of its parts;* according to the second, *number is in itself competent to express every magnitude.* These two principles adhere closely together, for to affirm the first is to claim that the infinite can be explained by a numerical operation, and to affirm the second is to claim that the whole is constituted by a multitude of parts. These two principles are thus resolved in the common postulate that *number sovereignly governs Nature and our understanding,* that it forces the latter to deny what, on the contrary, seems to be invincibly affirmed in it, namely, that substance is absolutely indivisible and the mode infinitely divisible. From this there results an apparent antinomy of which we can only rid ourselves by submitting the pretensions of number to a critique. This is why it is necessary to seek its origin and its nature, that is, to effect its genesis.

* * *

XVI.—Number, and with it measure and time, are thrust upon most minds as being *the highest ideas of understanding and the fundamental laws of Nature.* They owe this prestige to their extreme

41. *Ep.,* 12 (G., IV, 59, line 17).
42. Cf. *Ep.* 12 (G., IV, 59, lines 10–11).

abstraction, universality, and usefulness, as well as to the necessity of the relations they command. Yet, in spite of these fine appearances, they are intruders, who, fraudulently introduced into the intellect, have done nothing but precipitate and consummate the ruin of our knowledge.

These three notions [i.e. number, measure, and time] actually have nothing to do with the understanding. They offer, rather, this threefold quality of being:

a) *Products of the imagination,* that is, Beings of reason[43] or rather of imagination.[44]

b) *Nothings of knowledge.*

c) Aids of the imagination (*auxilia imaginationis*), merely capable of facilitating the conception of *imagined things.*

a) *Products of the imagination.*—The imagination engenders all three by analogous processes. Time, which serves to determine duration, and measure, which serves to determine quantity,[45] can in a sense be conceived as differing only in the object to which they apply: time, being only measure applied to duration, "abstractly conceived as a kind of quantity,"[46] and number, conferring on measure the exactness which distinguishes it from simple evaluation. Time, measure, and number are thus in certain respects inseparable concepts resulting from similar processes of confusion, of abstraction, of limitation.

We would be mistaken, however, to give them a rigorously identical origin; if, for example, we were to imagine that time arises from measure, being either the number of movement (Aristotle) or the tracing of abstract space onto concrete duration (Bergson). On the contrary, they have a distinct origin, for they are founded, each one on something different, which is the object to which it is applied. Measure comes from *the abstract knowledge of what constitutes the essence of extended substance:* magnitude, separated from substance and grasped only in its modes as their common property, is posited with these modes, themselves abstractly known, as divisible, composite, multiple; one can thus delimit it in terms of measure. Time comes from *the abstract knowledge of the existence (or duration)*

43. *Ep.,* 12 (G., IV, 57, line 18).

44. *Ep.,* 12 (G., IV, 57, lines 7–8): ". . . *potius imaginandi modos.*"

45. *Ep.,* 12 (G., IV, 57, lines 1–2). Contrary to Hobbes, and in accord with Descartes and Leibniz, Spinoza identifies *quantities* and *magnitudo.*

46. *E.,* II, xlv, S.

of modes, which, grasped independently of the eternal things from which it flows and from the order of Nature which determines it, is conceived as contingent, variable, and divisible at will; it is thus possible to delimit it in terms of time.[47] Finally, number comes from *the confused knowledge of multitude and of the differences among singular things:* successful in retaining in things only that by which they similarly affect our Body, that is, their general characteristics, the imagination divides them into classes where they subsist only as unities without intrinsic difference, capable of being counted.[48]

Each of these processes does indeed have its own physiognomy. Nevertheless, they are subject to one another; and all of them presuppose a foundation of discontinuity, the principle of discrete unities. For if time and measure are used to explain continuous quantities: duration and magnitude (number explaining discrete quantity),[49] this is possible only on condition that the limits by which these quantities are fragmented into discontinuous parts be introduced into the quantities themselves. All are thus amenable to the deficiency peculiar to the imagination, incapable of conceiving substance and modal distinction, both of which exclude discontinuity.

b) *Nothings of knowledge.*—This is what flows immediately from their genesis. From their enveloping the general concept, which is only the mental correlate of a residual generic image born of the confusion of cerebral impressions, there results: *a*) that they are not ideas, since they do not represent real objects outside us;[50] *b*) that they are without truth, inasmuch as truth is defined by the conformity of an idea to its object;[51] *c*) that they cannot properly be said to be false, but only neither true nor false.[52]—They are thus, in the most rigorous sense of the term, *nothings of knowledge.* Thus, inasmuch as Thought is conceived as expressing itself essentially in knowledge, they can be termed "modes of imagining rather than modes of thinking."[53]

c) *Aids of the imagination.*—Foreign by nature and by origin to knowledge and to truth, being in no way ideas, these Beings of rea-

47. Cf. V above.
48. *Ep.,* 12 (G., IV, 56); *E.,* II, xl, S. 1 (G., II, 120–121).
49. *C.m.,* I, 1 (G., I, 234, lines 12–16).
50. *C.m.,* I, 1 (G., I, 234).
51. *E.,* I, Ax. 6.
52. *C.m.,* I, 1 (G., I, 235, lines 16–18).
53. *Ep.,* 12 (G., IV, 57, lines 6–8). Cf. *TdIE* 46 (G., II, 32, lines 31–35).

son could not be *instruments of the understanding*. But, as they allow us to "imagine more easily," they are instruments of the imagination. Indeed, introducing into "imagined things," that is, into the qualitative and heterogeneous perception of corporeal affections, the homogeneity of similar parts and the discrete character of identical unities, they permit us to "retain" them better, and by establishing "comparisons" and "relations" among them, to "explain" them better.[54]

Since these are pragmatic instruments by which we can more easily orient ourselves in the universe of sensible things, among which our Body is located, with which it is constantly interacting, and upon which its life and death depend, one must admit that if they are not true, they have no need to be true, because, for instruments of this sort, it is sufficient that, in their own sphere, they be *efficacious*. It is thus literally "to apply oneself to derationalizing with one's imagination," to make of these instruments *ideas* presiding over the knowledge of things as they are in themselves. And we should not be surprised that every science of nature may be thus overthrown from top to bottom: "It is thus not astonishing that all those who have attempted to conceive the course of nature with the aid of similar notions, which are still wrongly understood (since they are held to be the contrary of what they are, namely, to be ideas of pure understanding), find themselves entangled in inextricable difficulties out of which they can emerge only by destroying everything and by admitting the worst absurdities."[55]

XVII.—Affirming the sovereignty of number and of related notions, in effect, shatters Nature, for it establishes everywhere the discrete. First, this means pulverizing substance, reducing it to a collection of finite substances, whereas finite substance is a chimera as absurd as the square circle. In addition, this means implicating substance in the contradiction of the infinite and the divisible, to which it is foreign, since it is absolutely indivisible. Next, this means disuniting the modes into a multitude of really separate parts, whose number, however great it may be, could not be infinite, since the infinite and number are mutually exclusive. This also means emptying each mode of its internal infinity, because if the infinite is not in the whole it cannot be in the part. In a similar manner, it means refusing to admit that modes of different magnitudes can envelop

54. *K.V.*, I, 10; *C.m.*, I, 1 (G., I, 234–235).
55. *Ep.*, 12 (G., IV, 57, lines 8–12).

unequal infinites, because if the infinite must in each be inferred from the multitude of its parts, the number of these parts must, as infinite, be the greatest of all in each—in other words, the same: an absurd consequence since, at the same time, it would have to be different according to the magnitude of each. Finally, it is to cut into pieces duration, which, at the base of all things, is in itself indivisible and infinite, and to claim to reconstruct it by their aggregate. Hence the impossibility of understanding how duration elapses. How, for example, can an hour pass if we cut it in two, then these two halves in two, and so on to infinity? In order to avoid dividing it indefinitely, will we reduce it to a multitude of indivisible instants? But this would be claiming to construct it of nothings of duration. We could just as well "hope to form a number by adding zeros."[56]

This is because "neither number, nor measure, nor time, since they are only aids to the imagination, can be infinite, otherwise number would be number no longer; nor measure, measure; nor time, time. As a result, one sees clearly why many people, confusing these three beings of reason with real things of whose true nature they were ignorant, have denied the Infinite."[57] But to deny the Infinite is to deny self-sustaining existence and, consequently, God, and, consequently, the Universe, since causing oneself and causing things is in God one and the same act: *"Eo sensu quo Deus dicitur causa sui, etiam omnium rerum causa dicendus est."*[58] Thus, the genesis and the critique of number lead to the most drastic of conclusions, since they finally force us to recognize that in affirming the validity of number we subscribe, without suspecting it, to the most radical of negativisms.

XVIII.—This terrible fall of number, hurled from the heights of the intelligible to the lower depths of the imagination and of biological utility, establishes a vigorous contrast between the mathematical philosophy of Spinoza and those of the philosophers of his time. Moreover, it opens an abyss between arithmetic and geometry,

56. *Ep.,* 12 (G., IV, 58, lines 14–15).
57. *Ep.,* 12 (G., IV, 58, lines 34 to 59, line 4). There is an agreement between Spinoza and Aristotle on the finite nature of number. But Aristotle draws from this the negation of the actual infinite, which would have to have an infinite number of parts—which is absurd, since number is finite. Cf. *Physics,* III, 5, 204b 7–10 and VIII, 8, 265a 9–11. In the same order of ideas, he substitutes the contiguous for the continuous (*Physics,* IV, 11, 219a–219b).
58. *E.,* I, xxv, S. (G., II, 68, lines 6–8).

which is proposed as a model to metaphysics in the *De intellectus emendatione* and which, in the *Ethics,* effectively provides its method.

But then how could Spinoza have preserved for number, at least implicitly,[59] its dignity as an *eternal truth,* with all the privileges which flow from it? A simple product of the imagination, having no support other than the existing Body, must it not also be unrelated to eternity? Is it not expelled from human and divine understanding, that is, from what is true? Must we not wonder then if number, although possible only through imagination, does not presuppose also, in spite of everything, a certain intervention of reason? Is not the *Being of Reason* in general opposed to fiction insofar as the latter "depends upon the will alone unguided by reason,"[60] and does this not allow the presupposition that such a Being, as its name indicates, must, on the contrary, depend upon the will guided by reason? Truth is denied in the case of number because it is not an idea and because truth is defined by the conformity of the idea to the thing; but, on the other hand, do we not give the name of *eternal truths* particularly to *axioms* which are only relations and not ideas, while it is only secondarily accorded to ideas?[61] This is a thorny question, which we will try to clarify elsewhere,[62] and where we must, more than ever, refrain from being "concerned more with words rather than with things."

XIX.—In this action brought against number, mathematicians, "provided that they have clear and distinct ideas," are, contrary to what one might think, on the side of true philosophers.[63] They indeed reject the four propositions in which the pretentions it usurps are affirmed:

1. *Everything can be expressed by a number.*—A false assertion, since they perceive magnitudes that no number could express, for example, irrational magnitudes.

2. *Every Infinite is such that its magnitude is so excessive (nimia magnitudine) that we cannot perceive its limits, or that its variations are not contained between any boundaries.*—Another error, for there are infinite magnitudes which are contained between

59. E.g., *E.,* II, xlvii, S.
60. *C.m.,* I, 1 (G., I, 236, lines 13–14).
61. Cf. *Ep.,* 10, from Spinoza to de Vries (G., IV, 47, lines 18–21).
62. Cf. Gueroult, *op. cit.,* II, ch. 11.
63. Cf. *ibid.,* I, 583.

two extreme values (a *maximum* and a *minimum*) that we know in a precise manner, magnitudes which, however small they are conceived as being, always include an infinity of variations.

3. *Every Infinite is such that the multitude of its parts is such that we cannot succeed in assigning a number to it.*—An assertion which is no less false, for it follows from the preceding refutation that these magnitudes are infinite because it is contradictory to their nature that number be applied to them, and not because the multitude of their parts surpasses every assignable number.

4. *There cannot be unequal infinites.*—An affirmation which is authorized by the fact that every infinite can be expressed only by the greatest of all numbers, but which is false in its basis, since it presupposes the absurdity that number is applicable to the infinite.

* * *

XX.—The geometrical example used to illustrate case no. 4[64] is advanced in order to refute the false interpretation of case no. 3, namely, the second of the errors which have just been enumerated.[65] It thus concerns the second pair.

Given, for example (cf. *fig. 1*), two nonconcentric circles AD and BC, the smaller inscribed in the larger. It is evident that the sum of the inequalities of the distances included between them (that is, the sum of the variations of these distances) is an infinite. This infinite does not result from the excessive magnitude (*nimia magnitudine*) of the space interposed between them, since if we consider only a portion of it, as small as we wish, the sum of the inequalities of the distances always surpasses every number. Nor does it result (as is the case of the hyperbola) from the fact that the variations of distance are not included between a *maximum* and a *minimum,* for, on the contrary, there is a *maximum* (AB) and a *minimum* (CD) of distance,[66] both of them exactly determined for us. It results from the fact that the nature of the space interposed between the two nonconcentric circles does not allow a finite, determinate number of inequalities of distance. To maintain the contrary is to wish to make a circle not a circle.

If, then, these things can be called *indefinite,* it is because number cannot *equal* them, that is, *define* them, but not because they are

64. Cf. VII above.
65. Cf. XIX above.
66. Or a *maximum:* AB-CD and a *minimum:* zero.

in themselves deprived of true infinity. "Indefinite" refers here, then, not to the nature of the thing, but only to the "impotence of the imagination."[67]

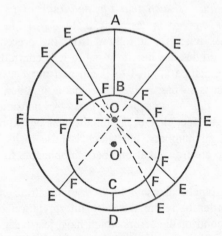

XXI.—However, Tschirnhaus observes, if we can agree that in this example the infinite is not explained by the excessive magnitude of the space which is here enclosed between two circles, nor by the indefinite variation of the distances between these circles, since this variation is included between a *maximum* and a *minimum*,—then we do not see how one thereby demonstrates that an Infinite is not inferred from the multitude of its parts.[68]

An unjustified objection, for the contrary is immediately apparent. To infer the infinite from the multitude of its parts is to say that this multitude is greater than any given multitude (than any assignable number) and that, consequently, it is impossible to conceive a greater multitude. Now, this consequence is false, since in the total space included between the two circles we conceive a multitude of parts two times greater than in half this space,—although, hypothetically, the multitude of the parts of half the space as well as of the total space is greater than any assignable number.[69]

The contradiction resides, then, in the following: that, on the one hand, on the basis of the multitude of the parts from which we would infer the infinite, we affirm that it is impossible to conceive a greater

67. *Ep.*, 12 (G., IV, 61, line 4).
68. *Ep.*, 80, from Tschirnhaus to Spinoza (G., IV, 331).
69. *Ep.*, 81, from Spinoza to Tschirnhaus (G., IV, 332).

multitude, and, on the other, we actually do conceive a greater one. This contradiction could be expressed a little differently (although Spinoza does not do so) in relation to the alleged number of the parts. If half the space included between the two circles and the whole of this space are both infinite, the number of the parts must in both cases be greater than any assignable number. It will thus not be greater in the whole than in the half—which is absurd. In other words, the number of the parts in the half would have to be at once equal and unequal to the number of the parts in the whole, since it would have at once to differ from it and yet to be the greatest of all, that is, the same.

XXII.—Thus, like Descartes,[70] Spinoza accepts infinites of different magnitudes, but for other reasons. As he understands it, the absurdities which flow from this, relative to number, give evidence that the infinite is conceivable only by the understanding and not by the imagination, mother of number; in short, that it is not incomprehensible, but only unimaginable. For Descartes, number is an idea of the understanding and not a product of the imagination;[71] as a result, these absurdities give evidence that the Infinite is not only unimaginable but incomprehensible. We cannot deny infinite number for the reason that it is an absurd concept for our finite mind, because when the infinite is in question, what is absurd for our understanding does not signify its impossibility in things.[72] Similarly, if we evoke the infinite power of God which incommensurably surpasses the capacities of our finite understanding, we conceive, in spite of the absurdity we see there, that this power could cause 2+3 not to equal 5, or a mountain to be without a valley.

In this way Descartes's flight from any mathematical speculation

70. Descartes, *Letter to Mersenne*, April 15, 1630 (Adam and Tannery, I, 146).

71. For Descartes, the *numbering number* is a universal which, like all universals (contrary to what Spinoza affirms), is produced by the *understanding alone*, which retains of the things it distinguishes only the relation (of duality, of triality, etc.) observed between them, disregarding their nature (*Principia,* I, 59; *A Regius* (Adam and Tannery III, 66, lines 7–8)). The *numbered number* is the distinction we notice between things (real distinction, modal distinction, and even a distinction merely of reason) (*Principia,* I, 60). In both cases, the imagination does not intervene.

72. Descartes, *Letter to Mersenne*, April 15, 1630 (Adam and Tannery, I, 147): "What reason is there to judge if one infinite can be greater than another? Seeing that it would cease to be infinite if we were able to understand it."

on the infinite is explained, although his genius had begun to explore these paths.[73] In this respect Spinoza is, against him, on the same side as Leibniz. Yet, he is a hundred leagues from Leibniz when he reduces number to a finite being of the imagination.[74] This depreciation of number, of arithmetic, of all symbolic thought, and the correlative exaltation of geometrical thought—prized to an extreme, insofar as it is considered as effecting the genesis of the thing in itself— agree with his conception of the true idea as *adaequatio,* that is, as the intuitive grasp of the totality of reasons or "requisites" of the thing,—in opposition to the Leibnizian notion of the true idea as oblique expression, necessarily symbolic, of a reality which, remaining in itself always inaccessible to intuition, can be grasped only by blind thought by means of an algorithm.

XXIII.—The meaning of the geometrical example previously invoked, generally wrongly understood, has been vitiated in its principle through errors in translation. At least two of these, one minor, the other major, may be examined here.

1. The words *"quantumvis parvam ejus portionem capiamus"* have generally been translated as "however small we may conceive *it"* or "we may suppose *it,"* *it* designating the *space interposed* between the two circles.[75] This space is then smaller as these two circles themselves are smaller or as the inscribed circle is larger. But the correct translation is: "However small be the part that we may consider of the interposed space," that is, whether we retain only half, a fourth, a thousandth, etc. *Letter* 82, to Tschirnhaus, authenticates this meaning.[76]

2. In the passage *"Omnes inaequalitates spatii duobus circulis AB et CD interpositi,"* Hegel and the commentators who followed him translate *"inaequalitates spatii,"* not as *"inequalities of distance,"* but as *"unequal distances."*[77] The example must thus be understood in the following manner:

73. Cf. Vuillemin, *Mathématique et Métaphysique chez Descartes* (Paris: P.U.F., 1960) and Y. Belaval, *Leibniz critique de Descartes* (Paris: N.R.F., 1960), pp. 300 f.

74. On the subject of the greatest of all numbers in Leibniz and in Descartes, cf. Belaval, *op. cit.,* pp. 221, 266 f.

75. Tr. Appuhn, III, p. 155; Pléiade, p. 1156.

76. Cf. XXI above.

77. "Die ungleichen Abstände des Raumes," Hegel, *Geschichte der Philosophie* (1844), Part III, sec. 2, p. 342; "La somme des distances inégales," trans. Appuhn, III, pp. 154–155. Cf. Pléiade, p. 1156.

Given segments having one endpoint on the circumference O and the other on the circumference O′, where we consider the sections EF of the radii of O, limited by the circumference O′, then CD<EF<AB (cf. *fig. 1*); the sum of the segments EF is then an end-to-end placement of segments of a transfinite number (according to current terminology). And this sum is infinite.

This interpretation is not acceptable. Certainly, the sum of the segments EF is infinite; certainly, too, their sum remains infinite whatever the smallness of the spaces considered. But, since it would be equally infinite if the two circles were concentric and if all the segments EF were equal, it is clear that the infinite sum of the unequal segments EF is not related to their inequality and is not delimited by the *maximum* and the *minimum* of their variations.

If, on the contrary, it is a question, not of the sum of the segments EF, but of the sum of their inequalities, it is evident that the two circles could not be concentric, for in this case there would be no inequalities among the segments EF. It is just as evident that the sum of their inequalities is necessarily contained between the *maximum* and the *minimum* of the variations of the segments EF.[78] We see then that the example can illustrate the thesis that any portion of space envelops an infinite divisibility, inexpressible by number. Indeed, the distance D′B (cf. *fig. 2*) determined by the difference between the *maximum* and the *minimum* appears equal to the sum of the variations of—

EF:D′B=AB−CD=(AB−E_1F_1)+(E_1F_1−E_2F_2)+(E_2F_2−E_3F_3)+ (E_3F_3−E_4F_4)+(E_4F_4−CD)—a banal equality as long as one considers a finite number of intermediary positions given to EF. But when EF varies continuously from AB to CD, the sum of the variations, that is, the integral of the differentials of EF (when E is on the arc of the circle $\overset{\frown}{AC}$) will still have as its value the value of

$$D'B= \int_{E\epsilon\overset{\frown}{AC}} d\,(EF)$$

As we see, it is a matter, not of an infinite sum of finite quantities, but of a sum of differentials or of variations. And we then understand by what natural connection the geometrical example is immediately

78. This is the point Spinoza stresses: *"Utrumque enim in hoc nostro exemplo habemus, maximum nempe AB, minimum vero CD," Ep.* 12 (G., IV, 60, lines 2–4).

applied to physics: "(the sum) of the variations that matter in motion can encounter in space which is limited in this way (also surpasses) every assignable number."[79]

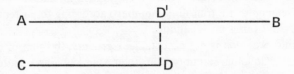

Here, Spinoza indeed pursues Descartes's vortical ring with its constriction, where the necessity imposed upon matter in order to overcome this constriction of dividing itself endlessly compensates for the narrowness of place with the greater speed of its smaller parts. The two nonconcentric circles represent this vortex as Descartes represents it in article 33 of part II of the *Principles*,[80] and as Spinoza has reproduced it in his *Principia philosophiae cartesianae*,[81] where, taking up anew the very term Descartes used: *inaequalitates* (*locorum aut motuum*), he distinguishes between *inaequalitates spatii* and *spatia inaequalia*.[82] The geometrical example expresses in a universal and abstract manner the concrete reasoning of physics. Indeed, given: 1. that matter moves inside vortical rings comprising constrictions; 2. that, as a result, the same quantity of this matter must, in the same period of time, move across unequal spaces (*inaequalia spatia*) included between a *maximum* and a *minimum* (the largest and the smallest width of the canal); 3. that in virtue of the infinite divisibility of space,[83] the multitude of these spaces surpasses every number; 4. that in each of these spaces the same quantity of matter, in order to continue to advance, each time must lose an infinitely small part of itself corresponding to the progressive narrowing of the canal, and to compensate for this its speed must increase each time to a correspondingly infinitely small degree,—then we see that between the *maximum* and the *minimum* the sum of the *inaequalitates*, that is, of the inequalities or differences of variation of the volume of matter as

79. *Ep.*, 12 (G., IV, 59, lines 14–16).

80. Descartes, *Principia*, II, 33 (Adam and Tannery, VIII, 59).

81. *Desc. Princ. Phil.*, II, 9, and 9, Lem. (G., I, 198–199).

82. *Desc. Princ. Phil.*, II, 10 (G., I, 199): "*Spatium inter A et B erit ubique inaequale, inter A et B indefinita spatia minora atqua minora . . . , etiam ipsius inaequalitates, indefinitas,* etc."

83. *Desc. Princ. Phil.*, II, 5 and 5, S. (G., I, 190–191).

well as of its speed, in short, the sum of the small parts of diminished extension, just like the sum of the small degrees of accumulated speed, is an infinite, inexpressible in terms of number.[84]

We must thus substitute for "sum of unequal distances," which would correspond to *"omnia spatia inaequalia,"* the translation true to the text: *"omnes inaequalitates spatii,"* "sum of the inequalities of distance."

When we have made this rectification, the difficulties vanish. Considering the two segments AB and CD as located on a secant which pivots around the center O, we add their successive *differences*[85] and obtain in *absolute values:*

$$\int_{E \epsilon \overset{\frown}{AC}} d\,(EF)$$

All the particularities of the text are thus explained. As it is a question, not of the sum of the distances, but of the sum of their inequalities, we understand that nonconcentric circles are necessary in order to circumscribe the infinite between the boundaries of a *maximum* (AB) and a *minimum* (CD): if, indeed, the circles were replaced by hyperbolas,[86] the variations of the distances (represented by the differences of straight lines parallel to the nontransversal axis of symmetry), having no *maximum,* would be without limits.

Finally, we rediscover here the problem of divisibility, for the example returns to show that the determinate distance AB—CD, namely D'B, includes an actual infinity of infinitely small distances, and consequently is indivisible into discontinuous parts; or, also, that the distance CD is a minimal quantity obtained by continuously diminishing the infinitely small parts of AB, the sum of these diminishments being a definite integral, that is, a finite quantity D'B resulting from an infinite summation of differentials.

* * *

XXIV.—The solution to the problem of the Infinite, due to a clear and distinct idea of substance, puts an end to all antinomies. These

84. *Desc. Princ. Phil.,* II, 8–11 (G., I, 196–200).

85. The term "difference" is used by Descartes in connection with hyperbolas to express the inequality of the distances (cf. *Dioptrique,* Disc. 8 (Adam and Tannery, VI, 178, lines 11–12)).

86. This is the case referred to, among others, by the remark: *"Neque etiam idcirco concluditur, ut in aliis contingit, quod ejus maximum et minimum non habeamus."* (*Ep.* 12, G., IV, 60).

antinomies, which permit the opposition of the Infinite and the finite, spring from the obliteration of the understanding, the expression of the Infinite, by the imagination, the expression of the finite. Far from causing their opposition to vanish by suppressing the first in favor of the second, the imagination transforms it into an irremediable conflict, for the Infinite, wrongly understood in us, subsists no less truly in things, and its negation by our mutilated knowledge amounts to nothing other than to confer upon it the properties of the finite. Thus, refusing to submit itself to violation, it obstinately affirms its presence on every occasion by causing to arise, from the depths of the alleged solutions dictated by the imagination, the fundamental absurdity which is at their source. The defenders of the finite, moreover, involuntarily give evidence of this absurdity when they are obliged, with Descartes, for example,[87] to recognize, somewhat in spite of themselves, the reality of the Infinite to which they "submit" their mind as to the incomprehensible. And the final reason for their absurd position comes precisely from the fact that they believe our understanding to be incapable of comprehending the Infinite; whereas it is understanding, that is, power of truth, only through the original comprehension which it has of the Infinite and which conditions that of every other thing, and although its ideas are adequate, that is, infinite in it as in God.

But, after the understanding has been returned to its authentic constitution, substance, by the same stroke, is restored to its true nature, and since its infinity as well as its indivisibility are grasped genetically from its necessary existence, they are imposed upon us in their full intelligibility. In this way light penetrates Metaphysics.

Seeing, from this point on, that this absolute indivisibility must subsist at the base of all things, we see clearly and distinctly that modes are infinitely divisible and, consequently, continuous. We then exclude—in accord with Zeno, defending the continuity of the Parmenidean sphere against the numerical discontinuity of the Pythagoreans, but defending it ourselves for genetic reasons and no longer only *per absurdum*—discontinuity, atomism, number. We understand genetically how the infinite is in the larger as in the smaller, and how—as Descartes recognized without understanding it—matter in motion must be able to divide itself endlessly when it must circulate

87. The expression "defender of the finite" can be accepted only to the degree to which our understanding, for Descartes, is made to know only finite things and not the infinite, which we cannot *understand,* but only *intend.*

within the constrictions of the vortical rings. The antinomy regarding the divisibility of matter is then resolved in favor of the Infinite. Thus, light penetrates Physics as it penetrates Metaphysics.

In the same fashion the antinomy regarding the first beginning of the world is resolved. If, indeed, we tried to reduce to a certain number all the movements in matter which have occurred up to the present, and their duration to a determinate time, the attributes of substance, limited to a determinate number, would not be infinite. As a result, we would deprive substance itself of a part of its existence, and we would make it finite, for, nothingness having no properties, substance must cease wherever its properties, that is, its affections, cease. But it would then annihilate itself, since every substance is destroyed as soon as it is assumed to be finite. The universe, that is, the whole of finite modes, is thus an infinite and has never begun.[88]

Finally, infinity and indivisibility, unveiling the true nature of my duration, render it intelligible like all the rest.

My duration is my existence posited by the immanent and eternal act of substance. This act is identified with my existence, for it constitutes it from within; an indivisible act, for substance does not divide itself; an act which is complete in my existence and entire in each of its moments, since it is indivisible. Each of the moments of my real duration is thus an actual infinite. It never *really* divides itself in them; otherwise the indivisible act, complete in it, would itself be really divided, which is absurd. Two consequences result from this:

1. The Cartesian problem is reversed: we no longer have to explain how beings, by themselves unstable, are maintained at every instant as if at arm's length from nothingness by the divine omnipotence, but rather how beings, which of themselves would endure indefinitely, are suddenly annihilated. As a result, we also see that if each instant encloses in itself the infinite, as Leibniz will intend, it is in a different sense, for it encloses only the infinite of the cause which sustains it and not, at the same time, the infinity of all the predicates, past and future, of my existence. Indeed, the infinity of these predicates and my existence itself do not depend solely on God insofar as he causes my essence absolutely and sustains my existence from within, but also on the determination of this divine cause by an infinite chain of finite causes transcending my essence and its sufficient cause.[89]

88. *Ep.*, 12 (G., IV 60, lines 9–16). Cf. *E.*, I, xvi, Dem. and *E.*, I, xxi, Dem. 2.
89. Cf. *E.*, I, xxviii and *E.*, II, xi, C.

My essence then includes only the reason of what defines it *sub specie aeternitatis,* that is, as understanding (the reason, Leibniz will say, of what belongs to it *sub ratione generalitatis*), and not the reason of the predicates of its existence, that is, of what imagination perceives (contrary to Leibniz, who, in place of Spinoza's singular essence, substitutes individual substance, sufficient reason of all its predicates, that is, of all that belongs to it *sub ratione possibilitatis*). The reason for all its predicates is not in itself, but in that infinite chain of causes external to it which God must necessarily produce in order to make it exist. Hence, every instant of my duration envelops, not the infinity of past and future moments of this existence, that is, the infinity of its predicates, but only the identity of the indivisible duration of my existence, directly expressing the infinity of its cause, whose eternity, although having no common measure with the succeeding instants, is nevertheless immanent to them.

2. From the fact that the changes I perceive in my existence do not ever really divide it and are only changes of modes, my duration can only be continuous, and it is absurd to see discontinuity here. We make it so, nevertheless, whenever we confuse it with time, the imaginative aid which serves to measure it. Finite, like any measure, time, in order to measure it, endeavors to reconstruct it by joining finite fragments end to end, fragments which are really separate one from another, inert, because detached from the act which makes them exist, in short, discontinuous. This is an effort as impossible to realize as that of expressing extension by a number, since here no more than elsewhere can we succeed in engendering the infinite with the finite, nor the indivisible with the divisible, nor the continuous with the discontinuous, nor the unity of an act with its dead and isolated fragments, nor rational activity with imaginative passivities, nor an adequate idea with inadequate ideas.

Thus it is sufficient that general concepts, beings of the imagination (totality seen as the aggregate of discrete parts, atoms, number, measure, time, etc.), be exorcised for the problems to vanish. Substance being clearly and distinctly conceived, Nature, then freed of the veils which hide it from us, reveals from this moment on, in its principle as in its modes, the unity of an infinite without break or fault, the object of a unique and transparent truth.

The Ontological Argument in Spinoza

WILLIAM A. EARLE

The ontological argument is universally discredited today, generally on logical grounds. It has become a platitude to assert that existence cannot follow from essence, that all analytic propositions are to be interpreted as hypotheses having no existential import. Our platitudes, however, would be falsehoods resting on an inadequate metaphysical analysis for a series of thinkers including Anselm, Descartes, Spinoza, Leibniz, Hegel, and Bradley. At each period the contemporaries of these men raised our objections for us and these objections were not unknown to the philosophers who rested their entire work on the ontological argument. At each period these philosophers insisted that the objections rested on a misunderstanding of precisely what the argument did and did not assert. Such misunderstandings will occur as long as we abstract the ontological argument from its metaphysical context; that is, as long as we alter the significance of the relevant terms. Since this entire context is probably clearest in Spinoza, I should like to reexamine the ontological argument as it occurs there in order to determine whether we are not committing the same errors of misinterpretation as did his contemporaries.

But before a discussion of the ontological argument proper, I should like to clarify the relation of this paper to that argument. I do not intend to "prove" the ontological argument in a direct fashion, since such a procedure would be in direct contradiction to the assertions of the argument. The argument states in some fashion that the existence of God or substance follows from his essence alone; to attempt then to give further grounds for the existence of God than those asserted by the argument would be to destroy that argument. The argument must stand or fall by itself; the only function of this discussion is to elucidate the argument, and not to prove it.

Briefly the argument states that there is an essence whose existence follows necessarily from that essence. That is all. It does *not* say: I have an idea of such an essence, and therefore God must exist

Philosophy and Phenomenological Research 11 (1951), pp. 549–554. Reprinted by permission of the author and of *Philosophy and Phenomenological Research*.

as cause. Nor does it say: there are certain finite things, hence there must be a necessary being as cause. These are both variants of the cosmological argument, and although used by Spinoza, were considered by him to be *a posteriori* and of inferior certitude. Both rest upon a certain empirical fact, the existence of a certain sort of idea or of finite things; and both employ certain notions of causation which we cannot analyze here. But these considerations are irrelevant to the argument in its pure form, which asserts only that there is an essence which necessarily involves existence.

Spinoza does not assert that *all* essences involve existence, nor that essence as such involves existence. Here he would insist that most essences do not and cannot involve existence. The question concerns only one special essence, the essence of substance, or of that "which is in itself and conceived through itself." This one, Spinoza asserts, must involve existence; and to see why, we must know what Spinoza means by the terms, "essence," "existence," and "substance."

Let us first examine the notion of essence. Essence, for Spinoza, is not a purely logical term, the mere object of any definable sign. Essence expresses something *positive,* it expresses power or reality. It is certainly not what Santayana for example means by essence, a term wide enough to include square circles, as well as negations of these, etc. "Non-chair" for Santayana is an essence in the same sense as chair, though for Spinoza it would be a mere fiction of the mind, a mere word. From such a conception we could derive no positive properties; we would know only what the thing was not. "Positive" and "negative," however, are slippery terms, since a word verbally negative may express something positive, as does the word "infinite," for example. Essences cannot be self-contradictory; and since the entire course of nature follows analytically from God who does all that he can do, it follows that there are only essences for those things which were, are, or will be. Anything else must either contradict itself, or contradict what exists. Such unrealizables will be mere fictions of the mind or compositions of words.

Secondly, and more importantly, an essence is *not* an idea, or a psychological state of some sort. Spinoza distinguishes between the *idea* and the *ideatum.* The idea of a circle would therefore have two aspects: it is, to be sure, an idea, a mode of thought; but it is the idea *of* a circle which is not a mode of thought, but a determinate mode of extension. The circle is round, and all its radii are equal, whereas it would be absurd to speak of an idea as being round or having radii. Thought and extension have distinct properties, and neither is to be understood in terms of the other. This distinction is clear *within* the idea; an analysis of the idea itself will exhibit these two aspects. An idea of a house for example is clearly in one sense a psychological act, a mode of thought; but the idea is *of* something which is made of stone, wood, and bricks, and not ideas. The essence of house or of circle, therefore, neither is nor involves the notion of thought. It is independent of that psychological act which thinks it, and this can be seen within that psychological act itself. This distinguishability of idea and ideatum is essential to the objective and independent validity of thought. A geometer resolves the circle into its proper elements, planes, lines, and the central point; at no point need he mention the thought which is thinking all this. No geometry will be found to posit among its principles ideas as such or anything else psychological. Geometry and logic are sciences independent of psychology, studying objective relations among the things posited.

Not all *ideata* are essences of course. But here we are interested in those *ideata* which are essences and their structural and essential independence from the psychological act by which they are thought. That they are independent can be guaranteed within thought itself simply by the complete analysis of the essence thought of.

These relations hold even when we take as the object of some thought thought itself. If I have the idea of an idea, then the thought which I am thinking of is independent of the particular act of thought by which I think it. Now this should not be understood as asserting that we can think of essences without thinking at all; such would be obviously nonsense, and is asserted by nobody. But it *would* be asserted that there are aspects within any idea which are logically, structurally, and essentially independent of the act which thinks them, that such a distinction can be demonstrated within thought itself (by the reduction of the particular essence to its principles), and that the independence of any eidetic science from empirical psychology depends upon this distinction.

The conclusion of all this is simply that essences are not ideas, although sometimes ideas are ideas of essences; the essences do not require that particular act of thought for their definition, and hence are structurally independent. This is a first step in the perception of the independence of essence: its independence from mind; it does not yet demonstrate that there are essences which are as a matter of fact existentially independent of everything.

Essences then are independent of the psychological act which thinks them; but, considered in themselves, they may be dependent upon other essences, or they may be absolutely independent. The essence of circle depends, among other things, on the essence of plane, of line, etc., since these other essences would figure in its definition. This order of derivation is of course logical, but it is mirrored in the level of existing things: an existing circle depends on an existing plane. The essence of island requires the essence of circumambient water; and so an existing island requires existing circumambient water. The order of essences and things is one and the same. A thing is a mode when it is conceived through another, and the essence of that mode will depend on the essence of that through which it is conceived. And just as the independence of essence from thought is discoverable within thought itself simply by the analysis of the essence, so the dependence or independence of the essence from other essences will be discoverable within thought alone by the adequate analysis of that essence. An independent essence will be one which is *conceived through itself* and which *is* in itself. These phrases clearly express the same thing: since things will depend *existentially* upon precisely those things on which their essences will *essentially* depend, independence of essence is the same as independence of existence. The discernment, therefore, of an essence which is thought through itself will be at the same time the discernment of that which exists through itself; defining the essence is precisely this act of discernment; hence as soon as God or substance is defined as being precisely that essence which is thought through itself, i.e., which is essentially independent, it is seen at the same time that he must exist.

But what kind of existence does such an essence have? Here again we must not import into Spinoza's system conceptions of existence fundamentally foreign to it. For Spinoza there are two sorts of existence: eternity, and duration. Duration is that existence which modes have, and is measured by time; eternity is the existence which independent essences have. When Spinoza speaks of the existence of God he is not attributing to God some sort of surd, some irrational, brute, simply given mode of being; the existence of God, he tells us, *is nothing but his essence:* they are one and the same thing. To assert God's existence, therefore, is to frame an analytic proposition. One is not adding an extrinsic property to an essence; ultimately the argument is simply the reaffirmation of the absolute independence of God's essence. It is analytic, and therefore requires no additional grounds.

To attribute to God an existence which would add a new determinant to his essence would be to attribute to him the existence appropriate to modes, duration. We cannot know by an analysis of the essence of modes whether they exist or not; we must consult the order of nature which is to say, for finite minds, we must consult experience. Hence to interpret the ontological argument as attempting to prove a synthetic proposition by something like "rational intuition" is to misinterpret it completely. The argument was never anything but an analytic assertion. Whether such a proposition, along with the metaphysics derived from it is held to be "interesting," "fruitful," or "useful" or not depends on what sort of knowledge one is seeking; the ultimate use of such knowledge or any knowledge is a question which more properly falls within ethics, and is a question not neglected of course by Spinoza.

The existence of God is therefore his eternity, and his eternity is again the radical independence of his essence. He is substance, and substance is that which is and is conceived through itself. So again we see, now by an explication of the term, "existence," that the argument is analytic. But why, it may be asked, do we not end with nothing rather than infinite substance consisting of infinite attributes, each one of which expresses infinite essence? This would be an objection only so long as we forgot Spinoza's conception of essence; it is positive rather than negative, and expresses, therefore, some positive reality, rather than the mere negation of something which would as a matter of fact be nothing but a fiction, and a fiction which more clearly than anything else *depended* on something else, namely *everything* else. In a metaphor, substance at this level is like a light shining in a dark space; since the essence in question has already subsumed everything else under it as a modification, there is nothing left which can contradict or oppose it; it is free to expand out infinitely. And as darkness cannot quench light, neither can non-being destroy the being of substance.

The existence of God is thus an eternal *subsistence*. The existence or duration of modes on the other hand will differ from the eternity of God to the degree that their essence differs from his essence. Since modes are derived essentially, their existence will also be derived, that is to say, they will be dependent upon the rest of the universe; existence does not follow immediately from these essences but only from the existence of their causes, which are, in turn, dependent upon *their* own causes, etc.; existence for modes will therefore be transitory. Since the existence of a mode cannot follow from its essence, propositions asserting its existence will be synthetic, and experience will be needed by any finite mind in order to ascertain its truth. We can therefore see why existence will be a brute fact, a surd, when it is asserted of modes by finite minds; such properties will be consequences of Spinoza's general conception of the relation between substance and modes. But if we were to *begin* with existence conceived after the fashion of duration, then clearly we could never arrive at the notion of eternal subsistence. The ontological argument asserting eternal subsistence would then be interpreted after the model of modes, and would always be absurd, a "synthetic" proposition, and wholly undemonstrable. On the other hand, beginning with the notion of an eternal subsistence, one can, if Spinoza is correct, derive a notion of existence or duration which is appropriate to our experiences of finite things.

In terms of this conception of the ontological argument, let us further consider some objections which have been made. The contention has been made, for example, that since the existence of God follows from his essence or definition, anything could be defined into existence, by simply including "existence" in the definition. Thus we might define a hippogriff as a "combined griffin and horse which exists." Would not it then analytically follow that such a creature must exist? The reason that such a being could not exist for Spinoza is *not* that the combination of horse and griffin violates some supposed rule of nature; such we could not know by reason alone. Rather it is because the combination of these two terms combined with the notion of existence itself contains a contradiction. The first part of the definition, horse and griffin, determines a mode which intrinsically depends on other things, ultimately on the whole circumambient universe; to now assert that such a mode existed in itself would make it independent of that universe. Similarly with the example of the "most perfect island, one of whose perfections is existence." An island is a piece of land surrounded by water. Its essence requires the essence of water, and its existence depends on the existence of the water. To then add that such an island existed in itself would be to contradict what we posited in the first part of the definition. (And if the island had only *dependent* existence, the point is granted: the island would only exist contingently.) Clearly the same argument would apply to any mode defined into existence. Existence follows only from certain essences, those namely which express infinity, independence, and substance.

Kant, in the portion of the *Critique* devoted to the refutation of the ontological argument, has no trouble disposing of it under the interpretation that it presents a synthetic judgment. But, if it is analytic, he says, then either the conception in your mind is identical with the thing, or else you have given us nothing but a "wretched tautology." Clearly, the argument *is* analytic; that it thereby implies that the thing, God, is identical with your conception has already been disposed of; and that it is a tautology is true, but whether it is "wretched" or not will depend on what value we wish to place on the analytic clarification of existence.

The Ontological Argument in Spinoza: Twenty Years Later

WILLIAM A. EARLE

The ontological argument has, of course, a long and venerable history; its "refutation" also has a long if not quite so venerable history. No sooner did Anselm formulate it than its "refutation" appeared, and the story is repeated through Descartes, Spinoza, Leibniz, Hegel, Bradley, through our own times. It looks like an argument, hence appeals to logicians; it uses the term "therefore," hence invites a purely formal analysis. But then it may not be an argument at all, and "therefore" may have other uses than the syllogistic. In any case, it would be foolish to formalize what has not been understood; and the understanding of what it says and what it does not say, introduces us at once into those metaphysical *systems* where it plays a central role. Spinoza was singularly explicit about that context; it therefore might be worth while examining the ontological argument within the context of a system where its meaning might become visible. The argument is here held to be strictly valid, and the career of both it and its refutations to be less that of a recurring malady of human reason itself, than the appearance and disappearance of certain principles of philosophical hermeneutics. If the essence of that argument is an intellectual intuition, is it really a discursive argument? And if it explicitly purports to be true of one unique "entity," God, what claims upon it can be made from a logic which, in its formalization, ignores this decisive difference in content? But before we go into the matter, it should be clear that the function of this discussion cannot be to "prove" the validity of the argument; if the argument is indeed sound, it then requires no additional proof and would be incompatible with any. Our purpose then is strictly interpretive, and no interpretation serves as a premise for what it interprets.

The ontological argument has had a variety of formulations: some speak of a "most perfect Being than which nothing more perfect can be conceived," but what is "perfection" and doesn't this version make reference to our capacities? Others speak of a Being which "cannot

---

This essay was written especially for this volume.

not be," putting it all negatively as if the life of this Being consisted in unsuccessfully trying to commit suicide; others call it a "necessary Being," suggesting to some that it is necessitated by others, hence contingent upon them; or that Being whose "*idea* implies its existence," making the Being dependent upon certain contingencies of sentience.

But the subject of the argument in Spinoza's language is God, Substance or *Natura naturans,* all taken as synonymous. It is neither the *idea* nor the *verbal definition* of it, although there is such an idea and such a definition. Spinoza defines "Substance" as "that which is in itself and must be conceived through itself." At first sight the definition seems a bit too lengthy; obviously nothing which was not in itself *could* be truly conceived through itself, and what has Substance got to do with how it must be *conceived?* Besides, the very sense of "in itself" implies that it is not "in another." But this seems to involve Substance itself in negative relations to its own modes, hence logically dependent upon them, a dialectical situation beloved of Hegel. The same would hold of anything whatsoever said about Substance; if we declare it to be ontologically "most perfect," we relativize it against the less perfect; if its essence implies its existence, we imply an initial distinguishability of essence and existence only to deny it; if we find it necessary, we envisage it against a domain of pure possibility where it *could* not be, and thus deny the very sense of the problem. The truth then is that Substance is strictly ineffable though equally strictly "conceivable." Everything then which is said *about* Substance has a peculiar sense; it will be the negation of a negation. In a word, the term can only be brought into discursive language, hence made effable, by denying something falsely said of it. Hence the infinite possible versions of the ontological argument. God or Substance is *not* a mere idea, a mere representation, a mere word, a mere possibility, a mere essence, or merely something "better" than hitherto envisaged. Each version raises the possibility of Substance being *that* and denies it. The forms of the "that" which Substance is not are as infinite as possible categories of the finite: space, time, relation, causation by another, etc., right on through the very idea of substances, which must be taken in a different sense when applied to Substance Itself. Hence all these descriptions must be understood in a preeminent sense, through an infinite analogy, when said of that which is called Substance. For Spinoza, since Substance is the very origin of things, and its idea the source of all intelligibility, that which is this origin and source cannot be really clarified through its own partial effects and modes. On the contrary, good philosophical method demands the opposite; and yet the origin of things, while in itself decisively ineffable, is held by Spinoza to be the subject of an "adequate idea." How indeed can that which is strictly ineffable to discursive language be adequately grasped, to such an extent, that nothing else can be understood except through it?

A few distinctions are in order. Spinoza distinguishes *idea* from *ideatum;* idea is a mode of thinking, ideatum is what the idea is of, which need not be a mode of thinking at all. If I form the idea of a circle, my idea is a thinking about a circle which is not in the least a mode of thinking, but something extended. It has a center and circumference and the radii are equal; none of these properties are true of the *idea*. But if I should form the idea of an idea, the ideatum would itself be a mode of thinking, like the idea of it. I form an adequate idea of an ideatum, when the idea grasps the ideatum itself, and not a part, aspect, phase, or property of it. How does the idea *know* that it grasps its ideatum adequately? No external criteria would be relevant, Spinoza explains in the *Emendation of the Understanding.* Truth is a measure of itself and the false, and self-evident truth is found in the *initial* relation of idea to ideatum. The ideatum, whatever it is, is already something, has, as ideatum, a sense or essence. Now either all of that is grasped by the idea or not; and the idea knows that in the very act of having an ideatum in the first place. Thus if I form the idea of one mode, as given mode it implicates other modes as well as Substance, which are not present in the initial idea although implicated by it. I therefore have a self-declared inadequate idea, knowable by the idea itself. Of what *could* I form an adequate idea? Obviously only of that which is "in itself"; the adequate ideas of other things will relate them back to the primordial in-itself.

What the adequate idea is adequate to, its ideatum, is called Substance. *Substance itself* then is the ideatum; the idea has not grasped therefore a "representation" of, an image of, nor a universal concept of Substance, but Substance itself "in person." Substance is not a universal, substantiality, or deity, but itself a "singular," an "individual," in the preeminent senses mentioned above. But an idea of a singular individual, indeed unique in this case, is an "Intuition," and not a universal concept. Hence the adequate idea in question is an *intellectual intuition,* precisely that which Kant denied to man but reserved as a possibility to God. For Spinoza, man's idea of God is one and the same as God's idea of Himself; hence the intellectual intuition which is expressed by the ontological "argument" is the participation by that idea which is the human mind in God considered as thinking of Himself. They are not two ideas which resemble one another, but one and the same.

But if we take a step backwards from this purely immanent or phenomenological analysis of the situation, we might ask how any such thing is possible. The claim is indeed extraordinary although guaranteed by internal analysis. And so we might ask, what is mind such that it can have any such intellectual intuition of Substance itself? Mind, says Spinoza, is the idea of the body. And at first sight this would seem to instantly obviate any possibility of an intellectual intuition of Substance which is eternal and infinite, and confine the mind's capacities to the sensory on the one hand, and the universal or conceptual on the other. Is not the body a finite mode, inherently dependent upon other physical bodies and their interaction? The modifications in my own body worked by external bodies and forces I am aware of as sensations; the ideas of these sensations are nothing but the ideas of "conclusions without the premises," hence taken by themselves, "inadequate"; the premises are of course the infinite concatenation of causes which produced those sensory effects I am aware of. Even my idea of my own body, which constitutes my mind, is inadequate; the body cannot be conceived through itself since it is not through itself but an effect of circumambient nature. Conceptualization from such data of sensation, in terms of their common properties, number, motion, etc., are clearly nothing in themselves, but *entia rationis,* useful but not beings. In such a situation, how could mind form by intellectual intuition the idea of Substance itself? Clearly, because our account of the epistemological situation is so far inadequate. The mind is the idea of the body, that is, there is one mode of Substance which expresses itself either as body or as its idea, mind. But to suppose the body is an independent thing, finite and merely lost among other finite modes, is to misunderstand the body. The body was never anything but a mode of Substance in the first place; and similarly the mind is not absolutely finite, since the absolutely finite is equally a contradiction in terms. Hence on both scores, mind and body, Substance is already implicated; body is a mode of Substance, its idea, mind, is the same mode thinking, and therefore dependent upon Substance. The idea of Substance then is *possible* ontologically; whereas a body not the body of Substance or a mind which excluded the idea of Substance are *not possible*.

The role of intellectual intuition of Substance is, obviously, decisive in any "rationalism." The epistemological fear within rationalism is that its adequate or its "clear and distinct" ideas are nothing but that, and in effect that the mind is enclosed within its own objects, its own representations, constructions, or constitutions; that the whole structure of knowledge might be an elaborate fiction, or that it bears nothing but a hypothetical relation to Being itself. The problem then is to find if possible that idea which is the idea of something which *is,* an idea which *knows of itself* that it is true. At that point, the magic circle of mere representations would be broken, and the ideas of mind would be anchored in reality. Descartes isolated the *cogito ergo sum* as one such anchor; it is a reflective idea, it is not a discursive syllogism, and each time it is enacted, it supplies an intellectual intuition of the being of the very ego thinking it. The ontological "argument" serves a similar function; the discernment of the idea of Substance or God, is the discernment of that idea which adequately grasps Being, not its image, representation or concept, but Substance itself.

The intellectual (or "rational") intuition of Substance is the idea of an infinite singular. It is then small wonder that such an "object" is ineffable; it would share ineffability with all singulars, but now in an infinitely enhanced degree. But "ineffability" conceals some curious reversals of meaning. If nothing drawn from either sense perception or the common notions drawn therefrom can be applied to Substance except by way of negating what is already negative in them, it might seem that the idea of Substance, far from being "adequate," was the least adequate of all, everything said about it being true only by way of infinite analogical remotion. On the other hand, for the rationalists, the exact opposite is the truth; it is not Substance which is obscure but *everything else* commonly taken to be clear on grounds of familiarity as with common notions, or vividness, as with perceptions. *Red* is, measured against Substance, a most inadequate idea, no matter how bright it is; and the common conceptions, such as thing or substance, motion and number, no matter how universally illustrated, remain obscure until seen *sub specie aeternitatis,* that is, from the angle of Substance.

Looked at finally, the various versions of the ontological argument all serve the same purpose: to discriminate among things that which is Substance. This unique Being independently of which nothing else can be or be conceived, has obviously unique "properties." Its mode of being is, Spinoza says, *eternity* and not temporal existence, which he reserves for modes of substance. Its being will be necessary and not contingent upon others. It will be "most perfect" ontologically, absolute and not relative, an "immanent cause" of all other things, and the "cause of itself," hence, we might as well say, "omnipotent." Its "essence implies its necessary being"; only that *sort* of thing could have necessary being, and necessary being could only hold for that sort of thing. In a word, the essence and being of this Being are identical; essence and existence are only distinguishable for modes of substance. And so, again and again, the various versions of the "argument" only serve to indicate that what is distinguishable for modes is not for Substance. Essence and existence here are the same; cause and effect are the same; and finally the world and its divine principle are the same taken in different ways, *natura naturans, natura naturata.*

But whereas we have no hope of surveying or comprehending the "face of nature," we do have the possibility of an intellectual intuition of its active principle. Substance then, as the immanent cause of all things, must be, as an idea, the ground of anything claiming to be knowledge. The order of ideas must be the same as the order of things. That idea from which all other true ideas must be deducible "in a geometrical manner" must itself contain the guarantee of its own truth *within* it. At this point, the ontological argument only indicates that such an idea is true of or adequate to its intended ideatum.

Nothing whatsoever in the ontological argument, purely understood, depends upon premises to the effect that I or someone else *actually has* such an idea at any given time. Nor can the effect of the argument be to render the being of Substance dependent upon our sentience. If no one had such an idea, nothing follows except that no one would know of Substance; Substance itself timelessly exists, and if finite sentience were obliterated, the only thing that would "know" of the being of Substance would be Substance itself, if "knowing" is still the appropriate term. For Spinoza, thought is an attribute of Substance, and "there is" eternally an idea of Substance, God's idea of himself. This idea, as we mentioned above, is *identical* with man's idea of Substance. There is but one such idea, a divine idea, which the human mind can participate in. It would carry us too far afield to discuss "ideas," which for us are almost virtually exclusively "psychological events," dependent for their actuality upon living organisms, in their older sense an ontological perfection, hence not so much dependent upon brains as rendering anything like a functioning, signifying mind possible.

No doubt at all, some of the misinterpretations of the very sense of the argument arise from suspicions of what might be thought to follow. Is Substance a secret surrogate for Jehovah or Christ? Precisely what passion should be poured into the term; or what existential relevance does Substance have? But here again Spinoza has responded in advance. The fifth book of the *Ethics* is devoted to man's *freedom,* a book not sufficiently studied by those who imagine that Spinoza is a "determinist" in a fatalistic sense. The freedom of man consists precisely in the rational intuition of Substance, "God's idea of himself," and the comprehension of himself and all other things as following from that unique essence-substance in which he participates. The reenactment by man of an infinite thought of an infinite Substance may be hopelessly useless for the projects of the *Lebenswelt,* since it is not one of them and could only look like an "escape hatch" to the devotees of Sartre's *engagement.* And yet Spinoza defines it as "blessedness," not a "pleasure," but freedom itself; put otherwise it is for us an act of transcendence, not from one misery to the next, but precisely from the oppressive finality of the *Lebenswelt,* by a "reinterpretation" of it from the standpoint of a rational intuition of *Natura naturans,* another name for the eternally creative Substance which cannot not be, and in which we participate.

Eternity and Sempiternity

MARTHA KNEALE

I

In the first part of the paper I shall discuss whether an eternal object can or must be also sempiternal. The question has at least historical interest, since philosophers and theologians have held widely differing views on it. I believe that it is also of logical interest and I hope that this will emerge in the course of the discussion.

Of the two notions with which we are concerned, that of sempiternity is comparatively simple. A sempiternal object is one which exists at all moments of time. This definition holds whether we believe time to be finite in one or both directions or infinite in both. But the notion of eternity is far less clear. William Kneale[1] has argued that the theological notion of eternity arises from a self-defeating attempt to combine the notion of life with that of the timeless existence of the Platonic Forms and he traces the attempt back to Parmenides and Plato. I accept the history he gives as at least plausible but I should like to make a further point. The alleged contradictory combination was already present in the word *aiôn* which Plato uses in the *Timaeus* for eternity. R. B. Onians[2] has argued plausibly that this word originally meant the spinal marrow, which was held to be in a special way the vehicle of a creature's life. He remarks, "It is not difficult to see how a word designating the life 'fluid' might come to mean the life which the fluid represents and so the lifetime temporally considered, the lifetime dependent upon it . . . . . The temporal suggestion appears gradually to have increased by popular association of the word with *aei, aiei* (always) till at last it meant 'eternity.'" If Onians is right then the word *aiônios,* which

Proceedings of the Aristotelian Society 69 (1968–69), pp. 223–238. Reprinted by courtesy of the Editor of the Aristotelian Society. © 1969 The Aristotelian Society.

1. William Kneale, "Time and Eternity in Theology," *Proc. Arist. Soc.,* LXI (1960–61), 87–108.

2. R. B. Onians, *Origins of European Thought* (Cambridge: Cambridge University Press, 1954), p. 209.

Plato uses in a seminal passage of the *Timaeus*[3] to express the nature of that which is merely imitated by time, would carry with it the connotation of "life" and it is noteworthy that Aristotle's only uses of the word in the *Metaphysics*[4] are applications of it to God and the intellect.[5] In arguing for the everlastingness of the heavenly bodies and of the *ouranos* (the heavens) itself, he uses the less emotive terms *aïdios* and *aei on* (always existent).[6]

It is clear that at least some ancient philosophers held that there are some sempiternal objects. As we have seen, Aristotle says that the heavens in general and the stars and sun in particular are sempiternal. Similarly Epicurus and his followers held that the primordial atoms are everlasting, but if we take Lucretius as typical of them, they made no distinction between eternity and sempiternity. He says of the atoms

> Sunt igitur solida primordia simplicitate
> nec ratione queunt alia servata per aevum
> ex infinito jam tempore res reparare.[7]

("The primordial things are therefore of solid simplicity, for they could not otherwise remain, through endless duration (*aevum*) and repair things from infinite time")
and also

> quae quoniam sunt
> illa quoque esse tibi solida atque aeterna fatendum.[8]

(For which reason you must also admit that they (the atoms) are solid and eternal.)

Again it is not at all clear to me that Aristotle would have drawn any distinction in meaning between *aïdios* (sempiternal) and *aiônios* (eternal) beyond the fact that usage restricts the application of the latter to what is alive.

Plato, however, in the *Timaeus* passage already mentioned seems to draw a sharp distinction in that he maintains that past and future tenses are not applicable to what is *aiônios*. Of this one can say only

---

3. Plato, *Timaeus,* 37C ff.

4. Aristotle, *Metaphysics,* 1072b 29 and 1075a 10.

5. Cf. also a curious discussion in *De Caelo,* I, 9, 279a 22–29, where Aristotle seems to attribute the similarity of the words *aiôn* and *aei* to divine inspiration. This offers some support to Onians.

6. Aristotle, *Metaphysics,* 1050b 22 ff.

7. Lucretius, *De Rerum Natura,* I, 548.

8. *Ibid.,* I, 627.

that it *is*, *i.e.*, as we should say, that it is timeless. Now the most obviously timeless things for Plato are Forms and mathematical objects (if there are such), but to these Aristotle applies the same word that he applies to the sun and the stars, *aïdios*.[9]

I have given these facts about ancient thinkers to show how the notions of eternity and sempiternity first came into western thought, but my main concern is to consider the logical relation between the two. It is clear that we have six possible relations to consider. The two notions may be identical, they may be different but mutually entail each other, there may be entailment one way or the other, there may be mere compatibility or there may be incompatibility. As it happens three of the possible views are already expressed by the authors we have considered. For Plato eternity and sempiternity are incompatible because eternity excludes succession, before and after, while these are plainly entailed by sempiternity; for Epicurus and his follower Lucretius the terms express a single notion; while for Aristotle they are at least compatible. The life of God is both *aiônios* and *aïdios*.[10] It is difficult to be more exact about Aristotle's views, but I shall later show that he may have held that there is a two-way entailment between eternity in one sense and sempiternity.

Turning to modern times we find that for popular theology the two are at least compatible. If any object is held to be eternal, that object is God. Yet we sing

> Before the hills in order stood
> Or earth received her frame
> From everlasting Thou art God
> To endless years the same.

Here sempiternity is plainly attributed to God, while I believe that the somewhat mysterious present tense of the third line indicates His eternity. Again we experience no shock of incongruity when Hamlet expresses the wish that "The *Everlasting* had not fixed His canon 'gainst self-slaughter."[11] Clearly "the Eternal" and "the Everlasting" are equally satisfactory designations for God. I think that the vague thought behind the utterances of popular theology is that God's eternity entails his sempiternity. In short there is a one-way entailment, for the reverse does not hold. Something, *e.g.*, the atoms of the old atomic theory may be sempiternal without being eternal.

9. Aristotle, *Physics*, 252b, 1–5.
10. Aristotle, *Metaphysics*, 1072b 29.
11. *Hamlet*, Act I, Scene 2, 132.

It is obvious that we cannot determine which of these possible views is correct without being clearer about the notion of eternity. Considering all the texts, it seems to me that there are two qualities different from sempiternity which are at different times connoted by the word "eternal" and its equivalents. The one is timelessness, the manner of existence attributed to the Platonic Forms, and the other is necessity. In much of traditional theology the eternal being is also the necessary being. The extra connotation of life which is conveyed by the Greek words *aiôn* and *aiônios,* I believe to be a philological accident, as suggested by Onians, but it undoubtedly made it easier for later theologians to regard God as the unique eternal object. Boethius, indeed, introduces the notion into his definition of eternity: *Aeternitas est interminabilis vitae tota simul et perfecta possessio*[12] ("Eternity is the endless and perfect possession of life all at once"). This definition is defended by St Thomas in Part I, Quaestio X, Art. 1 of the *Summa Theologica,* although, in his own statement, he does not use any word equivalent to "life" but insists simply that eternity is *tota simul* (all at once).

It should be remarked, however, that in other places Aquinas, as often, attempts to combine a Platonic and an Aristotelian point of view. In *Summa Contra Gentiles* I, 15 he says both *Tempore igitur non mensuratur. Igitur in ipso non est prius et posterius accipere* ("[God] is not measured by time. Therefore we cannot attribute before and after to him") and also . . . *quia quod semper fuit, habet virtutem semper essendi. Est igitur aeternus* ("because what always was has the power of always being. It is therefore eternal"). I agree with Professor Kneale that this notion of life "all at once" is self-contradictory, and I would emphasise the point further by saying that to contrast eternity with time by saying that it is *tota simul* is self-defeating because *simul* is itself a temporal notion. Things in time happen either successively or together (*simul*) and to say that the parts of time, past, present and future happen together is to deny the necessary condition of simultaneity. The point can be brought out more clearly if we attempt to develop in detail the simile which Boethius uses to make his conception of eternity plausible.[13] God's providence, he says, is the cognition of the lowly details of this world as from a high mountain. He does not elaborate the simile

12. Boethius, *De Consolatione Philosophiae,* V, 6.
13. *Loc. cit.*

further but presumably what he means is that the man on the top of the mountain can see the bends and ups and downs of a road all at once whereas the traveller on the road sees only a limited stretch at a given time. But when we come to think it out, the simile does not help. The spectator on high sees the road all at once but he does not see the traveller in all positions at once. This would be a contradiction. His perceptions must be as successive as the positions themselves. The only way to evade the contradiction, as far as I can see, is to regard the traveller in Minkowski fashion as a four-dimensional extended object, but then in order to account for *his* successive awarenesses we have to postulate something like J. W. Dunne's serial time and this involves a vicious infinite regress.

I conclude that timelessness as the *totum simul* of time is a self-contradictory notion and we must either find a different meaning for it or identify it with necessity. When people call objects such as numbers "timeless" perhaps all they mean is that these and the relations between them are somehow necessary, but it may be that they have in mind another and vaguer notion which is connected with the "timelessness" of mathematical truths. I will now try to give more precision to this notion of timelessness, and it will turn out rather surprisingly that it is either identical with the notion of sempiternity or that the two notions entail each other. As far as I can see, all that is meant by calling mathematical truths "timeless" is that there *is no point* in asking when two and two are four in the way that there is point in asking when the daffodils are in bloom. But this does not mean that it is not the case that two and two are four to-day, that they were four yesterday and that they will be four to-morrow. These statements are not meaningless or untrue, but simply so obvious as to be pointless. I would go so far as to say that it is true that to-day two and two have been four for a day longer than they were yesterday and similarly that, if God exists, he has existed a day longer to-day than he had existed yesterday. I admit that such remarks seem paradoxical, but they are neither meaningless nor untrue. It seems to have been the belief that they are meaningless which led Spinoza (who will be the subject of the second part of this paper) to make a sharp distinction between duration and eternity and thus to make the final section of the *Ethics* intolerably obscure. He says, for example, in *E.*, I, xxxiii, S. 2 that there is in eternity neither *when, before* nor *after* (*At cum in aeterno non detur quando, ante nec post*). There is one way of taking this remark which makes it quite true and harmless. If it means that there is no sense in asking when eternity begins or ends, then it is perfectly just. If there is an eternal object, *e.g.,* God, then there is obviously no sense in asking when he began to exist or when he will cease to exist. Since he is *at* all times, he is not *in* time, but this is not to be confused with saying that he does not exist at any time, *i.e.,* not yesterday, to-day or to-morrow. Similarly two and two were four yesterday, they are four to-day and they will be four to-morrow. Timelessness is lack of limitation of existence in time; it is not failure to exist at all times. *Mutatis mutandis* this holds of timeless truths. This is difficult for me to express, as I reject the notion of truth-at-a-time. But more of this later.

The argument which led Spinoza and has led many others to deny that an eternal object exists at a given time is of a type which has seemed to some very modern. It was much favoured by the late Professor Austin and its general form is: "There are no conceivable circumstances in which it would be pointful to utter the sentence S. Therefore the sentence S is meaningless." Using this kind of argument, Austin denies in effect that "He sat down intentionally" in normal circumstances expresses any proposition at all, let alone a true proposition.[14] It seems to me that this type of argument has been sufficiently dealt with by Professor J. R. Searle in his paper "Aberrations and Assertions."[15] As he remarks, it depends on confusing the conditions under which it is correct (conventionally or socially) to assert that-*P* with the conditions under which it is true that-*P*. It is very rarely, if ever, socially correct to assert that two and two are four on Wednesdays, because this suggests that they might be something else on other days. Nevertheless, it is perfectly true. In a way my point is the reverse of Professor Searle's. He is arguing against Austin's slogan "No modification without aberration" that adverbial modifications such as "voluntarily" yield sentences which express perfectly good propositions even in non-aberrant circumstances, while I am arguing that temporal modifications express perfectly good propositions even in aberrant uses, for the ordinary

14. J. L. Austin, "A Plea for Excuses," *Proc. Arist. Soc.,* LVII (1956–57), 1–30, repr. in J. L. Austin, *Philosophical Papers* (Oxford: Clarendon Press, 1961), pp. 123–152.

15. J. R. Searle, "Aberrations and Assertions" in *British Analytical Philosophy,* ed. B. Williams and A. Montefiore (London: Routledge & Kegan Paul; New York: Humanities Press, 1966), pp. 41–54.

non-aberrant use of time determinations is to report events or describe states which occur at a definite, or endure for a limited time. The sort of argument dealt with by Professor Searle seems to me to be the only sort of argument that has ever been put forward for denying that the so-called timeless truths hold at all times; and as I think that Professor Searle has shown that it is not a good sort of argument, I am ready to maintain that the so-called timeless truths do hold at all times and that, if such holding involves the existence of timeless objects, these will also be sempiternal objects. But does it involve the existence of timeless objects? I have so far avoided this question. Let us admit that "Two and two are four" expresses a timeless truth. Does this involve us in saying that the number two is a timeless object? I see no reason so far for being committed to this Fregean conclusion; for, as Descartes remarked, the truths of arithmetic are hypothetical, and I believe that to say "Two and two are four" is to make a statement about all possible pairs of objects.

The answer to the question whether there are timeless objects is obviously determined by the exact sense we attach to the word "object" and is perhaps best approached indirectly through the notion of a timeless truth, which I will now try to make precise. I will take as an instance the assertion of the existence of a quality, *e.g.*, the assertion that there is such a thing as saintliness, taken not in the sense that there are saintly people but that it is possible that some people should be saintly. The only clear sense which I can attach to the assertion that this is a timeless truth is that the words in which it is expressed express a true proposition at whatever time, wherever and by whomsoever they are used, provided only that the words used retain their present sense. In this the sentence differs from many sentences of everyday speech which are now generally recognised to be capable of expressing propositions of different truth-value in different circumstances. The expression of a truth in all circumstances is a necessary but not a sufficient condition for the expression of a timeless truth by a sentence; for it is also shared by Quine's "eternal sentences,"[16] which do not express timeless truths but are simply artificial devices for expressing in the timeless present propositions that would normally be expressed by the use of tenses. It seems that Quine is mistaken in supposing that his eternal sentences

16. W. V. O. Quine, *Word and Object* (Cambridge: Technology Press of M.I.T., 1960), p. 193.

contain no device that takes the place of tense; for they contain dates, and a system of dates can be used only by referring directly or indirectly to an origin which is related to the time of utterance of the sentence in question.[17] By a timeless truth therefore I mean a true proposition which needs neither a system of tenses nor a system of dating for its expression. Does the existence of such sentences entail the existence of timeless objects? Shall we say that saintliness is such a timeless object? This seems to me to be a not very important question. Its answer depends on a choice as to how we use the word "object." The important question for me is whether, if we say that it is a timeless object, we must also say that it is a sempiternal object, and I hold that we must accept the second thesis because the only clear criterion for the existence of a timeless object is that any sentence which can be used to assert its existence must not require a device like tense or date but express a true proposition whenever, wherever and by whomever spoken. By this criterion saintliness is a timeless object, and so, contrary to what I suggested before, are numbers. Moreover, rather unexpectedly, there may be (I don't say there are) timeless physical objects. For suppose there were exactly *n* Epicurean atoms, then the sentence "There are exactly *n* atoms" would express a true proposition whenever, wherever and by whomever uttered. It may be thought that this conclusion constitutes a *reductio ad absurdum* of my criterion of timelessness, and perhaps there is a better and tighter criterion of timelessness which would avoid this conclusion, but at the moment it seems to me that the notion of timelessness is otiose and could well be allowed to collapse either into that of sempiternity or that of necessity.

I now turn to this latter notion. There is a difference between a timelessly true and a necessarily true proposition. The proposition that there are exactly *n* Epicurean atoms would, if true, be timelessly true, but obviously not necessarily true, whereas the proposition that there is such a property as saintliness is necessarily true, since it is analysable into a modal proposition, which like all true modal propositions is necessarily true. Similarly propositions which are simply about numbers or other mathematical objects are, if true, necessarily true. I say "simply" in order to exclude propositions which are ex-

17. This point is argued in detail in a paper, "Propositions and Time," by W. and M. Kneale forthcoming in a volume on the philosophy of G. E. Moore edited by A. Ambrose and S. Lazerowitz.

pressed by such sentences as "I am now thinking about the number two," which is neither necessary nor timeless.

In so far then as I have been able to find a precise definition of timelessness, it both entails and is entailed by sempiternity. What remains for us to consider, then, is the relation between necessity, the other constituent of the notion of eternity and sempiternity. The position I want to uphold is that necessity entails sempiternity but not *vice-versa*.

The first point is clear in relation both to necessary truths and to necessary objects. For example, it is a necessary truth that two and two are four. Now suppose it to be the case that at some time they are not four; since *ab esse ad posse valet consequentia,* it is possible that they should not be four. We have thus a contradiction, and it must be the case that two and two are always four. Similarly, if there is a necessary object, *e.g.,* God, then there is a true proposition expressible by the sentence "God necessarily exists." Now suppose God not to be sempiternal; obviously there will be a true proposition expressible, according to the time of utterance, by "God did not exist," "God does not exist," or "God will not exist." It follows that "Possibly God does not exist" expresses a true proposition, so that again we have a contradiction. Therefore if God is eternal, in the sense of "necessary," he is also sempiternal. This proof holds whatever object we substitute for God and therefore any necessary object is also sempiternal.

But is the sempiternal also necessary? There are passages in Aristotle which suggest that he held this view, but even those who attribute it to him do not hold that it is true.[18] It is indeed highly paradoxical, being equivalent, as can be shown by simple contraposition, to the proposition that whatever is possible sometimes exists. My conclusion about the notions we have been discussing is therefore as follows. Timelessness is either identical with sempiternity or they are mutually entailing. Necessity entails sempiternity but not *vice-versa*.

18. For a full discussion of these passages, see J. Hintikka, "Necessity, Universality, and Time in Aristotle," *Ajatus,* XX (1957), 65–90, and "An Aristotelian Dilemma," *Ajatus,* XXII (1959), 87–92, and C. J. F. Williams, "Aristotle and Corruptibility," *Religious Studies,* I (October 1965), 95–107 and (April 1966), 203–215. Either an identification of or a mutual entailment between necessity and sempiternity is also sometimes maintained by medieval philosophers. See, *e.g.,* Duns Scotus, *Opus Oxoniense,* Dist. II. Quæstio 1, article ii, in *Duns Scotus, Philosophical Writings,* ed. by Allan Wolter, O.F.M. (Edinburgh: T. Nelson, 1962), p. 55.

II

In western philosophical tradition we have found two strongly opposing views. According to the one (held by Plato, Augustine,
Boethius and St Thomas in his Platonic moods) eternity and sempiternity are incompatible, while according to the other (held by
Aristotle, Epicurus, and St Thomas in his more Aristotelian moods)
eternity, whether as timelessness or necessity is either identical with
sempiternity or related to it by mutual entailment. Now Spinoza was
subjected either directly or indirectly to the influence of both these
views,[19] and I wish to use the results of my first part to suggest a
new interpretation of his *Ethics,* Part V, propositions xxi and following, a section which commentators have found peculiarly baffling.
Their bafflement arises from the following facts. There are many
passages in which Spinoza connects eternity with necessity and suggests that only God and His attributes are fully eternal and necessary.
The connexion is made in the definition of eternity itself, *Per
aeternitatem intelligo ipsam existentiam quatenus ex sola rei aeternae
necessario sequi concipitur.*[20] ("By eternity I understand existence
itself in so far as it is conceived as following from the definition of
the eternal thing alone.") We are told in *E.,* I, xxiv that the essence
of things produced by God does not involve existence, in other words
that they are not necessary, and *E.,* II, Ax. 1 tells us that men are
among those things. *Hominis essentia non involvit necessariam existentiam, hoc est ex naturae ordine tam fieri potest, ut hic et ille
homo existat, quam ut non non existat* ("The essence of man does
not involve necessary existence, that is, in the order of nature it can
equally come about that this or that man should exist or not exist.")
Yet we have in *E.,* V, xxiii, S. *Sentimus experimurque nos aeternos
esse* ("We feel and know by experience that we are eternal.") It is
true that the demonstration to which this is a scholium attributes
eternity to the human *mind* alone, but on the face of it the human
mind is no less a created thing than the human body. This is one
contradiction: Man both is and is not necessary and eternal. But
there is also a second apparent contradiction. Much of the language
in which the eternity of the human mind is explained is appropriate to

19. For possible lines of transmission see H. A. Wolfson, *The Philosophy of
Spinoza* (Cambridge, Mass.: Harvard University Press, 1934), Ch. 10.
20. *E.,* I, Def. 8.

duration. Proposition xxiii, itself says *Mens humana non potest cum corpore absolute destrui; sed eius aliquid remanet quod aeternum est* ("The human mind cannot be absolutely destroyed with the body but something of it *remains* which is eternal.") The verb *remanere* certainly suggests duration, and again it is stated explicitly at the end of the Scholium to *E., V, xx*, which is the introduction to this section of the *Ethics* that "it is now time to move to those things which pertain to the *duration* of the mind without relation to the body."

The reaction of commentators to these contradictions has for the most part been to say that, when Spinoza in this section uses the language appropriate to duration, he does not mean what he says but is obliged to speak metaphorically. All he is saying is that at certain moments of our lives we are aware of necessary truths and so in a certain sense experience eternity. Thus Pollock:

> Spinoza's eternal life is not a continuance of existence but a manner of existence; something which can be realised here and now as much as at any other time and place; not a future reward of the soul's perfection, but the soul's perfection itself.[21]

and more recently Hampshire:

> The possible eternity of the human mind cannot therefore be intended by Spinoza to mean that I literally survive, as a distinguishable individual, in so far as I attain genuine knowledge, for in so far as I do attain genuine knowledge, my individuality as a particular thing disappears and my mind becomes so far united with God or Nature conceived under the attribute of thought.[22]

These writers have been influenced, I believe, not only by those passages in which Spinoza draws a sharp line between duration and eternity, but also by the thought that Spinoza could not be putting forward anything so vulgar as the doctrine of personal survival after death. But this seems to me precisely what Spinoza is putting forward. Hampshire's view that *qua* eternal the individual human mind is lost in the divine consciousness must be wrong; for the premiss to the argument for the eternity of the mind reads *In Deo tamen datur necessario idea, quae huius et illius corporis humani essentiam sub specie aeternitatis exprimit*[23] ("There exists necessarily however, in

21. Stuart Hampshire, *Spinoza,* p. 275.
22. *Ibid.,* p. 131.
23. *E., V, xxii.*

God an idea which expresses the essence of *this and that* human body under the form of eternity.") It is the eternity of the idea of *this and that* human body, *i.e.,* of *this and that* human mind which is precisely in question. Again Spinoza expressly connects the intellectual love of God which accompanies the eternity of the mind with the third kind of knowledge (*scientia intuitiva*) which is knowledge of individuals.[24]

But if we reject the Pollock-Hampshire interpretation of this section of the *Ethics,* what better have we to offer? I think that no interpretation can be given which is consistent with *everything* that Spinoza says because in the course of his philosophical life, perhaps even during the writing of the *Ethics,* which continued for a number of years, he changed his mind about the relation between eternity and duration. What I shall put forward as an interpretation of this section is what I think Spinoza would have put forward had he had the time fully to think out and the liberty fully to express what he is here trying to say.

First, a conjecture as to history. I think that Spinoza began with a Platonic view of eternity as timelessness sharply separated from duration. I have already quoted one passage to this effect from the *Ethics.*[25] There is an even more striking expression of the same view in the *Cogitata Metaphysica,*[26] an early work which is of doubtful authority for Spinoza's mature views. Here he explains what he means by *aeternitas* and uses precisely the kind of argument which is exploded by Searle in order to distinguish this notion sharply from that of duration. If, he says, we separate God's essence from his existence, we are tempted to ask whether God has existed for a longer time since he created Adam than he had before, which has the same kind of absurdity as saying that the essence of the triangle or the circle, considered as an eternal truth has existed longer now than it had at the time of Adam. This way of thinking persists into the *Ethics,* as we have shown, but by the time he came to write Part V, I think that Spinoza was thinking in a more Aristotelian way. He thought that eternity was essentially necessity, that he can prove the necessity of the human mind and from this the sempiternity of the human mind. I say deliberately "sempiternity" rather than "survival" because there are two curious passages which suggest the pre-

24. *E.,* V, xxiv and xxxiii.
25. *E.,* I, xxiii, S. 2.
26. *C.m.,* II, 1.

existence as well as the post-existence of the human mind. The first occurs in *E.,* V, xxiii, S. "Although we do not remember that we existed before the body, nevertheless we feel our mind to be eternal," which strongly suggests that its eternity entails the pre-existence as well as the post-existence of the human mind. The second is in the Scholium to Proposition xxxi, where he says that he proposes to consider the human mind *as if* it had just begun to exist and to understand things under the form of eternity. This, he suggests, is false, and what follows is not that the mind *sub specie aeternitatis* has no duration but that its duration is endless in both directions like that of Aristotle's *ouranos.* How could Spinoza have reached this strange conclusion? He began, I think, with a theological premiss, one so deeply ingrained by his religious and philosophical training, that it was impossible that he should call it in question, namely the omniscience of God. He identified God with the universe for reasons which have some plausibility but which are not germane to the present question. The universe, therefore is omniscient. Everything is known, including the human body and the reason why any particular human body is a part of the universe. This knowledge, in the case of each human body *is* the corresponding human mind, or at least that part of it which is eternal. There is in God the knowledge of the essence of each human body, which is different from the essence of every other human body and this knowledge is necessary, *i.e.,* eternal and therefore sempiternal. Only for the brief space of our physical lives is it combined with the confused perceptions and passive emotions which torment our bodily existence. Otherwise through endless time it endures in the enjoyment of that complete understanding which even in this life is our highest satisfaction. How, then, in eternity, or rather in sempiternity, we may ask, does one human mind differ from another? Spinoza gives no answer, but it is possible to give one. The system of truths about the universe is like that of axioms and theorems in a logical system. It may be arranged in many different ways. A given human mind, I suggest, is that system of knowledge which has the existence of God as its first premiss (this is common to all), the existence of other parts of the universe as intermediate premisses, and the existence of its own body as conclusion. Thus every human mind is in a way the same system of knowledge as every other human mind, but it is the system arranged in a different way. Hence our individuality, not merely in this life but sempiternally.

There are a number of ineradicable flaws in this system, but it is not, I think, an ignoble one. There are reasons why Spinoza, even if he had thought it out in full clarity, which I suspect he had not, would have shrunk from expressing it with full openness. For it entails two doctrines of extreme unorthodoxy, and *pace* Pollock,[27] Spinoza did wish to be read and to secure a hearing. It is obvious, for example, that he is being tactful towards Christianity in the *Tractatus Theologico-Politicus*. The two unorthodox doctrines entailed by the second part of *Ethics V* are the pre-existence of the human soul and the doctrine of universal salvation. Spinoza is committed, like Origen, to the view that even the devil (if there is one) must have *beatitudo* in the end, and not only at the end but also at the beginning and presumably throughout most of the temporal duration of the universe. Of these two unorthodox doctrines, the second was the more hateful to Spinoza's contemporaries. This is shown by the fact that the politic Leibniz, who dared to put forward a kind of pre-existence, felt bound, in spite of his general optimism, to maintain that the number of the damned is far greater than the number of the saved at least as regards the inhabitants of this planet.[28] There is no wonder that Spinoza, if he held the doctrine, should have presented it in a somewhat veiled manner.

Had his attempt succeeded, it would have been an enormous triumph. He would have shown that a pure naturalism can offer the certainty of salvation in place of the hope put forward by revealed religion, and yet give equal encouragement to virtue and piety; for, as he himself emphasises, he has shown in Part IV and the earlier propositions of Part V that, even in this life, virtue is our only blessedness.

27. Hampshire, *op. cit.*, p. 276.
28. Leibniz, *Theodicy*, 19.

Spinoza's Proof of Immortality

ALAN DONAGAN

Spinoza's uncompromising declaration that "the human mind cannot be absolutely destroyed with the body; but something of it remains, which is eternal" (*E.*, V, xxiii),[1] has turned out to be an embarrassment. It appears to hold out to everybody the hope of an infinitely prolonged life after death. Many of his admirers, finding themselves unable to ascribe to him what they dismiss as a "popular travesty of the philosophic conception of 'eternity,'"[2] have battered his text with the hermeneutical blunt instruments of post-Hegelian theology. Others, conceding that he meant what he wrote, have written it off as an aberration, in which "the mystic simply abandons the structural order of his metaphysics."[3] Both parties agree that his affirmation of personal immortality, taken at face value, is irreconcilable with the rest of his system. In this paper, I shall try to show that it is not.

Since Spinoza spoke not only of an "eternal" part of the mind as "remaining" after the death of the body, but also of "the duration of the mind without relation to the body" (*E.*, V, xx S), I begin by investigating his use of the words "eternity" (*"aeternitas"*) and duration (*"duratio"*), and of the related word "time" (*"tempus"*).

In an invaluable chapter, H. A. Wolfson informs us that "the term eternity started on its career in the history of philosophy with two meanings," a Platonic one and an Aristotelian one. To the Platonists, "eternity is the antithesis of time and it means the exclusion of any kind of temporal relations"; to the Aristotelians, "eternity is only endless time."[4] Against Wolfson, most commentators have

---

This essay was written especially for this volume.

1. Throughout this paper, unless otherwise indicated, references to Spinoza's writings are to Carl Gebhardt (ed.), *Spinoza Opera,* 4 vols. (Heidelberg: Carl Winter, 1925), and translations from them are my own.

2. H. H. Joachim, *A Study of the Ethics of Spinoza* (Oxford: Oxford University Press, 1901), p. 295.

3. L. S. Feuer, *Spinoza and the Rise of Liberalism* (Boston: Beacon Press, 1964), p. 224.

4. H. A. Wolfson, *The Philosophy of Spinoza* (Cambridge, Mass.: Harvard

agreed with H. H. Joachim that Spinoza conceived eternity Platonically, as "timeless necessity of being, [which] has nothing to do with lasting through an 'infinitely long' time."[5] And indeed there are passages which appear to verify this interpretation, such as the remark that "eternity can neither be defined by time, nor have any relation to time" (*E.,* V, xxiii S). However, attention to Spinoza's usage shows this appearance to be an illusion.

He had no term for "time" in what I take to be its fundamental ordinary sense: namely, that in which it stands for the passage of the future into the present, and of the present into the past.[6] (Hereafter, for brevity, I shall refer to time, in this sense, as "temporal passage.") In his system, time is subordinated to existence, whether of substance or of its modes. He would have dismissed speculation about the passage of time in empty space as metaphysically ridiculous. That is why his fundamental temporal concept was that of continuation of existing (*continuatio existendi*): "continuation" being understood as indifferent to temporal direction, so that in his usage, one can speak of cockroaches as continuing to exist *before* the genesis of man, as well as *after* his extinction. That is also why he did not perceive that continuation of existing is equivalent to the existence of something through a passage of time, and therefore presupposes the more primitive concept of temporal passage.

He himself used the Latin synonym for "time" (*"tempus"*) in a deliberately restricted sense. The one passage I know of in the *Ethics* that throws light on this sense is little more than an allusion:

> Besides, nobody doubts that the way in which we imagine time is this: we imagine some bodies to be moved, with respect to others, more slowly, or more quickly, or equally quickly (*E.,* II, xliv, cor. 1, S).

University Press, 1934), vol. I, p. 358. Cf. William Kneale, "Time and Eternity in Theology," *Proc. Aris. Soc.* 61 (1960–61), esp. 97–107.

5. Joachim, *Ethics of Spinoza,* p. 298. For references to commentators agreeing with Joachim, see Martha Kneale, *Proc. Aris. Soc.* 69 (1968–69), 234–235 [this volume, pp. 227–240], and E. E. Harris, *Monist* 55 (1971), 672–674.

6. Cf. J. M. E. McTaggart, *The Nature of Existence* (Cambridge, England: Cambridge University Press, 1927), vol. II, p. 10: "the distinction of past, present, and future is as *essential* to time as the distinction of earlier and later, while in a certain sense it may . . . be regarded as more *fundamental* than the distinction of earlier and later." Cf. also C. D. Broad, *Scientific Thought* (London: Routledge & Kegan Paul, 1923), pp. 57–58, and Peter Geach, "Some Problems about Time" in P. F. Strawson (ed.) *Studies in the Philosophy of Thought and Action* (Oxford: Oxford University Press, 1968), esp. pp. 176–179.

This echoes the following analysis in his *Cogitata Metaphysica,* which a letter of April 20, 1663, to Lewis Meyer, shows to have expressed his own view.[7]

> [I]n order that [a quantity of duration] be determined (*determinetur*), we compare it with the duration of other things which have a certain and determinate motion (*motus*), *and this comparison* is called *time* (*C.M.*, I, 4).

This analysis tells us what *a* time is: namely, an interval of duration measurable by a clock. It analyzes the sense of "time" in which it is said that *the* time Michelangelo took to paint the ceiling of the Sistine Chapel was four and a half years.

Unless the distinction between "time" in the sense of temporal passage, and "time" in Spinoza's restricted sense, in which times are measurable intervals of duration, is kept firmly in mind, what Spinoza wrote about time and eternity will be seriously misunderstood. For example, if "time" were to be taken in the former sense, his remark that "eternity cannot be defined by time" (*E.,* V, xxiii S) would contradict an Aristotelian definition of eternity as "endless time." However, if it be taken in his own sense, the latter one, it is perfectly consistent with such an Aristotelian definition; for endless time is not definable by any measurable interval of duration.

Since, for reasons we have touched on, Spinoza conceived duration as enduring existence and eternity as eternal existence, his definitions of duration and eternity are only indirectly related to time in the sense of temporal passage.

> Duration [he wrote] is indefinite continuation of existing (*existendi continuatio*). *Explicatio.* I say "indefinite," because [such continuation] can by no means be limited (*determinari*) by the nature itself of the existing thing, or even by its efficient cause, which indeed necessarily posits (*ponit*) the existence of the thing, but does not take it away (*tollit*) (*E.,* II, Def. 5).

Here enduring existents are differentiated from nonenduring ones as being existents whose continuation can possibly have a limit.

7. "Furthermore, time arises because we can determine duration . . . as we please, namely, when . . . we separate it from the mode by which it flows from eternal things; time [arises] . . . in order that . . . duration may be determined in such a manner that, as far as it can be, we may imagine it easily" (*Ep.,* xii; *Spinoza Opera* IV, pp. 56–57).

What existents are excluded by this differentia? In view of Spinoza's definition of eternity, it is natural to answer that they are eternal existents.

> By "eternity" [he wrote] I mean existence (*existentiam*) itself, inasmuch as it is conceived to follow solely from the definition of an eternal thing. *Explicatio.* For such existence, like the essence of a thing, is conceived as an eternal truth; and therefore cannot be explained through duration or time, although a duration may be conceived to lack a beginning and an end (*E.,* I, Def. 8).

Taken in conjunction with his definition of duration, as its *explicatio* invites us to take it, this definition contrasts eternity with duration, as existence which, being necessary, cannot have a temporal limit—whether a beginning or an end—with existence which, being contingent, can have such a limit. In effect, it treats eternity as necessary continuation of existing. However, in referring to eternity, Spinoza shunned the word *"continuatio,"* presumably because it presupposes a point of reference from which existence "continues" before or after; for he held that no moment in eternity is privileged. It is therefore closer to his usage to say that eternity, as he conceived it, is equivalent to necessarily omnitemporal existence, understanding "omnitemporal" as meaning "at all moments in the passage of time."

In the letter to Lewis Meyer already mentioned, Spinoza amplified this:

> I call the states (*affectiones*) of substance "modes" [he wrote]; and their definition, inasmuch as it is not the definition itself of substance, can involve no existence. From this it follows that, although they exist, we can conceive them as not existing. From this, in turn, it follows that we, when we attend solely to the essence of modes, and not to the order of the whole of nature (*totius naturae*), cannot conclude from the fact that they now exist (*existant*), either that they will exist (*extituros*) hereafter or that they will not, or that they have existed (*extitisse*) herebefore or that they have not. From this it plainly appears that we conceive the existence of substance as *toto genere* different from the existence of modes. And from this arises the difference between *eternity* and *duration.* For through duration we can explain only the existence of modes; [we can explain the existence] of substance, however, through eternity, that is, [through] infinite enjoyment of existing (*fruitionem . . . existendi*), or, in strained Latin, *essendi* (*Ep.,* xii; *Spinoza Opera,* IV, 54–55).

Here what distinguishes eternity, the existence of substance, from duration, the existence of finite modes, is not timelessness as opposed to temporality, but necessity of existence as opposed to its merely contingent continuation.

It may be objected that, by explaining eternal existence as "conceived as an eternal truth," Spinoza, wittingly or unwittingly, committed himself to a Platonic conception of eternity as timelessness. Thus E. M. Curley has argued that

> . . . whatever follows logically from something which is logically necessary must itself be logically necessary. If Spinoza regards the existence and causality of God as being strictly logically necessary, then he has to say that the infinite modes are eternal [in the sense of timeless], whether he wants to or not.[8]

But why has Spinoza to say that? Must logically necessary truths be timelessly true? Martha Kneale has forcibly argued that not even truths about timeless objects are timeless. In her opinion, which I share, the proposition that $2+2 = 4$ was true yesterday and will be true tomorrow.[9] Moreover, even conceding that logically necessary truths are timeless, it would not follow, because a truth is timeless, that it must be about timeless objects. If we provisionally accept Spinoza's view that it is a logically necessary truth that an infinite substance exists, we have not the slightest reason to doubt that it may not also be a logically necessary truth that an infinite substance exists at all times.

Nor can there be much doubt that some of Spinoza's descriptions of substance and its modes presuppose that they exist in time. Not only did he remark that "an infinite thing must always (*semper*) necessarily exist" (*E.*, II, xi Dem.), but, in his first theorem about the infinite modes, he laid it down that "all that follows from the absolute nature of any attribute of God must always (*semper*) exist and [be] infinite, or (*sive*) is through that same attribute eternal and infinite" (*E.*, I, xxi). Curley himself acknowledges the justice of Wolfson's observation that the word "always" ("*semper*") implies temporality: "omnitemporality to be sure, but temporality none the

8. E. M. Curley, *Spinoza's Metaphysics: An Essay in Interpretation* (Cambridge, Mass.: Harvard University Press, 1969), p. 107.

9. Martha Kneale, *op. cit.*

less."[10] And only by resorting to such speculative interpretations as Hallett's of motion and rest as not spatio-temporal, or Curley's of modes as not individual things, but certain sorts of fact,[11] can we resist the conclusion that, since Spinoza held the immediate infinite and eternal mode of extension to be motion and rest, he must have conceived at least one eternal mode as being in time. The concept of timeless existence may be intelligible; that of timeless motion is not.

This conclusion is confirmed by a careful scrutiny of the textual evidence offered against it. Of the passages in the *Ethics* which at first glance appear to presuppose a Platonic conception of eternity, I know of none which, read in context, is not consistent with the conception of it as necessarily omnitemporal existence. Spinoza's well-known remark that

in eternity there is no *when, before,* or *after* (*E.,* I, xxxiii S 2),

is a good example. It occurs in the following passage:

Furthermore, all God's ordinances (*decreta*) have been ratified from eternity (*ab aeterno*) by God himself. For that it should be otherwise would argue imperfection and inconstancy. But since in eternity (*in aeterno*) there is no *when, before,* or *after,* it follows solely from God's perfection that God can never ordain anything else (*aliud*), nor ever could have; and that God did not exist before his ordinances, nor can exist without them (*E.,* I, xxxiii S 2).

Here Spinoza shows that God cannot ordain at one time what he does not ordain at another, by pointing out that what is true of an eternal thing is true at all times: such questions as "When was this true of it?" "Was this true of it before that?" and "Will this be true of it after that?" are all inapplicable to an eternal thing. What is being repudiated is inconstancy; and to deny that something is inconstant suggests, not that it is timeless, but that it is at all times the same: without weariness or shadow of turning. However, there is a complication.

As Wolfson observed, if there is an eternal part of the mind, it follows from Spinoza's conception of eternity as necessarily omnitemporal existence, not only that that part of the mind must exist

10. Curley, *Spinoza's Metaphysics,* 107; cf. Wolfson, *Philosophy of Spinoza,* vol. I, pp. 376–377.

11. H. F. Hallett, *Aeternitas: a Spinozistic Study* (Oxford: Oxford University Press, 1930), pp. 84–85; Curley, *Spinoza's Metaphysics,* p. 75.

after death, but also that it must have existed before birth.[12] Although Spinoza did not expressly avow such pre-existence, he argued against prenatal reminiscence in a way that presupposed it.

[I]t cannot happen [he wrote] that we recollect that we have existed (*extitisse*) before the body, because no traces of it are to be found in the body, and eternity can neither be defined by time nor have any relation to time (*E.,* V, xxiii S).[13]

But is not this an argument that prenatal reminiscence is impossible because it implies time, and "eternity can . . . [not] have any relation to time"? No. But to explain why, I must touch on the complication mentioned above. Although God is the fundamental eternal thing, not everything that is true of God is so by the necessity of his nature, or, as Spinoza put it, *sub quadam aeternitatis specie* (*E.,* II, xliv, Cor. 2). Some things are true of God "inasmuch as he is modified by a modification that is finite, and has limited (*determinatam*) existence" (*E.,* I, xxviii Dem.): as, for example, that God is the immanent cause of (and hence is related to) this finite mode and that, whose durational existence is "a certain form of quantity" ("*quaedam quantitatis species*") "(*E.,* II, xlv S)." This puts it beyond doubt that Spinoza held that God, the infinite and eternal substance, has relations to time, inasmuch as he is modified by certain finite modifications. He must therefore have intended his remark that eternity cannot have any relation to time to be understood as qualified. His text indeed suggests such a qualification, and only one: namely, "*sub specie aeternitatis.*" Accordingly, I submit that his remark should be understood as meaning that eternity, *qua* eternity (or an eternal thing, *sub specie aeternitatis*), cannot have any relation to time.

If this is correct, then Spinoza's argument in *E.,* V, xxiii S comes to this: the eternal part of a man cannot, *sub specie aeternitatis,* leave traces in his body; for leaving such traces would be an event in time. But it does not follow that the eternal part of a man may not be related to time by forming part of a human mind actually existing for a time. All that follows is that, if something eternal forms part of something existing for a time, then it does not do so *sub specie aeternitatis,* that is, by the necessity of its eternal nature. This conclusion, as we shall see, Spinoza unreservedly accepted. That a given eternal idea

12. Wolfson, *Philosophy of Spinoza,* vol. II, pp. 296–297.
13. Cf. Wolfson, *Philosophy of Spinoza,* vol. II, pp. 296–297; and Martha Kneale, *op. cit.,* p. 236 [this volume, 239].

forms part of a human mind actually existing for a time depends, in his view, not on the necessity of its nature, but on what finite durational modes God is modified by.

It is now time to investigate what Spinoza took the eternal part of the mind to be.

Natura naturata, as Spinoza described it, is a system of infinite and finite modes, which is truly conceived in each attribute that expresses an eternal and infinite essence (*E.,* I, xxix S). Of these attributes we know two, extension and thought; and, according to the theorem "the order and connection of ideas is the same as the order and connection of things" (*E.,* II, vii), every mode that is conceivable in the attribute of extension is also conceivable in the attribute of thought. However, while acknowledging that all the finite modes of nature are in diverse degrees animated (*animata*), in the sense that each is conceivable in the attribute of thought, Spinoza did not jump to the conclusion that for every material object (*corpus*) there is a corresponding mind (*mens*). He recognized no mode in the attribute of thought as being a mind, unless, under the attribute of extension, it is a body so apt (*aptus*) to do and undergo many things that its action is to a very great degree independent of the action of other bodies; and he recognized no bodies as satisfying this condition except living human bodies (*E.,* II, xiii S; cf. IV, xxxvii S1).

A body's aptness to do or undergo something depends on what Spinoza called its (actual) power of acting (*potentia agendi*) (cf. *E.,* II, vii C.; III, xi). As he used the word, *"potentia"* fundamentally means power displayed in doing something. In God there is no *potentia* that is not exercised. Hence God's power and his action are not really distinct: whatever he has power to do, he does. Apparently it is otherwise with finite things, but only apparently. As we usually think of it, the same power in a finite thing may be displayed in a variety of incompatible ways: thus, an athlete who has the power to run the first hundred yards of a mile race in eleven seconds, may also have the power to run the whole race in four and a quarter minutes, but not the power to do both in the same race. Here Spinoza would say that an athlete's body is "apt" for doing both. Again, a man's body may be apt for doing many things while actually doing none of them: it does not lose its aptness for doing them when he falls asleep. Nevertheless, it does not follow, in Spinoza's view, that the power of acting of a finite thing is not necessarily exercised.

Finite things differ from infinite ones in that their power of acting is limited by other finite things. To say of an athlete who ran the first hundred yards of a mile race in fifteen seconds that he had the power to do it in eleven is loose: if he did not do it, it was because the relevant finite modes conditioning his existence conditioned him to do something else, for example, to run the race in four and a quarter minutes, and so deprived him of the power to do what otherwise he might have done. Strictly speaking, everything at every moment exercises its full power of acting.

Taken strictly in this way, the whole of a thing's power of acting is identical with what Spinoza called the *"conatus"* whereby it strives to persevere in existence, and which he held to be its actual essence (*essentia actualis*) or essence-as-existing (*E.,* III, vii).[14] However, in an earlier discussion of essence in his proof that an infinite substance exists, he departed from this strict usage, according to which a power is necessarily exercised, and spoke of a finite thing's essence as a power of existing (*potentia existendi*) which would bring about its existence unless other things, incompatible with it, had a greater power of existing (*E.,* I, xi Dem. and S).

This deviation in usage is enlightening. Spinoza had laid it down that, if an essence were such that its existence would not in itself involve a contradiction, then what would call for explanation would be not so much its existence (if it existed), as its nonexistence (if it did not). Let us call such essences "intrinsically possible." His idea evidently was that an infinite substance would bring about the existence, as a finite mode, of every intrinsically possible finite essence, unless its other finite modes made it impossible to do so. Here Spinoza anticipated Leibniz: his infinite substance necessarily brings into existence the most perfect intrinsically possible system of modes (*E.,* I, xxxiii S 2). *Natura naturata* is therefore what Leibniz would have called the best of all possible worlds. And, although strictly speaking only the essences of modes in the most perfect possible modal system have power of existing, every intrinsically possible essence has it loosely speaking: that is, every intrinsically possible essence has conditional power of existing—it would exist if some

14. For Spinoza's use of *"essentia,"* both with and without such qualifying epithets as *"actualis"* and *"formalis,"* see Wolfson, *Philosophy of Spinoza,* vol. II, pp. 292–293. Wolfson correctly treats "essence," unqualified and variously qualified, as standing for one or another kind of existence. It is equally correct to treat those kinds of existence as kinds of essence.

finite existent did not prevent it. Essences possessed of power of existing only in this loose or conditional sense are not actual.

In this theory of finite essences, two points are cardinal to Spinoza's conception of the eternal part of the human mind.

The first is that essences are individual. Nothing but confusion can result from interpreting Spinoza according to the Aristotelian-Scholastic notion that, for example, Socrates and Plato are individuated by their matter, and share a common essence, *humanity*.[15] He held that, as existing individuals, Socrates and Plato are distinct actual essences or *conatus*. A living individual man is identical with his actual essence. Furthermore, since the only difference between an actual essence and the essence of a nonexistent individual is that the latter is merely a conditional power of existing, of which the condition is unfulfilled, the essence of a nonexistent individual is also individual.

The second point is most conveniently made in terms of Spinoza's implicit distinction between actual and formal essences. Since the very same essence (for example, that of Socrates' body) may be actual at one time (say, 424 B.C.) but not another (now), it is useful to have an epithet to indicate when an essence is being spoken of with no implication that it is actual. Spinoza used *"formalis"* ("formal") for this purpose. Hence, in speaking of essences of individuals merely as they are contained in the divine attributes, without any implication as to whether the divine finite modes are or are not permitting them to be actual, he called them "formal essences" (*"essentiae formales"*) (*E.*, II, viii). The idea of an actual essence is therefore composite, and may be analyzed into the idea of a formal essence, and the idea of other existents being such as not to prevent its existence. Spinoza presupposed an analysis of this kind when he declared that "something of the human mind" is eternal, namely, the idea of the essence of the human body, and went on to discuss the conditions under which the eternal "part" of the human mind is its greater part (*E.*, V, xxiii, xxxix). These passages are unintelligible

15. Aquinas distinguished *essentia ut totum* (as not cutting out designation of matter, but as containing it implicitly and indistinctly) from *essentia ut pars* (as cutting out designation of matter), and considered the essence of Socrates and Plato to be humanity only in the sense of *essentia ut pars*. See St. Thomas Aquinas, *Opuscula Philosophica* (*De Ente et Essentia*, II, 15), ed. R. M. Spiazzi (Turin and Rome, 1954), p. 9. Spinoza rejected both this distinction, and the distinction of form and matter from which it derives.

unless the idea of the essence of a human body is part of the idea of that human body actually existing: that is, unless the idea of its formal essence is part of the idea of its actual essence.

The answer to the question what Spinoza took the eternal part of a mind to be has now been anticipated. It is: the idea of the (formal) essence of its body. To understand it, however, we must go into his conception of an individual human mind.

Every finite mode which, as extended, is a living human body, is also, as thinking, a human mind. And, believing that, of the various modes in the attribute of thought (*modi cogitandi*), that which he called "idea" or "concept" is fundamental (*E.*, II, Def. 3, Ax. 3), Spinoza concluded that the primary constituent (*primum quod . . . constituit*) of an existing human mind must be a complex idea, having an existing human body for its object (*E.*, II, xi). Since every human body interacts with other bodies, a complex idea having an existing human body for its object will contain derivative ideas of those other bodies, the adequacy of which will be proportional to that body's power of acting (*E.*, II, xv–xvii). And, since to every idea there corresponds an idea of that idea, *ad infinitum,* every human mind will contain ideas of itself and of other minds (*E.*, II, xxi S).

Spinoza's general theory of the individuation of human minds is not hard to make out, although he wrote little about it. Since human minds are ideas, and not substances, theories of the individuation of substances do not apply; and since modes in one attribute are not intelligible in terms of any other attribute, human minds cannot be individuated by directly referring to human bodies. However, while ideas cannot be individuated by relations to bodies as such, it does not follow that they may not be individuated by bodies considered as their objects or *ideata*. And that was Spinoza's view. He held that human minds are complex ideas individuated by their primary constituents: ideas of existing human bodies.

Consider the most difficult case, that of two minds each of which contains ideas of exactly the same objects as the other. Let A be a mind having for its primary constituent the idea of the existing human body O_a, and B a mind having for its primary constituent the idea of the existing human body O_b. And let both A and B contain ideas of the objects O_a, O_b, O_1, O_2, . . . O_n, and no others. Of these ideas, some will be adequate, since every human mind has an adequate idea of the essence of God (*E.*, II, xlvii); and some not, since every human mind largely perceives its own body and external bodies "after the common order of nature," and, inasmuch as it does so, has inadequate ideas of them (*E.,* II, xxix S). Let us also suppose that *A* and *B* contain the same adequate ideas. They will nevertheless be distinct individuals, because, although they contain both the same adequate ideas, and inadequate ideas of the same objects, *A*'s inadequate ideas of objects all derive from an inadequate idea of O_a, together with certain adequate ideas, while *B*'s inadequate ideas of these same objects all derive from an inadequate idea of O_b, together with the same adequate ideas. Thus, if *A* and *B* both contain the following ideas and no others:

Adequate ideas of O_k . . . O_n, and inadequate ideas of O_a, O_b, O_1, O_2 . . . O_j,

then the structure of ideas constituting *A* will be:

Idea of O_a and ideas of O_k . . . O_n, from which are derived ideas of O_b, O_1, O_2, . . . O_j;

whereas the structure of ideas constituting *B* will be:

Idea of O_b and ideas of O_k . . . O_n, from which are derived ideas of O_a, O_1, O_2, . . . O_j.

Hence every mind is individuated by containing a nonderivative inadequate idea of its own body.[16]

Spinoza's proof that something of the mind remains, which is eternal, confirms Wolfson's emphatic statement that he conceived immortality as "personal and individual."[17] For in it, he set out to show, not that ideas which are common to different minds remain after death, but that a part of the individuating primary constituent of each mind does so, a part which retains its individuality.

His line of reasoning was as follows. The primary constituent of each human mind is the idea of a certain human body actually existing, which deeper analysis has shown to be the same as the idea of a *conatus* constituting a certain actual essence. Every idea of such an

16. Martha Kneale has given a different account of how, in eternity, one human mind differs from another (*Proc. Aris. Soc.* 69 (1968–69), 237 [this volume, p. 239]). One difficulty with her account is that it does not provide for the survival of the human mind as an inadequate idea of the essence of its body (see below, p. 257).

17. Wolfson, *Philosophy of Spinoza,* vol. II, p. 295.

actual essence is composite, and consists, first, of the idea of a formal essence, and secondly, of the idea of other existents' being such as to exclude everything incompatible with the existence of that formal essence. Every such composite idea is also inadequate—"mutilated and confused" as Spinoza used to say (cf. *E.*, II, xxxv),—because each man's ideas, both of his own body, and of other existents' being such as to permit it to exist, are mediated through his inadequate ideas of his body's modifications (*E.*, II, xix). The form which a man's inadequate idea of his body's actual essence takes is his awareness of his body's present existence, an awareness which involves both a sense of his body, and of its external circumstances. Plainly, a man's complex idea of his body's actual essence—his awareness of its present existence—endures only as long as his body itself endures. As a complex whole, it cannot remain after his body is destroyed. Nor can the second of its two parts remain: a man's idea of other existents' being such as to permit his body to exist is mediated through ideas of the modifications of his body as now existing. But it is otherwise with the first of its parts. For a man's idea of the formal essence of his body, while mediated through ideas of its modifications, is not mediated through ideas of them as now existing. Spinoza maintained that this part of every mind is eternal.

There is, however, an obvious objection. A fundamental theorem in Spinoza's system is that "the order and connection of ideas is the same as the order and connection of things" (*E.*, II, vii). Does it not rule out the possibility that an eternally existing idea of the essence of a body should correspond to a body which, having been destroyed, does not exist at all?

The answer is found in Spinoza's general theorem about God's knowledge of nonexistent individuals, of which his proof of immortality is a fairly straightforward application. That theorem is as follows:

Ideas of nonexistent individual things (*rerum singularium*) must be comprehended in the infinite idea of God (*Dei infinita idea*), just as formal essences of individual things or modes are contained in the divine attributes (*E.*, II, viii).

Unfortunately, Spinoza's "proof" throws almost no light either on what he meant by this, or on why he said it. He was content to remark that it is "obvious" (*"patet"*) from the preceding theorem, and would be understood more clearly from the preceding scholium. But the preceding theorem, that "the order and connection of ideas is the same as the order and connection of things," is the very one that gave rise to difficulty in a specific case, and its scholium contains nothing expressly about nonexistent individuals or their formal essences.

To understand what Spinoza had in mind, we must go back to what he wrote about nonexistent things in his proof that an infinite being exists. There, it will be remembered, he maintained that, if an essence is intrinsically possible, then its nonexistence must be explained by the existence of other things incompatible with it (*E.*, I, xi Dem.). Consider the essence of a nonexistent individual, say of a volcano like Vesuvius in all respects, except that its long quiescence in the pre-Christian era was disturbed, not by the eruption of A.D. 79 described in a letter of the younger Pliny, but by a nonexistent earlier eruption in 45 B.C., described in a nonexistent letter of Cicero. Spinoza held that this intrinsically possible counterpart Vesuvius does not exist only because its existence is incompatible with that of the actual Vesuvius. Yet this counterpart Vesuvius, and innumerable other counterparts, are "contained in" the divine attribute of extension as formal essences: that is, they are intrinsically possible finite modes of extension. However, and this is crucial, they are contained only in the attribute. They are neither among its finite modes, nor part of either of its infinite modes—*motus et quies* or *facies totius universi;* for both finite and infinite modes are actual existents, and our counterpart Vesuviuses are mere possibilities.

Yet, astonishingly, as Spinoza saw, if this is true then the very theorem that the order and connection of ideas is the same as the order and connection of things, entails that what, in the attribute of thought, corresponds to a mere possibility in the attribute of extension, must be more than a mere possibility. It is true that, just as our counterpart Vesuvius is not among the finite modes of extension, so it is not among the finite modes of thought. However, it is no less true that just as any finite mode of extension excludes the existence of incompatible finite modes, so the idea of such a mode implies the idea of the nonexistence of modes incompatible with it. Hence the true idea of a Vesuvius quiescent in the circumstances of 45 B.C. implies the idea of the nonexistence of a Vesuvius erupting in those circumstances. Both *ideas* are actual, although the *ideatum* of one of them is the nonexistence of something. And since the actual idea of the nonexistence of a Vesuvius erupting in 45 B.C. includes as a part the idea of the formal essence of such a Vesuvius, the idea of that formal essence must also be actual. Such actual ideas of the formal essences of nonexistent individuals, since they cannot be finite modes of thought, must form part of an infinite mode of it, a mode which Spinoza referred to as *"Dei infinita idea."* This infinite mode of thought must contain, *inter alia,* an actual idea of the formal essence of every individual body, existent or nonexistent.[18] In Leibnizian language, it must contain an idea of every intrinsically possible physical world. But, while all those possible physical worlds, except one, are merely possible, the ideas of each and every one of them must be actual.

Once it has been grasped that the identity of the order of ideas and the order of things not only does not forbid that there should be actual ideas of the formal essences of nonexistent things, but on the contrary demands it, Spinoza's proof of immortality is simple (*E.,* V, xxiii Dem.). When a living human body is destroyed, the corresponding mind, as nonderivative idea of that body actually existing, perishes with it; for they are the same finite mode in two distinct attributes. However, that mind, as actual essence, had as a part the idea of the formal essence of that body. And the idea of that formal essence belongs to God *sub specie aeternitatis:* it is part of the infinite idea of God, which is an eternal mode of God in the attribute of thought. Therefore the part of a man's mind which consists in the idea of the formal essence of his body must be eternal: it must have pre-existed his body, and cannot be destroyed with it. Q.E.D.

Conceivably, somebody might object that Spinoza's proof fails because of an equivocation. The expression "idea of the formal essence of a human body" may stand both for an adequate idea in the mind of God, or for what we have seen to be a necessarily inadequate one in the human mind which has an idea of that body as its primary constituent. How can the eternal existence of an adequate idea of something be imagined to guarantee the survival of an inadequate idea of that thing?

Spinoza's reply to this objection has two stages. First, so far as it is

18. Wolfson persuasively identifies this infinite mode of thought with the immediate infinite mode referred to by Spinoza as *"intellectus absolute infinitus"* (*Philosophy of Spinoza,* vol. I, pp. 238–241). Others have supposed it to be a mediate infinite mode, corresponding to *facies totius universi* (cf. Joachim, *Ethics of Spinoza,* pp. 94–96, and H. F. Hallett, *Benedict de Spinoza,* London: Athlone Press, 1957, pp. 31–32).

positive, an inadequate idea of something does not differ from an adequate one. "Nothing in ideas, on account of which they are said to be false, is positive" (*E.,* II, xxxiii). Every man's idea of his own essence must be to some extent positive, and to that extent it is part of the adequate idea in the divine intellect, and not different from it. Secondly, there are two senses in which an idea of the formal essence of a given human body is in God: (1) inasmuch as God is infinite, and has ideas of all intrinsically possible things; and (2) inasmuch as God constitutes the essence of the human mind which has an idea of that body as its primary constituent (*E.,* II, xi Cor.; cf. xxiv–xxx). It is only in the first sense that God's idea of the formal essence of a given human body is adequate. Spinoza was quite willing to say that, inasmuch as God constitutes the essence of the human mind of which the idea of that body is the primary constituent, his knowledge is inadequate (e.g. *E.,* II, xxx Dem.). In the latter sense, a man's idea of the formal essence of his own body will survive in the infinite idea of God exactly as he has it.

Confronted with a philosophical proof of something they hope to be true, most plain men become impatient, less because they impugn its soundness, than because they suspect that in it the character of their hope has been subtly transformed. The God of the philosophers, they complain, is not the God of Abraham; and the immortality of the philosophers is not the life of the world to come, in the heavenly city. Spinoza could not have denied that the character of the immortality he offered to demonstrate differs from that promised by the saints and prophets. Like other philosophers, he professed to have understood what the inspired have only seen in visions. Yet I think he would have claimed that immortality as he understood it preserves much of the substance of what plain men have hoped for.

The superficial differences, however, are great. As ordinarily imagined, not only will life after death be different in kind from life on earth, and in some cases at least, far better; but it will also be a continuation of life on earth, in which we shall retain memories of our earlier state. Spinoza, as is well known, denied that there would be memory in the life after death (*E.,* V, xxi), and this has tempted some commentators to conclude that he thought of life after death as Aristotle did in *de Anima:* as a life of pure thought, in which all awareness of self-identity has disappeared.

Our analysis has disclosed something quite different. We must remember that Spinoza did not think that our sense of self-identity, even in this life, depends on memory. A man knows his own identity to the extent that the primary constituent of his mind, his idea of his own body, is adequate. And, however inadequate it is, that idea is individual.

We can go further. A man's idea of the essence of his body changes during his life, and in that change there is loss as well as gain. However, God's idea of that essence, inasmuch as God constitutes the essence of that man's mind, is eternal and cannot change; hence it cannot be the idea which that man has of it at any given moment during his life. Can it be anything but the ordered totality of those ideas? If it cannot, it is reasonable to infer that Spinoza conceived the eternal self-knowledge of each man as being complete in a way in which his durational self-knowledge cannot be; for it is an idea of his body's essence through his whole life. Yet that idea not only need not be a memory-image, it cannot be, because it cannot correspond to physical traces in the brain.

Eternal self-knowledge, while more complete than any durational self-knowledge, can contain no element that is not present in durational self-knowledge. Nobody can accomplish anything after death; and nobody will know anything after death that he did not know at some time during his life. That is why Spinoza thought it all-important to attain wisdom in this life. No wisdom, and no virtue that a man attains in this life will be taken away from him; but neither will anything that he does not attain be added to him.

For this reason, I think Martha Kneale was mistaken in attributing to him the hideous hypothesis of universal salvation.[19] It is true that he dismissed all doctrines of retributive punishment in the afterlife (cf. *E.*, V, xli S). Just as the good will not be externally rewarded, so the wicked will not be externally punished. However, Spinoza did not think it to follow that we shall all be saved. First, he drew attention to the fact that "he who changes from an infant or a young boy to a corpse, is said to be unfortunate (*infelix*)," because "his mind, considered in itself alone, knows almost nothing of itself, of God, or of things" (*E.*, V, xxxix S). Yet the mind of a young child, even though undeveloped, may be at peace with itself. Secondly, he argued that *beatitudo* is not the reward of virtue, but virtue itself (*E.*, V, xlii). By parity of reasoning, vice, the contrary of virtue, is also the contrary of *beatitudo*. The destiny of the wicked is the same as that of

19. Martha Kneale, *op. cit.*, 237 (this volume, p. 239).

the good: perpetual inadequate self-awareness. But what is *beatitudo* for the good, because it involves understanding and love of God, and acquiescence in the course of nature, will be confusion and frustration for the wicked.

Spinoza and the
Theory of Organism

HANS JONAS

I

Cartesian dualism landed speculation on the nature of life in an impasse: intelligible as, on principles of mechanics, the correlation of structure and function became within the *res extensa,* that of structure-plus-function with feeling or experience (modes of the *res cogitans*) was lost in the bifurcation, and thereby the fact of life itself became unintelligible at the same time that the explanation of its bodily performance seemed to be assured. The impasse became manifest in Occasionalism: its tour de force of an extraneous, divine "synchronization" of the outer and the inner world (the latter denied to animals) not only suffered from its extreme artificiality, the common failing of such *ad hoc* constructions, but even at so high a cost failed to accomplish its theoretical purpose by its own terms. For the animal machine, like any machine, raises beyond the question of the "how" that of the "what for" of its functioning—of the purpose for which it had thus been constructed by its maker.[1] Its performance, however devoid of immanent teleology, must serve an end, and that end must be someone's end. This end may (directly) be itself, as indeed Descartes had implied when declaring self-preservation to be the effect of the functioning of the organic automaton. In that case the existence as such of the machine would be its end—either terminally, or in turn to benefit something else. In the former case, the machine would have to be more than a machine, for a mere machine cannot enjoy its existence. But since, by the rigorous conception of the *res extensa,* it cannot be more than a

---

Journal of the History of Philosophy 3 (1965), pp. 43–58. Copyright by the Regents of the University of California. Reprinted from the *Journal of the History of Philosophy,* vol. III, no. 1, pp. 43–58, by permission of the Regents.

1. The concept of "machine," adopted for its strict confinement to efficient cause, is still a finalistic concept, even though the final cause is no longer internal to the entity, as a mode of its own operation, but external to it as antecedent design.

machine, its function and/or existence must serve something other than itself. Automata in Descartes' time were mainly for entertainment (rather than work). But the *raison d'être* of the living kingdom could not well be seen in God's indulging his mechanical abilities or in the amusement of celestial spectators—especially since mere complexity of arrangement does not create new quality and thus add something to the unrelieved sameness of the simple substratum that might enrich the spectrum of being. For quality, beyond the primitive determinations of the extended per se, is the subjective creature of sensation, the confused representation of quantity in a mind; and thus organisms cannot harbor it because as mere machines they lack mentality, and pure spirits cannot because they lack sensuality, or the privilege of confusion and thereby of illusion with its possible enjoyment. And as to their intellectual enjoyment, even that, deprived of the thrill of discovery by the same token, would pale in the contemplation of what to sufficiently large intellects is nothing but the ever-repeated exemplification of the same few, elementary (and ultimately trivial) truths.

There remained, then, the time-honored—Stoic as well as Christian —idea that plants and animals are for the benefit of Man. Indeed, since the existence of a living world is the necessary condition for the existence of any of its members, the self-justifying nature of at least one such member (= species) would justify the existence of the whole. In Stoicism, Man provided this end by his possession of reason, which makes him the culmination of a terrestrial scale of being that is also self-justifying throughout all its grades (the end as the best of many that are good in degrees); in Christianity, by his possession of an immortal soul, which makes him the sole *imago Dei* in creation (the end as the sole issue at stake); and Cartesian dualism radicalized this latter position by making man even the sole possessor of inwardness or "soul" of *any* kind, thus the only one of whom "end" can meaningfully be predicated as he alone can entertain ends. All other life then, the product of physical necessity, can be considered his means.

However, this traditional idea, in its anthropocentric vanity never a good one even where it made sense, no longer made sense in the new dualistic and occasionalist setting. For man, the supposed beneficiary of living creation, i.e., of all the other organic mechanisms, was now himself an inexplicable, extraneous combination of mind and body—a combination with no intelligible relevance of the body for the existence and inner life of the mind (as also, of course, vice versa). Therefore, even if it was shown that the existence of the organic world was necessary for the existence of human bodies, as indeed it is, it could not be shown that the existence of this very body was necessary for the existence of "man" considered as the thinking ego. Furthermore, the very distinction of man's body within the animal kingdom, viz., to be at least partially an organ of mind—that distinction for the sake of which Descartes had been willing to brave the contortions of the pineal gland doctrine—was also nullified by the occasionalist fiction, in which the human body became no less completely an automaton than all other organisms. Thus, the existence of the entire living kingdom became utterly unintelligible as to purpose and meaning as well as to origin and procreative cause. A vast scheme of delusory "as ifs" superseded all question of real issue in the working of things.

All this amounts to saying that the main fault, even absurdity, of the doctrine lay in denying organic reality its principal and most obvious characteristic, namely, that it exhibits in each individual instance a striving of its own for existence and fulfillment, or the fact of life's willing itself. In other words, the banishment of the old concept of appetition from the conceptual scheme of the new physics, joined to the rationalistic spiritualism of the new theory of consciousness, deprived the realm of life of its status in the scheme of things. Yet, since sheer unrelatedness never satisfies theory, and since the irrepressible evidence of every one of our psycho-physical acts obstinately contradicts the dualistic division, it was inevitable that attempts were made to overcome the rift.

For this there were in principle three ways open, each of which was in fact chosen at one time or another: to accord primacy alternatively to matter or to mind, or to transcend the alternative by a new concept of substance. The third choice was Spinoza's, in one of the boldest ventures in the history of metaphysics. Its important implications for a philosophy of the organism, only partially explicated by Spinoza himself, are seldom noticed.[2]

2. Some excellent observations on the biological aspect of Spinoza's metaphysics, with special reference to modern developments in the physical and biological sciences, are found in Stuart Hampshire, *Spinoza,* pp. 75 ff.

II

Let us briefly recall the general principle of Spinoza's system. Its basis is the concept of one absolute and infinite substance, transcending those specifications (viz., extension and thought) by which Descartes had distinguished between different kinds of substance. Besides difference of kind, the oneness of Substance also excludes plurality of number: the infinity, being non-partitive, leaves no room for the existence of finite substances. Thus whatever is finite is not a substance but a modification or affection of infinite substance— a "mode." This is to say that individual being is not self-subsistent but inheres in the self-subsistent as a passing determination thereof. On the other hand, the infinity of the one substance involves an infinite number of "attributes" expressing the nature of that substance—each adequately insofar as it is itself infinite and in this conforms to the infinity of substance (as, e.g., the infinity of space does for the attribute of extension), but inadequately, namely incompletely, insofar as it expresses it only under this form. The sum of the attributes is the essence of substance itself, thus each attribute is "part" of the essence (or, the essence in one aspect) and as such complementary with all the rest. The same can also be stated by saying that the attributes all together "constitute" the essence, not however additively, but as abstract moments that are only abstractly separable. Individual existents, then (the "modes" mentioned before), are variable determinations of substance *in terms* of its invariable attributes (*"this* particular cube," *"this* particular thought"); and each individual affection of infinite substance as it occurs is exhibited, equally and equivalently, throughout all its attributes at once. Extension and Thought are two such attributes, the only ones of which *we* are cognizant. Thus, while the "modes" (affections) are what really happens to substance, the particular actualities of its existence, the "attributes"—e.g., extension and thought—are the universal forms in which such actualities manifest themselves and under which they can be conceived with equal truth by any finite mind that enjoys cognition of some of these forms. Since, in the human case, this is limited to the two indicated, our world consists in fact of body and mind, and nothing else.

The point for our context is that what to Descartes and to Cartesians like Geulincx were two separate and independent substances—

as such requiring for their existence neither each other nor a ground common to both[3]—are to Spinoza merely different aspects of one and the same reality, no more separable from each other than from their common cause. And he stresses that this common cause—infinite substance or God—*is* as truly extension as it is thought, or, as truly corporeal as mental; but there is as little a substance "body" as there is a substance "mind." Now since both these attributes express in each individual instance an identical fact, the whole problem of interaction, with which Occasionalism had to wrestle, or of the interrelation generally between the two realms, vanished. Each occurrence (mode) as viewed under the attribute of extension is at the same time, and equivalently, an occurrence viewed under the attribute of thought or consciousness, and vice versa. The two are strictly complementary aspects of one and the same reality which of necessity unfolds itself in all its attributes at once. It would even be too disjunctive to say that each material event has its "counterpart" in a mental event, since what externally may be registered as a parallelism of two different series of events is in truth, that is, in the reality of God or nature, substantially identical. Thus the riddle created by Cartesian dualism—of how an act of will can move a limb, since the limb as part of the extended world can only be moved by another body's imparting its antecedent motion to it—this riddle disappears. The act of will and the movement of the body are one and the same event appearing under different aspects, each of which represents in its own terms a complete expression of the concatenation of things in God, in the one eternal cause.

III

Spinoza's central interest, it is true, was not a doctrine of organism, but a metaphysical foundation for psychology and ethics; but incidentally his metaphysical basis enabled him to account for features of organic existence far beyond what Cartesian dualism and mechanism could accommodate. In the first place, Spinoza was no longer compelled to view those complex material entities we call organisms

3. They do require the latter in the extraneous sense of first having had to be created and then continuously to be confirmed in existence by God: but the *creative* (as well as preserving) cause is not an immanent cause; and insofar as those things were created *as* substances, they were precisely created as self-subsistent, however revocable that subsistence may be.

as the products of mechanical design. The idea of a purpose, in analogy to man-made machines, was replaced by the eternal necessity of the self-explication of the infinite nature of God, that is, of substance, that is, of reality. Therefore, what mattered in the understanding of an organism was no longer its lesser or greater perfection as an independent piece of functioning machinery, but its lesser or greater perfection as a finite "mode," measured by its power to exist and to interact (communicate) with the rest of existence, or, to be a less or more self-determined part of the whole: on whatever level of such perfection, it realizes one of the intrinsic possibilities of original substance in terms of matter and mind at once, and thereby shares in the self-affirmation of Being as such. And the principle of infinite reality, involving infinity of possible determination, would account for the wealth and gradation of organic forms. The purpose, then, is not ulterior and certainly does not lie in man, but lies entirely in the infinite self-expression itself; and even this does, strictly speaking, not merit the term "purpose," since it is governed by the immanent necessity of the absolute cause.

Secondly, the very image of "machine" could be dropped. Here we must note one of the inherent limitations of that image, quite apart from the psycho-physical question. The model—meant from the outset for animals and not for plants—provides: (a) for a connected *structure* of moving parts, such as levers, hinges, rods, wheels, tubes, valves; and (b) for the generation of *movement* from some source of power, such as the tension of a spring in a clock, or the heat of fire in a steam engine. Though the latter, or any combustion engine, was unknown to Descartes, he anticipated the model when he declared heat to be the moving force in the animal machine, and this heat to be generated by the "burning" of food. Thus the combustion theory of metabolism complements the machine theory of anatomical structure. But metabolism is more than a method of power-generation, or, food is more than fuel: in addition to, and more basic than, providing kinetic energy for the running of the machine (a case anyway not applying to plants), its role is to build up originally and replace continually the very parts of the machine. Metabolism thus is the constant becoming of the machine itself—and this becoming itself is a performance of the machine: but for such performance there is no analogue in the world of machines. In other words, once metabolism is understood as not only a device for energy-production, but as the continuous process of self-constitution of the very substance and form of the organism, the machine model breaks down. A better analogy would be that of a flame. As, in a burning candle, the permanence of the flame is a permanence, not of substance, but of process in which at each moment the "body" with its "structure" of inner and outer layers is reconstituted of materials different from the previous and following ones, so the living organism exists as a constant exchange of its own constituents, and has its permanence and identity only in the continuity of this process, not in any persistence of its material parts. This process indeed *is* its life, and in the last resort organic existence means, not to be a definite body composed of definite parts, but to be such a continuity of process with an identity sustained above and through the flux of components. Definiteness of arrangement (configuration) will then, jointly with continuity of process, provide the principle of identity which "substance" as such no longer provides.

On these lines indeed, Spinoza seeks to answer the problem of organic identity. Substance cannot by the terms of his ontology furnish such identity, because substance is not individual, and the organism is an individual. What is individual is a "mode," and so must be the organism as a species of individual. In fact, it is under the title of "individuality," i.e., in considering what makes an individual, and not under the title of "living things" in particular, that Spinoza treats the phenomenon of organism. Now *any* mode of universal substance, whether simple or complex, whether brief or enduring, is an individual (by definition, for to be a "mode" means just to be a distinct occurrence in the eternal self-unfolding of infinite being), and is this in all of the attributes if in any one of them. In that of extension this means to be a *body,* either simple or composite, *distinct* from other bodies. Since this distinctness cannot lie in its substance (by which on the contrary it is one with all), it must lie in its modal *determinations,* such as figure and motion, and in their interaction with other instances of determination in the same attribute. The continuity of determinateness throughout such interactions (a continuity, therefore, not excluding change) bespeaks the self-affirming "conatus" by which a mode tends to persevere in existence, and which is identical with its essence. Thus it is the *form* of determinateness, and the *conatus* evidenced by the survival of that form in a causal history, i.e., in *relation* to co-existing things, that defines an individual. All three— form, continuity, and relation—are integral to the concept of an individual and provide a clue to the meaning of its identity. The manner of "relation," i.e., of the causal communication with the environment in acting and suffering (affecting and being affected), depends on the given *form* of determination, i.e., on the kind of body involved: the affections of a simple body will simply reflect the joint impact of the environment, fusing the many influences into one, without discrimination of the various individual agents; whereas composite bodies of a certain kind, as we shall see, may embody the affections of the environment differentially in their condition and thus also act on the environment differentially. Here we note one divergence from the machine model, to be taken up later: the point of such compositeness, i.e., of degree of complexity, is not variety of mechanical performance by a self-contained automaton, but range and variety of reciprocal *communication* with things, or, the manner of being part of the whole while yet being something apart from the whole.

IV

However, the interactional aspect (the being part of a whole) is based on the formal nature of the individual; and as this may be composite, and is so in all cases of higher relatedness, we have first to consider the meaning of compositeness as such, or, the manner in which an individual itself can be a "whole" of its own parts, a "one" of many. This—as the parts of a composite are in turn individuals— is the same as asking how a plurality of individuals may be so united that all together form a larger (and higher-order) individual. Now any union of individuals must be in terms of interaction, i.e., of mutual determination; and if it is more than a haphazard collection, the order of grouping may engender an *order* of interaction such that the *total* of mutual determinations will be a *form of determinateness* itself. But form of determinateness, as we have seen, is precisely what defines "individual," as it constitutes the distinctness of a mode: and thus a body composed of many and diverse bodies (which again may be "composite to a high degree") may truly be an individual—if this total *form* of multiple inner relations maintains itself functionally in the interactions of the compound with the outside world, thereby testifying to a common conatus of the whole.

The possible advantage of such compositeness in terms of the external relations of an individual has been provisionally indicated and is not our concern at present. What matters now is the new possibility of "identity" opened up by the concept of individual here expounded. If it is the (spatial and dynamic) *pattern* of composition and function in which the individuality of a composite consists, then its identity is not bound to the identities of the simpler bodies of which it is composed; and the preservation of that identity through time rests with the preservation of the pattern rather than of the particular collection presently embodying it. The identity of a whole is thus compatible with a change of parts; and such a change may even be the very means by which the identity of certain individuals is sustained.

This train of thought obviously permits an understanding of organism quite different from the Cartesian one and, we think, more adequate to the facts; and this even in terms of "extension" alone, i.e., without the full benefits of the doctrine to be reaped from complementing the physical facts with those in the attribute of "thought." The main propositions touching upon the physical side of organism are found in Part II of the *Ethics,* entitled "Of the Nature and Origin of the Mind" and thus pre-eminently dealing with the mental side. However, from Proposition XI onward, Spinoza deals with the soul-body problem, and in that context makes certain statements concerning the type of body that corresponds to a soul or mind, and the type of identity that pertains to it. They are Lemmata 4–7 after Prop. XIII—as follows:

LEMMA IV. If a certain number of bodies be separated from the body or individual which is composed of a number of bodies, and if their place be supplied by the same number of other bodies of the same nature, the individual will retain the nature it had before without any change of form.

DEMONSTRATION. Bodies are not distinguished in respect of substance (Lem. I);[4] but that which makes the form of an individual is the union of bodies (by the preceding definition).[5] This form,

4. LEMMA I. Bodies are distinguished from one another in respect of motion and rest, quickness and slowness, and not in respect of substance.

5. DEF. When a number of bodies of the same or of different magnitudes are pressed together by others, so that they lie one upon the other, or if they are in motion with the same or with different degrees of speed, so that they communicate their motion to one another in a certain fixed proportion—these bodies are said to be mutually united, and taken altogether, they are said to compose one body or individual which is distinguished from other bodies by this union of bodies.

however (by hypothesis), is retained, although there may be a continuous change of the bodies. The individual, therefore, will retain its nature with regard both to substance and to mode, as before.— Q.E.D.

LEMMA V. If the parts composing an individual become greater or less proportionately, so that they preserve towards one another the same kind of motion and rest, the individual will also retain the nature which it had before without any change of form.

LEMMA VI. If any number of bodies composing an individual are compelled to divert into one direction the motion they previously had in another, but are nevertheless able to continue and reciprocally communicate their motions in the same manner as before, the individual will then retain its nature without any change of form.

LEMMA VII. The individual thus composed will, moreover, retain its nature whether it move as a whole or be at rest, or whether it move in this or that direction, provided that each part retain its own motion and communicate it as before to the rest.

Lemma 4 refers to metabolism, 5 to growth, 6 to movement of limb, 7 to locomotion. There follows an important scholium to this whole series of lemmata.

SCHOL. We thus see in what manner a composite individual can be affected in many ways and yet retain its nature. Up to this point we have conceived an individual to be composed merely of bodies which are distinguished from one another solely by motion and rest, speed and slowness, i.e., to be composed of the most simple bodies. If we now consider an individual of another kind, composed of many individuals of diverse natures, we shall discover that it may be affected in many other ways, its nature nevertheless being preserved. For since each of its parts is composed of a number of bodies, each part (by the preceding lemma), without any change of its nature, can move more slowly or quickly, and consequently can communicate its motion more quickly or more slowly to the rest. If we now imagine a third kind of individual composed of these of the second kind, we shall discover that it can be affected in many other ways without any change of form. Thus, if we advance *ad infinitum,* we may easily conceive the whole of nature to be one individual whose parts, i.e., all bodies, vary in infinite ways without any change of the whole individual.

After this, a number of postulates deal with the human body in particular, of which we quote postulates 1, 3, 4, and 6.

POST. 1. The human body is composed of a number of individual parts of diverse nature, each of which is composite to a high degree.

POST. 3. The individual parts composing the human body, and consequently the human body itself, are affected by external bodies in many ways.

POST. 4. The human body needs for its preservation many other bodies by which it is, as it were, continually regenerated.

POST. 6. The human body can move and arrange external bodies in many ways.

V

If we ponder these statements in the total context of Spinoza's theory, we realize that, for the first time in modern speculation, an organic individual is viewed as a fact of wholeness rather than of mechanical interplay of parts. The essence of organic being is seen, not in the functioning of a machine as a closed system, but in the sustained sequence of states of a unified plurality, with only the form of its union enduring while the parts come and go. Substantial identity is thus replaced by formal identity, and the relation of parts to whole, so crucial for the nature of organism, is the converse of what it is in the mechanistic view. There, the finished product, the complete animal machine, is the sum of the component parts, and the most elementary of such parts, the simplest units of matter, are the ultimate and the only true subjects of individuality. Identity then, as identity of individual corporeal substances, comes down to the mere inert persistence of matter, and from this basic type of individuality and identity every other individuality and identity in the extended realm is derived. Conversely, identity in Spinoza's theory of individuality is the identity of a whole which is so little the mere sum of its parts that it remains the same even when the parts continually change. And since the individual is a *form of union,* there are qualitative grades of individuality, depending on the degree of differentiated order, and quantitative grades, depending on the numerical extent of inclusion (both scales, on the whole, tending to coincide)—so that the All forms a hierarchy of individualities, or wholes, of increasing inclusiveness culminating in the most inclusive one, the totality of nature as such. Within a certain range along this line are those grades of individuality, i.e., of complexity of organization, which we term "organic": but this is a matter of degree only, and on principle all nature is "alive." On whatever level of compositeness (but the more so, the higher the level), the various orders of individuality exist essentially in the succession of their states, i.e., in the continuous series of their changes, rather than in any momentary structure which a mechanical analysis into elements would reveal. The specifically "organic" bodies, then, are highly composite minor totalities of subordinate individuals which again are composed of lesser ones, and so on. In such a stratification, the variability of being which compositeness enjoys as such, is communicated upward cumulatively, and with each supervening level is raised to a higher power, so that the uppermost level representing the totality in question is the beneficiary of all its subordinate members.

Thus the concept of organism evolves organically, without a break, from the general ontology of individual existence. Of every such existence it is true to say that as a modal determination it represents just one phase in the eternal unfolding of infinite substance and is thus never a terminal product in which the creative activity would come to rest.[6] While a machine certainly is such a terminal product, the modal wholes, continuing their conative life in the shift of their own parts and in interchange with the larger whole, are productive as much as produced, or, as much "natura naturans" as "natura naturata."

VI

So far we have dealt with the phenomenon of life in the attribute of extension only, that is, with life as represented by organized bodies. If we now turn to the inward aspect, the progress of Spinoza's monism over Cartesian dualism becomes even more manifest. Extension as a whole, as we have seen, represents but one attribute by which the infinite essence of substance is of necessity expressed. It is equally expressed, with equal necessity and equal validity, by the attribute of thought. This means that to every *mode* of extension there corresponds a mode of "thought" which is only another aspect of the same underlying cause complementarily expressed in either way. Now

6. That activity, being that of substance as a whole, can of course in its universal movement overrule any individual conatus, and inevitably does so sooner or later.

since individuals are modes of the one substance, and in each such mode substance is affected throughout its attributes, it follows that *any* individual in the world of bodies (and not just a certain class of individuals) has its co-ordinate counterpart in an individual of thought. This principle discards two connected Cartesian ideas at once: that "life" is a fact of physics alone, and that "soul" is a fact of man alone: according to the first, life is a particular corporeal *behavior* following from a particular corporeal structure which distinguishes a *class* of objects in nature, viz., the natural automata; according to the second, "soul," equated with consciousness of any kind, be it feeling, desiring, perceiving, thought (anima = mens = cogitatio), as such not required for physical function of any kind *and thus not for life,* is absent in animals and present in man, but is neither in *his* case a principle of "life," which remains a purely behavioristic phenomenon in all cases. To Spinoza, soul still is not a principle of life considered physically (as it was to Aristotle), but neither is life itself mere corporeal behavior. The concurrence of outwardness and inwardness is here no longer a unique arrangement in the case of man, nor even a distinctive mark of the whole class of things normally called "animate": as the essence of substance, that concurrence is the pervading trait of all existence. Yet the universality of the principle by no means obliterates those distinctions in nature by which we speak of animate as against inanimate things, of sentient as against merely vegetative organisms, and of conscious and reasoning man as against unreasoning animals. On the contrary, for the first time in modern theory, a speculative means is offered for relating the degree of organization of a body to the degree of awareness belonging to it.

Let us recall that dualism did not offer such a means, i.e., did not provide for an intelligible relation between the perfection of a physical organization and the *quality* of the life supported by it: all it provided for was the relation between organization and observable behavior. The wealth of gradation in the animal world between the most primitive (i.e., simple) and the most subtle (i.e., complex) structure could not be overlooked but had to remain meaningless. Since no other kind of soul but the rational was recognized, all the mechanical perfection displayed in animal organisms amounted just to a gigantic hoax, as no higher type of experient life corresponded to greater excellence of mechanical performance. Thus the very perfection in terms of external construction and function mocks all justification in terms of lives and purposes. Even in man, as noted before, there is no intelligible connection between the excellence of his body and the uniqueness of his mind, as these two are only extraneously joined together. On materialistic premises such a connection was plausible enough, since mind, if it is a function of the brain, must needs be determined in its quality by the quality of the brain. But this plausibility is paid for by too heavy a price in difficulties concerning the nature of mind itself. Spinoza's psycho-physical parallelism offered an ingenious theory of connection between grade of organization and grade of mentality without violating the principle of non-interaction between the two sides. That such interaction cannot be is no less axiomatic to him than to the whole Cartesian school: "The body cannot determine the mind to thought, neither can the mind determine the body to motion nor rest, nor to anything else, if there be anything else."[7] The positive complement of this negative rule is thus stated for the corporeal side: "A body in motion or at rest must be determined to motion or rest by another body, which was also determined to motion or rest by another, and so on ad infinitum."[8] At least in this application to the physical realm, the ontological rigor of the rule admits no exception; and we may add that none of the leading thinkers of the period down to, and including, Kant ever challenged the validity of it. The reasons for thus ruling out of court the most insistent evidence of common experience —that fear or love or deliberation can determine action and thus be causes of bodily motion—cannot be discussed here: we just note that they commanded overwhelming consensus. But if interaction is ruled out, the alternative need not be mutual independence or unrelatedness of the two sides. The Occasionalists, in their attempt to account for the prima facie facts of interconnection, acquiesced in a mere externality of correlation, which was no less miraculous a coincidence for the fact that God saw to its happening time and again. This unsatisfactory construction Spinoza replaced by an intrinsic belonging-together of mind and matter, which gave causal preference neither to matter, as materialism would have it, nor to mind, as idealism would have it, but instead rested their interrelation on the common ground of which they both were dependent aspects.

7. *E.*, III, ii.
8. *E.*, III, Lem. 3.

VII

Applying this formula to the doctrine of organism and the diversity of biological organization, of which man represents one, and perhaps the highest, degree, we have to ask more concretely in what the correlation of mental to physical modes consists. Spinoza answers that the "soul" is an individual mode of thought, that is, an "idea" in God, whose one and continuous object (*ideatum*) is an actually existing individual body. This "idea" of one determinate body, if it is as sustained as the existence of its object, must of course be a *series* of ideas, corresponding to, and concomitant with, the series of states in which the pertaining body exists; and it must at each moment be a *complex* idea, in accordance with the complexity of the body. What is represented in the idea is the total state of the body at each given instant. Now that state of the body is determined by two factors: (1) by what it is in itself, its own formal nature, that is, by the form or pattern of its composition; and (2) by its affection from outside, i.e., the influence of other bodies on its condition. Thus the state of a body represents at each moment itself *and* those bodies of the surrounding world which do affect it at that moment. And it does represent the latter insofar as they affect it, which they do again, not only in virtue of their own power or their own intrinsic nature, but also in virtue of the way in which the affected body can be affected: that is, its own organization determines the manner in which other things besides itself can be represented in its own state.

Now, clearly, degrees of organization can be understood precisely as degrees of the faculty of a body to be affected more or less variously, distinctly and thus adequately by other bodies individually (being in any case affected by them collectively). Thus a more differentiated, because more complex organization—for instance, of the sensory apparatus—would make for a more perfect, that is, more differential way in which the body receives the affections from other bodies. In brief, degree of organization may mean degree of discriminatory sensitivity—both understood in strictly physical terms (as, e.g., in a camera). Now, since the soul is nothing but the correlate "idea" of an actually existing body, the degree of distinctness, differentiation, and clarity enjoyed by this idea is exactly proportionate to the state of the body that is its sole object. Thus, although the immediate object of the soul is only the co-ordinate body, which is the same mode of substance in terms of extension that the soul is in terms of thought, yet through this body's being affected by other bodies and affected in different degrees of perfection according to its own organization (and to circumstances), the corresponding mental state will have mediate awareness of the world—as represented through affections of the body—in different degrees of obscurity and clarity, of limitedness and comprehensiveness. Therefore "soul" is granted to animals and plants on exactly the same principle as to man, yet not the same soul. The soul, being the equivalent of the body in a different attribute, or the expression of the same mode (determination) of substance of which the body is the expression in extenso, must be completely conformal to the kind of body whose soul it is, and there are as many kinds and degrees of soul as there are kinds and degrees of vital organization.[9] The two are in each case just the two equivalent aspects of one and the same basic reality, which is neither matter nor mind, but is equally expressed by both.

The general principle is stated in the famous Prop. vii of Part II, the *Magna Carta* of "psycho-physical parallelism": "The order and connection of ideas is the same as the order and connection of things." With reference to the human mind, the doctrine is expressed in the following propositions of the same part:

PROP. XI. The first thing which forms the actual being of the human mind is nothing else than the idea of an individual thing actually existing.

PROP. XII. Whatever happens in the object of the idea constituting the human mind must be perceived by the human mind; or, in other words, an idea of that thing will necessarily exist in the human mind. That is to say, if the object of the idea constituting the human mind be a body, nothing can happen in that body which is not perceived by the mind.

PROP. XIII. The object of the idea constituting the human mind is a body, or a certain mode of extension actually existing, and nothing else.

SCHOL. Hence we see not only that the human mind is united to the body, but also what is to be understood by the union of the mind

9. This, incidentally, is the first theory after Aristotle's to show why a human soul cannot be transposed into an animal or vegetable body, i.e. which excludes the *possibility* of metempsychosis. Leibniz's *Monadology,* while avoiding most of the pitfalls of Cartesian dualism, falls short of Spinoza on this point.

and body. But no one can understand it adequately or distinctly without knowing adequately beforehand the nature of our body; for those things which we have proved hitherto are altogether general, nor do they refer more to man than to other individuals, all of which are animate, although in different degrees. For of everything there necessarily exists in God an idea of which He is the cause, in the same way as the idea of the human body exists in Him [which idea is the human mind]; and therefore, everything that we have said of the idea of the human body is necessarily true of the idea of any other thing [being the "mind" of that other thing]. We cannot, however, deny that ideas, like objects themselves, differ from one another, and that one is more excellent and contains more reality than another, just as the object of one idea is more excellent and contains more reality than another. Therefore, in order to determine the difference between the human mind and other minds and its superiority over them, we must first know, as we have said, the nature of its object, that is to say, the nature of the human body. . . . I will say generally that in proportion as one body is fitter than others to *do or suffer many things* [*severally*] *at once,* in the same proportion will its mind be fitter to perceive many things at once; and the more the actions of a body depend upon itself alone, and the less other bodies cooperate with it in action, the fitter will the mind of that body be for distinctly understanding. We can thus determine the superiority of one mind to another; we can also see the reason why we have only a very confused knowledge of our body. . . .

PROP. XIV. The human mind is adapted to the perception of many things, and its aptitude increases in proportion to the number of ways in which its body can be disposed.

PROP. XV. The idea which constitutes the formal being of the human mind is not simple, but is composed of a number of ideas. [This follows from the high degree of compositeness of the human body.]

PROP. XVI. The idea of every way in which the human body is affected by external bodies must involve the nature of the human body and at the same time the nature of the external body.

DEM. All ways in which any body is affected follow at the same time from the nature of the affected body and from the nature of the affecting body; therefore, the idea of these modifications necessarily involves the nature of each body; and therefore the idea of each way in which the human body is affected by an external body involves the nature of the human body and of the external body.

COROLLARY 1. Hence it follows, in the first place, that the human mind perceives the nature of many bodies together with that of its own body.

COR. 2. It follows, secondly, that the ideas of external bodies indicate the constitution of our own body rather than the nature of the external bodies.[10]

VIII

The conclusion from these general propositions, regarding the question whether animals have souls, that is to say, whether they feel, strive, perceive, even think in a way, is stated by Spinoza in no equivocal terms. Since mind is not a species of substance, defined by fixed attributes like reason and intellect, but itself a total attribute of infinite substance, and as such admits on principle of the same infinity of different modes as extension has in its own sphere, animals can obviously enjoy a degree of mind congruent with their bodies without any prejudice to the distinctive characteristics of the human mind, as congruent with its body. Thus we read in Part III:

PROP. LVII. The affect of one individual differs from the corresponding affect of another as much as the essence of the one individual differs from that of the other.

SCHOL. Hence it follows that the affects of animals which are called irrational (for after we have learnt the origin of the mind we can in no way doubt that brutes feel) differ from the affects of men as much as their respective natures differ from human nature. Both the man and the horse, for example, are swayed by lust to propagate, but the horse is swayed by equine lust and the man by a human one. The lusts and appetites of insects, fishes, and birds must vary in the same way; and so, although each individual lives contented with its own nature and delights in it, nevertheless the life with which it

10. The following quotation from *Ep.* 66 may here be added as a succinct summary of Spinoza's doctrine of mind: "The essence of the mind consists in this alone that it is the idea of an actually existing body; and accordingly the mind's power to understand extends to those things only which this idea of the body contains in itself or which follow from it. But this idea of the body involves and expresses no other attributes of God but extension and thought. Hence I conclude that the human mind cannot apprehend any attribute of God save these two."

is contented and its joy are nothing else but the "idea" or soul of the individual [body] in question, and so the joy of one differs in character from the joy of the other as much as the essence of the one differs from the essence of the other. . . .

The last scholium, in conjunction with that to Prop. xiii of Part II, clearly establishes the principle of an infinite gradation of "animateness," co-extensive with the gradation of physical composition, for which the entirely simple is merely a limiting case: even this would not be devoid of a minimum of inwardness, since to its distinctness, such as it is, there must correspond the idea "of" it in God—and this is its "thought" or "soul." Note how in Spinoza's logic a *genitivus objectivus*—the idea of this body—turns into a *genitivus subjectivus* —this body's thought. On the lowest level, this "thought" will not be more than an infinitesimal feeling, but even this will be compounded of an active and a passive aspect: namely, on the one hand, self-affirmation, whose physical equivalent is the *vis inertiae* (both expressing the conatus for self-continuation), and on the other hand, experience of otherness, or, perception, whose physical equivalent is the subjection to outside forces (both expressing the integration into the sum of things). Each thing asserts itself, but all things around it assert themselves, and in the case of the very simple, low-grade individual (illustrated perhaps by the atom), completely at the mercy of external impingements, the compound assertion of all others in its dynamic condition all but submerges its self-assertion, so that the active aspect will be at a minimum; and correspondingly, the very experience of otherness (its "affects") will not rise beyond an indiscriminate fusion of mere passivity: its perception will be as indistinct as its selfhood. Only complex functional systems afford the inner *autonomy* that is required for greater power of self-determination, *together* with greater variety of inner states responding to the determinations which impinge on it from without. The mental equivalent of both is, on the active side, higher degree of consciousness with its affirmation and enjoyment of *self,* and, on the passive side, greater distinctness of perception with its understanding (and possible mastery) of *things.* The idea of *power* is fundamental in the evaluation of the corporeal as well as of the mental side and furnishes the standard of perfection: the power of the body to exist, persist, to do and suffer many things, to determine others and itself, is at the same time affirmation of that power by the mind which is the "idea" of that body.[11] And since degree of power is degree of *freedom,* it is true to say that higher organization of the body, and correspondingly greater complexity of its idea, mean greater freedom of the individual both in body and in mind.

The phrase "fitness to do or suffer many things" expresses Spinoza's insight into the essentially dual character of the organism: its *autonomy* for itself, and its *openness* for the world: spontaneity paired with receptivity. Their concurrent, indeed interdependent, increase is a seeming paradox, since openness in perception means exposure to affection, thus determination from without, contrary to the self-determination which autonomy of action would imply and all conatus must seek. Yet increase in *passive* power is asserted by Spinoza together with increase in active power to be the mark of higher fitness of an organism and thus of its perfection. Here is proof of his profundity. For this dialectic is precisely the nature of life in its basic organic sense. Its closure as a functional whole within the individual organism is, at the same time, correlative openness toward the world; its very separateness entails the faculty of communication; its segregation from the whole is the condition of its integration with the whole. The affectivity of all living things complements their spontaneity; and while it seems to indicate primarily the passive aspect of organic existence, it yet provides, in a subtle balance of freedom and necessity, the very means by which the organism carries on its vital commerce with the environment, that is, with the conditions of its continued existence. Only by being sensitive can life be active, only by being exposed can it be autonomous. And this in direct ratio: the more individuality is focused in a self, the wider is its periphery of communication with other things; the more isolated, the more related it is.

This dialectic of individual life in the world Spinoza has seen, and provided for in his system, as neither Descartes before him nor Leibniz after him did.

11. Compare Spinoza's restatement of his principle of the degrees of mental perfection as *related* to, though not causally dependent on, degrees of bodily perfection, in the Explanation at the end of Part III: "Since the essence of the mind consists in its affirmation of the actual existence of its body, and since we understand by perfection the essence itself of the thing, it follows that the mind passes to a greater or less perfection when it is able to affirm of its body, or some part of it, something which involves a greater or less reality than before."

The Two Eyes of Spinoza

LESZEK KOLAKOWSKI

It is only with the greatest of difficulty that monistic doctrines are capable, in their constructions, of rescuing the idea of negative freedom, and one may well doubt whether anyone at all has succeeded without the sacrifice of coherence in attaining this goal.

If one excludes the conceivable, but never seriously projected, model of perfect solipsism, then monistic thought, that is, the attempt at a general relativization of all qualities of being to a single primordial being, inclines irresistibly toward agreement upon the disappearance of the whole range of subjectivity, understood as an irreducible domain. For monism aims at a construction whereby subjectivity will always appear as a certain particular state or arrangement or manifestation or phenomenon of something which is not subjective at all, and whereby, therefore, subjectivity can be defined without residue in terms of the object.

Hence belief in freedom, understood as a negative quality of the subject, is belief in absolute beginnings, in perfect primordiality, in the primordial spontaneity of at least certain acts of a consciously acting subject. This belief implies that when we try to seek into the reasons of our free decisions, we always come to a point where the question breaks off irretrievably, where the final reason of wanting is wanting itself and nothing more. "Why is it that I want thus, and not another way?"—one may always ask, and one may sometimes find an answer, but each answer will be a new "I want," and after a certain number of questions, each more hollow than its predecessor, the chain of explanation comes to an end and only one thing remains: "I want, because I want."

An action on the part of a subject to which one attributes the capability of avoiding determination or the power of refusal in the face of a question about the reason of a personal choice—this action, then, must pass for an absolute, that is, for an initial reality, which each time brings into existence some new thing which creates its own

Translated by Mr. Oscar Swan from L. Kolakowski, "Dwoje oczu Spinozy," *Antynomé wolnósci,* Wilna, 1966, pp. 219–229, by permission of the author and his agent.

self and which ever so often opens up in the *massif* of reality an unforeseen crack or idiopathic whirlpool. There are, therefore, as many absolutes as there are subjects conscious and capable of choice; at each point of subjectivity in the universe the unity of the divine absolute or the absolute of nature breaks down. The difficulties of many scholastics who sought a noncontradictory formula which could have reconciled the monopolistic primordiality of God with the freedom of an *ex nihilo* choice, differentiating, but not differentiated, in advance, may be appreciated from that point of view. Also the ultimate sterility of these attempts and the eternal instability of all solutions, as well as the scantiness and carelessness of the attempts which Christianity in all its variations undertook to evade taking as mutually exclusive the almightiness of God and human freedom: these too have their roots in the same monistic temptation that the doctrine of the creation contains.

Cartesianism freed itself from these intricacies thanks to the epistemological proviso to which, in its *cogito,* it gave expression. Since we may, since we are even compelled, to rescue our own existence, as an existence we have experienced, as an initial and incomparably irresistible point of thought about being, it will not only be easy to attribute to this epistemological primacy an ontological sense, but we simply will not be able to do otherwise. For if it were appearance that is "given" in the most primordial sense, then each passage from appearance to thing would be false. Cognitive absoluteness of an act of thought directed toward one's self endows that act with authority, so that it may also reclaim for itself a certain absoluteness in the existential order. Freedom, then, is not beset at the outset by the snares of God's grace; instead, one can found it earlier, before any kind of knowledge about grace reaches us. To have freedom, it is not necessary to search for evasions. Cartesian freedom knows no limitations and in its negativity it is constituted from the beginning as a talent so unremovable that man adds his own fiat to God's each time he acts freely; he is therefore equal at each moment to the creator, when, by the power of his self-defining creativity, he passes from nondifferentiation to differentiation.

The fundamental discontinuity of the Cartesian construction continues to remain without signs of improvement. How, then, will we reconstruct the physical world when absolute initialness has become reserved for act, in which experience in relation to itself acquires distance in order to catch itself for a moment in a splitting reflection?

The famous argumentation which lifts itself up to God and takes his truthfulness as witness in order to save our belief in the reality of earth and heaven immediately displayed to its critics so many striking flaws that, among the adherents to the Cartesian doctrine, the majority preferred to disavow it. In a monumental wave of reconstruction, even the first observers unmasked the organic incapability of its initial assumption to permit the rebuilding of physical existence. Freedom, hence negativity, which defines human existence in its independence, thus remained a reward promised to those who, confronted with the question of the reality of the world, suspend their opinion.

Thus Cartesianism split philosophies into those which begin to spin their thread from thought as experienced and only return to the world thanks to the violation of rules of proof, and those which, beginning from being itself, constituted without anyone's cognitive help, are incapable of breaking through to subjectivity and leave human existence on the level of the thing, or provide another kind of reality only through arbitrary decree.

It seems that the difficulty with Spinoza's metaphysics is exactly the opposite to that of the Cartesian. The latter tried to rebuild the world, accepting the experienced *cogitationes* as a raw datum; the former, at least in the version of the *Ethics,* established an absolute single being, a divine substance, as a starting point, in an ontological proof definitively confirmed the material of thought, and then wrestled in vain with the act of self-knowledge when it tried to place it in the metaphysical picture. What, then, of the fact that human existence is not simply a body, but a soul, existentially identical to the body, since it shares with all things—modifications of infinite substance—that participation in the ideal or "mental" quality, which embraces all individual existences? We are a "soul" in the original meaning, namely, insofar as each thing is a soul. In our own individual way we are a soul according to Spinoza only insofar as, besides the idea contained in us, there is the idea of this same idea, hence self-knowledge, a self-knowledge unattainable for other things. But what is the metaphysical reason for that addition? None other than precisely that in God is present the idea of everything, hence also the idea of the idea. Indeed one might suppose that from this point of view there is no reason to deny to the idea of anything at all that duplication, thanks to which ideal existence—or the exceptionless participation of the thing in the logical order of existence—becomes, in addition, a self-knowing being, not only knowing something, but also knowing that it knows. Spinoza did not take note of the absurd consequence which his metaphysical doctrine as such irresistibly suggested; instead, he differentiated man's existence with the aid of an artificial limitation, completely deprived of reason within the structure of his metaphysic. So it was with just cause that he was criticized for haziness on this point and with just cause also that he was reproached for that fundamental inability for any kind of theoretic decision which could legitimize the subjective territory within being; not without cause, finally, did his critics assert that if one holds truly to metaphysical assumptions, human existence cannot be re-created within their boundaries other than through purely material, empirical qualities.

Freedom of the absolute and its immanent necessity are no different in essence according to the Spinozistic analysis from that freedom which the Platonizing scholastics attributed to the divine creator. For the specific nature of divine existence does not allow, according to Spinoza, absolute being to be free in the sense in which nondetermination is attributed to human activities according to current popular opinion. For the absolute is not subject to the succession of time—which, after all, derives in a natural manner from its ultimate perfection. A being for which the past is one thing and the future another would indeed have to mediate in some way its own cognitive bond with the world, would have to have at its disposal memory or foresight, and would have then to take up a position in regard to the sphere of events with which it is establishing a mediate relation through recollection or projection; its knowledge about the world would not be a direct participation in the course of events or a contemplation that is actual, but would demand a differentiation between that which can be and that which is in fact. Since it is impossible in God to think of the difference between possibility and actuality, it is also impossible in him to think of the relation of temporal succession. By the same token it is also impossible to imagine that he ever had at any moment at all the gift of free decision in the face of a situation where he would not be differentiated beforehand—precisely because no "beforehand" enters in, because absolute being must be definitively actualized. It seems that "divine freedom" designates nothing more than that very circumstance, that God is not in any act of his constrained or inclined toward anything by situations external to him or by commands—a characteristic which in an obvious way belongs to his position of absolute creator. Thus in fact, in relation to the absolute, a distinction between what is free and what is necessary becomes nonsensical, and Spinoza is saying nothing more than this when he calls his God free and at the same time attributes absolute ineluctability to his actions. He is free, because he is not coerced by anything; he is tied to his own necessity, because he is always actualized. Being self-exhaustive in his immobile self-identity, God-Nature appears to human perception only in a temporal succession of individual events, causally connected but materializing in time one after another. In the thing itself, however, the past and the future are fulfilled on equal footing, because they are fulfilled in nature, and outside of nature—the single genuine concrete, the single self-dependent existence—there is nothing, and nothing deserves the name of being in its basic meaning.

There cannot be, therefore, any fissure in being which would break apart its primordial self-identity, no imaginable opening through which something that is not yet defined would have to be defined only in time. Also unimaginable is purposeful activity of being—as if one were free to think that the absolute sets some kind of goal for itself, that it therefore aims at the filling up of a lack in one's own existence, or desires a satisfaction which it has up till now not known. Purposefulness is evidence of imperfection; it is blasphemy then for one to set up a purposefully operating absolute. In the world in which we live, everything has really already happened, and there is no hope that a freely self-defining spontaneity will be able suddenly to dig out a hole in the succession of events or to interrupt their continuity: that would be equivalent to supposing that by a capricious decision one might so bring it about that from a certain statement something did not result which was a logical consequence of it. For the course of physical events proceeds with exactly the same inevitability with which inferences follow from premises in Euclid's *Elements*. So the very nature of the absolute renders impossible purposefulness in nature and fortuity in the world—unless one considers "fortuitous" simply everything whose causes or reasons are unknown to us, thereby relegating fortuity to our own ignorance, but not to the property of being itself.

In the light of these principles, the absurdity of the idea which ascribes to a human being free will in the popular sense is so clear, that it would not be worth while to unmask it especially, if it were not for the special role which this prejudice plays in collective life, upheld by theologians in opposition to common sense. To shatter that prejudice appears to Spinoza a task so easy that it is hardly worth the effort, and the abundant space which he devotes to this matter results only from the social importance of the question, not from his philosophical concern. For it is obvious—since everything is in God and anything beyond God is impossible to conceive, and since, further, God necessarily exists—that every manifestation of his indifferent creative might is equally inevitable; in particular, that "will and understanding are to the nature of God as motion and rest." Human behavior, then, does not differ from others as far as its definiteness, its supposed nondetermination, its conjectured control over itself, and the fictitious power of its purposeful decisions are concerned. Whatever can happen, must happen, whatever need not come to pass, cannot come to pass. Between impossibility and necessity there is no middle ground in being itself—at the most it is only in our fragmentary knowledge about the world.

If, therefore, we free ourselves from Spinoza's vocabulary, we will say this: to the world it is indifferent that we are a part of it; it does not contain itself any intent, benevolent or hostile, directed toward man, it has realized in its perfection everything which can come into existence, it has no intentions of changing anything in consideration of human suffering and it is after all simply unthinkable that it would or could do this. There is no providence in the world which could keep guard over our life, there is no protection, no reward and punishment, there is no good and evil, there is no justice or injury. Good and evil, justice and injury are only present in the domain which has been called to life by ourselves for our own needs; nature is not interested in our constructions.

But the peculiarity of human existence, even if it is not metaphysically legitimized by anything—its capacity for experiencing itself—is not only the source of our individuality, but also the source of false fancies concerning precisely this individuality. The world knows everything, but does not know that it knows. Man knows insignificantly little, but knows that he knows and that he does not know. His physical actions are subject to the same necessity as the motion of the wavy surface of the ocean or the falling away of a rock from a cliff. If that rock were equipped with the same self-knowledge of its own movements as man, it would imagine in the same way that by the power of free decision it would rather roll downwards than fly upwards. There is exactly the same amount of freedom in our own actions: powerless but self-deceiving self-observation, thanks to which we dream in our pitiable pride that we ourselves are the creative source of the mechanical motion which the totality of our physical actions exhausts. An observer of one's own body, which he watches as though through a glass—for there is no causal link between thought and motion—imagines that he is guiding it, like a boy who commands the thunder to crack, but gives his command precisely at the moment when the thunder is beginning.

Would it be the case, then, that we are not responsible for our own body, agitated, apart from our decisions, by the pressure of displaced bodily parts? Once more, according to Spinoza, the question is incorrectly posed. If someone asks whether one should render evildoers harmless in the name of the collective need, he should be answered affirmatively, not, however, for the reason that the evildoer has described himself "freely" within his evildoing, but simply because we must oppose circumstances which aim against our desires for self-preservation. In the same way, we stamp underfoot poisonous snakes, not asking about their freedom, in the same way that we move aside a rock which is lying in our path. And if someone insists on equating responsibility with indeterminateness of decisions and a lack of causal differentiation in our actions, then it is clear that responsibility, understood in this way, is not present in the world outside of our own fancy.

An evil doctrine, a forlorn philosophy—said his enemies. I know not whether good or evil—replied Spinoza; it is enough that it is true.

But it is a misfortune to live in a world arranged like that, they insisted. Knowledge of the truth cannot be a misfortune, a life of illusion cannot be happiness, answered the philosopher. But anyway, why is it a misfortune? To understand correctly the universe in its infinite perfection, in its total self-sufficiency, means at the same time to love it exactly the way it is. This is not love in the everyday meaning of an affection which we harbor for another person, hoping for reciprocation. Love that is rational—because only from understanding, only from intellectual effort can that particular affection grow—does not demand reciprocation, because it knows that the absolute is not subject to affection. It is, at all events, a happy love, because it can never be disappointed and it permits one to free himself completely from vain expectations of a world different from the way it is. The understanding of necessity, the Stoics' freedom, may be called freedom in the sense in which freedom is total spiritual independence of situations over which we are not able in any case to have control. Thus we rise to a position of observation, from which human passions, quarrels, despairs, sufferings, and basenesses can be considered with the same dispassionate equanimity with which we spin our chains of ratiocinations about geometrical abstractions. The result is worth the effort: we cast off vain sorrows, the sad feeling that we are somehow to blame for fate, or that this or that is due us from the world, embitterment at unsuccessful undertakings, indignation in the face of human baseness, outrage at the sight of evil, barren and ineffectual pity—all this will be spared us. Accessible to us will be the feeling, full of joy, that we are a small part of the infinite whole, with whose extra-temporal and eternal existence we can in some measure identify ourselves, since we are able to understand that existence. Fear of death, the nightmare of oblivion or damnation, will become extinguished, because in a world to whose inevitability we become genuinely attached, death will appear as an unforestallable component of a wonderfully consistent whole.

The philosophy of a masochist—so the eminent historian Lewis Feuer comments upon this vision of the world; are we to be glad of the fact that the absolute world is limitlessly indifferent to us and must we love it without being able to count upon reciprocation? Are we to adore an order of things which destroys us with the same inevitability as the wind knocks leaves from a branch, and which always and eternally must cast its irresistible force upon our frail powers?

Let us rather say: the philosophy of a resigned mystic, who clothed his personal mysticism in a Cartesian conceptual framework, a philosophy of escape, a theory of freedom attainable through the spiritual negation of the finite order of the world.

But we know, of course, that this is only one face of Spinoza's world. The same man who commanded us to humble ourselves in ecstasy before the unchangeable order of once-and-for-all foregone events, who commanded us to adore a perfectly indifferent divinity and to look for liberation in intellectual adaptation to a world in which everything has already occurred that can occur—this man was also an aggressive theoretician of the liberal party in the Netherlands, a defender of tolerance and political freedom, a partisan supporter of the republican movement, the author of the *Theologico-political Treatise,* a scathing critic of churches and theologians.

This difference in attitude is to be explained to some extent by chronology, but not entirely. In the metaphysics itself one can catch the most general formula of that ambiguity which turns up both in the life of the philosopher and in his moral philosophy. Perhaps it is impossible to reconcile a view of the world in which all individual things have no existence of their own, but are utterly absorbed by the divine absolute, with that other one, where each thing contains in itself an unchanging instinct for self-preservation and yields to destruction only under constraint of a superior force. Both these trends find expression in the recommendations which in turn command man to flee before his own finiteness and to seek liberation in the ultimate intuition which unites him with the absolute, and then advise him to be mindful of his self-interest, of the preservation of his body and soul, not hesitating in case of need to make use of silence, subterfuge, and half-truths.

To be sure, these differences of perspective may be explained in part by the fact that the greatest goods of life, attainable only through the persistent efforts of the intellect, according to Spinoza, are in any case to be allotted only to a few. Those for whom everyday affections do not overshadow the genuine order of goods cannot be at odds with each other; not that this is a transcendental order, established by nature in normative form, but because "good" means a quality completely consistent with human nature, something that intensifies existence or nourishes the soul. Such people appreciate those values that everyone may enjoy on an equal basis, those the possession of which by some does not curtail their possession by others; values of a cognition adapted to the thing itself, of a cognition in the perspective of eternity. There are, however, few such people, and there is no reason to limit reflection on the human world to affairs that are important only for that élite.

Collective living demands rules which appeal to the factually active, most commonly met inclinations of human nature, and require that, whether we praise them or blame them, we must, as a reality, take cognizance of them. It is improper to imagine to ourselves that a world of social arrangements can be sensibly projected in reliance upon the supposition that everyone can be free in the sense in which freedom is participation in the cosmic indifference of the perfect being.

Let us consider, then, the freedom which does not depend on a purely cognitive relationship to such a world as is given, but to that second, more modest, kind—freedom in the same sense that Hobbes used that word but still without contradicting the rigorousness of his own belief in universal causality. Freedom thus understood is not a quality of man—whether innate or acquired—but a quality of the situation in which the human individual circulates, namely, it is simply the absence of obstacles which would not allow him to do exactly what he wants to do (a condition which does not require, of course, that his desire be a spontaneity unordered by conditions). The main question in this area concerns precisely this: since there is no superior law which could limit an individual in anything *a priori,* or could regulate the individual's actions (the scope of rights is equal to the scope of power), how can one arrange it so that collective life, limiting as little as possible the freedom of individual actions, would at the same time avert the universal war which would otherwise necessarily arise?

The answer is simple—at least in its general theoretic formulation: remove the tyranny of the churches, competing with the power of governments; resist the pretensions of the clergy, who in the name of the infallibility of their dogma try to shackle the entire world in the collar of their catechisms; establish religious tolerance and freedom of speech for everyone; maintain free trade and free thought; combat fanaticism, superstition, aspirations to a monopoly on truth. But even these rules require limitations: the complete freedom of religious belief cannot be so understood as to extend to everything that someone's caprice would want to recognize as part of the religious code—for then license would know no limitations. It is necessary to have a certain form of official religious cult—a frequently recurring idea at that epoch among people who were tired and disenchanted with one-and-a-half centuries of religious wars. Such a cult, subordinate to the sovereignty of civil authority, hence incapable of being changed into clerical despotism, would be extremely poor as far as material content goes and would comprise only such beliefs as everyone would accept, although each could interpret them in his own fashion: even the philosopher himself would agree that God exists and that he rewards or punishes for human actions, although in the current sense he does not believe in God, much less in his legislative and executive power. But it is not that that is important; let each person grasp the truths of faith as he wishes, as long as he has preserved fidelity to his obligations before his fellow men, has worked side by side with them in mutual enterprises, and has held back from inflicting suffering and injury. An official religion in its effective contents would be no different, then, from a collection of rudimentary regulations of customs and manners, and would not threaten the tolerant structure of the government. The Bible is suitable for use in such a cult—not because it contains any sort of truths about the world, because it does not contain any, but because recorded in it are the simplest sorts of instructions concerning human coexistence, which a simple man can more easily swallow in the form of anecdotes than if he had to laboriously arrive at them through philosophical inquiry. It is certain at the outset that the majority of the human mob will preserve its superstitious beliefs, that it will preserve its faith in God, the father and protector, governor of the world, faith in the continuance of the individual after death, in heaven and hell. But there is nothing wrong in this if such faith—as long as it is free from fanaticism and hatred for those of other faiths—accomplishes what cannot be accomplished on a collective scale through philosophical reflection, that is, if it restrains harmful passions and subdues innate greed, thirst for power, selfishness.

This is the way it looks when we place Spinoza's adjurations in the purely philosophical order in which his moral philosophy belongs. They are then vague and sterile, somewhat banal; it is otherwise when we attempt to understand them also from the perspective of the political conflict with which the writings of the philosopher were entangled.

Up to the time when the curse of the Jewish community reached him, Spinoza moved about in an atmosphere of republican free thought. Above all this was the result of his contacts with Francis van dan Ende; this ex-Jesuit, scoffer, political radical, enemy of the Church and of monarchy, believed in the absolute sovereignty of the people, and later, involved in a conspiracy against the king in France, he bore witness to his convictions, giving up his head beneath the axe. It is quite possible that Spinoza's religious views served rather as a pretext for his excommunication, the real reason being his republican opinions which somehow came to light—dangerous for the unity of the Jewish community, which traditionally sympathized with the House of Orange. Won over to the side of cosmopolitan free thought, the young philosopher soon came into contact with leaders of the republic—the form of government then in power in the Netherlands, but always shakily, always at odds with the aspirations of the Calvinistic clergy and the monarchical pretensions of the House of Orange. The *Theologico-political Treatise* was at the same time a criticism of the Jews who pretended to a select place in history, a criticism of Christianity and its pretensions to infallibility, a criticism of the churches as disseminators of superstition and obscurantism, a defense of tolerance, democracy, a republican style in politics. It corresponded in its essential shape to the doctrine which was being espoused by the brothers de la Court—theoreticians of the Republic —in their political and economic dissertations. Thus the leading idea of the work was not revolutionary; rather it contributed to the strengthening of the factually governing, though weak and badly organized, party, supported by the interests of the liberal, peacefully inclined, tolerantly oriented commercial elements in the most developed cities of the United Provinces. The population, however, in its majority, was undesirous of an enlightened governing élite, and several times it betrayed its sympathies, fostered by all possible means by the Calvinist clergy for the princes of the House of Orange. The Protestant customs, so hated by the philosopher, effectively organized the resentments of the underprivileged classes and in moments of disrupted equilibrium provided the chances for the mass support for a conservative revolution which did in fact come about, in the year 1672, at a moment of military defeat. The freethinking patriciate, the tolerant republicans, the sympathizers with Arminianism in theology—all these turned out in time of crisis to be without popular support. The leaders of the republican oligarchy, the brothers de Witt, fell victims to a vicious mob and were pulled to pieces on the streets of the Hague by the fanaticized crowd. The question of democracy had to be considered all over again. If democracy had to depend on the unbridled force of a rabble yielding submissively to the cries of demagogues, what sort of arguments could be cited in its favor by the philosopher, a sympathizer with the liberal and freethinking, but prosperous regents? Spinoza defended democracy in his *Treatise,* published in 1670. In no place, however, did he defend revolution in the name of democracy; important for him was not merely freedom, but also stability of authority, hence he deemed it better to obey tyrannical governments than to overthrow them by force. After all, the democracy which he defended was from the beginning, as he understood it, a system of reason rather than a system of power exercised by the majority; from the beginning also, suspicion, or even contempt for the ignorant mob radiates much too clearly from his writings for him to pass for the spokesman of the revolutionary tribunals. He was more concerned with disseminating the *feeling* of freedom than freedom itself, so that, in accordance with the advice of the master of Florence, rational authority would direct people in such a way that it would *seem* to the subjects that they were really in control of themselves. For a measure of genuine freedom and a measure of good judgment, Spinoza was never able to find a harmonious formula, just as he was not able to find one which would have united his advice for tolerance without contradicting the need for the stability of governments. At a time when all the condemned political tendencies of that day had found a voice—the independent role of a regular army, the theocratic aspirations of the clergy, the fanaticism of the rabble—the theory of freedom needed revision. Spinoza undertook this in part in his unfinished *Political Treatise,* which poses questions articulated in a somewhat different way than the renowned earlier dissertation, published in the name of the continued existence of republican power. True to his refusal to undertake active political dissent, the philosopher started to consider, not so much what form of government in general is the most perfect, but rather in what way the continuance of various particular forms of government can be preserved—including the monarchical—together with the simultaneous maintenance of such a sum of political freedoms as are conceivable in given circumstances, always assuming that among the people, blind passions and unthinking desires will always be stronger than sober reflection and rational calculation. One should not, therefore, project anything based on the assumption that human behavior will be subject to the force of reason, but rather harness these untamed emotions and exploit them in the service of the public good.

Let us summarize.

Freedom as Spinoza understands it, if it is possible at all, is no quality of human nature, is not, in particular, a capacity for unconditioned spontaneity, that is, so-called free will; the will is a theoretical abstraction: there exist only individual acts of wishing, and these are ordered inevitably by the entirety of the situation in which they occur.

Nor can freedom be a right of man, which in the name of higher values it would be necessary to reclaim, for there are no rights different from the force with which each person is capable of imposing his own desires upon actual situations.

We are free in our voluntary agreement upon eternal and unchanging harmony of an indifferent and aimlessly operating nature.

This is negative freedom—independence from superstition, from anger, from despair and vain sorrow, from fear of death and the threat of hell. It is also positive freedom: the happiness of taking conscious part in the eternal essence of the highest being, with which the effort of ultimate intuition and intellectual love for the cosmic order unite us. Such freedom is attainable at the cost of resignation— not from external goods only, but also from personal self-assertion, hence simply from individuality. Theoretically available to everyone, in fact it is perhaps only the lot of a select few. It is the highest result of intellectual effort, it is then available and may be complete independently of any situation of one who possessed it. It is limitlessly resistant to the pressure of events, insensible to the blows of predestination.

But it is not thus that Spinoza characterizes freedom where he most frequently has recourse to this word. *Free* is the thing whose actions are not ordered by the pressure of external circumstances. Freedom so conceived thus also characterizes a situation, but a situation which understanding alone does not assure. God is free in this sense, but can one ascribe freedom thus understood to human existence? The philosopher answers in the affirmative, not noticing, it appears, the contradictions between this belief and his own assurances of the powerlessness of human existence in the face of external causes, of the inevitable, observational, but never causative, role of consciousness in physical actions. Between the utterly interiorized freedom of a Cartesianizing mystic and the positive freedom which confirms individuality in its instinct for self-preservation, there is no point of conciliation. These are the two faces of Spinoza's thought —one directing a retreating glance toward the all-engulfing power of the absolute, the other concentrated on a view of the world of finite things, observed through the rationalistic dispassionateness of a scientist. The inconsistent silhouette of the philosopher, apostle of deduction and unsuccessful imitator of Euclid in the area of metaphysics, can be explained by the inconsistent thread in his biography. His connections with the petty bourgeois mysticism of the freethinking sectarians and his connections with the republican bourgeoisie probably determine the dual track of Spinoza's thought, at least in its leading tendencies.

That same coexistence of motifs poorly suited to one another can be noted in his political doctrine, hence in the theory of freedom viewed as a situation of an individual confronted by social institutions. The competition between inconsistent tendencies reveals itself there as an unceasing vacillation between sympathy for the disinherited and hatred for the ignorant rabble full of incalculable impulses, between the desire for the broadest tolerance and the demand for the preservation of a stable oligarchy of sensible people, unreceptive to fanaticism and dogmatism.

The chimerical and plainly fantastic hope that reason would be able to capacitate man to everything to which profitable emotions could push him, is at the least so limited that it relates at the outset only to a few. Thus Spinoza does not have any pretensions that one could adjudicate upon political systems with its help. But the supposition obtrudes itself that those freedoms which he preserves for the spiritual aristocracy and those which he would want to defend for simpletons are not coterminous at any point. An act of free identification with idealized cosmic order already assumes that value in the presence of which all others wane and grow indifferent; a sage does not experience any lack and it is uncertain in what respect bondage and physical constraint could lessen his authentic freedom. One in turn for whom the immediate freedoms of political life are an essential value, one for whom freedom must be secured, since he himself is unable to secure it, is probably already unable to avail himself of the most perfect form of liberation.

Thus there is no harmony in the final version of Spinoza's doctrine, and its ambiguity and internal dissension bear abundant fruit in the following century. In a simplified schema the "German reception," or, more generally, the pantheistic reception, takes from the philosopher the motif of the whole and the part, hope for ultimate reconciliation with the absolute through the mystical renunciation of individual affirmation. The "French reception" fortifies the threads of republican free thought, generalizes the slogans of liberty, repeats with satisfaction the sallies against the clergy and the church. The optics of a political radical and the optics of a metaphysician trying to tame infinite being: two points of view so different that it would indeed be highhanded to reproach the inconsistency of the philosophy on this point and its lack of a synthetic portrait of the world: as if anyone in history had actually succeeded in bringing that double observational standpoint—directed toward being and toward the object—into union with one another. After all, Spinoza said, or rather repeated after Epictetus, our entire happiness or misery depends exclusively on the quality of the thing to which we address our love:

and he conceded at the same time that he had not at all managed to rid himself of attachment to those paltry goods which rational sense commands us to repudiate. He was thus conscious of the fact that the metaphysical eye does not converge with the scientific or the political eye; he looked with one and the other, and saw with each in a different way. Thus he saw even freedom alternately, now in haughty resignation from everything that the world of objects can present, now in a situation amid objects among which one can pick by dint of understanding and sensible effort. He knew that he was, whether or not he wanted to be so, a part of the human world, embroiled in its conflicts, responsibilities, and disturbances, and at the same time he desired—the mystic who had cast aside God and had repudiated belief in immortality—to negate his finitude and to somehow touch being itself. He even imagined that he had attained his goal, but at times he was brought into confusion by the gnawing questions of his penetrating friends. Whether he died with a feeling of satisfaction or of defeat, we will never learn.

PART THREE
The Nature of Man and Society

Spinoza and the Idea of Freedom

STUART HAMPSHIRE

I believe that everyone who has ever written about Spinoza, and who has tried to interpret his thought as a whole, either has been, or ought to have been, uneasily aware of some partiality in his interpretation, when he turns once again from his own words to the original. Certainly this is my own position. When the study of Spinoza is reviewed historically, one sees that each commentator, unconsciously faithful to his own age and to his own philosophical culture, has seized upon some one element in Spinoza's thought; he then proceeds to develop the whole of the philosophy from this single centre. Spinoza as the critic of Cartesianism: Spinoza as the free-thinker and destroyer of Judaeo-Christian theology: Spinoza as the pure deductive metaphysician: Spinoza as the near-mystic, who imagines a level of intuitive understanding beyond discursive reason: lastly, Spinoza as the scientific determinist, who anticipates the more crude materialists, and the more crude secular moralists, of the nineteenth century: as the precursor of George Henry Lewes. All these masks have been fitted on him and each of them does to some extent fit. But they remain masks, and not the living face. They do not show the moving tensions and unresolved conflicts in Spinoza's *Ethics*. They remain interpretations that have been imposed from outside. They smooth over and cover up the opposing strains within the original thought. His writing has a hard, finished, unyielding surface. One can return to it again and again without ever being sure that one has penetrated to the centre of his intentions. He could only state; he could not loosely explain, or betray his intentions in an approximation. Yet I have the persisting feeling—I cannot yet properly call it a belief— that in the philosophy of mind he is nearer to the truth at certain points than any other philosopher ever has been. I do not therefore propose historical accuracy and historical justice as motives for returning once again to the original *Ethics* at one of its most diffi-

Proceedings of the British Academy, 46 (1960). Reprinted by permission of the author and of the British Academy.

cult points. Rather I believe that there is something very relevant to moral and political philosophy at this time to be learnt from an entirely literal, unprejudiced, and uncondescending attention to Spinoza's idea of freedom. Perhaps his conception of freedom is after all a valid one; and perhaps we are now in a better position than our ancestors to find the true significance of it.

The two most obvious facts about Spinoza are the two most important facts in understanding his intentions: first, that his definitive philosophical work was justly called *Ethics:* second, that the only evaluative distinction finally recognized in his philosophy, other than the distinctions between true and false, and between adequate and inadequate, ideas, is the distinction between freedom and servitude. These are the terms, positive and negative, in which a man, and a man's life, his actions and passions, are to be finally judged. These are the terms in which a wise man reviews and criticizes his own conduct, his own emotions and attitudes, and it is by reference to this contrast that he will, if he is wise, make his own decisions. A man is wise in proportion as his thought at all times proceeds by active reasoning from premises that are well known to him as self-evident truths. These self-evident truths are necessarily available to him, as instruments for his enlightenment, among the many confused and inadequate ideas that he must also have. They are necessarily available to every thinking being, as the reflections in his thought of the universal and unchanging features of the natural order of extended things. His inadequate ideas reflect only his particular and temporary standpoint as one extended thing among others. If once he concentrates his attention on these timeless truths, independent of his own standpoint and perceptions, and argues carefully from them, he cannot help coming to the conclusion that human conduct has to be judged, and his own decisions made, by reference to this single standard, the standard of freedom of mind as opposed to servitude of mind; and he will unavoidably agree that the distinction between freedom and its opposite is the distinction between active reasoning, internally determined, and the mind's passive reception of ideas impressed upon it from without.

"He cannot help coming to the conclusion," "He will unavoidably agree that it *must* be interpreted"—here already there are the signs of necessity. As soon as we start to argue strictly, these and other signs of necessity will always enter in. As will be seen later, these marks of necessity, rightly understood and in the appropriate context, are the marks of freedom and activity of mind. The mind is active and free when, and only when, the argument is strict, when the conclusion of a passage of thought is internally determined by the thinking process itself. A man whose attention has been drawn to self-evident, primary truths, the terms of which he understands, will unavoidably follow a continuous train of thought and will unavoidably affirm the necessary conclusions. If he fully understands, he has no choice. If he has a choice, and if he can doubt and hesitate until he settles the matter by a decision, his conclusion will be determined, at least in part, by something that is external to the thinking process itself.

Some of these primary truths are concerned with the notion of cause or of explanation, in the widest sense of these words. In the widest sense of the word "cause," anything that is an appropriate answer to the question "Why?" gives a cause, irrespective of the category to which the thing to be explained belongs. The question "Why?" may, for example, be asked with reference to a belief, a human action, a human attitude or sentiment, the existence of a physical object, or the properties of numbers and geometrical figures. Anything that counts as an answer to the question "Why?" is an explanation, whether true or false, of the belief, action, attitude, sentiment, physical object, or mathematical entity. In the vocabulary that Spinoza inherited, the word "cause" can be substituted for the word "explanation," without prejudging any questions about the type of explanation appropriate to these different cases. The distinguishing of different types, or categories, of causes, which is the distinguishing of different types or categories of explanation, has always been the proper work of philosophy, and of that reflexive knowledge that is peculiar to philosophy. Spinoza draws these distinctions between types of explanation in the *Ethics,* adapting an inherited scholastic vocabulary for his own purpose.

Let us assume the standpoint of an individual thinker, a finite mode, with his necessarily limited knowledge. Reflecting on the range of his knowledge, he will find at least one clear distinction: the distinction between an understanding of causes that is complete and self-justifying, and an understanding of causes that is not complete and self-justifying. There are ideas in reference to which the question "Why is it so?" receives a complete answer, in the sense that, in looking for the explanation, we arrive at self-evident truths, and definitions, in a finite number of steps. There are other ideas in reference to which the question "Why is it so?" leads us back along an infinite series of ideas, with no final and sufficient explanation to be found within the series, however long we continue. So much is common to Leibniz and Spinoza. They diverge when they specify the limits of application of the two orders of explanation, the complete and the incomplete. For Spinoza the fundamental difference between the two orders of causes is the difference between the series of eternal things and the series of things that come into existence and pass away at a certain time. There is no further difference between the two orders of explanation which is not entailed by this primary difference. There is no ultimate contingency in the existence of things in the common order of nature, no contingency imputable to a creator's free choice among logically possible alternatives. The difference is only between that which is eternal and that which is finite in its existence. The existence of things that are not eternal, and that occupy a determinate position in the time-order, can only be incompletely explained. There must always be an infinite regress of causes required to explain why this particular thing exists at this particular time. The existence of this thing was contingent upon the prior existence of some other thing and so on *ad infinitum.* No limit can be set on the universe of individual things that come into existence and pass away. But there are objects conceived as eternal things, about which it does not make sense to ask when they came into existence and when they will perish: numbers, for example, or the whole of extended Nature, which can be referred to as a thing, as *Res extensa.* About such things an explanation can be given of why their properties must be ordered as they are, an explanation that will terminate in self-evident, primary propositions defining the nature of the objects referred to.

This distinction between the two orders of explanation, the two kinds of answer to "Why is it so?", the temporal and the non-temporal order, corresponds to Leibniz's distinction between truths of reason and truths of fact, and also to familiar post-Kantian distinctions between analytic and synthetic propositions. But it is a different distinction, not the same distinction with a different label. Every philosopher has to draw some similar line between the two types of knowledge. As the chosen ground of distinction differs, the line will fall in a different place and will suggest different groupings and exclusions. Spinoza expresses the distinction, not only as a distinction between different types of object, eternal things and finite things, but also as a distinction between the ways in which any given subject-matter can be studied. Whether we are inquiring into human emotions, including our own emotions, or into the nature and movements of physical objects, we can always, if we choose, look for the eternally valid laws that explain the variety of human emotions and the movements of physical objects. We can always regard the particular case of an emotion or of a physical movement, occurring at exactly this time and soon to disappear, as an instance, or illustration, of a constant, unchanging pattern. Such a pattern has its own ultimate explanation in the permanent structure of things. We can always regard the thing to be explained *sub specie aeternitatis,* without attention to the date on which it occurred, or to the standpoint from which it was observed, and not *sub specie durationis,* which would involve explaining its place in the time-order that leads up to this particular occasion. If we are interested only in ourselves and in our own environment, and therefore in the occurrence of the emotion, or of the physical movement, at this particular time, and if we wish to trace the causes in their historical sequence up to this moment, we will of course need to invoke the eternally valid laws in looking for the historical explanation of this particular case. But the interest is then an historical interest, and this is an interest that can never be finally satisfied. Some uncertainty will always attach to any historical explanation that we attempt. Some of the infinitely numerous factors, which should ideally have been mentioned, have always eluded us. We fall into error, and an error that has serious consequences in our practical activities, if we do not always bear in mind the intrinsic difference between the two types of explanation, the two orders of causes, the intellectual order and the common order of nature. We must always be aware of the incompleteness and necessary uncertainty of any historical explanation of things in the common order of nature. Intellectually, the error is to take some cause picked out from the temporal sequence of events and to concentrate our attention upon it as *the* cause, and then to suppose that we can know that, if only this had been different, which it might have been, the effect would never have followed. Then it will seem to us contingent that things happened as they did. But the appearance of contingency is due to the necessary limitation of our knowledge, to our incapacity to follow to its conclusion every path of investigation, where the paths are infinitely many. When we isolate some one cause as the sole object of interest, and think of it as something that really might have been different, we are simply failing to realize the infinite complexity of the connections between things in the temporal order. Practically and morally, the corresponding error will be to love or to hate with blind concentration the particular thing which, through weakness of mind, has become isolated in our thought from the infinitely complex network in the common order of nature. Instead of being detached and sceptical in reflecting on the infinite complexity of the causes, we shall be uncritically certain that we have identified the original good or evil within our own environment. We shall therefore for a time tend to act as if our welfare depended solely on the destruction or preservation of this particular thing. Our conduct will for a time correspondingly exhibit the same blind and helpless partiality, the same imaginative obsession with one thing, suggested to us by our environment, as the true cause of our present pleasure or suffering.

Most men spend their lives in an alternation between one object and another as the temporary object of desire or aversion, absorbed in their own partial view of their own environment, and unable to see this environment, and their own passive reactions to it, as formed by a concatenation of causes that extends infinitely in every direction. They have therefore no consistent plan, no stable and central direction of their interests. This alternation of desires, this fluctuation of the mind, is the state of fantasy, obsession, and unenlightenment. The mind is then to a greater or less degree disintegrated, in the sense that the succession of its states is not determined by the subject's own activity of thought. Their states of mind are only to be explained as more or less unconnected responses of their imagination to the stimulus of the environment, which evokes desires and aversions that have no adequate foundation in the subject's own directed reasoning. This condition of unfreedom, of slavery to the passions, is the equivalent in Spinoza of the heteronomy of the will in Kant. But it is not an enslavement of the will, but rather of the understanding. The remedy is the correction of the understanding and an appeal to its natural powers. The remedy is available to everyone who is able to reflect upon, and who never forgets, the two levels of explanation, the two orders of causes, and therefore the two kinds of knowledge which each man necessarily possesses. As long as a man is reflectively aware, whenever he thinks, of the nature of his own thought, as either actively directed towards eternal and demonstrable truths, or else as absorbed in uncriticized fantasies traceable to his own sensations and memories, he is not misled either in that which he claims to know with certainty, or in that which he considers desirable or undesirable, as good or bad. He will reflectively examine the reasons for his own desires and aversions, and he will distinguish those that are to be explained as the effects of events on his imagination, from those that are explained by an active consideration, independent of his own situation, of the tendency of an object to serve the purposes common to all thinking beings as such. Because he knows when he truly knows and when he only incompletely knows, he always knows when he has an entirely sufficient reason for his actions and attitudes, and when he has not. As he is by nature an active thinking being, he will prefer the type of explanation of things that is complete and intellectually satisfying when it is presented to him. As a body naturally tends to maintain itself, and restore itself, against the effects of the environment, so correspondingly a mind tends to assert its power of thought, and to prefer rational argument, whenever it is presented, to the passive association of ideas in the common order of nature. But we need to be awakened to the recognition and the use of the powers that our minds possess. This is part of the work of a philosopher, which includes, as in the example of Spinoza's own writing, exhortation, a call to reflection, alongside purely intellectual analysis.

Perhaps this picture of the free man as self-directing, as an integrated mind with a continuous controlling reason, is so far a clear one. But the notion of freedom itself is still unclarified: what is the precise connection between a man's knowledge of the distinction between different levels of knowledge and his freedom in action? The connection is to be found in Spinoza's theory of individuals. Like every other identifiable particular thing in the natural order, a man tries in his characteristic activity to preserve himself and his own distinct nature as an individual, and to increase his own power and activity in relation to his environment. This trying (*conatus*), or inner force of self-preservation, is that which makes any individual an individual. Regarded as a physical organism, his overriding interest is to preserve his own stability as a distinct organism in relation to the physical environment. Regarded as a thinking being, his overriding interest is to preserve the coherence and continuity of his own thought against the flow of unconnected ideas which are his perceptions, sensations, and imaginations. The conatus of the individual, conceived as a physical organism, is the body's tendency to repair itself and to maintain itself in relation to the environment. The conatus of the individual, conceived as a thinking being, is the *vis animi,* which is the essential and natural tendency of the mind to assert active thinking and knowledge against the passive association of ideas in imagination. The more the sequence of a man's own ideas can be explained without reference to causes outside his own thinking, the more active and self-determining he is, regarded as a thinking being. The more active and self-determining he is, to that degree also he can be more properly regarded as a distinct thing, having an individuality that sets him apart from his particular environment. The more self-determining and active he is, and the more free, in this sense of "free," the more he can be regarded as a real individual, real as an individual thinking being.

Because a thing's reality as a distinct individual depends on its activity and freedom, Spinoza must take the word "free," rather than the word "good," as the fundamental term of evaluation. He is a scholastic and an Aristotelian in taking it for granted that praise and evaluation of a thing are necessarily an assessment of the degree to which it realizes its nature or essence in its activity. The nearer a thing approaches perfection in the activity proper to it, the more praiseworthy it is. He takes the virtue, objectively regarded, of any thing to be the same as the perfect realization of its nature. But, unlike Aristotle, he identifies the essential nature of any individual thing with its individuality, with that which makes it a distinct individual: and this is its power of self-maintenance in relation to other things. Its virtue is its power as an individual. A particular thing's nature or essence is its nature or essence as a distinct individual rather than as a specimen of a kind. Peter or Paul are therefore not to be judged as being more or less good men, that is, as realizing more or less completely the potentialities of their species. They are to be judged as more or less complete individuals, that is, as more or less distinguishable as active agents from the temporary influences of their environment in the common order of nature. A man's natural tendency or conatus is not to make himself a good or perfect specimen of his kind, to realize in his activity some general ideal of humanity, but rather to preserve himself, this individual, as an active being, who is, as far as possible, independent in his activity. He has achieved virtue, and succeeded in that which he necessarily desires, when, and only when, he is comparatively free and self-determining in his activity. He would be a perfect being, if he were perfectly self-determining, active, and free. His happiness, and enjoyment of action, does not depend on a choice of ends of action that he, as an individual, has to make and that he is free to make: the choice of whether to pursue the ideal of excellence that is proper to his species. In the last analysis, and speaking philosophically, there is no such choice of an ideal or end. Philosophically speaking, the choice is of the right means to an end that is already determined for him by his nature and appetites as an individual thinking and physical thing. The real choice is between the first step of reflection, preliminary to the use of his intellectual powers, and an undirected passive response to experience. His desires, as they emerge into consciousness, are determined by the thought of the causes of his pleasure and suffering. If the thought is confused, and is largely fantasy, he will pursue, *sub specie boni,* temporary ends, which, by the laws of his nature, must lead to frustration, instability, and suffering. Therefore he needs to be stirred to take this first step of reflection. His happiness consists in his sense of his activities as having their originating cause within him, and in his enjoyment of his own activity as unimpeded activity. He is frustrated, and therefore suffers, when his activity is not self-directed, but is rather the immediate effect of causes external to himself. The suffering is the loss of his sense of his own power and vitality as a distinct and active being.

The notion of an individual nature or essence may be found altogether obscure. We can, I think, still attach a sense to the notion of the essential characteristics of a species, and to the judgement of individuals as more or less perfect specimens of their kinds. But can we intelligibly speak of an individual or particular thing becoming more or less of an individual? Spinoza provides a criterion by which the approach in perfection of an individual *qua* individual is to be judged: the criterion is the degree to which the individual is active and self-determining. Any thing that is identifiable as a particular thing can be judged by this single criterion, irrespective of the kind to which it is allotted within conventional classifications. One may review the scale of the increasing activity and self-determination of particular things, and therefore of their increasing individuality, from physical objects of various orders of complexity, to living organisms, to human beings. Human beings, at the top of the scale, can be completely self-determining when their activity is continuous thought, with each idea following its predecessor, in the intellectual sense of "follow" as well as in the temporal sense. At such moments—and the moments cannot be indefinitely prolonged—men rise above their normal human condition as finite modes.

In the ordinary vocabulary we conventionally classify things into kinds according to their typical human uses. Spinoza demands that, as moralists and philosophers, we should see through these anthropocentric classifications to the true individuality of particular things. When we group them into kinds, we should follow this single principle in differentiating the kinds: their characteristic power and form of self-maintenance as individuals. From the standpoint of the true natural philosopher, the natural order should be seen as a system of individuals within individuals, of increasing power and complexity, each type of individual differentiated by its characteristic activity in self-maintenance. The more fully we study and understand particular things, not as specimens of the conventionally recognized kinds, but as types of structure each acting and maintaining their identity according to the laws of the type, the more we shall understand Nature as a whole. This is the form in which natural knowledge, objectively valid for the whole of Nature, is properly to be expressed. Psychology as a science can be no exception.

There is one case in which each man is well qualified to achieve such a true understanding of an individual: himself. Starting from this secure example, he can work outwards towards a true and objective understanding of Nature as a whole. He will become dissatisfied with the conventional classifications of things by their ordinary human uses, and he will find a more objective and truly scientific principle of classification in their various modes of self-maintenance. Spinoza's objective study of the emotions, the outline of a psychopathology, illustrates these principles. There are systematic connections, laws of unconscious memory, to be found behind the conventional classifications of the passions. Systematic knowledge of these laws is the necessary first step to useful self-knowledge.

It is now possible to state the connection between a constant awareness of the distinction between adequate and inadequate knowledge and the notion of freedom. We need to apply the doctrine of the individual as essentially active to a thinking being who is a person. For every belief that I have, and for every claim to knowledge that I make, there is an explanation of why I have this belief and why I claim to have this knowledge. Every passion that can be attributed to me is a pleasure or a pain combined with an idea of the cause of this pleasure or pain. There must therefore be an explanation of my having this idea about the cause of my pleasure or suffering. Suppose then that I am at all times asking myself the question —Is the sequence of ideas that has terminated in this idea a self-contained sequence that, by itself, completely explains my idea of the cause? In other words, was the conclusion reached by a rational process? Or must I mention ideas that are associated in my experience, but that are without intrinsic connection, in explaining my conclusion? Under these conditions of self-conscious reflection, I never affirm a proposition, or commit myself to a belief, without qualifying it as adequately or inadequately founded. If this condition were fulfilled, I could not be a victim of those passions that consist in the association of my pleasure or suffering with the idea of a particular transient thing, or person, in the common order of nature as its adequate cause. And when I say that I *could* not be a victim of the passion, the impossibility here is a logical impossibility. The unexamined links of association, which are necessary to the belief that is part of the passion, depend for their existence on my not being reflectively aware of them. As soon as I am self-consciously aware of them, I must then know that it is only through the fantasies engendered by my particular history that my present pleasure or suffering has become associated in my mind with the idea of these particular things or persons, which I now in consequence hate or love. If I actively inquire into the true causes of my pleasure or suffering, the passive association of ideas is broken, and the attention focused on the particular thing, or person, as the adequate cause is dissolved. An emotion necessarily involves a thought of the cause or occasion of the pleasure or unpleasure, and it is in this sense directed towards an object. Spinoza's theory of the emotions represents them as states of pleasure or unpleasure, and of desire and aversion, combined with a thought of the causes, simple or complex, of the pleasure or unpleasure. To change the accompanying thought is therefore to change the emotion, and therefore to change the desire or the aversion that determines conduct. Suppose that I am angry with someone and am angry about something that he has done. To be angry is to be displeased and to be disposed to injure someone, together with the thought that he has been the cause of injury to me. When I consider my true interests as an active thinking being, and also examine a train of unconscious associations that leads to the idea of him as the original cause of my displeasure, and recognize the inadequacy of the idea, the passion of anger disappears. When I realize the contributing causes of my displeasure in my own unconscious memories and consequent dispositions, the idea of an adequate external cause disappears, and there is nothing left to be angry with. When on reflection I realize that no one external thing can be isolated as the cause of my displeasure, I not only realize my error in imagining a simple external cause of my state: I open the way to the activity of intellectual inquiry, regarding this particular case wholly as an instance of general laws. I thereby substitute the active enjoyment of my own powers of thought for the suffering associated with my imagination of an adequate external cause of my displeasure.

To interpret Spinoza as expecting emancipation solely from an intellectual understanding of causes is not entirely correct. It is equally incorrect to represent him as defining freedom simply as knowledge of the causes that determine my emotions and actions. Reason is the expression of my primary desire of self-assertion as a thinking being, of the urge to extend my own activity and freedom as far as I can. I am to the highest degree free when I am engaged in an intellectual inquiry, and when the subject of this inquiry is the order of my thought, as an instance of something that may be understood *sub specie aeternitatis,* and not as it is affected by particular causes in the common order of nature. My happiness then consists, first, in immunity from hatred of particular things, and from the other negative and depressive passions, as an immunity that an adequate understanding of causes necessarily brings: secondly, it consists in the positive enjoyment of my own freedom *as* freedom, as the active exercise of the power of thought. These two necessary conditions of happiness, which may be distinguished in other philosophies, are inseparable, even if distinguishable, in Spinoza's thought. He is often represented as implausibly asserting that knowledge of the causes of suffering by itself brings liberation from suffering. This is a double over-simplification. First, the liberation consists in the substitution of a free activity and of self-assertion, which is as such enjoyable, for a passive reaction, which is as such depressing and frustrating. Secondly, in the definition of any of the passions the pleasure or suffering, and the thought of its cause, are indissolubly connected. If the confused thought, or imagination, of an external cause is replaced by thought in an intellectual order, an active emotion replaces a passion.

We may now ask whether, and with what qualifications, this idea of human freedom is still defensible, and whether it suggests the true grounds of our present interest in the freedom of the individual as the main end of policy, both in private and political affairs. Let it be remembered that a man is most free, according to Spinoza, and also feels himself to be most free, when he cannot help drawing a certain conclusion, and cannot help embarking on a certain course of action in view of the evidently compelling reasons in favour of it. He has a compelling reason for following a certain course of action when he knows with certainty that it will promote his power and freedom as an active thinking being, and therefore that it will promote his enjoyment of his own existence. Then he cannot hesitate. The issue is decided for him without any need for the exercise of his will in decision, exactly as the issue is decided for him when the arguments in support of a theoretical conclusion are conclusive arguments. The only difference between theoretical conclusions and practical decisions is that the latter are always governed by the agent's desire for his own good, rationally or irrationally interpreted. When a man finds himself divided in mind between conflicting and inconclusive arguments, and between conflicting inclinations, he is, and feels himself to be, so much less a free man in his affirmations and in his actions. In such a case that which has determined his final decision, whatever it is, must be, at least in part, external to his own thought. In such cases some explanation could always in principle be given, a cause found in the common order of nature, for his deciding as he did. But it would not be a complete explanation of the right kind, namely, something that was present to his mind as a universally sufficient ground. He was moved to affirmation or action by something that was outside the rational sequence of thought. He was not entirely active and self-determining, but, at least in part, unknowing and passive in his motivation, since that which moved him to action was below the level of conscious thought. He was not altogether free in his decision, and he knows and feels that he was not, because he did not himself recognize its necessity. When some part of the explanation of my believing something, or of my doing something, is to be found in a cause unrecognized by my reason, and in something external to my thought, I had not sufficient grounds for my belief or action. If I have a full awareness of the adequate explanation of my affirming or acting, I necessarily have sufficient grounds for my affirmation or action. The knowledge of the necessity of affirming something, or of doing something, by itself converts an external cause into an inner ground of affirmation or action. If I know clearly why I believe something or why I am doing something, I must have my own sufficient reasons for affirming or doing. If I cannot completely explain why I reach the conclusion, and if I allow that there are other possibilities open to me, my conclusion, whatever it is, will have been motivated by something other than my own reasoning.

It should now be evident that the too simple question "Was Spinoza a determinist?" admits of no clear answer. The doctrine of the two orders of causes, the intellectual and the temporal orders, by itself makes the question indeterminate—almost meaningless. But there is a question that always lies behind any mention of "determinism" and that certainly is worth asking: "Did Spinoza provide clear and acceptable grounds for familiar moral distinctions? Or is his idea of human freedom incompatible with the acceptance of any familiar moral distinctions?" We cannot answer without considering the concept of morality itself: what kind of classifications of men and of their activities are to be counted as moral classifications, as resting on moral distinctions? There is no philosophically neutral answer to this question. Following Kant, one may distinguish between the moral and natural qualities of men on the basis of some doctrine of the will, which is taken to define the domain of the moral. And there is certainly no place for any such distinction as this in Spinoza's thought. Or one may so restrict the notion of morality that nothing counts as a moral judgement, or as a moral choice, unless the free choice of some specific end, or specific standard, of human activity is prescribed, an end or standard that all men, as men, unconditionally ought to aim to achieve or to conform to. If, following Spinoza, the freedom of the individual, as an individual, is taken as the supreme evaluative term, and not the goodness of a man, as a man, one cannot properly speak of a specific end, or specific standard, of human performance which each man ought to achieve or to conform to. Within the terms of his metaphysical theory, there is no sense in saying that men ought to be free, that they ought to be self-determining, integrated in mind and constant in their desires, and actively rational, in an unconditional sense of "ought." The unconditional injunction to them to pursue a certain end implies that they have a choice among various possibilities, and that they may make the wrong choice, unless they are enlightened by the moralist.

Philosophically speaking and in the last analysis, they have no such choice of the ultimate ends of action. They are all, the virtuous and the vicious, the enlightened and the unenlightened, in any case trying to survive as active individuals and are trying to assert their power and freedom as individuals. The only question that arises, either in their own decisions or in judgement upon them, is— "How completely are they succeeding in asserting themselves as self-determining individuals? How can they become more successful than they are in maintaining and extending their own freedom and activity?" Of the ideally free man one can say that he will necessarily have certain virtues—for instance, the virtues of liberality and benevolence. In this sense there is indeed a standard or norm of conduct: that we can specify the dispositions that are inseparable from freedom of mind, and therefore we can specify the essential public and private virtues. Spinoza clearly explains in the Preface to Part IV of the *Ethics:* although the words "good" and "bad" indicate nothing positive in the things to which they are applied, we do indeed need to retain them in use, because (I quote) "we want to form for ourselves an idea of man upon which we may look as a model of human nature." This is part of the technique of self-improvement, a preparation for the life of reason. And he explains again in Part V that reflection upon maxims of virtue and wise conduct is a useful starting-point for the life of reason. But it is, strictly speaking, a misstatement, a philosophical error of the kind that occurs only in speaking to the unenlightened, to represent the virtues of the free, rational man as duties imposed upon us, or as appropriate matter for unconditional moral imperatives. There is no law, and therefore there are no duties, other than the natural law of self-preservation, which states that we try to extend our power and liberty as far as we can. How far we can, and by what methods of intellectual discipline, is the proper subject of any book that has the title "Ethics." Its conclusions are properly called the dictates of reason. Most of the duties recognized in conventional morality are in fact irrational foreshadowings of behaviour that would be the natural and unconstrained behaviour of a free man. He has his own adequate reasons for being a peaceful, friendly, just, and co-operative member of society. He may need to appeal to the myth of the moral law to persuade the mass of his fellow citizens to co-operate in civil society. Some of the conventional virtues of civil society, those associated with renunciation, unworldiness, and repression, are not virtues but defects. They are signs of weakness and of failure in the individual's realization of his own vitality as an individual. They have been taken for virtues, when myths of a transcendent God and of another world have been taken seriously as metaphysical truths. Preoccupation with death, and with human weakness, and with the passage of time, rather than with the enjoyment of present activity, are the emotional counterparts of these false philosophies. In a well-known and significant paragraph,[1] Spinoza says that the attitude of the severe moralist, which issues in denunciations of the vices and vanities of man, and of the common conditions of human life, is always the mark of a diseased mind. Pathos and virtue are opposed to each other, because, for Spinoza, virtue is energy—in a rather more precise sense than Blake intended.

There is therefore a sense in which Spinoza is representing the study of ethics, in the then dominant Christian and Jewish tradition, as one immense error, as the pursuit of a harmful illusion. The illusion is that various goals or ends of human effort, towards which our actions might be directed, are open to us for decision and for appraisal, and that the discussion and comparison of the various ends of action is the proper subject-matter of ethics. The ultimate ends of action are not open for decision or discussion. They are fixed by the laws of our nature as mind-body organisms struggling to preserve ourselves against our environment. That which we generally take, in our ignorance of these natural laws, to be our own free decision between alternative ends is to be explained as the complicated working of these laws in our own individual psychology. They are laws governing increases and decreases of vitality in the mind-body organism, and, derivatively, of unconscious appetites and conscious desires. I am only self-directing and independent when I am actively studying the laws of nature themselves, free from any concentration of interest exclusively on myself and on my relation to other particular things. Unless I continually reflect in this detached, philosophical manner, my particular judgement of ends of action, of good and bad, will correspond only to my particular desires and needs, due to the complications of my particular environment, and to the fantasies that have arisen from this history. I am deceived, if I do not discover the element of fantasy, and of unconscious memories, in my original judgements of value. Moral argument, that which replaces the traditional free

1. *E.*, V, x, S.

discussion of ends of action, should be an attempt to bring to light, and to recognize, our own motives and their sources, and thereby to make our pursuit of our own safety, and the enjoyment of our own activity, fully self-conscious and therefore fully rational.

I think it is at least possible that Spinoza is right in his opinion that traditional ethics is the pursuit of an illusion, and that gradually, in the course of years, he may be shown to be right. But for him of course this conclusion was not opinion, but knowledge. Nor did he think that it required, or could receive, confirmation from further observation and scientific inquiry. I am assuming a view of his philosophy, and of philosophy itself, which was not his, and which many living British philosophers would certainly not accept: the view that a philosophy such as his, which began with a claim to final truth demonstrable by *a priori* argument, is to be judged now as a speculative anticipation of truths that may gradually be supported by scientific inquiry, and by accumulating human experience. The confirmation, if it comes, will not be like the confirmation of an empirical hypothesis. It will not be direct confirmation, which leaves one with no reasonable alternative other than to accept the hypothesis as true. Rather the confirmation would be that some notions closely resembling Spinoza's key notions become widely accepted as peculiarly appropriate in studying and in evaluating human behaviour. New psychological knowledge might fit better into this framework than into any other, and psychologists themselves, and those who must now be directly or indirectly influenced by them, might come to employ concepts closely akin to Spinoza's. Certainly anyone who altogether rejects Spinoza's naturalistic standpoint, and anyone who has some religious and transcendental ground for his moral beliefs, would remain unpersuaded: and, given his premises, justifiably so. But those of us who have no such transcendental grounds may at least pause and consider the possibility that much of our habitual moralizing about the ends of action is altogether mistaken. Certainly we should not deceive ourselves by dismissing Spinoza as the kind of determinist who allows no possibility of deliberate self-improvement, as if this were the dividing line between him and the traditional moralists. It is not. An unprejudiced reading of the introduction to the *De Intellectus Emendatione,* and of Part V of the *Ethics,* will show that it is not. The dividing line is his theory of individuals maintaining themselves as individuals and of the mind and body as the two aspects of a single organism; and this line can be traced back to his nominalistic logic and to his philosophy of nature.

I have elsewhere suggested that there is an illuminating, and more than superficial, resemblance between Spinoza's and Freud's conception of personality. The more closely one considers this resemblance, the more clearly it appears to be traceable to common philosophical beliefs, which lie far below the surface of a shared terminology. That simple, misleading question "Was Spinoza, was Freud, a determinist?" has to be put on one side, and for the same reason, in both cases: that determinism, as a label, is associated with a particular model of the type of explanation to be aimed at in individual psychology and in the assessment of character: and this is a type which was certainly not theirs and which they had no interest either in accepting or rejecting. A determinist, as this label is commonly understood, has the single idea that any human behaviour is to be explained by well-confirmed natural laws which, taken together with a statement of initial conditions, exhibit the behaviour, whatever it may be, as always in principle predictable. This is not the kind of understanding, and of self-understanding, that is proposed by Spinoza and Freud.

Let me briefly list their points of agreement. First: there is the "economic" conception of the mind: that any individual is a psychophysical organism with a quantity of undifferentiated energy that appears in consciousness as desire and, below the level of consciousness, as appetite. This is the instinctual energy that must find its outlet, however deformed and deflected it may be by its interactions with the environment. Desires and appetites are projected upon objects, as objects of love or of hate, in accordance, first, with the primary economic needs of the organism, as objects promoting or depressing its vitality, and, secondly, upon objects that are derivatively associated, through the complex mechanisms of memory, with increase or depression of vitality. Following this conception of a person's undifferentiated energy of self-assertion, Spinoza's account of passive emotions, and of the laws of transference that govern them, is very close to Freud's mechanisms of projection, transference, displacement, and identification, in forming the objects of love and aggression. Second: that the way towards freedom and self-direction is through the recognition of the unreality of the causes with which an individual associates pleasures and sufferings. A man's discrimination between good objects and bad objects will be explained to him as imaginative projection upon reality of unconsciously remembered incidents in his personal history. Third: the purpose of such an explanation is to give him an overriding interest in the objective order of things, an interest independent of his own fantasies and of the passive association of ideas. The recall to reason is a recall from fantasy, and from the attachment to past experience through unconscious memories, towards an active and present enjoyment of his energies. He therefore becomes free to direct his mind naturally to its proper objects, instead of endlessly and helplessly repeating patterns of pursuit and aversion that originally established themselves below the level of his consciousness. Fourth: in his original state of uncriticized passive emotions, based upon fantasy, and the projection of his conflicts on to external objects, a man necessarily follows contrary and violently conflicting inclinations, and not a stable and consistent policy. Taken as a whole, his behaviour, in realizing his own desires, is therefore self-defeating. He is in this sense a divided and disintegrated personality. Freedom consists in the integration of all his desires and aversions into a coherent policy, the policy of developing his own powers of understanding, and of enjoying his active energies.

The point of philosophical interest here is the conception of mental causation which in turn determines the conception of freedom as the proper subject of ethics. For both Spinoza and Freud, the starting-point was the individual who, although part of the common order of nature, has to assert his individuality, his activity as an individual, against the common order of nature: in later, un-Spinozistic language, to assert the self, as agent, against the not-self, the external reality which resists him. His only means of achieving this distinctness as an individual, this freedom in relation to the common order of nature, is the power of the mind freely to follow in its thought an intellectual order. Then the flow of his reasonable thought and his reasonable action is predictable with greater certainty than when his thoughts and actions were determined by causes external to his own thinking. Spinoza and Freud alike argued that it is the common condition of men that their conduct and their judgements of value, their desires and aversions, are in each individual determined by unconscious memories. This is the nature of the passions—that their objects can be explained only from knowledge of unconsciously remembered satisfactions and frustrations in the individual's history, and not from the properties of the objects themselves. The future activity of a reasonable man is predictable on the basis of his present activity, while the future of the man who is a slave to his passions is to be inferred only from the fantasies that he formed in the remote past. When a man's thought follows the objective order of things in nature, he is, and knows that he is, for a time an autonomous individual, asserting his own power and independence of mind. I repeat "for a time." For neither Spinoza nor Freud were optimists. Freedom is at the best only intermittent and partial, and the general condition of men, as parts of nature, is one of fantasy and of passion determined by unconscious memory and therefore by conflict and frustration. But Freud's was certainly the deeper pessimism. Attending to the evidence of fact, he found no reason to believe that the mere force of intellect and of reflection could by itself open the way to self-knowledge, and therefore to freedom of mind. And one traditional form of philosophical writing, which still survives in Spinoza, is disappearing from our literature: the exhortation addressed to reason, the call to reflection on the right way of life, which used to be the preface, as in the *De Intellectus Emendatione,* to intellectual analysis.

Spinoza's philosophy can be construed as a metaphysical justification of individualism in ethics and politics. In so interpreting him, we only follow his design of his own work, which has never, I think, been treated with sufficient seriousness, largely because the attention of political philosophers has been concentrated on the more crude and inapplicable metaphysics of Hobbes. Whatever may be our judgement on the metaphysical premises from which it was deduced, Spinoza's theory of the passions is indeed a justification for taking the freedom of the individual as the supreme goal of political action. The now prevailing liberal conceptions of freedom, based on an empiricist philosophy, leave a mystery: why is the individual's act of choice, free from outside interference and threats of force, the supremely valuable activity of a man? Mill himself drew his answer from his utilitarian philosophy. The freedom of the individual was not for him a supreme and absolute end, but rather a means to the general progress of mankind. The individual's freedom of choice is a means to diversity and experiment, and diversity and experiment are means to the discovery of the most desirable forms of life. There is nothing in this philosophy that requires that the freedom of any individual is as such to be respected before all other things. Perhaps a revived doctrine of natural rights could give a sense to the absolute, as opposed to the conditional, value of the freedom of the individual. But no sense is given to the notion of natural rights within the empiricist philosophies of this time. If every man is by the law of his nature as an individual trying to assert his own power and freedom, in Spinoza's sense, in his thought and action, there is indeed a natural basis for the insistence on freedom as the supreme value in politics as in personal morality. The pursuit of any incompatible end will only lead to conflict and violence.

I return to my starting-point. It is, I think, at least possible that Spinoza has presented the outline of a defensible conception of individual freedom as the ultimate value in politics. In the *Tractatus Theologico-Politicus,* particularly in Chapter 20, he undertakes to show both that a civilized social order, based on freedom of thought and toleration, is a necessary condition of the use of reason, and therefore of the individual's fulfilment and enjoyment of his active powers: also, and more important now, to show that violence and social conflict are the projections into the external world of conflicts of passion within the individual. The first demonstration is in its conclusion, though not in its method, a commonplace. The second is not. We continue to speculate without conviction about freedom and social co-operation in the traditional terms of political philosophy, without any serious attention to the psychopathology of the individual, and as if all the discoveries in clinical psychology in the last fifty years had never been made. And this is, I think, why political philosophy seems now dying or dead, and lacks all conviction, except as an interpretation of the past. It has lost contact with the revolutionary and relevant moral science of its time. It is contrary to reason, and contrary also to John Stuart Mill's own principles in philosophy, that we should still cling to Mill's definition of freedom, when the philosophy of mind upon which he based it is discredited. We thereby preserve the letter, and lose the spirit, of empiricism, and of the liberal beliefs that were derived from it.

Spinoza's Account of Imagination

R. G. BLAIR

It did not occur to Spinoza that the ideal of a perspicuous insight into the nature of reality as a whole might represent an incoherent demand. He had no need for areas of theoretical assumptions based only on intelligent speculation, because the ontological argument was valid, God necessarily existed, and all true propositions could be deduced with the help of propositions about the necessary nature of God.

In his system there can be no empirical contingencies as we usually think of them. Nevertheless, determined thoughts and impressions can still be erroneous. In fact, three levels of knowledge are distinguished: the highest knowledge, intuitive knowledge of the essences of individual things; reasoning about things in general; and the weakest kind, imagination. One may speculate that, while it seems odd to class imagination as a bad sort of knowledge, the distrust of all intuitions which could not be rigorously demonstrated to reveal something true represented an attempt at intellectual honesty in a world still ruled by religious bigotry and political authoritarianism. Speculation was indeed not persecuted automatically in seventeenth-century Holland, but immediate suppression of undesirable thoughts was the order of the day in Europe as a whole.

Like Descartes, Spinoza regarded it as his philosophical duty to eradicate as many sources of possible error as he could discover. Imagination had to be accepted as a fact of life, yet treated with profound distrust. Pure thought could lead one out of its toils along the road to true knowledge and blessedness. That thought was, however, a determined process. Spinoza did not stop to consider whether there was not, as many philosophers today would maintain, a logical error in supposing that one can know that one has arrived at a piece of true knowledge by a determined process of thought.

The word "imagination" is inherently ambiguous. I shall be concerned not with imagination as a faculty which is exercised by an inquiring or original mind, but with the simple ability to produce

---

This essay was written especially for this volume.

visual or other sensory images—in other words, with a psychological datum which, as we shall see, it is not altogether fanciful to discuss in terms of physical processes in the body. It is this sort of account that Spinoza gives in the *Ethics*.

One early proviso. It seems that all everyday perceptions are also cases to be included under the head of imagination in Spinoza's system, since they are certainly not cases of reasoning about things in general (i.e. scientific thought); and intuitive knowledge of the essences of individual things is something to which one can only attain when one has already progressed to a high stage of mental development. Thus children's perceptions are no better than images, since children are not capable of reasoning about their perceptions in the required manner. However, it is clear that Spinoza's contempt for imagination is founded in the confusability (as he supposes) of images with perceptions, and this is, intuitively speaking, likely to be especially true of children, if it is true at all, since their experience of telling the one from the other is limited. In this way one may assume that childish perceptions are impressions of dubious status in Spinoza's system; and even adults' perceptions are cases of imagination insofar as the knowledge gained from them does not constitute an adequate idea of their determined causes. The account he gives of imagination, however, presupposes that images and percepts are in fact different kinds of entities or events and known so to be. Even if both are cases of "imagination," images, unlike percepts, have as their objects things which do not exist or are not present.

In a deterministic system, in which all statements are ultimately statements about the nature of God, the account of any particular feature of the world must be seen as both an empirical and a logical one. We can make sense, at least, of the notion that all features of the world are determined by previous features of it. That is just the classic determinist position. The explanation of any feature is then the locating of the causes which are responsible for it, and the causes can only be discovered by empirical investigation. In Spinoza's system, however, any feature of the world is to be accounted for by logical argument about the nature of God. That any feature is as it is is not merely causally determined; it is also logically necessary. This is a way of looking at things which we can now hardly take in at all. In the account of imagination we shall see Spinoza tacitly abandoning it when he introduces postulates about how the body works[1] for which no genuine *a priori* arguments are offered.

The account of imagination does, however, follow another pattern with which we are familiar. It *describes* our conscious experience of the world, and then *explains* it by reference to the causes of its occurrence. Mere reports by ourselves of our experiences may be said to occur on the lowest level of knowledge. These reports may then be shown to be very misleading in the light of explanation of a general scientific kind on the second level. Till this point all is clear and acceptable. Then we remember that the highest level of knowledge is one on which we are taken away from general explanation to a special insight, which we have as much into other individual people and things as we do into our individual selves. In theory it is on this level of deductive essentialism or existential logic that the propositions of the *Ethics* are asserted, for that is the level of true philosophy. In practice, however, not all philosophical reasoning leads us to third level insights, if such an insight is possible at all, even in Spinoza. The account of imagination we shall be considering, for example, seems to consist of second level generalizations. First level reports of what images are like give way to a putative explanation of them as bodily occurrences.

II

According to Spinoza, to have an image is to undergo a bodily process or to be in a particular bodily state. It is a passive affection of the body to which it succumbs for physical reasons, and this produces an image as an idea in the mind. (In Spinoza's monistic philosophy an expression about an image as an affection of the body always has corresponding to it an expression about that image as an idea of the mind.)

This account is basically the same as that given of perception. Thus Proposition XIV of the second part of the *Ethics* states: "The human mind is adapted to the perception of many things, and its aptitude increases in proportion to the number of ways in which the body can be disposed." And in the same way the mind can *imagine* many things when the body is affected in various ways. Proposition XVI tells us: "The idea of every way in which the human body is affected

1. *E.,* II, xiii.

by external bodies must involve the nature of the human body, and at the same time the nature of the external body." In imagination two bodies are again involved, although the external body is now required for the description of the image only because the subject's previous perception of it when present allows him to imagine it when absent.

Proposition XVII shows how Spinoza believes that we can distinguish an experienced percept from an experienced image. "If the human body be affected in a way which involves the nature of any external body, the human mind will contemplate that external body as actually existing or as present, until the human body be affected by an affect which excludes the existence or presence of the external body." Thus, although images and percepts have a similar physiological basis (one, presumably, we should now say, which is connected with brain processes) the experience of an additional affect will characterize the image as only an image. Two complementary ways are here suggested in which we may make the required distinction. (It should be noted that Spinoza claims only to have provided one reasonable explanation of images among others, though he believes this to be "not far from the truth."[2]) Either we may actually have a bodily experience which shows us that the imagined object is absent—for example we may try to touch it and fail. Or, since the bodily affect will produce an idea in the mind, we may *think* that the object must be absent, because we have failed to touch it or had some bodily experience which told us we were imagining something.

There is of course something radically false about this account. It simply misrepresents the experience of imagining. Firstly, it is not true that we need suppose that any idea which enters our heads is of a real object. We do not naturally "posit the existence," as Spinoza claims, of ideas which are in our minds. And secondly it is false that we need either to perform psychological experiments or reason from them in order to tell the difference between images and percepts. No reflection is required, and no experimentation. The difference is given absolutely in the feel of the experience itself.

For the proof of Corollary XVII ("The mind is able to contemplate external things by which the human body was once affected as if it were present, although they are not present and do not exist."), Spinoza has recourse to the postulates already mentioned. This pas-

2. *E.,* II, xvii, S.

sage is really only a modish piece of primitive physiology which deals with the "hard," "soft," and "fluid" parts of our anatomies. It is, however, most interesting that the principle invoked to explain the causation of imagery by the interaction of the soft and fluid parts is that of the response of "contemplating the external body as present" being conditioned to stimuli with which it was not initially associated by a Pavlovian generalization of responses to substituted stimuli. (Fluid motion S′ associated with fluid motion S continues to evoke the same R, though fluid motion S alone was actually the motion of perception.)

In this account imagery is the result of the "spontaneous motion" of the body fluids. It simply happens to the subject, and he does not bring it about. This is, of course, absurd, since it can hardly be the case that, whenever I deliberately call up an image of a past event, the bodily fluids just happen to indulge in spontaneous motion. On the other hand, it is no doubt very prudent of Spinoza to say that we must distrust imagination, if this means distrusting the spontaneous motion of bodily fluids.

This account does not allow us to conceive of one possible way in which it might be reconciled with our obvious ability to know an image for an image instantaneously. For it might be that, as children, we really do have to carry out experiments to make the distinction. Perhaps we even learn that there is a distinction at all by experiment. But, if so, we certainly learn so thoroughly that, in a short space of time, experiment ceases to be necessary. Spinoza's account, however, maintains that all "human minds" continue to be dependent on the "affect" which will tell them an image is only an image, and this must be false. We do not sit around wondering whether we are imagining things any more than we do whether we are dreaming. (Certainly we do in mists, twilight, etc. But these are really cases of possible hallucination. Here the original classification of images together with percepts and false percepts as "imagination" can be seen to injure Spinoza's view of images.)

I do not wish to imply that Spinoza's account, revised in the sense of the last paragraph, need be taken very seriously. Indeed I agree with those phenomenologists and other philosophers who maintain that imagination and perception are categorically different. On the other hand, a theory of imagination fitting comfortably into the framework of Spinoza's account is popular among some experimental psychologists even today. For instance, in *Learning Theory and the*

Symbolic Processes, O. H. Mowrer quotes with approval from a paper entitled "Images as Conditioned Sensations" by C. Leuba:

> Our experiments indicate that after an inadequate stimulus has been presented a number of times, while an individual is experiencing certain sensations, it will by itself automatically, and without the intervention of any conscious processes, produce those sensations. An image can, therefore, be considered as a conditioned sensation.[3]

Mowrer, himself, then writes:

> Although cast in the vernacular of the modern conditioning laboratory, the notion that an image is a conditioned sensation . . . squares not only with common sense but also, as we shall presently see, with certain classical psychological notions. An image, in common parlance, is some object which an individual "sees" or otherwise "perceives" without the object being objectively present. By a word, another image, or some other stimulus, the individual is *reminded* of the object and reacts somewhat *as if* it were actually present. In other words, a *part* of the total experience produced by the object itself is here being aroused as a learned, conditioned response; and this response we call an image—and the process of its arousal, *imagination*.[4]

The philosophical weakness of this account is that the "inadequate stimulus" may be without any but the most fortuitous connection with the imaginative response. If a man's eating of an orange has been associated with his reading *The Times,* he should, after a while, every time he picks up *The Times,* be at least disposed to savor the absent ascorbic taste of orange flesh. (I say "disposed" because there may be many types of interference which cause the conditioned sensation to fail—a hot fire, a good meal, etc.)

In this way of looking at imagination, all its phenomena are reduced to the level of seeing palm trees when one remembers a day on a tropical island. If one has only seen a palm tree in films, then one cannot, strictly speaking, imagine a palm tree, but only a cinematic palm tree. There is also no account of the characteristic feeling that imagination is free from all external influences which, as we shall see, Spinoza himself regards as being in a certain sense very important. On the other hand, Mowrer's restrictive account is not obviously un-

---

3. O. H. Mowrer, *Learning Theory and the Symbolic Processes* (New York: Wiley, 1960), p. 166.

4. *Loc. cit.*

acceptable for a limited range of memory-like images—i.e. involuntary images. And it also has an ingenious answer to the problem of distinction between percepts and images which is still acute even for this limited range of phenomena: an image is the conditionable and conditioned *part* of a sensation.

> One would not want a sensation, in its totality, to be conditionable, for this would lead to a full-scale hallucination. When, therefore, things work out right, we experience just enough of the original sensation to know what it is but *not* enough to make us think that we are actually having it again. In other words, we know it is "all in your head" instead of "out there."[5]

III

Spinoza's system cannot teach us much today if it is taken as a whole. Philosophy, as he understood it, is no more. From his point of view, human experience has become chaotic; Nature is no longer a coherent whole. His God inevitably does not exist, and the world is not a determined part of that God. On the other hand, the extent to which he prefigured particular trends of thought which are still with us is quite remarkable. In this light, the latter part of Scholium XVII of the second part of the *Ethics* deserves to be quoted in full:

> In order that we may retain the customary phraseology, we will give to those affections of the human body, the ideas of which represent to us external bodies as if they were present, the name of *images of things,* although they do not actually reproduce the forms of the things. When the mind contemplates bodies in this way, we will say that it imagines. Here I wish it to be observed, in order that I may begin to show what *error* is, that these imaginations of the mind, regarded by themselves, contain no error, and the mind is not in error because it imagines, but only insofar as it is considered as wanting in an idea which excludes the existence of those things which it imagines as present. For if the mind, when it imagines non-existent things to be present, could at the same time know that those things did not really exist, it would think its power of imagination to be a virtue of its nature and not a defect, especially if this faculty of imagining depended upon its own nature alone, that is to say, if this faculty of the mind were free.

5. *Ibid.,* p. 167, footnote.

I have suggested elsewhere[6] that this scholium represents a mirror-image of the account developed by Sartre in which the faculty of imagination is seen as manifesting human freedom. The absurdity of that view resides in the extraordinary move from the phenomenological assertion that we experience the freedom of our conscious minds to the metaphysical dogma that we must always therefore be free in our actions. Sartre simply disregards the obvious point made, for example, by Spinoza, that imagination is not a trustworthy guide to hard facts. Nevertheless, it would not be difficult for him to support his claim by reference to Scholium XVII. For surely the mind, when it imagines, *can* "at the same time know that those things (which it imagines) do not really exist." This is a sort of conscious certainty we do habitually experience. Recognizing this fact would not show for Spinoza that men are free in the full-blown Sartrean sense. It would, however, show that they possess greater guarantees against self-deception than Spinoza supposes. They would thus be more luminously and directly conscious of the workings of their own minds. For Spinoza that would mean that they possessed greater "freedom."

Freedom as self-knowledge and the awareness of necessity has always been widely regarded as Spinoza's most attractive idea. It is the foundation of his moral philosophy, according to which the good man is always active in striving to realize his own perfection but is also resigned to his fate in that he realizes that the world is wholly determined. Professor Hampshire compares Spinoza's belief that self-knowledge is the bringer of contentment with the Freudian view that the revelation of the meaning of one's past for one's present emotional life is the healer of psychic disorders.[7] This is a most valuable comparison, although it might be thought that Spinoza's pantheism suggests rather a comparison with the psychology of Jung. The similarities between Spinoza and Freud are, firstly, their location of a determined process as governing a man's life; to have Freudian self-awareness is to recognize the force of the libido, and to have Spinozistic self-awareness is to recognize one's *conatus,* or striving, toward the goal of self-perfection: and secondly the belief that to be deceived about oneself is morally wrong, because it impedes the growth of both happiness and moral and intellectual maturity. Where Freud sought to re-

6. R. G. Blair, "Imagination and Freedom in Spinoza and Sartre," *Journal of the British Society of Phenomenology,* 1 (1970), pp. 13–16.

7. Stuart Hampshire, *Spinoza,* pp. 106–109.

place unconscious sufferings by conscious self-insight, Spinoza saw a willing and resigned participation in the perfection of one's essential nature as the goal of life.

One should not go too far in the comparison of Spinoza and Freud, however, for those less cautious than Professor Hampshire might conclude that the insight one gains into one's own life is similar for both men in a respect in which it is radically different. Freud did not suppose, as would be necessary to make the analogy complete, that a particular experience in childhood followed by logical and causal necessity from previous states of God or Nature. On the contrary, if a child was assaulted by its father, that was an unfortunate and unusual occurrence. It is not necessary to an appreciation of Freud to suppose such a thoroughgoing determinism that nothing could ever have been other than in fact it was. The insight one gains, if one is such a child, is merely enough to tell one that there is a causal connection between the event (or often the imagined event) and one's present distress.

It is true that some types of traumata, while not following inevitably from the very nature of things—i.e. there are human institutions which avoid them—are very deeply engrained in most societies. The inevitability of the Oedipus complex is given in most social setups. Still more general features of the world, such as the sexual differences between men and women, do apparently present the basis for ineradicable traumatic possibilities. In these last cases one might claim that analysis consists of becoming reconciled to certain basic features of the world. On the whole, though, the analyst must be said to explain the mere contingent effects of certain adventitious experiences. It is the relief provided by an empirical causal analysis which is held to be the psychotherapeutic healer. Nobody gains insight into the logical necessity of his experiences, for they are not in fact necessary, although, of course, they do have causes.

IV

Spinoza's account of imagination as a conditioned sensation applies only to one of the vicious variety of contexts in which we use the term. Because of his Pavlovian requirement one cannot imagine without also remembering. Can such an account really tell us anything one way or the other about freedom? It is fully analogous to the

Sartrean account, for Sartre too is speaking primarily of visual or other sensory images. Strictly speaking, he claims that the necessity of freedom can be apprehended on the basis of the phenomena of visualizing etc. alone, without invoking any propositional imagination or suppositions. But why should a succession of images convince a man of his freedom, even if he is never in any doubt as to whether they are not in fact percepts? It is only if he can conjecture their being translated into reality that he might surely be (however implausibly) supposed to have such a conviction.

The mere ability to produce an image at will—i.e. not as the result of motions of the fluid parts of the body etc.—seems no more likely to convince me of my freedom than the ability to produce a pleasant sensation by scratching my back. For that sensation of pleasure is undoubtedly gratuitous and need never have been. I produce it just as freely as I do or do not freely produce my images. It is, rather, the apparent freedom of our propositional imaginings, our ability to think imperious Caesar dead and turned to clay before he dies, and the rational flow of our thoughts in an ordered way, the causes of which seem so impossible to determine, which *seem* to give us an area of freedom. The rationalism of Spinoza and Freud which stresses that imagination is often just fantasy should still, however, tell us that all we have managed even then to establish are certain unstable impressions of a seeming freedom.

The good man, according to Spinoza, must strive to perfect his nature. If, therefore, he concluded that imagination *was* a "virtue" of his nature "and not a defect," he would be committed to developing his power of imagining, even if this only consisted in keeping in good practice at evoking images of past events. In point of fact, however, the process of gaining self-awareness will inevitably lead to the realization that imagination is a "defect," and he will be equally committed to a struggle to eradicate his images.

It is perhaps unfortunate for Spinoza that images are connected in his account with memory, which is surely also an untrustworthy faculty. The good man might find himself attempting to eradicate his memories and hence his past. Here too, however, we may well think that Spinoza's high valuation of critical honesty is inspiring. It is true of him, as of so many other philosophers (and indeed perhaps of most men), that his negative "virtues" are greater than his positive ones. The inquiring, anti-authoritarian urge for honesty is more admirable than the Yoga-like cult of self-perfection. And yet Russell's evaluation of him as the "ethically supreme" philosopher is so fully appropriate at a time when moral philosophy has become concerned with good manners rather than with good lives.

Action and Passion: Spinoza's Construction of a Scientific Psychology

MARX WARTOFSKY

1. *Introduction*

Spinoza's construction of a scientific psychology is one of the most striking historical examples of the heuristic function of metaphysics in the genesis of scientific theory.[1] It is, at the same time, an example of how the requirements of a scientific theory are related to the construction of a metaphysics. That these two propositions are not mutually exclusive, I hope to show in this essay; and that they are both true requires us only to believe that science and metaphysics mutually interact, and help to shape each other, especially in those periods of great discovery and courageous theorizing which mark the youth of a new science.

What is at issue in this essay is Spinoza's claim that a science of human nature is continuous with a science of nature; that human action and passion are as subject to universal laws, and therefore as subject to rational understanding, as is the motion of bodies, in physics, or the relations among points, planes, and solids in geometry. To understand Spinoza's claim, I hope to specify the particular *Problematik* with which he was presented by Cartesian psychology, and to show the forcefulness both of his methodological and psychological insights. But beyond this, I hope to make clear a programmatic point: to show how Spinoza's conception of a science of psychology is related to his metaphysics, and in particular to his ontology of the person, as a natural individual continuous with all of nature, yet distinct as a conscious organism, i.e. as organized matter which thinks and feels, and which acts in order to survive, or to preserve its individuality.

To begin, I will consider the phrase "scientific psychology," both with respect to the notion of a method or a kind of knowledge, and with respect to the specific characterization of its domain. I will then

---

This essay was written especially for this volume.

1. See my "Metaphysics as Heuristic for Science," in R. S. Cohen and M. W. Wartofsky, eds., *Boston Studies in the Philosophy of Science*, vol. III (Dordrecht: D. Reidl, 1965), pp. 123–170.

present the *Problematik* or problem-setting of Spinoza's construction, and then proceed to the reconstruction of Spinoza's psychology as a theoretical system, embedded in and supported by a metaphysics. Here, the notions "action" and "passion" will be seen to be theoretically central, as will the epistemological notions "adequate" and "inadequate ideas." Finally, after a consideration of Spinoza's "mechanics" of the affects, or emotions, I hope to point to the relevance of Spinoza's program for contemporary psychology.

2. *"Scientific Psychology" in Historical Context*

The phrase "scientific psychology" I take here as expressing a historical conception, and not some canonical contemporary "science." First, it can hardly be claimed that there is a canonical "scientific psychology" today. Second, the shifting conception of what is canonically "scientific," in general, cannot be understood as more than an arbitrary sequence of fads and faiths, unless the genesis of our contemporary conceptions is understood historically. To this end, the theory of science which I want to present, specifically, is that which developed in the crucible of seventeenth-century philosophical debate and scientific discovery, and to which Spinoza's most crucial contribution was his psychology. How this theory of science comports with our own theories is a separate and difficult question, about which I will say very little here. A general methodological approach to the question of what constitutes a Spinozist "scientific psychology" begins with the question, *first, of what constitutes scientific knowledge* for Spinoza; and *second, of what constitutes the specific domain, or the specific object of this knowledge.* To the first question, the answer is Spinoza's own characterization of scientific knowledge as the "second kind of knowledge," namely, that which realizes the lawful connections between phenomena, and comprehends the causal or determinate manner of these connections. In practice, such comprehension or understanding is exhibited in the formal statement of these connections in a deductive system, such that the implicit conditions of the famous theorem (*E.*, II, vii: "The order and connection of thoughts is the same as the order and connection of things") are fulfilled. Scientific knowledge, therefore, is the affirmation of true thoughts, i.e. of those which are in agreement with the order and connection of things; nor is this simply an ordering sequence; the "connection" is causal, determinate, and in Spinoza's special sense, necessary; namely, it follows from the nature of Substance itself. The way things are, they are necessarily; and so, a science, as the systematic idea of nature, is a knowledge of this necessity *as* necessary, and not simply under the form of contingency. (*E.,* II, xliv, & Cor. 2. Dem.) The limits of a science are therefore the limits of the clear and distinct, i.e. the "adequate" ideas we can have, and are therefore related to the conditions and limits of our knowledge. Spinoza's conception of scientific knowledge is therefore closely related to his psychology, insofar as the psychological theory gives us in turn an account of the genesis and constraints on our knowledge.

This brings up, quite specifically, the related question of the domain or the object of a science; since what can be known of a particular domain or object depends on the way in which knowledge of it is possible. In the case of psychology, the domain or object of knowledge is man's conscious action, i.e. human activity itself, insofar as it is an object of consciousness, and can come to be known in accordance with laws and principles. More precisely, for Spinoza, psychology includes the mind's knowledge of its own body, insofar as this body undergoes changes in its "power of acting"; and the mind's knowledge of its own affections, insofar as these are conceived as affections of the mind itself. The first of these constitutes the domain of imagination, perception, and the emotions; the second, of thought proper. Spinoza offers us both a theory about how such knowledge (of the emotions and perception and of thought) is possible—this is the epistemological groundwork of his psychology—and also, a psychological theory of emotion and thought—that is, an account of the *laws* of emotion and of thought, as natural phenomena, and therefore as part of a general science of nature; in particular, that part of it which is the science of man.

3. *Spinoza's Problematik*

The *Problematik* of Spinoza's psychology is posed by Cartesian psychology and its metaphysical framework: namely, by mind-body dualism. Insofar as this concerns Descartes's psychology, it can be summarized by two basic ideas: first, that the science of bodies, in their motion and interaction, is a mechanical physics, whose ontology is that of inert matter, whose principle of motion lies outside itself. Animal bodies are subject to the same mechanism as the rest of physical nature; and insofar as animal bodies are affected by motion or change, this motion or change can be understood as a composition of motions of the parts of animals, and of the interaction of these bodily parts with external bodies. Second, however, insofar as these motions or changes affect conscious beings, the mode of this affect is by mechanical and causal interaction of bodily affections with the soul, by the mediation of the pineal gland. But as opposed to the inert and extended property of matter, in which only efficient causes operate, and in which all motion is that of moved movers, the soul or thinking substance has its principle of motion in itself, and is, as soul, fully self-determined, and in this sense has agency, will, and freedom.

In Descartes's psychology, therefore, the automatism of body is sharply contrasted with the autonomy of the soul; the science of the one is mechanics; of the other, autonomous reason. The psychology of Descartes poses a double problem: first, insofar as it is psychology proper—i.e. insofar as it deals with *psyche* or *soul* in itself, it deals with the interaction of the bodily affections with the soul only at its margins, if at all. Second, if psychology is to deal with this interaction, it is faced with the inordinate metaphysical difficulties of the interface between mutually exclusive ontologies and mutually exclusive methodologies: how can the mechanical interact with the autonomous, the extended with the nonextended, the finite with the infinite, the determined with the free?

This excursus sets the problem of Spinoza's psychology sharply, and also permits a characterization of his solution to it: not only the bodily affections but those of the mind as well are to be included in the science of mechanism. The continuity of sensory perception, emotion, and thought is to be reaffirmed. But such a reaffirmation cannot be achieved simply by methodological fiat; rather, the metaphysics of Descartes has to be fundamentally revised, and the ontological dualism overcome, so that a methodological monism can be asserted. If no domain is to be immune to the mathematical method, and to explanation in terms of efficient causes which this method offers, then mind, no less than body, must be adequately conceived as determined to its activity by causes. But if mind is to be conceived, as it must be, as an activity whose principle of motion and change is in itself, then so too must body. The dualism of inert substance on the one hand and self-active substance on the other, must be exchanged for a monism of self-active substance, whose modes of activity are differentiated but whose principle of activity is not. Such a self-active principle must be such that its existence and its activity are one and the same; it must be therefore *causa sui* in the special sense of an *active causa sui;* its being must be identical with its activity; and it must, at the same time, be one, and yet be self-differentiated; its "parts" must therefore be conceived not as simple mechanical divisions, but as partial expressions of the whole.[2] Spinoza therefore sets himself the task of constructing a psychology which, unlike Descartes's, includes the soul within the context of a science of mechanics and yet retains its self-activity. Both mind and matter therefore need to be recast for the requirements of this monism; and the continuity of the bodily affections with the mind's activity has to be systematically worked out. So, too, the consequences and limits of mechanism itself are tested, and the inadequacy of mechanism begins to be shown. In effect, then, Spinoza's extension of mechanism begins to transcend this mechanism itself and therefore to strain the very conception of the prevailing scientific methodology.[3]

I am arguing that Spinoza's metaphysics was not a philosophical or theological exercise in its own right; but rather, that its motivation was the problem of a consistent scientific methodology which would include the domain of psychology; that the metaphysics was in the service of this aim. It may be argued that this view fails to grasp the essentially ethical motive in Spinoza's thought. But the continuity between the ethical and the scientific in Spinoza, as in Aristotle, lies in the conception of the ethical as that activity which is in accordance with the nature of man, and the discovery of this nature and of its proper activity is the task of rational science in the service of man's well-being. Moreover, Spinoza's conviction is that a wrongly con-

2. This mereological principle is best expressed, perhaps, in Giordano Bruno's phrase, "wholly in the whole, and wholly in every part of the whole" (*De Immenso et Innumerabilibus,* II, xiii, cited by H. F. Hallett, *Aeternitas,* Oxford: Clarendon Press, 1930, pp. 155–156). We know that a related solution is sought by Leibniz, in the *Monadology,* and it shares much in common with Spinoza's; but it does not share Spinoza's insistence on the equal ontological status of matter with that of mind.

3. See my earlier discussion of this point, in "Diderot and the Development of Materialist Monism," *Diderot Studies* II, ed. N. Torrey and O. Fellows (Syracuse: Syracuse University Press, 1952), pp. 279–327. There, I attribute mechanistic limits to Spinoza's view, based on the most explicitly mechanistic of the formulations in the *Ethics,* (*E.,* II, Axiom 2, Lemma 3, following Schol., Prop. xiii), and counterpose Leibniz, Maupertuis, and Diderot to Spinoza. I now think Spinoza himself strains and breaks the limits of this classical mechanism.

ceived morality, based on superstition, fantasy, wishful thinking, is the product of human ignorance, and only the critique of this superstition frees man for his proper activity, in which alone his happiness and well-being reside.

That Spinoza fails in his task, that his monism suffers from inconsistencies and obscurities, that his psychology itself founders on the discontinuities of body and mind, as he himself conceives them, is the burden of much of Spinoza criticism. Yet the towering attempt at a system, and the power of its monistic imperative still provide, to my mind, one of the most viable heuristic guidelines in the formulation of a contemporary science of psychology.

4. *The Theoretical Construction, I: Bodies, Minds, and Ideas*

I will treat Spinoza's psychology principally from the point of view of its systematic construction. The theory of action and passion in Spinoza is in effect his theory of the nature of the person and the primary theoretical construct of his psychology. To Descartes's divided being, constituted by body and mind, Spinoza counterposes an active, integral organism, which is essentially body, constituted of parts. This composite body is identical with its activity, or more precisely, with its power to act. Moreover, this composite is not merely an aggregation of parts, but an individual thing. (See Spinoza's arguments on composition, *E.*, II, xiii, Def. following Axiom 1, and Lemmas 5, 7; Schol.; Post. 1.) Identical with this composite or organic individual is the human mind, which is, in Spinoza's phrase, the idea of this body. It is one and the same thing, as body, conceived under the attribute of extension, and as mind, conceived under the attribute of thought or consciousness. The person, or the human individual, is therefore a body-mind, that is to say, a determinate mode of substance, conceivable under both attributes, but self-identical, under both. As a determinate mode of substance—that is to say, an individual thing—it is by definition finite. And here, the crucial nature of finite existence, or of the modes, in Spinoza, is the metaphysical clue to his psychology. "Every determination," says Spinoza, "is a negation." That is to say, determinate being is "caused" by something external to it, which defines its limits, makes it the particular individual it is, and characterizes its powers to act. No determinate being can act with infinite power, precisely because as determinate, its power (and synonymously, its existence) is bounded by its (necessary) relations with all other determinate things. As determinate, it is essentially *interactive,* or is both caused *by* and is the cause *of* other things. Nothing is undetermined, for then it would not exist, or be an individual. But everything (short of Substance itself) is both *determined* and *determining;* passive, insofar as it is determined by something other than itself; active, insofar as it determines some other, or itself. Only the whole system or universe of such interactions has no delimitation, since by definition it is the whole, and there is nothing external to it. This infinite being, or substance, therefore, doesn't "act" *on* anything, but is identical with all of the internal activities of its modes; not only is it infinite activity, in this metaphysical sense, but it is infinitely self-differentiated activity, since the chain of causes, according to Spinoza, is infinite, without beginning or end. (See, e.g. *E.,* I, xxviii & II, xiii, Lemma 3, for Spinoza's rejection of infinite regress arguments.)

In what sense, then, can a body or an individual be active, if its activity is fully determinate—i.e if it is caused to act by other individuals with which it interacts? Here the very language and conception of mechanism are strained beyond limit. For, being the very individual it is, is not simply constituted as the set of determinate relations it has with everything else in the universe—though it is also that; rather, the quality and character of its relations, or its actual and potential interactions with other things are also determined by its own composition, i.e. by the simple or composite bodies which constitute it. The dialectical dilemma of a thing *constituted* by no more than its relations was resolved by Leibniz in his postulation of the monads as dimensionless, mathematical points. This relational *existence,* however, sacrifices the materiality of the basic individuals of the system. By contrast, the simplest bodies, for Spinoza, are extended, and therefore, so too are the composites. They are material bodies which, by virtue of their power to affect other bodies, are active, and by virtue of their capacity to receive the actions of other bodies, are passive. Insofar as such a body acts, therefore, the cause of its activity is in itself, and can be conceived clearly and distinctly by the mind, as following from the nature of the body. In Spinoza's language, "we act when anything is done, either within us or without us, of which we are the adequate cause, that is to say . . . when from our nature anything follows, either within us or without us, which by that nature alone can be clearly and distinctly understood" (*E.,* III, Def. 2). But in fact, Spinoza goes on to say that though the mind *is* the idea of the body, and is thus necessarily aware of everything that happens in its object, it comes to know its object, i.e. its body, only by virtue of its awareness of changes in the body, i.e. of modifications or affections of the body. On the one hand, what we can know clearly and distinctly of the body is what Spinoza calls common notions—i.e. those ideas which all men have in common, concerning body, and what is common both to our own bodies and to external bodies. But insofar as we have an adequate idea of the body, this idea must be the idea of the body as an adequate cause, that is to say, of the body acting in accordance with its nature. And thus, we cannot have an adequate idea of the body insofar as it is affected by other bodies external to it. But since the body, as determinate, is what it is in its interaction with other bodies, and its determination or modification by them, we cannot have an adequate idea of the body, short of having an adequate idea of the whole system of interactions. Thus the finitude of the body is at the same time the finitude of the human mind. Its knowledge of itself, as an individual, is forever limited by its partiality with respect to the total scheme of things. But this knowledge is not as such false, thereby, it is only the *occasion* of falsity, or the possibility of error.

The upshot is that the body is the adequate cause of its actions only as it is seen as substance acting, in one of its modifications, i.e. only as the whole system of interactions is expressed in it, or only as the mind can come to conceive it under the form of necessity or under the form of eternity. Insofar as the mind is the idea of the body, and the body is a determinate body or an individual in a system of such individuals, the mind is, as is the body, a finite mode, a part of this system. What it can come to know is the systematic interrelation of all other bodies to its own, but only insofar as the mind's own body is affected by these interactions. Therefore, it can never come to know external bodies (or causes) in themselves, but only by the effects they have on the mind's body. This knowledge, Spinoza says, is knowledge which the mind *necessarily* has, since it *is* the idea of the body, and is not a separate or derived reflection *of* the body. In effect, the identity and being of the mind is the consciousness of bodily affections; or better, *is* these bodily affections conceived under the attribute of thought. Thus, the mind cannot *but* have ideas, and thus has them necessarily (*E.*, II, xii). But from this necessary knowledge of one's own bodily affections, it does not follow, says Spinoza, that we have *adequate* ideas of the external bodies insofar as these are the sources of these affections. And insofar as the body is affected from without, the knowledge of the bodily affection itself is inadequate since it is not itself the cause of its affections, but only their partial cause.

The individual human body as a finite mode of substance is part of a system of such bodies; and thereby, interaction and interdependence are the very modes of existence of such bodies [Postulate 4, following *E*. II, xiii]. Yet, Spinoza's notion of such bodies as composites of bodies, and as composites of composites, constituting at each level of organization a unity or an individual, permits him to ascend from "simple bodies" to the one "individual" comprised of the system as a whole, and therefore, to the idea of that one individual as the idea of the whole, whose awareness of that whole (its "body") is an awareness of an infinitely differentiated unity; moreover, of this unity as containing all of its differentiation as *self*-differentiation, and therefore as its own activity (since nothing is external to it), of which it necessarily has an adequate idea. At this limit, as Spinoza expresses it, mind achieves "the intellectual love of God," or contemplates itself accompanied by the idea of God as cause. It achieves, in effect, knowledge of individual objects as they are in themselves, by virtue of this knowledge of the "third kind," or intuition (*E.,* II, xlvii and Schol.).

Short of this state of blessedness, with which Spinoza concludes the *Ethics,* there is the finitude of human existence, as its necessary condition. Spinoza relies here on common sense as much as on metaphysics; or rather, his metaphysics simply states, in systematic and abstract fashion, the requirements of common sense: as individuals, we are dependent upon and interdependent with other individuals. As human beings, our existence *is* in this interaction, both as bodily beings and as conscious beings. The consciousness of our interdependence is not simply a condition of the finitude of our minds, but equally (and identically) the condition of our bodily existence. But precisely because of this necessary condition of dependence upon others, and because we can have adequate ideas only insofar as these are of our own activity, or what follows from our own natures, then insofar as we interact with external individuals, our ideas are inadequate or confused; and we are, by nature (the nature of our finitude or dependency), condemned to inadequate ideas of this interaction. We are therefore the subjects of passions as well as actions, and therefore, insofar as we are human, we suffer. For the passions according to Spinoza (in common with Descartes, and a long tradition) are those affections of the body of which we are not ourselves the cause, except partially; or are those changes in our power of acting which are, in part at least, impressed upon us from without. Since by definition such affections are known only inadequately, then insofar as we have an inadequate idea of anything, we suffer or are subject to the passions, and in proportion to the number of inadequate ideas we have.

Thus, Spinoza's theoretical construction of a science of psychology begins with his notion of body, of the action of bodies and of affections of the body. A body, however simple, is extended; and moreover, is identical with its activity, or power of acting. As an individual, short of being the composite and unique individual which is the universe itself (conceived under the attribute of extension), a body is part of a system of bodies; and is itself constituted as a system of bodies, which are its parts, insofar as it is not a simple body. Human beings, since they are neither atoms or simple bodies, on the one hand, nor Substance itself, or God, on the other, are composites with bodily parts, and are, as individuals, part of larger composites or systems of individuals. It is this position midway in the scale of nature—neither its ultimate constituents nor the whole—which constitutes the ontological character of the human individual, or person; and which provides the theoretical framework for an account of him as a conscious being, whose agency is identical with his body's power of acting. This power of acting, or self-activity is, in Spinoza's terms, the "perfection," the "reality" or the "existence" of any individual. The more modes of acting an individual has, the more "reality" or "perfection" such an individual has. And this power of acting is therefore dependent upon the kinds and modes of interaction available to that individual. Thus, the dependency on other bodies, in a strange and dialectical sense, is the very condition of a body's activity, since its power to act is its power to affect other bodies; as, in turn, the power to act of these other bodies is their power to act on this (my) body. The fundamental mode of the existence of human bodies, as individuals, is therefore a relational mode, or one of interaction.[4]

Insofar as composite bodies are acted upon by other bodies, they undergo modifications or affections. Spinoza treats this in a thoroughly mechanistic manner, in that such affections are literally changes or "traces" impressed upon the body, or its parts. When such changes

4. Cf. Arne Naess, "Freedom, Emotion and Self-Subsistence," and Jon Wetlesen, "Basic Concepts in Spinoza's Social Psychology," both in *Inquiry*, Vol. 12, no. 1 (Spring 1969).

or modifications disrupt the "proportion of motion to rest," which
is the equilibrium-condition for the continued existence of an individual—i.e. when the composite relation of motion and rest of the parts
of the body is disturbed—then the individual, as *that* composite, may
be destroyed. But short of this, the impressions or traces left on a
composite individual by the actions upon it of other external bodies
are affections which are necessarily "known" in the body, as the idea
of that body, or the mind. The mind's awareness of such affections
(or "the idea of these bodily affections") is, according to Spinoza,
the very essence of what it is to be a mind; and in this sense, the
mind is the "idea of the body." But Spinoza's theory of how these
affections come to be known depends on a mechanism of bodily
affections which produces "images"—on Spinoza's account, a kind of
physiological "echo" effect, whereby an impression made by an external body, striking on the "fluid parts" of the body, causes a deflec-
tion in the plane of the "softer parts," and thereafter the fluid parts
"by their own spontaneous motion" are reflected in the same way
(i.e. by an equal angle of reflection) by this changed plane, as they
were upon their original incidence. By this "angle of incidence equals
angle of reflection" mechanism, together with a notion of a reverbera-
tion or continuing "spontaneous motion" of the fluid parts, Spinoza
constructs a theory of reflection, or image-formation, whereby the
affection of a body by an incident body may be continued when the
incident body is no longer acting or present. In short, Spinoza proposes both a "trace" theory of images, and a mechanism for memory
—i.e. of the persistence of images when the actions or bodies originally
producing them are no longer present. A bodily affection is therefore,
literally, a change in the bodily constitution; and the awareness of
this change is the imagination, i.e. the mind's idea of this change
formed necessarily. What is important in Spinoza's theory is that
the mind is not *caused* to become aware of an image, by the change
in the body; this latter is the Cartesian model of mind-body interaction. Rather, for Spinoza, the mind's idea of this bodily affection
is just this very affection itself, conceived under the attribute of
thought. It is, therefore, identical, as idea, with the bodily affection.
Therefore, too, images are veridical, for Spinoza; they cannot be mistaken because, in effect, they are the ideas of bodily affections, and
are so necessarily; i.e. they cannot be otherwise than as they are.
Spinoza says, "these imaginations of the mind, regarded by themselves, contain no error, and . . . the mind is not in error because

it imagines, but only insofar as it is wanting in an idea which excludes the existence of those things which it imagines as present" (*E.,* II, xvii, S.). Error, for Spinoza, is negative, a deficiency, rather than a positive activity of the mind.[5] Thus the imagination, in presenting things which are absent as if they were present, is the occasion for, but not the cause of, error insofar as the mind is wanting in an idea which "excludes" (in Spinoza's terms) the idea of the presence of the imagined thing.

In connection with his theory of imagination, and the derived theory of memory, Spinoza develops an associationist mechanism, whereby the simultaneous action of two or more bodies on the affected body generate an association in the mind of the image of one with the other. In the proposition (*E.,* II, xviii) where he proposes this, he talks only of simultaneity; in the Scholium to that proposition, he talks also of associative memory in terms of the concatenation or order of the bodily affections. Here (in defining memory as "a certain concatenation of ideas, involving the nature of things which are outside the human body, a concatenation which corresponds in the mind to the order and concatenation of the affections of the human body"), he adds the idea of a sequence-association as well as a simultaneity-association.

The importance of this theory of image-formation and of imagination is that, in it, the image always carries with it the idea of an external body; and therefore, though the mind knows its own body only in the ideas it forms of the bodily affections, it has also the idea of external bodies as part of its idea of these affections, insofar as these affections are images. Moreover, the idea of the body is thus mixed with the idea of external bodies, as affecting it. And thereby, the mind knows its own body not as the adequate cause of these affections, but only as the partial cause. It therefore has, in Spinoza's terms, a confused knowledge of the bodily affections, since they do not follow simply from the nature of the body itself, or from its activity alone, but also from the action upon it of other bodies. Insofar as these actions upon it change or affect the body's power of acting, they also affect the mind's power of acting—i.e. they are the condition of inadequate ideas, or the limits upon the mind's clear and distinct ideas. For, Spinoza argues, "the mind doesn't know itself except in-

5. However, see G. H. R. Parkinson's discussion of some difficulties in Spinoza's theory of falsehood and error: *Spinoza's Theory of Knowledge* (Oxford: Clarendon Press, 1964), esp. pp. 120–127.

sofar as it perceives the ideas of the affections of the body" (*E.,* II, xxii). In this second-order knowledge, whereby the mind knows not only the bodily affections, as ideas it has of them, but also knows the *ideas of these ideas* of the bodily affections, the mind in effect knows itself. But as these ideas of ideas are themselves tainted with the inadequacy of the bodily affections, since they are not causes of themselves, the mind necessarily has inadequate or confused knowledge of itself as well (*E.,* II, xxix). In this condition of what Spinoza calls "external perception" he locates the Passions, and relates them to inadequate ideas, i.e. to confused knowledge.

One may ask why Spinoza essays such an elaborate theory of bodies and bodily affections as a condition for a psychology, and especially for a psychology of the affects or the emotions. It is precisely because his theory of the affects is intended to be continuous with his natural philosophy, his psychology continuous with his physics. The groundwork of Part Two of the *Ethics,* on bodies and their interaction, and on the identity of mind with the body's power of acting and its affections, is fully utilized in Part Three, "On the Origin and Nature of the Affects."

Several things may be noted here: first, that the metaphysical notions of adequate and inadequate causes has been "reduced" to a mechanics of bodily interactions. The reduction, however, has introduced the metaphysical notion of self-activity (the characterization of substance, as *Natura Naturans*) at the level of extended bodies, i.e. to individuated matter; and further, has defined body in terms of this self-activity, and of the limits imposed upon it, by the self-activity of other bodies. Second, by the mind-body identity, the adequate and inadequate causes have their counterpart in adequate and inadequate ideas. Further, the notions of action and passion are dependent upon the distinction between adequate and inadequate ideas (and concomitantly, adequate and inadequate causes). Finally, the whole structure of Spinoza's psychology rests on the analysis of action and passion, insofar as these are the systematic and theoretical concepts in terms of which the human beings' "power of acting" is defined. And this "power of acting" is identical with human existence and its psychological characterization—the human being *is* his activity, insofar as he is both agent and patient, in his interaction with other human beings, and with the things which are necessary for his existence. This activity is, according to Spinoza, self-preservative in its nature—it conduces to continue the human being in existence. Interestingly, Spinoza's rejection of all final causes yet preserves *this* one as the essential one: survival is the *conatus,* end and mode of human existence. What conduces to it is good; what affects it adversely is evil; but "good" or "evil" only insofar as the mind characterizes what it desires, or what gives it joy or causes sorrow. It is, for Spinoza, the primary affects of *desire, joy,* and *sorrow* which characterize the *conatus,* or the species of self-activity of the human being; and these, insofar as they enhance or increase the body's power of acting, or diminish it, lend it more "reality" or "perfection" or "existence," or less.

Spinoza will derive his ethical consequences from this *conatus,* just as Aristotle did, in the best naturalistic fashion. Happiness, after all, is that activity which is in accordance with man's nature. But man's "nature" is to survive, to persevere in existence; moreover, to "increase" his existence, or enhance it, by increasing the degree or amount of self-activity, or of action, and by diminishing the constraints on this self-activity, i.e. by controlling the passions. The remarkable thing, apart from questions of systematic success or failure, is the absolute *chutzpah,* the brashness of Spinoza's program: from the motions and interactions of bodies, to the psychology of the affects, to the therapeutic theory by which actions are enhanced and passions regulated, to the vision of blessedness and beatific virtue, all in one continuous sweep, deriving each later or higher stage from the one previous.

5. *The Theoretical Construction, II: Actions and Passions*

Spinoza begins his construction with a methodological claim: namely, that the affects should be treated in the same way, by a rational science, as any other natural phenomena; and this, for the reason that the human affects or emotions *are* natural phenomena, continuous with all of nature. In his celebrated phrase, man is not a "kingdom within a kingdom," but rather is wholly within the *one* kingdom, nature. He is not a disturbance or a break in the continuity and unity of nature; and therefore, there is no realm in which man has absolute dominion, or "freedom of will," in violation of the universal determinism of the natural world. Neither does man's capacity for folly and vice fall outside the dignity of a natural science:

> Nothing happens in nature which can be attributed to any vice
> of nature, for she is always the same and everywhere one. Her virtue

is the same, and her power of acting; that is to say, her laws and rules, according to which all things are and are changed from form to form, are everywhere and always the same; so that there must also be one and the same method of understanding the nature of all things whatsoever, that is to say, by the universal laws and rules of nature. The affects, therefore, of hatred, anger, envy, considered in themselves, follow from the same necessity and virtue of nature as other individual things; they have therefore certain causes through which they are to be understood, and certain properties which are worthy of being known as the properties of any other thing in the contemplation alone of which we delight. I shall therefore pursue the same method in considering the nature and strength of the affects and the power of the mind over them which I pursued in our previous discussion of God and the mind, and I shall consider human actions and appetites just as if I were considering lines, planes or bodies. (*E.,* III, "On the Origin and Nature of the Affects.")

Yet, it would be a mistake to take Spinoza's methodological reduction for an ontological reduction. Just as bodies are not lines, or planes, so too affects are not geometrical entities. The "universal laws and rules of nature" are not the laws of geometry; but the laws of geometry, of physics, and of psychology are universal, insofar as a common intelligibility underlies our understanding of them. This understanding has its most elaborated form in mathematics, in the method of demonstration from principles. It is this method, rather than the specific content of the mathematical principles, which Spinoza proposes here. Spinoza proposes, therefore, a unified science which would include previously separated domains. Analogously, the science of mechanics, in the seventeenth century, achieved a unification of the two discrete domains of Aristotelian physics, thereby accounting for both terrestrial and celestial phenomena by a unified set of principles and laws. But these unified principles bore only on *bodies* in motion or at rest. The realm of human action, insofar as it was conceived of as agential, was absolutely sundered from this mechanics. It is this breach between the domain of nature and the domain of mind, or human action, which Spinoza's monism is intended to overcome.

This program of unification is the methodological motive for proceeding "geometrically," i.e. by a deductive construction, in his theory of affects. Thus, he begins with the definitions of *adequate* and *inadequate causes, actions* and *passions,* and *affects.* We have seen that *adequate cause, adequate idea,* and *action* are parallel constructions, as are *inadequate cause, inadequate idea,* and *passion.* Spinoza defines *adequate cause* in terms of the concepts *effect* and *clear and distinct idea:* Thus, if an effect can be clearly and distinctly perceived, or understood by means of the cause, then the cause is adequate. Now adequate causes are not simply conceptual entities; that of which I can form a clear and distinct idea is actually existing (since clear and distinct ideas do not admit of falsity, or incompleteness). So the adequacy of the cause is to be understood ontologically, as entirely constitutive, by its action, of the effect. Partial constitution of the effect therefore yields inadequate causes, i.e. those whose effects cannot be understood by means of these causes alone. The notion "cause" therefore connotes efficacy in producing an effect. Or, it connotes an activity which is in itself either adequate or inadequate to produce or constitute an effect. Insofar as it is adequate, Spinoza calls it an action, and we are said to act "when anything is done, either within us or without us, of which we are the adequate cause"; and we are said to suffer "when anything is done within us, or when anything follows from our nature, of which we are not the cause excepting partially" (*E.,* III, Def. 2). What is "done," either within us or without us, insofar as it changes our power of acting, either increasing or diminishing it, is, in Spinoza's term, an *affect.* He gives the definition both in terms of modifications or affections of the body, and of the idea of these affections in the mind. In short, *affects* are changes in the person's life activity, enhancing or hindering it. They are never neutral, but entail some dynamic alteration of the vitality, the *conatus* of the person. If we identify the affects with the emotions, then it is clear that Spinoza holds that the life activity of a human being is constituted of a composition of such emotions. They are nothing but the variations in intensity and power of this life-force itself. Thus, we have a field theory of the emotions, in that the emotions are nothing but the dynamics of the life-force, *its* growth and diminution, as such. This stretches the concept of emotion beyond our present ordinary usage, however flexible this may be. For it says, in effect, that the principal characteristic of the person acting is his *power* of acting. His very existence *is* this power, both as it pertains to the body's activity and the mind's. And therefore, the split between the cognitive and the emotive or affective, or between faculties of thought and feeling, or more sharply, between thought and action, is systematically denied. Thought, as we shall see, is involved itself as a mode of this affective activity, or is this very activity itself insofar as it is reflected upon, or become self-reflective. In short, for Spinoza, thought *is* action, under the form of reflection; or is self-conscious action. The imagination operates as a mechanism whereby the affects are related to their objects, or to their imagined objects. Will is seen not as a separate faculty or agency, but only as the mind's affirmation or denial of truth and falsity. As such, the term *will* is an abstract characterization of the concrete and particular acts of volition, which are expressions of appetite or desire, when these are conceived under the attribute of thought alone. In this sense, Spinoza says will and intellect are the same, or a volition and an idea are the same (*E.,* II, xlix). Spinoza's conception of the person as a *conatus,* a life-activity striving to preserve itself in existence, places all of the usual psychological categories within this context, and sees them ultimately as the changes in the power of acting of this life-force, or as the conditions under which such changes take place.

From this glorious monism to the differential characterization of the affects, Spinoza proceeds proposition by proposition. But the details are subordinate to the systematic construction. Action and Passion are the crescendo and diminuendo marks, the dynamics of a life-activity. Ultimately, by virtue of the human body's dependency on what lies beyond it, and of man's consciousness of this dependency, man's actions are surpassed by the passions; he can never be the adequate cause of all the effects requisite for a life. Therefore, he can never be the master of himself, by an act of free-thought, or by sheer self-discipline. In Spinoza's terms (*E.,* IV, ii–iv) "we suffer insofar as we are a part of nature, which part cannot be conceived by itself, nor without the other parts," and "The force by which man perseveres in existence is limited, and infinitely surpassed by the power of external causes"; and further yet, "It is impossible that a man should not be a part of nature, and that he should suffer no changes but those which can be understood through his own nature alone, and of which he is the adequate cause." In short, man is bound by his finitude to the overwhelming power of the passions, and thus to inadequate and confused ideas.

In this darkest and most pessimistic portion of the *Ethics,* Spinoza proceeds again from his definitions and principles to an elaboration of the actual affects themselves, giving us the balance between those which are actions and those which are passions, and arriving at this by a calculus of the affects, or what we may characterize as a mechanics of the affects. Here, as in his discussion of the action and interaction of bodies, the model is one of the composition of forces or "motions," the primary "motions" or affects being three in number.

6. The Theoretical Construction III: The Affects

Spinoza, unlike Descartes and other previous theorists of the affects, fixes on three "primary affects." His is therefore the most economical construction, in terms of "primitives." He characterizes these as Desire (*Cupiditas*), Joy or pleasure (*Laetitia*), and Sorrow or pain (*Tristitia*). Desire is the *conatus* itself; namely the mind's consciousness of its own striving or effort to persevere in its being, to survive; but clearly, not simply a consciousness, but the striving itself *and* its consciousness. Insofar as this striving is related to the mind itself, Spinoza calls it *Will* (effectively, Will to Live); insofar as it is related to the body, it is called *Appetite;* but he says that these are the same, distinguished only in that desire is conscious appetite. Furthermore, he says that this Desire is the very essence of man "insofar as it is conceived as determined to any action by any one of his affections"; and further, "by the word 'desire' . . . I understand all the efforts, impulses, appetites, and volitions of a man which vary according to his changing disposition, and not unfrequently are so opposed to one another that he is drawn hither and thither, and knows not whither he ought to turn." (*E.,* III, The Affects, Def. 1 and Explanation). This first of the primary affects presents a special case, in view of our previous characterization of the affects as the dynamics of the life-force, or of the *conatus* itself. Some commentators[6] see in this an inconsistency in Spinoza. For either desire is the essence of man, or it is an affect, i.e. a modification of this essence. But it seems clear that the person's life-activity is not, itself, some abstract universal "force," or a merely formal essence, for Spinoza, but rather is the concretely constituted and alterable energy or activity of his existence. Thus, when Spinoza says that desire varies according to man's changing "disposition," he is saying no more than that man's power of acting changes, in accordance with the particular and concrete constitution of a man at a given time, or through some time. For Spinoza, dispositions are structures, and structures dispositions. To be consti-

6. D. Bidney, *The Psychology and Ethics of Spinoza* (New Haven: Yale U.P., 1940), pp. 100–111; J. Martineau, *A Study of Spinoza* (London: Macmillan, 1895), p. 260 (cited in Bidney).

tuted a certain way—i.e. for the composite human being to exist as that *particular* composite individual—is to be able to act a certain way. It is not the case that a given structure or composition "exists," and is only then affected by this or that desire, but rather that desire is the temporally indefinite (though finite) mode of activity which expresses, or is identical, as activity, with a given structure. As man's very essence, it is identical with his existence. One may say, with Spinoza, "no desire, no life." Now this *conatus,* which is the ongoing life-force or effort of a given individual which perseveres in existence, may be abstractly characterized as coextensive or identical with the existence or life of that individual. It is not thereby an abstract essence, but rather *is* the form and modification of this striving itself, in the course of a life. This is an exceptionally dynamic or energistic view of the person, as identical with his life activity; and of his modifications (bodily and mental) as themselves constituting this activity; and therefore of the person's constitution itself as a perduring unity through such changes. But this is, I think, precisely what Spinoza seeks, in breaking away from the mechanism of inert bodies, and the autonomism of a simple, undifferentiated mind, in which alone self-motion exhibits itself.

The relation of Desire to the other two primary affects, Joy and Sorrow, is also systematically complex. Spinoza's goal is not simply to give an account of Joy and Sorrow (or pleasure and pain), but rather to fix them, as affects, within the framework of a composite body (and its mind), acting and undergoing. Thus, in an echo of the Aristotelian account of pleasure and pain,[7] Spinoza sees Joy as "man's passage from a less to a greater perfection" and Sorrow as "man's passage from a greater to a less perfection." Since by perfection Spinoza means the same as reality or existence, or a man's power of acting, Joy is an increase in this power, Sorrow its diminution. Nor are these metaphors, for Spinoza, but literally the characterizations of the degree of autonomy a man has, i.e. the extent to which his actions proceed from his nature, or the extent to which he is the adequate cause of what he does, or of what happens in him. Thus, Desire and Joy, as primary affects, are capable of being actions, or active affects. But to the extent that Desire, Joy, and Sorrow are related to external objects, our knowledge of them is through the imagination, as we have seen; and to the extent of our dependency,

7. *Eth. Nic.,* 1152b ff.; *Rhet.,* 1369b 33 ff.

or the dependency of our ideas of these affects on what we know only inadequately, all such affects are passions and not actions.

Spinoza seems to be saying that even when our power of acting is increased, if this increase depends on what is external to us, or what doesn't follow from our nature alone—namely, on what is not entirely under the control of our own natures, or what derives from bodily affections caused in us, even partially, by external bodies—then the affects are in bondage to these externals. For mind, this means that we cannot have adequate but only confused ideas of what satisfies our desire, or causes us joy (or sorrow). This follows from the fact that the mind cannot have an independent and adequate idea of the external bodies with which the passive affects are concerned, but only an idea of the affections of its own body produced by the external body, and the imagination's positing of an actually existent and present body as the cause of these affections. Yet, for Spinoza, this dependency is not simply negative—it is so only in the case of sorrow or pain—but may be positive as well, in that even such inadequate causes may enhance or increase our power of acting, for else the concept of joy, or of its derivative affects (love, hope, confidence, self-exaltation, etc.) would be meaningless in the context of passive emotions.

There is a dialectical difficulty here, in that our power of acting is presumably that which conduces to our actions, not our passions, and is therefore enhanced by the clear and distinct, or adequate ideas we have of the causes of our affects. But insofar as these affects are passive, i.e. have at least part of their causes in external bodies of which we cannot have adequate ideas, they are limitations upon our activity, and are, as Spinoza says, passions. But how can passions increase our power of acting? Obviously, they cannot, on Spinoza's theory; yet the affect Joy and its derivatives plainly *are*, by definition, increases in our power of acting. Here Spinoza is ingenious, though I think not successful. The sense in which most passions *increase* our power of acting is the sense in which they are counterposed to other passions which *decrease* our power of acting; and the resultant effect of this composition of forces is a *lesser decrease* (by virtue of that, a relative increment) in our power of acting. Spinoza nowhere puts it in this way; yet, in his theory, an affect can be destroyed or delimited only by a stronger and opposed affect (*E.,* IV, vii). True ideas, he says, cannot alter an affect, insofar as they are true; but only insofar as these ideas (of good and evil) are considered as affects; that is, only insofar as they become affirmations of an increase in our power of acting. I take this to mean that the mere contemplation of a true idea by the mind is not yet an efficient cause at the level of affects, but that it needs to be embodied in our activity. What it proposes as good has to be embodied in our activity; what it proposes as good has to be desired, i.e. actively striven for; and what it proposes as evil, must become the object of our contrary striving. In Spinoza's terms, the good is simply the name we give to what it is we desire, or what, in the desiring, gives us joy, or increases our power of acting.

The primary affects, then, characterize the principal modes of human action and interaction. They constitute, as it were, the internal psychological life of man, in virtue of his relation to other things requisite for his existence.

Man is, on this view, a creature of needs, and of vital activity in the service of these needs. His whole psychic life is the mirror of this activity, or its double in consciousness. However, it is not that consciousness *reflects* these needs, but rather that consciousness *is* these needs themselves, under the attribute of thought.

What we have here, then, is a distinctive expression of the identity theory, not simply as a mind-body identity, but in this context, as an identity of thought and emotion, thought and joy, thought and sorrow, thought and desire. The radical consequence of this view is a rejection both of a mechanistic determination of psychic states by bodily states (an epiphenomenalist view too often mistaken for Spinoza's) and of a psychic determination of bodily states (the "free-will" views against which Spinoza argues). For if one takes the identity seriously, as Spinoza constantly reminds us to do, every change in a psychic state is a change in a bodily state, necessarily; but not causally. A change in the psychic character, or intensity, or quality of an emotion does not *lead* to a change in a bodily state; it *is* one. Thus, the mistaken notion that Spinoza proposes a parallelism as against Cartesian interactionism simply has the model wrong. There is a conceptual parallelism, insofar as we think of bodies and of minds. But what we think, under these two attributes, is not parallel, but identical. The import of this identity for a theory of emotion, its complexities and difficulties aside, is that it refuses to assign the study of the emotions either to an exclusively physiological, causal-determinist model of explanation, or to an exclusively descriptivist, phenomenological, or teleological model of explanation.[8] Spinoza eschews mind-body interaction of the Cartesian sort not because he insists on an autonomy of (somehow) "parallel" causal chains, but because he sees the emotions as variables in the dynamics of the life-activity of an integrated organism. The further import for a theory of therapy, regarding the emotions, is that any therapeutic effect must involve a change in the life-activity of the individual, and not simply either a change in a psychic state, or in a bodily state. Spinoza's analysis of the emotions is not simply a way of understanding the emotions, but by virtue of this understanding, a way of dealing with them therapeutically. The normative construction is already contained in his very definitions of the primary affects, and of action and passion. This, therefore, is no mere anatomy of the emotions or passions, but rather a guide for the improvement of life, insofar as our life-activity itself is constituted by the dynamics of action and passion.

The whole construction of the psychology thus depends on the conception of a bodily organism—a "complex body" or a "composite of composites"—adequate in its complexity to feel, to suffer, to enjoy, and to think. That Spinoza intended just such a materialism of emotional and psychic life (or just such a psychic and affective capacity for organized matter) is, I think, clear. And nowhere clearer than in his own paraphrase of the Identity theorem in Part II of the *Ethics* (*E.*, II, vii) in the Scholium on actions and passions in Part III: ". . . the order of the actions and passions of our body is coincident in nature with the order of the actions and passions of the mind" (*E.*, III, ii, Schol.). Moreover, in what follows, Spinoza presents his striking argument for the capacities of the body, to account for the highest human activities, such as architecture and painting, in terms of bodily activities. Here, Spinoza develops his most powerful argument for a materialist mind-body theory, precisely in the context of what would be considered distinctively "psychic" activities, and thus, presumably beyond explanation in terms of physiology. He does this

8. See, for a discussion on this point, L. S. Vygotskii, "Spinoza's Theory of the Emotions in the Light of Contemporary Psychoneurology," *Voprosy filosofii*, 1970, No. 6, tr. E. E. Berg, in *Soviet Studies in Philosophy*, Spring 1972, pp. 362–382. This essay by Vygotskii, excerpted from the last chapter of a monograph bearing the same title, is part of the last of a seven-volume collection of his work, presently in preparation, which will also include "Spinoza's Theory of the Passions." Vygotskii contrasts Kilthey and Lange, among others, with respect to "descriptive" (phenomenological) and "explanatory" (causal) psychologies of the emotions.

in answering a skeptical doubt that the body, in itself, could have such elaborate capacities:

> I scarcely believe . . . that, without a proof derived from experience, men will be induced to calmly weigh what has been said (about mind-body identity), so firmly are they persuaded that, solely at the bidding of the mind, the body moves or rests, and does a number of things which depend upon the will of the mind alone, and upon the power of thought. For what the body can do no one has hitherto determined, that is to say, experience has taught no one hitherto what the body, without being determined by the mind, can do and what it cannot do from the laws of nature alone, insofar as nature is considered merely as corporeal. For no one as yet has understood the structure of the body so accurately as to be able to explain all its functions . . . So that it follows that when men say this or that action of the body springs from the mind which has command over the body, they do not know what they say, and they do nothing but confess with pretentious words that they know nothing about the cause of the action, and see nothing in it to wonder at . . . But my opponents will say, that from the laws of nature alone, insofar as it is considered to be corporeal merely, it cannot be that the causes of architecture, painting, and things of this sort, which are the results of human art alone, could be deduced, and that the human body, unless it were determined and guided by the mind, would not be able to build a temple. (*E.*, III, ii, S.)[9]

9. Bidney draws a very different conclusion from this passage, and one which I think is wrong. He interprets it to show that, for Spinoza, there are bodily affects which do not involve coincident affects of the mind; or, in effect, that Spinoza is inconsistent here, since elsewhere Spinoza argues that all bodily affections are also affections of the mind, on the identity thesis. Thus, if Spinoza admits affections which are purely corporeal, as he appears to, e.g. in his sleep-walking example (*E.*, III, ii, S.), or in his account of such affects as trembling, paleness, sobbing, and laughing (*E.*, III, lix, S.), the identity is violated. I think, on the contrary, that the point of the passage is that, for whatever mental affections there may be (especially those which we are prone to think of as *independently* mental), there are yet bodily affections coincident with them; that the body is therefore complex enough, in principle, to support such complex affections. Therefore, the thrust of the passage is not to assert that there are no mental affections independent of the body. Yet, as Bidney points out, Spinoza has no theory of unconscious affections with which to cope with those modifications or changes of the body which remain beyond conscious life. I think, rather, that what is missing in Spinoza's account is a notion of threshold, or emergent level, beneath which bodies are not minded, but at which they are. This is suggested, however, in Spinoza's notion of the mind as the idea of a composite or complex

Now it would be puerile to interpret Spinoza as intending to argue here that the body is "just as capable" of building a temple as is the mind, or that a body without a mind could do so. The polemic here is against dualism, and for identity. Nor is it for some statically conceived and merely analytical or formal identity of mind and body; rather, Spinoza is arguing for the identity of the *conatus,* the striving, self-preserving and self-enhancing life-activity of a minded body. It is the identity of a power of acting, and in this context, the emotions or the affects are crucial, as we have seen, since they are in effect nothing but the variations in this power. Thus, in the same Scholium, Spinoza says:

> The decrees of the mind are nothing but the appetites themselves, which differ, therefore, according to the different temper of the body. For every man determines all things from his affect; those who are agitated by contrary affects do not know what they want, whilst those who are agitated by no affect are easily driven hither and thither. All this plainly shows that the *decree of the mind, the appetite, and determination of the body are coincident in nature, or rather that they are one and the same thing, which when it is considered under the attribute of thought and manifested by that, is called a decree, and when it is considered under the attribute of extension and is deduced from the laws of motion and rest, is called a determination.* (*E.,* III, ii, S.) [My emphasis—M.W.]

If we are to understand Spinoza's theory of the passions at all, this identity is all-important. For it is at this (systematic) point that the continuity of a science of nature with a science of man is affirmed. Since, in effect, the science of nature is a search for the rational (causal) connections among bodies, by means of which we come to understand nature under the form of law, the extension of this program to the human sciences cannot introduce a different or alien methodological principle. The human mind and in particular the affections of the mind, its changes in its power of acting, now fall under a double condition: methodologically, the mind too can come to be understood rationally, i.e. in terms of its determinations; but this methodological extension has its warrant in the ontological claim: since the mind is "nothing but" nature acting in a certain configuration, it is fundamentally no different from, and in fact, is identical

---

body. Spinoza is not a panpsychist, though the temptations to such an interpretation are great. Cf. D. Bidney, *op. cit.,* pp. 38–41.

with that nature which is also the subject of natural science; it is simply nature conceived under the attribute of thought. The enterprise, therefore, becomes a "natural philosophy of the mind," or a science of psychology whose *identical* counterpart is a scientific physiology. There are thus not *two* sciences, but one; and this one is simply conceived under alternative attributes.

In this sense, Spinoza is not arguing for a reduction of psychology to physics, but rather for an extension or elaboration of the physics of bodies to take into account the activities of those complex and composite bodies which constitute persons or human beings; a "physics" therefore, capable of explaining psychic function and human action. He uses the argument from complexity here, as a way of claiming for this complex organism those capacities for human action and art upon which his dualist opponents based their claims for free will and psychic agency. "I adduce also here the structure itself of the human body, which so greatly surpasses in workmanship all those things which are constructed by human art . . ." (*E.,* III, ii, Schol.). All this is therefore programmatic on Spinoza's part. His argument from ignorance (that we do not know the limits of corporeal activity) does not lead him, in the *Ethics,* to an actual examination of human physiology, which would begin to fulfill the program in actual research. Rather, he pursues his exploration at the level of psychological analysis, leaving it merely a programmatic claim that the "order of the actions and passions of our body is coincident in nature with the order of the actions and passions of the mind." I should rather say that this is more than simply a programmatic claim; for the metaphysical construction which Spinoza essays in the *Ethics* is made for the sake of supporting just this claim. And in this sense, I have argued that the metaphysics is for the sake of the scientific construction.

Spinoza's Moral Philosophy[1]

E. M. CURLEY

So, if there is any other, this manner of living is the best and is to be commended in every way.—*E.*, IV, xlv, C. 2, S.

Spinoza occupies a peculiar position in the history of philosophy. Nearly everyone is willing, if pressed, to concede that he is a philosopher of major importance, that in his system the philosophic ideal of presenting a coherent and reasoned picture of the universe and of man's place in the universe is realized to a degree that has few parallels. But hardly anyone is willing to devote to the study of his system the time and patience and care that most other major philosophers are granted as a matter of course.

This is particularly true of his ethical theory. It is a rare book on ethics which does not have at least a passing reference to Spinoza. But it is an even rarer book which has more than a passing reference. Those philosophers in our century who have been interested in ethical theory and who have gone to the history of philosophy—either to find a congenial ancestor or to add a scalp to their collection—have tended to go to Mill or Kant, to Plato or Aristotle, to Hobbes or Butler, to Hume or St. Thomas, but not to Spinoza. There are some notable exceptions to these generalizations. Most students of ethics will be familiar with C. D. Broad's chapter on Spinoza in his *Five Types of Ethical Theory*. But by and large what I say is true.

My purpose in this paper is to argue that it is not a good thing to ignore Spinoza in this way, that we have much to gain from trying to take a fresh look at him. I think we can make use of what has been said in recent years about the nature of ethical language to get a clearer idea of what Spinoza was about. We are now, it seems to me, in a better position to understand him than Broad was forty years ago. Conversely, I think we can also make use of what Spinoza says to raise important philosophical problems which are sometimes slighted in contemporary discussions. We may even find that Spi-

---

This essay was written especially for this volume.

1. This is a revised version of a paper read to the New Zealand Philosophy Association in Hamilton in May 1968.

noza's approach to the solution of those problems has something in it worth considering.

Let me sketch the way in which I intend to go about doing this. First I shall take up Spinoza's metaethical theory. Unlike some historical figures, who have had metaethical theories wished upon them, Spinoza does explicitly discuss the meaning of ethical judgments. Briefly his theory is this: when we say that something is good, we are not attributing a property to an object; we should not expect to find some property that is common and peculiar to all things that are good; nor are we saying that we have some kind of feeling or attitude toward the object; the judgment that something is good is a relative judgment—relative in a double sense; when we make this judgment, we are contending that the object bears a certain relation to a standard, that it conforms well to the standard; that is one sense in which the judgment is a relative one; but it is also relative in the sense that the standard to which we compare the object varies from one kind of thing to another—the standard to which we compare horses is different from the standard to which we compare men. The standard in each case is supplied by the general idea we have of the kind of thing in question. These general ideas Spinoza regards as confused and arbitrary. They vary from one person to another. The general idea that I have of horses is unlikely to be quite the same as the general idea that anyone else has of horses. And Spinoza does not seem to think that there is any possibility of one person's general idea being correct and another person's being incorrect. No standard occupies a privileged position. People's judgments will vary as their standards vary and that, it seems, is the end of the matter.

Such, in outline, is Spinoza's metaethical theory. The first part of the paper will be taken up in an attempt to show that this is really what Spinoza was saying, though, of course, he does not put the theory in quite that way. In the second part of the paper, my concern is this. The greater portion of Spinoza's ethical theory is devoted not to metaethics, but to normative ethics, not to the analysis of ethical judgments, but to the making of ethical judgments. He tells us that pity is in itself evil, that humility and repentance are not virtues, and that something which he calls the intellectual love of God is the highest good. This is puzzling. It is natural to suppose that when he makes these judgments he thinks that he is saying something which has some kind of objective status. If he does not think that these propositions have an objective status, i.e. if he does not think that they are the kind of proposition on which reasonable men ought to be able to agree, then these judgments would seem to be very much out of place in the *Ethics*. But the implications of his metaethical theory are such that it is very difficult to see how he could possibly have thought that his judgments were objective ones. The implications of his analysis of ethical language seem radically subjectivist. So in the second part of the paper I want to consider how Spinoza— or anyone who held similar metaethical views—might try to give his judgments an objective status.

But before considering that question, I must first amplify and justify the sketch I have given of Spinoza's metaethics. I said that, for Spinoza, the judgment that something is good does not attribute a property to an object. He expresses this view in various ways. In the *Short Treatise* he says that some things are in our understanding and not in nature.[2] These things Spinoza there calls entities of reason and he includes good and evil among them. In the *Ethics,* Spinoza's way of putting the doctrine is different. There he says that good and evil are only modes of thought, that they indicate nothing positive in things considered in themselves.[3] But I think what he is getting at is the view which we would now most naturally express by saying that goodness is not a property, or that "good" is not a property word. The grammatical form of "X is good" suggests that it is on a par with "X is yellow," or perhaps "X is 259-sided," but the grammatical form is misleading. That, in effect, is what Spinoza is claiming.

We can see this if we consider some of the arguments which Spinoza uses to support his view that good and evil do not indicate anything positive in things. One consideration he cites in its favor is that one and the same thing may at the same time be both good and either evil or indifferent. Music, he says, is good to a melancholy person, bad to one mourning, and neither good nor bad to a deaf man. This is the sort of argument which you might think would lead to a straight-forwardly subjectivist analysis, along the lines "X is good" means "X is pleasing to me."

But Spinoza has other considerations in mind as well which lead him to quite a different form of subjectivism. For instance, in a letter to Blyenbergh (19) he argues for the view that good and evil do not

2. *K.V.,* I, 10; G. I, 49.

3. The basic text for Spinoza's metaethics is the Preface to Part IV of the *Ethics.*

indicate anything positive in things on the ground that the same characteristics which we admire in animals we detest in men. He cites the bellicosity of bees and the jealousy of doves. The examples are, perhaps, unfortunate. It is not easy to see why anyone would admire those qualities even in those animals. But the same point can be made with a different example. It is no compliment to a man to say that he has all the virtues of a good dog. The docility we admire in a house pet we do detest in a man.

The kind of analysis to which this sort of argument leads is closer to Stevenson's second pattern of analysis than to his first, but it is closer still to Urmson's suggestive talk about grading. The point is this. We call things good in virtue of certain characteristics we take them to have. But "good" is not defined in terms of those characteristics. For the characteristics vary from one kind of thing to another and the meaning of "good" does not vary from one kind of thing to another.[4] The only thing a good man and a good dog have in common that sets them off from bad men and bad dogs is that each compares favorably with other members of its species. To say this is to say that there is nothing positive which they have in common. "Good" and "evil" are terms which we use to compare members of the same species with one another. A good X is one that compares favorably with other X's. A bad X is one that does not. The notion of "favorable comparison" is to be understood in terms of approximation to something we take as an ideal—our general idea of the species in question. A good X is one that comes fairly close to our general idea of the species X.

Spinoza regards general ideas as arbitrary and confused. This is one reason why I suggested that his metaethic was a form of subjectivism. First of all, he thinks of general ideas as being like general images which are formed from a multitude of particular images,[5] very much in the way that a composite picture of a number of men might be formed by photographing each of them separately on the same negative, using the technique of multiple exposure. It is not surprising, therefore, when he says that general ideas do not correspond to anything in nature, but are highly confused.

4. Hobbes seems also to have seen this. Cf. R. Peters, *Hobbes* (London: Penguin, 1956), pp. 162–165.

5. Of course, an image, for Spinoza, is a modification of the body, not an idea. Still general ideas are ideas of images formed in the suggested way, and will naturally possess corresponding defects.

Moreover, and this seems to me a more important point, the general idea of man that I have is going to depend on the nature of my experience of particular men. There is no guarantee that I will have encountered a random sample of men, and if the sample has been biased, then my general idea of man will reflect that bias. Again, the general idea which I form of men will depend in part on my own temperament and interests. I may have been struck by features of the men I have encountered which someone else would not have noticed, and I may have missed features someone else would not have missed. So these general notions are not formed by everyone in the same way. They vary from person to person, and as they vary, people's ethical judgments vary. Since none of them can be said to correspond to anything in nature, no one person's general idea is in a privileged position, and the same will be true of the ethical judgments which rely on these general ideas to supply a standard of comparison.

These subjectivist tendencies are reinforced when we consider the account Spinoza gives of how general ideas come to be used as ideals. This is clearly something which needs explaining if general ideas are formed in anything like the way Spinoza says they are. His description of that process suggests that my general idea of man will be the idea of a man possessing average height, average strength, average intelligence, average consideration for others, and so on—the average in each case being an average for that particular subclass of men whom I happen to have met. There does not seem to be any reason for giving men good or bad marks in proportion as they approach this average. Indeed there seem to be cogent reasons for not doing this. The average may be approached from either one of two directions—from "above" and from "below." The man who is very bright, very strong, very considerate of others, etc., may be as far from the average as the man who is his opposite in each of these respects. Yet both, if this is correct, would be equally bad men. The man of mediocre intelligence, strength, etc., would be a very good man. So it is difficult to see why we would use our general ideas as ideals.

The paradoxes which result from taking general ideas, so construed, as ideals no doubt account for Broad's curious misinterpretation of Spinoza on this point. According to Broad, when, on Spinoza's view, we say that Jones is a very good man, we are presupposing an arrangement of the members of the species man in an order determined by whether they perform the characteristic functions of men more or less efficiently:

> This series has neither in theory nor in practice a first or last term, or an upper or lower limit. Thus the notion of a "perfectly good" or "perfectly bad" man would be meaningless. But we can form the notion of an average or typical member of the species, though it is of course a fiction to which nothing actual exactly answers. A member of the species will then be called "good" if it performs the specific functions with decidedly greater efficiency than the average member and . . . "bad" if it performs them with decidedly less efficiency than the average member.[6]

This is just a mistake on Broad's part. Spinoza says quite explicitly that things are judged good or bad in proportion as they do or do not conform to our idea of the species in question. The general idea of the species does provide the series with an upper limit. A perfect man would simply be one who conformed exactly to our idea of man. It is no more meaningless to call a man perfect, on Spinoza's view, than it is to call him good. But though Broad is plainly wrong on the matter of interpretation, the theory he attributes to Spinoza looks rather more plausible at first than the theory Spinoza actually held. Why would anyone use his general idea of man as an ideal?

Spinoza does give an explanation of how this comes about, an explanation framed in terms of the notion of perfection. But for the most part what he says of perfection applies as well to goodness, if we make suitable modifications. The two notions are of the same type: both are modes of thought which we employ in comparing things of the same species to one another: both involve essentially reference to a standard. The chief difference between them is that perfection implies absolute agreement with the standard, whereas goodness implies only a more or less close approximation.

According to Spinoza, the notion of perfection—in ordinary language, at any rate—is tied up with the notions of purpose and intention. Initially, the term "perfect" was applied only to artifacts. A thing was called perfect if it was as its maker had intended to make it. A man builds a house. While it is in the stage of being built, it is imperfect. But once he finishes it, it is perfect—provided of course that the builder has succeeded in giving it the form he intended to.

6. *Five Types of Ethical Theory* (London: Kegan Paul, Trench, Trubner & Co., 1944), p. 46.

This sounds much more plausible in Latin, for the Latin word "perfectus" is simply the past participle of the verb "perficere," whose primary meaning is "to accomplish." Etymologically, "perfect" means "accomplished" or "finished" or "done thoroughly." It is a consequence of this view that strictly speaking we cannot say whether a thing is perfect or imperfect, good or bad, unless we know who made it and what he meant to make.

This original application of the notion of perfection is extended once we begin to form general ideas. We see a number of houses and we form a general idea of what it is for something to be a house. We grade houses as perfect or imperfect, good or bad, according to whether or not they conform to our general idea, even though in a given case we may not know who made the house or what specific kind of house he meant to make.

Presumably this is at least a halfway rational judgment. For though the builder of *this* house probably did not intend to build a house conforming exactly to my general idea of a house, still the features embodied in my idea of a house are features which I have found to be common to a number of houses. This means that they are likely to bear some relationship to the purposes for which people build houses. My general idea of a house gives me some guidance as to the builder's probable intention. If I find that his house lacks a roof, then I shall probably be right in judging it to be imperfect. I may be wrong. It may be that he is an eccentric whose only concern is to keep out the wind and not the rain. But probably he means to put a roof on his house, and just has not gotten round to it. So far as we consider the judging of artifacts, then, the use of general ideas as a standard seems to have some point.

But of course we do not judge only artifacts. We judge natural objects as well: horses and apples, sunsets and men. And here the use of general ideas as standards does not make sense. It would make sense on a teleological view of nature. If horses and men were God's artifacts, just as cars and houses are man's, then we might take the prevalence of certain features in a species as evidence of its creator's intentions. But this teleological view of nature and its attendant anthropomorphic conception of God are absurd. "We have shown in the Appendix of the first part of this work that nature does nothing for the sake of an end, for that eternal and infinite Being whom we

call God or Nature acts by the same necessity by which he exists."[7]
Hence our use of general ideas as standards for judging natural objects is entirely without foundation. And since the judging of one
particular kind of natural object—man—is what is at stake in ethics,
it is not easy to see how Spinoza could possibly suppose that any
ethical judgments ever are objective. We measure men by our general
idea of man and this is intelligible only on a discredited view of
nature.

The distinction which Spinoza draws here between artifacts and
natural objects is clearly analogous to that which Hare draws between functional words and words which are not functional. The
word "house" is a functional one. To know what it is for something
to be a house is, in part at least, to know what houses are for. This
knowledge carries with it, by implication, knowledge of the criteria
by which houses are judged good or bad. You do not really know
what it is for something to be a house unless you know what it is for
something to be a good house. By contrast, the word "sunset" is
not a functional one. Knowledge of the meaning of the word does
not carry with it knowledge of the criteria by which sunset fanciers
grade sunsets.

There are differences, of course, between the two distinctions.
Spinoza draws his distinction between different kinds of thing; Hare
draws his between different kinds of word. More importantly, Hare's
concept of a functional word explicitly includes the words for the
various kinds of roles which men play in society. Though carpenters
and secretaries would both seem to be, in Spinoza's sense, natural
objects and not artifacts, the words "carpenter" and "secretary" are
clearly functional words—their logical behavior is more like the logical behavior of "hammer" and "typewriter" than it is that of "sunset."
To know what it is for someone to be a secretary is to know what
it is for someone to be a good secretary, though we need not think
of secretaries as being the products of a divine craftsman in the way
that their typewriters are the products of human craftsmen.

But these differences between the Spinozistic distinction and the
Harean distinction are more superficial than significant. They are, or
seem to be, agreed on the point which is crucial for ethical theory:
that to know what it is for something to be a man is not necessarily to
know what it is for something to be a good man. And it strikes me,

7. *E.*, IV, Preface.

therefore, as quite appropriate that Hare, in attacking the views of Geach, should call to our mind the memory of Spinoza as he does in the following passage:

> Geach is the latest of a famous succession of thinkers who have systematically confused "what a thing can (or, alternatively, *can typically* or *does typically*) do" with the quite different notion "what a thing *ought* to do (or, alternatively, what it is *good* for it to do)." Plato was of course the principal culprit. The word "function" has perhaps been used to cover all these notions. The assimilation between them is only justified if we accept the assumed premise *Natura (sive Deus) nihil facit inane.*[8]

In stressing the differences between artifacts and natural objects, or between functional and nonfunctional words, and in questioning the teleological premise which underlies their assimilation, both Spinoza and Hare seem to place in jeopardy any claim that ethical judgments may have to objective status. For if, as they both seem to be saying, there is no set of criteria which occupies a privileged position as being, for some reason, peculiarly appropriate criteria for the evaluation of men, then it is difficult to see how one could ever hope for a rational solution to ethical disagreements.

So far I have been stressing the similarities between Spinoza's metaethical views and certain contemporary metaethical theories. And I think this is a useful thing to do for a number of reasons. For one thing it enables us to avoid the rather unhelpful classification of Spinoza as an ethical naturalist—a classification which Broad makes at the end of his *Five Types of Ethical Theory*. If we understand by an ethical naturalist someone who thinks that there is some property common and peculiar to all good things and who thinks that this common property may be identified with some empirical property which they have, then Spinoza is not in that sense an ethical naturalist. He may be an ethical naturalist in some other equally legitimate sense of that notoriously ambiguous term. I think he is. But he is not a naturalist in the sense defined; and this is a matter which is not merely verbal—for it means that his theory is not open to the telling objections raised against theories which *are* naturalistic in that sense.

Again, if you look at Spinoza in the way that I have been proposing, it seems to me that certain other aspects of his philosophy become more intelligible. Spinoza held, for example, that evil is

8. *Analysis* 18 (1957), 103–112, "Geach: Good and Evil."

merely a negation. This is a thesis which many people find very
mysterious. But if you view the terms "good" and "evil" as predicates
used not to ascribe a property to an object but to indicate that the
good or evil object conforms to some standard to a greater or lesser
degree, then the thesis that evil is only a negation is understandable.

Still, Spinoza does not develop his metaethical theory with anything like the subtlety and complexity we expect in a philosopher
nowadays. In stressing his similarity to contemporary thinkers there
is a danger of creating the impression that Spinoza was just doing
crudely the sort of thing people like Urmson and Hare now do with
more sophistication. This would be unjust. For Spinoza was also
concerned to do something quite different, something which places
him squarely within the Platonic-Aristotelian tradition that Hare is
so critical of, but something which he does in a peculiar way of his
own that is quite interesting.

Spinoza does not devote a great deal of time to the analysis of the
ordinary uses of ethical language. He thinks, not implausibly, that
the ordinary uses of ethical language are hopelessly confused in that
they employ standards of judgment for which no cogent justification
can be given. But he also thinks that it is possible to construct a
standard of judgment for which a cogent justification can be given.
Hence everything so far said about the apparently subjectivist implications of his metaethical theory has been misleading. Spinoza's view
—as I understand it—is not that normative judgments, including his
own, are inevitably subjective. On the contrary, it is only the judgments of the ordinary men that are confused and without solid
foundation. The normative judgments of the philosopher are—or can
be—solidly and unequivocally established. Whether or not we agree
that Spinoza is successful in carrying out his program, I think we
must agree that something like this was his intention.

We can see how Spinoza meant to go about laying a foundation
for ethics if we focus attention, not on the many general ideas of
human nature which confused men now use as standards in judging
other men, but on the one idea of human nature which clear-headed
men could use in judging other men (and themselves). After he has
argued in the *Ethics* that good and evil indicate nothing positive in
themselves, but are merely modes of thought, Spinoza goes on to say:

> Although this is so, we must nevertheless retain these words. For
> since we desire to form an idea of man as a model of human

nature which we may contemplate, it will be of service to us to retain these terms, in the sense I have mentioned. By *good,* therefore
I understand in the following pages everything which we know with
certainty is a means by which we may approach nearer and nearer
to the model of human nature we set before us. By evil I understand everything which we know with certainty to hinder us from
resembling that model. I shall call men more or less perfect or imperfect insofar as they approach more or less nearly to this model.[9]

Spinoza uses very similar language in the famous opening passage
of the *Treatise on the Correction of the Intellect.* After describing
his disillusionment with the "goods" pursued by the multitude—fame,
riches, and pleasure—Spinoza says that as his mind turned away from
its former, inherently unsatisfying objects of desire, the true good
became more discernible to him. "Man," he says,

> conceives a human nature much stronger than his own and sees that
> there is nothing to prevent him from acquiring such a nature. So he
> is spurred to search for means which will bring him to such a per-
> fection and calls everything which will serve as such a means a true
> good. The highest good is that he should arrive, together with other
> individuals if possible, at the enjoyment of such a nature . . . this
> is the end for which I strive, to acquire such a nature for myself and
> to endeavor that many should acquire it with me.[10]

Now it seems to me undeniable that when Spinoza talks of setting
before us a model of human nature, of conceiving a human nature
stronger than his present one, a character which he strives to attain,
both for himself and for others, he must be saying that we can form
an idea of human nature, which is rightly used as a standard of
judgment. Whatever may be the case about other ideas of human
nature, there must be something which gives this one a privileged
status.

Spinoza does not, in these passages, tell us much about the model
of human nature which is to be set before us, nor about how to attain
it. Filling in such details is the main burden of Parts IV and V of the
Ethics. When, at the end of Part IV, we are given a sketch of the life
of the free man—when we are told that the free man thinks of nothing less than of death; that, living among the ignorant, he strives as
much as possible to avoid their favors; that he endeavors to unite

9. *E.,* IV, Preface.
10. *TdIE,* 13–14, G., II, 8.

other men with himself in friendship; that he never acts fraudulently; that he hates no one, envies no one, is angry with no one, and so on—we are being given a description of that kind of human nature which we may take as ideal, as the standard for our judgments. These are the criteria by which we are to grade ourselves. This is the stronger human nature which Spinoza strives to attain for himself and endeavors that others should attain with him.

Clearly then, Spinoza is engaged in a project of commending a particular way of life to his fellow men. And the question we want to ask is how he would defend the claim that that way of life is an ideal. There seem to be two different but convergent strands in his thought at this point, one of which is much more important than the other.

The less interesting one occurs in the Preface to Part IV, where Spinoza writes that he understands the same thing by reality and perfection because

> we are accustomed to refer all individuals in nature to one genus, which is called the most general, viz. to the notion of being, which pertains to absolutely all individuals in nature. So insofar as we refer individuals in nature to this genus, compare them to one another, and find that some have more being or reality than others, to that extent we say that some are more perfect than others. Insofar as we ascribe something to them which involves negation—as do a limit, an end, impotence, etc.—we call them imperfect, not because something is lacking to them which is theirs, or because nature has sinned, but because they do not affect our mind to the same extent as those we call perfect.

I take it that Spinoza is not reporting on ordinary usage here, but is attempting to justify his own usage, both in the identification of perfection with reality (*E.*, II, Def. 6) and in the (equivalent) identification of virtue with power (*E.*, IV, Def. 8). But it is not easy to see what is the precise relevance of this introduction of the notion of the *summum genus,* Being. We might imagine that Spinoza has in mind something analogous to what occurs in his theory of knowledge. There the traditional instances of universals—man, horse, dog, etc.—are rejected as irrelevant to the scientific enterprise because of the inadequacy of our ideas of these universals. They are contrasted with the common notions like extension, and motion-and-rest, which are common to everything, can only be conceived adequately, and are fundamental to science. It is tempting to think that in his moral philosophy Spinoza meant to contrast our idea of the highest genus with our ideas of subordinate genera, and to argue that the idea of Being, because of its necessary adequacy, does provide an objective standard of judgment. Unfortunately for this line of reasoning, in the same passage in which Spinoza speaks so critically of our ideas of subordinate genera he also gives a similar account of the causation of our idea of Being, and says that the term "Being" signifies an idea which is confused in the highest degree.[11] So purely epistemological considerations do not seem able to account for the use of the idea of being as a standard. Indeed, such considerations would count against that use.

The other, more promising strand of thought invokes Spinoza's conception of human nature. The kind of life set before us as an ideal is prescribed by reason because it is the kind of life each of us, insofar as he acts according to his own nature and is not determined by external causes, necessarily seeks. This approach is summed up with characteristic conciseness in *E.*, IV, xviii, S.:

> Since reason demands nothing which is contrary to nature, it demands that everyone love himself, seek what is really useful to him, desire everything which really leads man to a greater perfection, and absolutely that everyone strive, insofar as he can to preserve his being. Indeed this is as necessarily true as that the whole is greater than its part (III, iv). Next, since virtue (by IV, Def. 8) is nothing but acting according to the laws of one's own nature, and one only endeavors to conserve his being (by III, vii) from the laws of his own nature, it follows that this endeavor to conserve one's own being is the foundation of virtue and that happiness consists in man's being able to conserve his being.

Now in a sense, there is nothing very novel about this argument. It is only a variation on the familiar theme of drawing conclusions about what a thing ought to do from what it does, a specimen of the well-known naturalistic fallacy, open to familiar objections. But if we examine the argument closely, we may find that there is something in the details of *this* variation which is novel and perhaps offers a way of coping with the familiar objections.

First, notice that the argument is not a simple inference from factual premises to ethical conclusions. Spinoza may proceed from "is" to "ought," but his premises include a formal ethical principle

11. *E.*, II, xl, S. 1, G., II, 121.

which many people would regard as unexceptionable.[12] I take it that the force of the statement that reason demands nothing contrary to nature is that

(1) Nothing which is (absolutely) impossible is obligatory.

"Contrary to nature," I suggest, means "contrary to natural law." And since natural laws, for Spinoza, are necessary propositions, an action contrary to nature is impossible—absolutely impossible, that is, and not merely impossible under certain given conditions. So the major premise is a form of the principle that "ought" implies "can."

The second premise—the "factual" one—is not, as it happens, stated in the passage quoted. But the argument plainly presupposes Spinoza's doctrine that "each thing, insofar as it can, endeavors to persevere in its being,"[13] and that "the endeavor of each thing to persevere in its being, is nothing but the active essence of the thing itself."[14] These propositions entail that

(2) Man necessarily endeavors, insofar as he can, to persevere in his being, i.e. that it is absolutely impossible that he should not so endeavor.

Spinoza's propositions, of course, are stated as very general ones, governing all individuals, and are not limited to stating something about men. Nevertheless, their main interest in this context lies in their application to man, and from that standpoint it will not matter greatly if they turn out to be false of other individuals, like spiders.[15]

The phrase "insofar as he can" translates Spinoza's "quantum in se est" in III, vi and this rendering calls for some comment. Both Elwes and White see Spinoza's use of the expression "in se est" as the use of a technical term and render "quantum in se est" by "insofar as it exists in itself." And while there may be good grounds for doubting that this is intended as a technical usage, I think their interpretive translation is fundamentally right. "Quantum in se est"

12. For a dissenting opinion, see E. J. Lemmon, "Deontic Logic and the Logic of Imperatives," *Logique et Analyse*, 8 (1965), 39–70.

13. *E.*, III, vi.

14. *E.*, III, vii.

15. Cf. Broad, *op. cit.*, p. 36. On the other hand, apparent exceptions in nonhuman nature do threaten the grounds Spinoza offers for the general form of the *conatus* principle and to that extent leave us without a reason (or without *his* reason) for believing it.

is used by Descartes in his discussion of the principle of inertia, where it clearly is not employed as a technical term.[16] Spinoza uses the same expression in his geometric presentation of Descartes when he offers his own proof of the principle of inertia. The *conatus* principle is conceived very much on the analogy of the principle of inertia and no doubt the use of "quantum in se est" is simply carried over from the one context to the other. Nevertheless, the force of the phrase in both cases is to suggest that if you consider an object in itself, without attending to any particular external causes, you will not be able to assign any reason for its changing its state— whether the change be in its motion-and-rest or in its "being."[17] So to suppose that an object unaffected by external particular causes would nonetheless change its state will involve a violation of the principle of sufficient reason. Now I have argued elsewhere that "existing in itself" means, for Spinoza, "existing independently of any external causes."[18] Hence, the Elwes-White translation is basically right in spirit.

The *conatus* principle (*E.,* III, vi) tells us how things act when they are not operated on by any external causes. It is this which licenses the identification in III, vii of the *conatus* with the active essence of the thing. All things are necessary, but some are said to be necessary in virtue of their essence or nature, and others are said to be necessary in virtue of their cause.[19] Since the perseverance of a thing in its "being" is not necessary by reason of any external cause, it must be necessary by reason of the essence or nature of the

16. Cf. Caillois' note to III, vi in Spinoza, *Oeuvres complètes,* ed. R. Caillois, M. Francès, and R. Misrahi (Paris: Gallimard, 1954, Pléiade edition). The relevant Cartesian text occurs in *The Principles of Philosophy,* II, 37. Spinoza's version of this is in his *Parts I and II of Descartes' Principles of Philosophy,* II, Prop. xiv.

17. Cf. Spinoza's demonstration of II, xiv in his *Descartes' Principles of Philosophy.* I leave aside here the question of what precisely Spinoza intends by "persevering in one's being." But it should be noted that as it is subsequently interpreted in Part III of the *Ethics,* it does not appear to be strictly a conservative principle, in the way that the principle of inertia is. It does not simply ascribe to things a tendency to maintain the *status quo,* but implies also a striving to increase the individual's power of action. Cf. *E.,* III, xii. This latter aspect is extremely important in Spinoza's psychology and is ignored here only for the sake of simplicity.

18. In *Spinoza's Metaphysics* (Cambridge, Mass.: Harvard University Press, 1969), Ch. 1.

19. *E.,* I, xxxiii, S. 1.

thing itself. It is, or exemplifies, a law of the thing's nature.[20] So it is absolutely necessary, not relatively necessary, or necessary under the given conditions.

Spinoza's argument concludes that reason "demands that everyone love himself, seek that which is really useful to him, desire everything which really leads man to a greater perfection, and absolutely that everyone strive, insofar as he can, to preserve his being."[21] If we telescope these various demands of reason into the final one, as I think we may, and if we translate talk about what reason demands into talk about obligation, as we did above in discussing the first premise, we may represent his conclusion in the following way:

(3) It is obligatory that man endeavor, insofar as he can, to persevere in his being.

The telescoping is legitimate, I think, because it seems likely that Spinoza would regard the other demands of reason as derivable from this one. The translation into the idiom of obligation is another matter, which I shall take up shortly. But the first thing to notice about this conclusion is that, *prima facie,* it is not validly drawn, not because it is an ethical conclusion, but because it looks like a stronger ethical conclusion than Spinoza's premises warrant. I have represented Spinoza as arguing, roughly, that impossible actions cannot be obligatory and that actions contrary to the preservation of our being are impossible. From this it does not seem to follow that *any* action is obligatory; all that seems to follow is that actions contrary to the preservation of our being are not obligatory, i.e. that actions in accordance with the preservation of our being are permissible. The most Spinoza has shown is that we may act in a certain way, not that we ought to.

Now this is plainly correct as far as it goes. It then becomes of interest to consider how Spinoza's premises would have to be strengthened to yield the conclusion he appears to want. One possibility is to add the premise that

(4) Some way of acting is obligatory.

We might then argue that since *some* way of acting is obligatory, and since no *other* way of acting can be obligatory because any other is impossible, Spinoza is, after all, entitled to conclude that

20. Cf. the *Metaphysical Thoughts,* I, 6, G., I, 248.
21. *E.,* IV, xviii, S.

actions in accordance with the preservation of our being not only may be done, but ought to be done.

Then the question becomes, Would Spinoza accept this further premise? Or, what amounts to the same thing, Is it legitimate to interpret his talk about what reason demands in terms of talk about obligation? Now it cannot be denied that Spinoza uses a great deal of language which sounds prescriptive. In the Scholium to *E.,* IV, xviii alone, he speaks of the precepts of reason, of what reason prescribes, of the dictates of reason, of what reason demands and so on. This sort of language is by no means unusual in his writing. On the other hand, it may be argued that to introduce the notion of obligation, and related notions like permissibility, is to presuppose a law conception of ethics which makes sense only if you conceive of God as a law-giver.[22] Now Spinoza explicitly rejects the conception of God as a law-giver—roughly on the ground that the notion of disobeying an omnipotent being is unintelligible.[23] So it might be said that if Spinoza's language is rendered in terms of obligations, permissions, etc., then an incoherence is introduced into his thought which it would be better to avoid.

This is part of the reason for the disposition of commentators to deny that Spinoza's moral philosophy contains any "oughts" or moral imperatives and to try to explain away the sort of language I have been stressing. To say that X is "dictated by reason," Wernham argues,[24] can mean one of two things for Spinoza.

(i) It may mean that X is dictated by the man's own reason, that he has an adequate idea of his own interest and sees X to be the necessary means to his interest. But if this is the case, he is "bound" to do X only in the sense that he cannot do otherwise. All men necessarily do what they think to be in their interest. There is no moral imperative and "to speak of [the] man's reason as issuing commands . . . is to use a misleading metaphor," since the language of commands presupposes an ability to disobey.

(ii) Or it may mean simply that X is, in fact, the necessary means to his true welfare, whether he sees it to be or not. To say that the

22. Cf. G. E. M. Anscombe, "Modern Moral Philosophy," *Philosophy,* 33 (1958), pp. 5–6.

23. Cf. *E.,* II, iii, S and the *Theological-Political Treatise,* Ch. 4, G., III, 62–65.

24. Benedict de Spinoza, *The Political Works,* ed. and tr. A. G. Wernham (Oxford: Clarendon Press, 1958). See particularly pp. 10, 19–20.

man is "bound" to do X in this sense is not to issue a moral imperative. For on this interpretation, the dictate of reason is quite compatible with the man's being causally determined to do not-X. This "ought" does not imply "can."

Wernham supports this interpretation with a good deal of textual evidence, and I have no doubt that it contains at least a part of the truth about Spinoza. But I cannot believe that it is the whole truth, or even the most important part. Spinoza is not engaged solely in the statement of eternal truths, he is also engaged in the advocacy of a particular way of living. No doubt we cannot use the model of a divine legislator to explain his deployment of concepts associated with a law conception of ethics. Still, before we concede too quickly that his moral philosophy contains (or can legitimately contain) no "oughts," we should see if there is not some other way of construing his prescriptive language so that it can embody genuine moral imperatives.

First of all, we must grant that Spinoza does not show himself to be very much interested in telling people to seek the preservation of their being. There would not be much point in prescribing a course of conduct people will necessarily follow anyway, and Spinoza is not one to waste words. He is much more concerned with telling us to cultivate certain "affects of the mind" as necessary means to that necessary end. His prescriptions, in Kantian language, are hypothetical imperatives with necessary antecedents, and so, in effect, categorical. If you want to "preserve your being," strive to hate no one. Well, you do want to preserve your being, and it is not a contingent fact that you do. It is, as a law of nature, absolutely necessary. So if the connection between antecedent and consequent is well made out, the command is not in any way conditional. The important thing, then, is to provide an intellectually compelling argument that the avoidance of hatred really is a necessary means to that end. This is the main motivation for the elaborate psychological apparatus of Part III.[25]

25. Kant, of course, is prepared to allow the existence of one end which can be presupposed as actual, and even necessary, in all rational beings. Cf. *The Foundations of the Metaphysic of Morals,* tr. L. W. Beck (New York: Liberal Arts Press, 1959), p. 33. His objection to treating imperatives prescribing means to that end as categorical seems to be that no one can be clear about what really will lead him to the end he seeks, and hence (I suppose) that no one can perceive "counsels of prudence" as unconditionally binding. I take it that Spinoza

But is it not quite possible that doing X should be a necessary means to my welfare and that I should nevertheless be causally determined not to do it? Yes, of course. Still, this need not prevent our saying that you ought to do X. Moral imperatives are rules of conduct which have a double generality. They prescribe a certain *kind* of conduct, not just particular actions, and they prescribe it to *all* men alike, not just to some. Both sorts of generality are relevant here.[26] It makes perfectly good sense to issue a general prescription to people to avoid acts of a certain kind, even if you know that some of them, in some circumstances, will be unable to comply. It is sufficient to give the prescription point if there are some circumstances in which some will be able to comply. A command which prescribed conduct that is absolutely impossible would be pointless. But a command which prescribes conduct that will only be impossible under certain conditions may be a perfectly sensible command.

Does this show that Spinoza's determinism is compatible with his espousing a hortatory ethic? I do not suppose that it does entirely. It may be replied that the distinction between what is absolutely necessary and what is only necessary under certain conditions is of no help. It does not matter that some actions are explained by reference to the thing's nature (and the absence of any countervailing external causes), whereas others are explained by reference to external causes. The fact remains that for Spinoza all actions are equally necessary. Of any action it may be said that it could not have been otherwise. That one has to add "under the circumstances" is irrelevant, since the same thing may be said about the circumstances.

At this point I think Spinoza's reply would be that we need to keep the question of whether people are to be blamed for what they do quite separate from the related questions of whether they may be exhorted to act in a certain way and punished for not so acting.[27] Blame is essentially retrospective, and the consideration, with re-

---

would join issue over the claim that "the task of determining infallibly and universally what action will promote the happiness of a rational being is completely unsolvable" (p. 36).

26. For a passage in which Spinoza shows himself alive to the importance of the second sort of generality, see *E.*, IV, lxxii.

27. These questions are commonly run together by Spinoza's critics, from Oldenburg to Copleston. Cf. the correspondence with Oldenburg, *Ep.*, 74, 75, and 77–79, and F. Copleston, *A History of Philosophy, Modern Philosophy: Descartes to Leibniz* (Garden City, N.Y.: Image Books, 1963), vol. 4, p. 254.

spect to a past action, that under the circumstances the action could not have been otherwise, is sufficient to render the blame irrational. Exhortation and punishment, insofar as they are rational, are prospective. They seek to provide circumstances for future action such that it will be as we would wish it to be. So Spinoza writes that

> this inevitable necessity of things does not destroy either divine or human laws. For whether the teachings of morality take on the form of a law from God himself or not, they are nonetheless divine and salutary,[28]

and that

> men can be excusable and nevertheless lack blessedness, and be tormented in many ways . . . he who goes mad from the bite of a dog is indeed to be excused, though he is rightly suffocated. Whoever cannot govern his desires and limit them from fear of the laws —though he is to be excused on account of his weakness—nevertheless cannot enjoy peace of mind and the knowledge and love of God, but necessarily perishes.[29]

As Spinoza remarks elsewhere, bad men are no less to be feared when they are bad by necessity.[30] So we may properly defend ourselves against them by taking whatever punitive action is necessary. Analogously, good counsel is no less good because it will be either necessarily acted on or necessarily not acted on. Where the offering of such counsel can contribute to providing circumstances sufficient for right action, we would be foolish not to offer it. Only when determinism is confused with fatalism, and we assume that people's actions will follow a certain path no matter what the circumstances are, can it seem irrational to offer prescriptions for conduct.[31]

This account of how Spinoza's prescriptive ethics may be reconciled with his determinism seems to me to move generally in the right direction. But it is still somewhat artificial in its concentration on action and in its tendency to overestimate the importance of exhortation. Spinoza, I think, would have had a great deal of sympathy both with the view of human nature, and also with the conception of the task of moral philosophy, recently advocated by Iris Murdoch. Miss Murdoch argues that most modern moral philosophy

28. *Ep.,* 75, G., IV, 312.
29. *Ep.,* 78, G., IV, 327.
30. *Ep.,* 58, G., IV, 268.
31. Cf. Copleston, *op. cit.,* p. 257.

—both in its analytic and in its existentialist wings—has been dominated by an entirely unrealistic picture of the nature of choice, has severed choice from its "continuous background" in the human personality, and has concentrated on "inspiring ideas" like freedom, sincerity, and the rational discernment of duty—which are not complex enough to do justice to what we really are. "The agent, thin as a needle, appears in the quick flash of the choosing will."[32]

By contrast, she argues for a view of human nature, in which man is seen as

> . . . much more like an obscure system of energy out of which choice and visible acts of will emerge at intervals in ways which are often unclear and often dependent on the condition of the system in between the moments of choice.

What is of primary importance, morally, is the quality of the consciousness from which action flows, and one of the main problems of moral philosophy is that of deciding whether there are

> . . . any techniques for the purification and reorientation of an energy which is naturally selfish, in such a way that when moments of choice arrive we shall be sure of acting rightly.

Where a person is subject to strong emotions, there is not much use in our addressing moral imperatives to him, or in his addressing them to himself. "What is needed is a reorientation which will provide energy of a different kind, from a different source." Moral philosophy should focus on enduring states of mind, rather than the moment of choice.

This conception of human nature is derived in the first instance from Freud, but there is surely a great deal in it which is derivable from Spinoza. What he is certainly most concerned with, in Part IV of the *Ethics,* is commending the gradual formation of a certain kind of character which will be less a prey to violent, destructive emotions. "The true knowledge of good and evil cannot restrain any affect insofar as that knowledge is true, but only insofar as it is considered as an affect."[33] So the "energy" of the individual, its endeavor to persevere in its being, requires to be put in the service of a better informed consciousness. And Part V of the *Ethics* is

32. See *The Sovereignty of the Good* (London: Routledge and Kegan Paul, 1970), particularly pp. 53–56, 70–71, and 83–84.
33. *E.,* IV, xiv.

specifically designed to describe techniques for the purification and reorientation of that energy.[34] The most important of these is that the mind should be filled with the intellectual love of God.

So far I have been arguing for a particular interpretation of the structure of Spinoza's attempt to provide a foundation for normative ethics. I have presented him as moving in a way that is not obviously invalid from a theory of human nature to prescriptive conclusions, provided that we understand his argument to rely also on certain ethical premises which are at least highly plausible. But I have not considered whether Spinoza's theory of human nature is defensible. Clearly this is an important question. Equally clearly, it deserves fuller treatment than there is space for here. But I would like to close by suggesting that it ought not to be dismissed as lightly as egoistic psychological theories sometimes are.

Forty years ago Broad thought that no modern philosopher need take the trouble to treat egoistic psychologies seriously. Though they might still flourish among bookmakers and smart young businessmen, they had been killed in "higher social and intellectual circles" by Butler. Butler's refutation is of interest now only because "all good fallacies go to America when they die, and rise again as the latest discoveries of the local professors."[35] That is as it may be, I suppose. If Broad were writing today, he would not need to go so far afield to find a venue for the resurrection of dead theories.[36]

The central objection to psychological egoism, I take it, is that it is either patently false or vacuous. It is patently false if it denies the possibility of distinterested action, and vacuous if it interprets the notion of egocentric action so broadly that nothing could count as a disinterested action. Now I do not think that Spinoza's version of egoism is faced with quite that dilemma. His doctrine that people strive for the "preservation of their being" cannot be directly refuted by confrontation with unanalyzed everyday experience, any more than the principle of inertia can. Both principles are protected from direct falsification by the qualifying clause, "quantum in se est." Both principles profess only to describe how things act insofar as they are not acted on by other things. If there is a danger of vacuousness, it arises from this qualification, and not from the fact that the goal of human action is specified in elastic and all-inclusive phrase-

34. See particularly *E.,* V, x, S and *E.,* V, xx, S.
35. *Op. cit.,* p. 55.
36. Cf. Murdoch, *op. cit.,* pp. 51, 78.

ology. The *conatus* principle could be rendered unfalsifiable by treating any deviation from the norm it describes as sufficient evidence that the individual is being acted on by external causes, just as the principle of inertia could be made unfalsifiable by treating any deviation from rest or uniform rectilinear motion as sufficient evidence of the operation of external forces. But in neither case is that necessary. If physicists were not successful in finding external factors to correlate in a law-like way with deviations from the principle of inertia, no doubt they would eventually give it up. Analogously, the fate of Spinoza's *conatus* principle would depend on whether or not it could be successfully integrated into a systematic psychology which would be able to account for apparent exceptions.

Whether or not there is, or is likely to be, any successful psychological theory incorporating an egoistic first principle very like Spinoza's is a difficult question, which had better be left for discussion on another occasion.

Spinoza and the Political Problem

HILAIL GILDIN

I

Spinoza's political philosophy is generally acknowledged to be greatly indebted to that of Hobbes. Spinoza appears to adopt wholeheartedly all of Hobbes's innovations in political thought. Like Hobbes he seeks a clear, precise, and effective solution to the political problems of men based on an understanding of men as they are and fit to be imposed on men as they are. Like Hobbes, he seeks to arrive at an understanding of the goals of political life by going back to a pre-political "state of nature" out of which man-made political orders emerge. Both speak of man's natural right to all things in the state of nature. Both speak of the transfer of this right to the sovereign power when men institute political societies. Both regard the attainment of peace and security as the purpose of political life. Finally, a considerable portion of the political writings of both is devoted to an attack on what both regard as erroneous views regarding the proper relation of religion to politics.

In spite of this broad area of agreement, Spinoza arrives at conclusions which are strikingly different from those of Hobbes. Spinoza manifests as decided a preference for democracy as Hobbes does for absolute monarchy. Spinoza rarely mentions absolute monarchy without criticizing it forcefully. Furthermore nothing in Hobbes appears to correspond to the central importance which Spinoza ascribes to granting men freedom of speech as a matter of principle. On the rare occasions on which Spinoza mentions Hobbes by name, he only does so in order to bring out the differences between them. Spinoza does not exempt Hobbes from the condemnation of all previous political philosophers with which he opens the *Political Treatise*.

A careful analysis of Spinoza's accounts of the state of nature and of the formation of society disclose significant differences between his views and those of Hobbes even where one would have thought their positions to be closest. The remarks that follow will be based

---

This essay was written especially for this volume.

on Spinoza's treatment of these subjects in the *Theologico-Political Treatise,* the only work in political philosophy which he lived to complete. The *Theologico-Political Treatise* does not set forth Spinoza's full political teaching. It does not present Spinoza's views regarding the institutions that well-formed commonwealths of various kinds must have. The *Theologico-Political Treatise* does, however, contain a clear analysis of what Spinoza thinks the political problem to be. It also proposes Spinoza's solution to a problem which he thought would have to be solved before the political problem could be solved: the problem of the relation between religion and political life. The principle underlying Spinoza's solution to this problem proves, upon analysis, to be identical with the principle that governs his recommendations for the construction of sound political orders.

In order to follow Spinoza's analysis of the political problem in the *Theologico-Political Treatise,* it is important to be aware of a certain peculiarity that characterizes his exposition. Spinoza begins his discussion of politics by describing the natural right of men in the state of nature, the misery that results from their exercise of that right, the desire of men to leave the state of nature, their agreement to transfer all their natural right to a sovereign charged with maintaining peace between them, and the sovereign's inability to maintain peace unless he can make breaches of the peace and disobedience to himself unprofitable through the use of coercion. Spinoza no sooner completes his presentation of this solution to the problems posed by the state of nature, a solution that cannot help reminding one in most points of the views of Hobbes, than he immediately proceeds to question it (201[9–14 and ff.]).[1] The grounds on which he questions it are that it fails to solve the political problem and that the analysis on which it is based even fails to catch sight of what the true problem is. This strange procedure is then repeated. In the next to the last chapter of the *Theologico-Political Treatise,* Spinoza discusses what authority the sovereign should have over the practice of religion. His initial solution to this problem again reminds one of Hobbes. Spinoza argues that the sovereign cannot do what he was brought into being to do unless he possesses complete authority, not over private religious convictions, but over any expressions of those convictions

1. All references to the *Tractatus Theologico-Politicus* in the text are to page and line numbers of Gebhardt's edition of Spinoza's Collected Works, Volume III.

in speech or action. In the immediately following chapter, Spinoza objects to the exercise of that authority and teaches that in a good commonwealth the sovereign will allow everyone to think what he wants and to say what he thinks, particularly with regard to matters of religion. The peculiarity we have been describing is neatly expressed in Spinoza's own outline, in the Preface to the *Theologico-Political Treatise,* of the argument of the last two chapters of that work: "After this I show that the holders of sovereignty are not only the protectors and interpreters of civil right but also of sacred right and that they alone have the right to decide what is just, what unjust, what pious, what impious. And finally I conclude that they can best retain this right and safeguard the dominion if everyone is allowed to think what he wants and say what he thinks (11[31]–12[2])." The following paragraphs will try to show that a proper understanding of the peculiarity under discussion will also shed light on Spinoza's understanding of the political problem.

II

Spinoza opens his discussion of politics in the *Theologico-Political Treatise* with an analysis of natural right. By natural right he means something broader than Hobbes did. Hobbes had deduced man's natural right to all things in the state of nature from the fact that it was a war of all against all and that in such a situation it was fully in accord with right reason for each individual to do whatever he thought best in order to preserve himself. Spinoza abandons the restriction that what is by nature right must be in accord with right reason. His account of natural right follows from his views regarding natural necessity, a necessity to which he believes man to be subject no less than anything else. Those who reject this view are accused by him of regarding man as "a state within a state." Spinoza equates natural right with the irresistible power of irresistible natural necessity. Natural right so understood is not confined to man. "Fish, for example, are determined by nature to swim, and big ones to eat smaller ones; and so fish take possession of the water, and big ones eat smaller ones with supreme natural right (189[15–17])." The application of this interpretation of natural right to man leads to the following result: "The right and precept of nature under which all are born and for the most part live, forbids nothing except what no one desires and what no one can do; it rejects neither strife, nor hatred, nor anger, nor deceit, nor anything whatever that appetite urges (190[30–33])."

Spinoza's equation of natural right with power leads to differences between himself and Hobbes regarding the best way to bring the state of nature to an end by putting natural right under some restraints. For Hobbes, this is accomplished by a contract through which men transfer the natural right to all things to a sovereign. Three well-known features of Hobbes's teaching regarding this transfer deserve notice here: (1) the right to self-preservation cannot be transferred to the sovereign; (2) the contract through which this transfer is effected is binding in conscience (even a promise made to a thief in order to save one's life is binding in conscience); (3) the fact that the contract is binding is not enough to guarantee its observance; to guarantee its observance the sovereign must have the right to punish violations of it by any penalty he thinks proper, including death. Nevertheless the binding character of the contract is not totally without effect. Hobbes wants the subjects to obey the sovereign not only because they are afraid of him but out of an understanding why they should obey him; he wants a special effort to be made to educate subjects in their duties by teaching them his doctrines.

Spinoza also believes, together with Hobbes, that men must transfer their natural right to do as they please to a sovereign if they are to surmount the miseries of the state of nature. Because natural right is power, this means that men must transfer to the sovereign their power to do as they please. Either this transfer takes place or it does not. If it does take place, men have no power to resist the commands of the sovereign, and it makes no sense to speak of their retaining any inalienable rights. If they do retain any rights vis-à-vis the sovereign, they also retain the power to disobey him, and the state of nature has not been effectively surmounted. For this reason, Spinoza speaks of men transferring *all* their power and *all* their natural rights to the sovereign (193[19]–194[5]). The example of how this is done which Spinoza finds clearest for his purposes is democracy, which he presents as a paradigm of what the correct solution requires rather than as the only regime compatible with the correct solution. In a democracy men transfer their natural right or power to all members of the society collectively. The collective right of the society to demand obedience from the individual has the same overriding superiority over his right to disobey as its collective power has over his power to disobey. What is true of democracy must be no less true of aristocracy and monarchy. Only a government with all the power of its subjects transferred to it can keep them from relapsing into the misery of the state of nature. Once the transfer has taken place, men must do whatever they are told to do by the sovereign. Spinoza assures the reader that men can do this without great peril to themselves at least in a democracy. The power and right of Spinoza's sovereign does not depend on men being bound by the promises they make to him. Spinoza discusses the case of the promise made to a robber in order to save one's life. He denies that such a promise is binding, not because it is made to a robber, but because natural right does not forbid deceit (192[10–16]). To be sure, if men on the whole were guided by reason, they would realize that deceit undermines the fabric of society and that it is therefore to be shunned as a great evil. But the lives men commonly lead is determined, not by reason, but by certain common passions and pleasures. To rely on the efficacy of moral convictions is to disregard the fact that men will never forego anything that their passions lead them to think good except out of hope of some greater good or fear of some evil. It is on this alone that obedience to the sovereign must be based. A commonwealth ruled in this way continues, in a sense, to remain in the state of nature which, in another sense, it surmounts, and its subjects continue to possess the natural right which, in another sense, they have transferred (see *Ep.* 50, beginning). What men do still is determined by what their passions lead them to think best for themselves, but the outcome of what they do is no longer strife engendered or intensified by hatred, anger, or deceit.

Immediately after completing his discussion of this solution to the political problem, Spinoza proceeds to raise serious doubts regarding its adequacy (Chapter XVII, beginning). He appeals to the actual practice of rulers, which he had largely ignored before. The continuing need for coercion indicates that the transfer of right or power to the sovereign is never completely consummated. Even with all the instruments of coercion at their disposal, there is a limit to what rulers can demand of their subjects without provoking a rebellion. The subjects continue to enjoy a latent power to rebel which cannot be taken from them. Spinoza goes so far as to maintain that rulers never are so firmly established that they do not fear overthrow by their subjects more than defeat by a foreign enemy. The continued need for organs of coercion as well as their inadequacy for securing complete obedience shows that the natural right of subjects has not been brought under complete control. The replacement of natural right by the right of the sovereign obtains *de jure* rather than *de facto;* it is to a considerable extent a fiction. This is true despite the great power rulers have of molding the souls of their subjects by remote control: most men can be made to believe, love, and hate what their rulers want them to. Yet the situation remains as it has been described. Every dominion depends on the faithfulness, virtue, and steadfastness of its subjects. But, however men may be brought up to believe that they should be faithful, virtuous, and steadfast, they remain wayward and corruptible, envious and mercenary, and prone to criminal innovations. At best, only limited transfers of natural right are possible. There is a dangerous gap between the degree of obedience that must be demanded for the attainment of peace and security and the degree to which this demand can be effectively met. This gap is an ineradicable vestige of the state of nature and its anarchy. It gives the ruled an opportunity to disobey their rulers. It makes rulers eager to forestall such disobedience by oppressing the ruled and reducing them to helplessness. Becoming aware of this gap makes it possible to reach a clear understanding of what the true political problem is and what the solution to that problem must accomplish. The true political problem is to eliminate the danger of tyranny and anarchy to which the gap under discussion leads, without eliminating the gap itself, and to make both rulers and ruled conduct themselves as the common good requires despite the continued existence of this gap.

The authority of the sovereign over his subjects is also threatened from another source. This source is what Spinoza calls superstition. The proper way of dealing with that threat is one of the major themes of the *Theologico-Political Treatise.* According to Spinoza all men are by nature prone to superstition (6[18–19]), and nothing can be done to liberate most men from their subjection to it. (12[10–11]). If men become members of a religious sect, there is always the danger that the leaders of that sect will seek to control its adherents by arguing that men must obey God and His interpreters in preference to their secular rulers.

In order to completely eliminate this danger Spinoza demands, as Hobbes had done before him, that the man or body of men which rules a society be given absolute control over the practice of religion. Spinoza demands more than the right to influence the religious observances of a society by determining what religious doctrines may be promulgated. He wants the ruler to have the right to exercise control over the practice of religion in his own name and on his own authority. Spinoza devises a series of arguments in support of this demand. The thread that runs through all of them is the supreme importance of political society for the practice of justice and charity, i.e. for the exercise of piety as Spinoza had defined it earlier in the *Theologico-Political Treatise*. Anything that weakens the commonwealth restores the condition from which it rescued man, a condition in which the exercise of piety is impossible. The highest exercise of piety is patriotic concern for the public welfare. It is the office, not just of anyone, but of the sovereign of a society, to decide what the public welfare demands. Obedience to God, therefore, means obedience to the sovereign of a society. God only rules over men through men with the right to give commands. There are no traces of divine justice except where just men rule. The civil authority has the highest and strongest claim to the obedience of all on grounds of piety as well as of expediency. It cannot secure that obedience if the control of religion is denied it. A large part of the obedience due it will fall to those who do exercise this control. To seek to restrict the civil authority's right to regulate religion is tantamount to sedition (Chapter 19).

Spinoza's demand that the sovereign openly control the practice of religion is reminiscent of his demand that it control everything simply, or that all the rights of its subjects be completely transferred to it. Both demands are no sooner made than they are withdrawn. The reason for their withdrawal is the same: it is by nature impossible for these demands to be met. The making of both demands served a purpose. It showed what a perfect solution required and what the consequences of its not being available were.

The two demands are in reality one. If a ruler could make his subjects think whatever he wished, his power over them could be complete. The core of natural right, at least among men, is the power that each individual has to judge things for himself and to seek to preserve himself in accordance with his judgments. The right to judge for oneself cannot be transferred in the sense that it cannot be directly subject to another's command. Even when one obeys an armed robber, one does so in the belief that it is safer to do so because the robber is armed. It is true that in claiming for the ruler the right to regulate the exercise of piety Spinoza explicitly denies him the right to interfere with an individual's private convictions about God (229[3–8]). But this restriction remains in force only as long as an individual keeps these convictions private. The moment he utters them publicly, attempts to convert others to them, or does anything else his convictions may demand of him, he invades the province of the civil authority unless he acts with its permission. However, Spinoza is aware that the civil authority could not prohibit the utterance of specific religious convictions and forbid specific religious ceremonies without branding these convictions and ceremonies as criminal. Those who sincerely espouse them cannot respect such a prohibition. They will view it as an invasion by the civil authority of a province over which it has no control. They will regard the civil authority not as a ruler to be obeyed but as a tyrant to be resisted, and if possible destroyed (244[3–18]). Even assuming the forbidden religion to be that of a minority, the civil authority will not be able to prohibit it in its own name. It will be compelled to justify its action by appealing, and therefore in a way submitting, to an authority different from its own, to the authority of the most powerful religion of the community, an authority that it will strengthen and inflame by its submission and appeal (225[17]–226[7], 244[13]–245[16], 247[1–17]). It appears impossible for the ruler of a society to secure obedience to his decrees about religion on the strength of his political authority alone.

The consequence of this impossibility could seem to be the insolubility of the political problem. This is so despite the fact that Spinoza does not deny the civil authority the power to rule the minds and souls of its subjects. Thus what the civil authority cannot accomplish in its own name, it may seek to accomplish by resorting to deceit. A king who succeeded in convincing his subjects that he was divine or semidivine could enjoy undisputed political and religious authority over them. Spinoza concedes that the worst inconveniences arising from the separation of political and religious authority could be removed in a monarchy (7[2–5], 74[8–32], 201[31]–202[35], 204[13]–205[14], 207[19–35], 239[19–32]). But Spinoza denies that monarchy solves the political problem. Despite all the devices that monarchs have employed, their dominions have continued to be threatened more by their subjects than by their enemies. While admitting that in many circumstances there is no alternative to absolute monarchy, Spinoza criticizes absolute monarchy because it leads to needless wars, to bloody struggles for the throne and to the oppression of its subjects, whom the monarch always attempts to reduce to slavery (7[6–12], 205[5–14], 224[3]–225[11], 236[16–24]).

According to Spinoza, the only satisfactory solution to the political problem is a commonwealth that is formed by a free people and that continues to depend on its support. In such a commonwealth there is less of a disparity between the right to rule and the power to rule than in an absolute monarchy. Only a free people can guarantee men the freedom from fear and the security lack of which compelled them to flee the state of nature. Moreover, only a free people can be fully trusted to care about securing these ends for all. The chief objection to this solution is the people's captivity to superstition. In the *Theologico-Political Treatise* Spinoza speaks more than once of the great disorders occasioned by this captivity. Rule by the superstitious people would seem to mean rule by those who know how to manipulate the superstitions of the people. How could Spinoza trust the people, which he believed to be ineradicably superstitious, to play the important role he assigned it in the political life of a free commonwealth?

Spinoza believed that all the politically undesirable by-products of the people's proneness to superstition could be eliminated by instituting freedom of speech and religion. If freedom of speech is granted to all sects as a matter of principle rather than of expediency, the chief hope animating sectarian disputes, the hope for a political triumph over other sects to be gained by becoming the only established religion, would be removed once and for all. The violence of these disputes would be reduced if the parties to them knew they could never expect to vanquish their opponents. Freedom of speech and religion could be expected to emancipate the multitude's love of strange and new religions (6[18]–7[5]). This would lead to the rise of strange and new sects. However, one cannot help wondering how much harmony Spinoza could expect to result from compelling many such sects to coexist peacefully. Had Spinoza not taught that the opinions which move one man to religion and devotion move another to laughter and contempt (11[1–8]; 176[33]–177[6])? Could harmony be expected to result from such laughter and contempt? Spinoza speaks of the violent anger and hatred with which sectarian disputes are conducted in the very passages in which he recommends freedom of speech and religion for all sects (225 f., 244 f., 246[19–25]). What could prevent the mutual ridicule of sects from continually provoking such disputes (212[25–30])? To understand Spinoza's answer to this question, one must bear in mind his teaching that men cannot respect things which excite ridicule or disgust.[2] In other words, sectarians situated as Spinoza would have them would unbeknownst to themselves be compelled to stress publicly (and even privately) those of their religious convictions which were in agreement with as many of their opponents as possible. They would be compelled to do this precisely in order to preserve their religious convictions against the contagious subversion of ridicule. They would have to do their best to keep out of sight, without even being able completely to remove, teachings that would excite their opponents to derision. In seeking to avoid the laughter of people whom they could no longer hope to destroy, they would, without realizing it, become converts to the Universal Religion Spinoza prescribes in the *Theologico-Political Treatise*. An increase in the number of sects would only hasten this process. In time, religion, separated from sectarian hatred and anger, would cease to be a source of political upheavals.

Unlike the solution to the problem of religion that was discussed earlier and that is associated with the name of Hobbes, the present solution can be established and enforced by the civil authority acting in its own name. The civil authority may not be able to prohibit a religion in its own name. But nothing prevents it from tolerating many religions in its own name. The more religions there are for it to tolerate, the easier it is for it to be tolerant. The supremacy over religion to which the civil authority could not lay claim directly, is now within its grasp through freedom of speech and religion.

The solution to the problem of religion serves both as a condition and as a model for Spinoza's solution to the political problem. Just as the problem of religion could not be solved by the kind of direct attack Hobbes had recommended,[3] and a way had to be found to achieve the same end by indirect means, so too a direct solution to the political problem cannot be given for the reasons discussed above. Here too Spinoza seeks indirect means to achieve the desired end. These means are delineated in great detail in his *Tractatus Politicus*. While this paper is not the place for a detailed discussion

2. *Tractatus Politicus*, iv. 4. Consider the implications for enforced toleration of *E.*, III, xxi and Corollary.

3. For whether Hobbes's last word on this subject is any different from Spinoza's, see Leo Strauss, *What Is Political Philosophy* (New York: Free Press, 1959), p. 186.

of Spinoza's proposals, it can be said that their general character is the same as the general character of his solution to the problem of religion: to concede to men the free play that cannot be taken from them and to channel the use they make of it. Both the *Theologico-Political Treatise* and the *Political Treatise* exhibit Spinoza's faith that the channeling for which he wishes could be effected.

BIBLIOGRAPHY

The titles listed here include a selection of commentaries and a very brief selection of recent journal articles in English which may help the student to embark on further reading. For a full bibliography of recent publications of works by Spinoza as well as of books and articles on his philosophy (including essays in collections on more general subjects), the reader is referred to the volume of essays edited by Freeman and Mandelbaum (see II below).

I. WORKS OF SPINOZA
   A. The standard edition is that of Gebhardt:
Spinoza Opera, ed. Carl Gebhardt (Heidelberg: Carl Winter, 1925). 4 vols.
   B. The most readily available edition of major works translated into English is the Dover edition of the Elwes translation:
Chief Works of Spinoza, tr. R. H. M. Elwes (New York: Dover, 1951). 2 vols.
Other works available in English include:
The Correspondence of Spinoza, tr. A. Wolf (New York: Russell and Russell, 1966).
Earlier Philosophical Writings: the Cartesian Principles and Thoughts on Metaphysics, tr. F. A. Hayes (Indianapolis: Bobbs-Merrill, 1963). (There are three recent versions of the *Cartesian Principles;* for details see bibliography in Freeman and Mandelbaum.)
Short Treatise on God, Man and His Well-Being, tr. A. Wolf (New York: Russell and Russell, 1967).

II. BOOKS ON SPINOZA
Curley, E. M., *Spinoza's Metaphysics: an Essay in Interpretation* (Cambridge, Mass.: Harvard University Press, 1969).
Fløistad, Guttorm, *The Problem of Understanding in Spinoza's Ethics* (Oslo: Institute of Philosophy, 1967, mimeographed).
Freeman, Eugene and Mandelbaum, Maurice, eds., *Spinoza: Essays in Interpretation* (La Salle, Ill.: Open Court, 1973).
Gueroult, Martial, *Spinoza. Tome I: Dieu* (*Ethique I*) (Paris: Éditions Montaigne, 1968). (Appendix IX translated in this volume.)
Hallett, H. F., *Benedict de Spinoza* (London: The Athlone Press, 1957). (Chapters I to III included in this volume.)
Hampshire, Stuart, *Spinoza* (New York: Barnes and Noble, 1961).
Joachim, H. H., *A Study of the Ethics of Spinoza* (New York: Russell and Russell, 1964, reprint of 1901 edition).

Strauss, Leo, *Spinoza's Critique of Religion,* tr. E. M. Sinclair (New York: Schocken Books, 1965).

Wolfson, H. A., *The Philosophy of Spinoza* (New York: Schocken Books, 1969). 2 vols. (Reprint of 1934 edition. Chapter I included in this volume.)

III. ARTICLES

A. Special issues of periodicals devoted to Spinoza:

The Monist, Vol. 55 (1971), no. 4. (Freeman and Mandelbaum is an expansion of this issue.)

Inquiry, Vol. 12 (1969), no. 1. (The articles of Fløistad and Parkinson included in the present collection are reprinted from this issue.)

B. Some recent journal articles:

Brann, H. W., "Schopenhauer and Spinoza," *Jl. Hist. Phil.* 10 (1972), 181–196.

Eisenberg, Paul, "How to Understand *De Intellectus Emendatione*," *Jl. Hist. Phil.* 9 (1971), 171–191.

Epstein, Fanny, "On the Definition of Moral Goodness," *Iyyun* 19 (1968), 153–169.

Fløistad, Guttorm, "The Knower and the Known," *Man and World* 3 (1970), 3–25.

Foss, Laurence, "Hegel, Spinoza and a Theory of Experience as Closed," *Thomist* 35 (1971), 435–446.

Gram, Moltke S., "Spinoza, Substance and Predication," *Theoria* 34 (1968), 222–244.

Hampshire, Stuart, "A Kind of Materialism," *Proc. A.P.A.,* 1970, 5–23.

Natanson, Harvey B., "Spinoza's God, Some Special Aspects," *Man and World* 3 (1970), 200–223.

Radner, Daisee, "Spinoza's Theory of Ideas," *Phil. Rev.* 80 (1971), 338–359.

Rensch, Bernhard, "Spinoza's Identity Theory and Modern Biophilosophy," *Phil. Forum* 3 (1972), 193–207.

Rice, Lee C., "The Continuity of 'Mens' in Spinoza," *New Schol.* 43 (1969), 75–103.